CHRONICLES OF SOCCER IN AUSTRALIA

The Foundation Years
1859-1949

CHRONICLES OF SOCCER IN AUSTRALIA

The Foundation Years 1859–1949

PETER KUNZ

FAIRPLAY
PUBLISHING

First published in 2019 by Fair Play Publishing.
Second Printing 2019.
PO Box 4101, Balgowlah Heights, NSW 2093, Australia.

www.fairplaypublishing.com.au
sales@fairplaypublishing.com.au

ISBN: 978-0-6484073-6-2
ISBN: 978-0-6484073-7-9 (ePUB)

© 2019 Peter Kunz
The moral rights of the author have been asserted.

All rights reserved. Except as permitted under the Australian Copyright Act 1968 (for example, a fair dealing for the purposes of study, research, criticism or review), no part of this book may be reproduced, stored in a retrieval system, communicated or transmitted in any form or by any means without prior written permission from the Publisher.

Front cover design and page layout by Leslie Priestley.

Photographs and memorabilia reproduced in this volume are from the National Library of Australia, the National Archives of Australia, South Hobart Football Club, Alamy and from the personal collection of Peter Kunz.

All inquiries should be made to the Publisher via sales@fairplaypublishing.com.au

NATIONAL
LIBRARY
OF AUSTRALIA

A catalogue record of this book is available from the National Library of Australia.

Contents

Foreword	ix
Introduction	1
Chapter 1 A Crowded Playing Field	4
Chapter 2 The Case for the Code 1859-1879	10
Chapter 3 Tentative Roots 1880-1899	17
Chapter 4 Fragile Consolidation 1900-1909	37
Chapter 5 Growth and Contraction 1910-1918	54
Chapter 6 Servicemen and Soccer during the First World War	75
Chapter 7 Friction and External Contact 1919-1929	79
Chapter 8 Australian International Matches 1922-1926	107
Chapter 9 The Women's Game	123
Chapter 10 High Hopes and Reality 1930-1939	129
Chapter 11 Australian International Matches 1930s	152
Chapter 12 Soccer in the Shadow of War	164
Chapter 13 Australian International Matches 1941-1945	181
Chapter 14 Servicemen and Soccer during the Second World War	184
Chapter 15 Enter the Immigrant 1946-1949	187
Chapter 16 Australian International Matches 1945-1949	205
Chapter 17 View to the Future	215
Acknowledgements	221
List of References	222
List of Clubs	230
About Peter Kunz	333

Foreword

There's an incredible piece of work set to hit your eyes in Chronicles of Soccer in Australia.

For me, there's no better way of understanding and appreciating something than to learn about the history of that something.

I accidentally became an Australian soccer football fan in my late teens, when I wandered into Lambert Park in inner-western Sydney to watch two teams I had barely knew existed - Apia Leichhardt and Marconi Fairfield. Until then my life was rugby league, Cronulla Beach, and school study. I knew nothing about soccer.

When I suddenly became hooked on this new atmosphere I was experiencing at Leichhardt, at a lovely old ground where you could almost smell a long and great tradition, I wanted to know more about the history of this sport - the teams, the players, the fans.

Just like I knew that the country's biggest rugby league competition kicked off with nine teams in 1908, or that surfing in Australia started with the visit of Duke Kahanamoku in the 1910s, I wanted to know the origins of soccer football in this country. How, from those beginnings, did it lead to this national league game I was now watching at Lambert Park in 1988? How long have they been playing this type of football at this venue? Who are these players?

Not satisfied with what information was available, I set about compiling the record in my own database about soccer in Australia. In time I became the go-to person for the statistical history of the game at the top level in Australia, especially its national leagues and national teams. The journey was challenging, but kinda fun, and I know how much time it takes.

Australian soccer fans bemoan the lack of manuscriptal history of their sport in this country.

They'll bemoan the sport itself for not doing enough to document and promote its history, saying that the sport can't be taken seriously if we don't know its history.

Well, it's up to fans to document the history - which is exactly what Peter Kunz has done. In a stunning way.

I first met Peter in the mid-1990s through his football-obsessed brother Chris, who has also done a great deal for football in this country including on the literary front. While I quickly realised Peter was a life-long and passionate fan of Australian soccer, I didn't realise how much Peter was putting into the game's history.

Documenting history is a challenge, especially when you're aiming to cover a lot of territory, and your information sources are scant. The effort to document pre-1950s soccer across Australia from a club perspective must have been huge. In my comparatively simple task of researching a few dozen Australian national team players from the 1920s, 30s and 40s I spent a ridiculous amount of time poring through archives of newspapers from the day. When I started flicking through Peter's manuscript I couldn't understand how, where, and for how long, it must have taken him to assemble this monumental piece of work on hundreds of clubs.

I assumed that Peter's focus would be on the states where I knew newspapers covered soccer better, especially Sydney and the Hunter region. But then I saw his chapters on Tasmania, Canberra and even the Northern Territory.

Gobsmacked. I had no idea football existed in some of these places back then let alone some of the fascinating insights such as the influence of the Chinese in Darwin's football history, or that the Coledale club sent off carrier pigeons to convey the half- and full-time scores against North Wollongong to its distant fans.

Peter shows us that the fascinating social and international dimensions of soccer in Australia have been there from the start. But Peter has gone well beyond 'the start'. His bold undertaking of covering club football in Australia up to 1949 reveals great insights into soccer and Australian society for the following decades.

Despite the detail, the book is easy to read, satisfying both the anorak and more casual history-minded reader alike. Peter Kunz has achieved something remarkable in *Chronicles of Australian Soccer*.

Andrew Howe
Adelaide, July 2019

Introduction

To many, association football, known as soccer, may just be considered a relatively simple and healthy sport played on a field with 22 participants hoping to score more goals than their opponents. To the enthusiast this is the sport in its pure essence, and indeed long may it remain so.

However in a historical context, the history and development of football in Australia is a fascinating insight into the mores and attitudes of Australia and its people. As in no other sport, football engenders debate about what it is to be an Australian and Australia's place in the world.

The virtues of geographic and cultural isolation as opposed to global engagement has been played out on Australian soccer fields. Attitudes to immigrants, race and class and the value of sport as a reflection of national culture are reflected within the sport of soccer 'down under'.

Documents relating to the early days of soccer are relatively scarce. As well intentioned as all involved with the sport have been, many local club officials or coaches were fully occupied developing their clubs or players. They did not have regard for posterity when it came to the preservation of historical records. A few were more prescient and carefully stored and archived information for future researchers.

If local coaches and officials were less to blame, more puzzling was the culpability of senior Australian soccer officials. Many failed to curate the objects of state or national importance which documented the game's successes. This usually was not wilful, but was an indication of a lack of respect for posterity or an archival trail.

It is a sporting legacy, expressed through history and its objects, which creates within the soccer public, the pride and passion necessary to sustain the sport into the future. Such attachment creates 'code allegiance', sells 'merchandise' and funds the future of clubs and national teams.

If Australians do not inculcate a love and respect their own football history, no other people are going to do this for us.

Our football traditions seemed hard both to initiate and maintain. Other nations with a football history no longer than ours have often managed to maintain cup and league competitions. Many competitions hark back to the 19th century with an unbroken chain of competition.

The history of Australian football is one littered with league and cup competitions that were begun in haste or fervour and were discarded almost at whim. The club listing at the back of this book attests to the fecundity of trophies and their evanescence.

In many cases a 'new broom' administration was ushered in, determined to put their stamp on history. It discarded a previous administration's competition arrangements, even if elements were logical, almost out of spite. They would 're-invent the wheel' and this cycle would repeat.

The Irish statesman, Edmund Burke said 'those who do not learn from history are bound to repeat it'.

Australian football suffered from two seemingly conflicting problems. One was the failure of administrators to learn from historical errors and the other was the failure of the same officials to maintain worthwhile traditions. Sometimes bad choices were made. Worthwhile traditions, rules or regulations were discarded while poor ones were maintained. As is often the case, such lessons were often only learnt in hindsight.

The intervention of two world wars, the Depression, bureaucratic infighting and the jealousies of other codes have added fuel to the unstable fire.

Such a paucity of cultural and historical awareness has led Australia to the situation, where today, it is one of the few countries which lacks a comprehensive national football museum. Some collections or objects are now stored in general museums or libraries, or in some private collections. Frankly, although safe, they will never be accorded the prominence they would deserve in a dedicated museum.

As most cultural institutions do not customarily 'de-accession' and pass collections to other institutions, collections already stored elsewhere are unlikely to form the nucleus of any future museum.

The aim of this book is to give an overview of the development of soccer in all the states and territories of Australia within the context of Australian history, politics and culture until 1949. The chapters have been divided into decades or relevant date periods, with the history of the game within each state explained. Local, state and international matches are highlighted.

Contemporary quotes have been chosen to add to the narrative. Such quotes and the language used, place the game in its historical context. In cases where articles or statements of the day are quoted, the sporting descriptor used to describe soccer or the other codes is what is in the original document.

The main subject of the book is the history and progress of senior men's club, state level and international football throughout Australia. However, I have also included information about the development of junior, amateur and women's football, as well as refereeing and coaching. All facets of football are equally important to the development of the sport, and assists a holistic view of those involved in the early development of the game in Australia.

I refer frequently to the actions of the other codes. Football has developed in Australia in tandem with the sports of Australian Rules football, rugby union and rugby league. No history of soccer in Australia can be written objectively without reference to other codes.

Much thought has been given to the word which I will use to describe the sport now officially named 'football' in Australia. From this point, I use the descriptor 'soccer' almost exclusively. By doing so, the sport can be differentiated easily from the other codes. In Australia, adherents of all codes, call their own preferred game 'football'.

Soccer during the period under examination, has also been referred to as 'London Football', 'British Association Football', 'British Football' or 'Association Football'.

I trust the purists who, as I, agree that soccer has more right to be called football than any other code, will understand my choice of nomenclature in this historical context.

The history which follows is dedicated to the memory of all *soccerites* (as early soccer enthusiasts were known) who established, fostered, played or supported *the beautiful game* in Australia in its formative years.

Peter Kunz
Canberra, July 2019

Chapter 1

A Crowded Playing Field

When soccer was established in Australia it did not have the 'football' field in isolation. It found it was competing for attention with another two codes, Australian Rules and rugby. The situation was different in England where soccer became officially established in 1863, prior to the establishment of rugby in 1875.

In many other countries where rugby did not take root, soccer became the first and often the only football code of note.

In fact it is one of the great curiosities of world sport that the two 'football' codes of England, that of soccer and rugby, in general had totally separate popular geographic markets. The exception has been Britain, and to a degree, France.

Rugby thrived in South Africa, Australia, New Zealand, Fiji, Samoa and Tonga and its influence created the dominant codes of American (US) and Canadian football. These were all countries where soccer was a minor sport. In just about every other nation soccer was the code of choice. The 'mother country' could harbour and nurture both, but it was as if the rest of the world could only chose and favour one code.

Soccer in Australia always faced more competition than in other countries. It now competes with three other codes for participants, grounds, spectators, money and media attention.

The history and fate of soccer in Australia is intertwined with and influenced by the history and existence of the other codes. A potted explanation of the relative geographic history of all four codes within Australia is in order.

The first football code played officially in Australia, and indeed the world, was Australian Rules. Australian Rules was devised principally by Thomas Wills and the first rules were in place by 1859. This is four years before the rules of soccer were codified by the Football Association in London in 1863, although a variant of soccer called Sheffield Rules had been played in England since 1853. Rugby was codified in 1875.

Wills wanted to develop a sport which could keep cricketers fit in winter. Having attended Rugby school in England, he did not want the code to be as rough as the form of football played at, and named after, that school. Unlike rugby or soccer, Australian Rules, though first played on whatever space was available, was soon played on oval shaped cricket pitches in winter. This made it the only code among the four in Australia which did not share a rectangular field.

Critically, Australian Rules was 'first in the field' to hold organised competitions compared with the other codes. The 'invention' and development of Australian Rules in Victoria prevented the spread of rugby from becoming a truly national sport. The dominance of Australian Rules and rugby from the outset ensured soccer would initially become the number two code in most Australian states. In New South Wales and Queensland it was to fall to third position once rugby had split into the two codes of rugby union and rugby league in 1908.

Historians talk of a 'Barassi line' (named after the Australian Rules player of the 1950s and 1960s, Ron Barassi) which geographically splits Australia roughly from north to south. This delineates between states or territories which adhere to either Australian Rules (Victoria, Tasmania, South Australia, Northern Territory and Western Australia) or rugby union and rugby league codes (New South Wales, Queensland and the Australian Capital Territory). Although the 'Barassi line' generally adhered to state borders, the Australian Rules code was historically prominent in the Riverina area of New South Wales and reached into the Australian Capital Territory.

This 'Barassi line' has remained virtually immutable, with the sole exception of the Australian Capital Territory, which until the 1970s was arguably an Australian Rules stronghold, but which now favours rugby union and rugby league, not least because both codes have teams in the national competition.

Australia did not become a federated Commonwealth until 1901. Before this date the various colonies maintained their colonial independence. In the states of New South Wales and Queensland it was rugby which took hold of majority support. Occasionally a certain fluidity existed among clubs as to whether to follow the rules of soccer or rugby in the northern states.

The fact that soccer was promulgated, at least officially, in Australia well after Australian Rules and rugby was unfortunate timing. It was the late arrival to a table hosting two competitors. It was regarded as an 'interloper' sport. In 1908 the 'footballing pie' was divided into four, not three, when rugby league made its debut.

The game in the 19th century was dominated by English or Scottish migrants. It was considered mildly 'ethnic' in Anglo-Scottish terms.

The social and sporting environment in which the sport of soccer found itself in Australia was, and still is, unique in the world. In no other country of the world do four codes of 'football' flourish. These challenges have done much to hinder the development of the sport, though the sporting and cultural environment has also made the sport and its followers resilient, determined and passionate.

At times, many within the sport have not made it easy to gain converts. Hostility from those outside the sport is one thing, but there was ample strife created within by soccer followers.

A reading of the administrative history of the sport in the Australian states contains a litany of various associations being formed to govern competitions. They would abort, split or re-form due to personal, philosophical, or ethnic animosities and ambitions.

A student of early Australian soccer history will often find that themes which many consider to be recent, or at least post World War II vintage, have their roots in earlier times.

Prior to World War II 98% of the population of Australia was comprised of those with Anglo-Saxon origins. Soccer was principally propagated and populated by migrants almost exclusively of English, Irish, Scottish and Welsh stock. Among these, the English and particularly the Scottish were the greatest contributors.

After World War II, migrants from the Continent of Europe and also from South America, Asia and Africa left their strong imprint and diverse playing styles, overlaying the original 'British' playing styles and philosophy.

Some current fans fail to realise that soccer has been a game propagated and played by migrants since its earliest days in Australia and this feature is not merely a post-World War II phenomenon.

Opposition to the sport from other codes and the incumbent media and general populace was evident from the earliest times. Sporadically, there were examples of harmony, sharing of facilities and general bonhomie. This was so especially if this suited the purposes of the entrenched codes. However rivalry and an element of dislike from the incumbent codes, though expected, was an element which was evident from soccer's nascence.

It would probably be true to say that in no other country in the world are attitudes by many acolytes of the major footballing codes so ardently held.

Religious sectarianism in Australia which pitted Protestants against Catholics has faded. However, it can be argued that what can be called *footballing sectarianism* is far more durable.

Soccer has been connected with the 'foreign' in Australia. It was often named by the administration, supporters and others as 'British football' at the turn at the twentieth century, a time of nationalism and a gradual withdrawal from British influence.

The rugby codes, though no less of British origin, were considered totally assimilated sports. Australian Rules, which drew its inspiration from a concoction of foreign codes, was promoted and propagated as a uniquely Australian game for Australians.

Antipathy towards soccer was also based on its working class roots. Most of the British sports which had been successfully transplanted to Australia were supported by the upper or middle classes. Such sports included cricket, tennis, hockey, rowing, golf, gymnastics and rugby. Australia Rules appealed to all classes from the rich to the poor in the southern states. By the time soccer was serious in joining the Australian sporting landscape in the 1890s it had already lost the support of the upper classes in Britain.

From the 1880s English and Scottish professional soccer teams attracting working class players. The playing of soccer, which had hitherto been a social pastime of middle and upper class amateurs became a profession for the most talented and determined working class players.

Working class players joined clubs which flourished in midlands and northern working class cities. These clubs could afford to pay players as their financial health was based on attracted broad working class support. The reaction of the university educated upper class was to leave soccer *en masse*. Without mass working class and some middle class support, it is doubtful if professional clubs in England could have afforded to attract the best professional players and maintain their grounds and infrastructure.

The exit of the upper class from the sport of soccer was, ironically, to ensure its vitality, international growth and economic strength. Middle class businessmen, engineers and other professionals were to travel to foreign countries, particularly in Europe and South America. While abroad they constructed railways, roads, buildings and other infrastructure. In their spare time they played soccer and developed soccer clubs.

It is, however, fascinating to ponder what would have happened if soccer had remained an upper class sport in Britain. Perhaps, like rugby, it would have found early acceptance in Australia and other English speaking nations which in reality spurned the sport. An inversion of the current world popularity of soccer may have occurred.

Australians, like those of many nations, revel in national simplifications or myths.

They pride themselves in being 'classless' but that statement seems a convenient sop to those marooned in the lower rungs of society, as much as it has been a smokescreen to cover the actions of the upper class. The Australian 'upper class' has always been as zealous to distance itself from the 'others' as in any other society. The British and Europeans, in their laconic acceptance of class distinctions, perhaps exhibit a more honest attitude to what in all societies is inevitable.

Soccer players and crowds in Australia would largely be drawn from English factory workers and Scottish miners. Many small businessmen of British origin donated cups or sponsored clubs. Conspicuous by their absence were big business and the cultural imprimatur of leaders of politics and society.

The working and lower middle class soccer supporters did not readily have the financial or social contacts to boost the game. Many influential Australians favoured one of the socially entrenched codes and were unlikely to favour or aid the 'interloper' code. Could it be that 'classless' Australia snubbed and stymied soccer based on class distinction as much as any other factor?

Australians cultivate the sense that they support the 'underdog'. Yet the 'underdog' code of soccer has had to continually fight for every centimetre or column inch for recognition and respect. So many supporters or officials have been so used to minority status that some almost fear the maximal potential which soccer may achieve. To lead boldly is challenging and there can be a modest comfort in being cocooned within the mediocrity of the also rans.

Within soccer, stresses were created because players, facilities, support and finances were often lacking. An added cross to bear for true followers has been a history of sporadic violence among some spectators and players.

The sport was inherently less physical than Australian Rules and more particularly the two codes of rugby. Violence by soccer players seemed more noticeable.

Many of the migrants who supported the sport were very passionate and vocal in supporting their teams. In many cases the immigrants from Britain, often mild mannered away from the pitch, gave vent to passion while on it or at the sidelines. This would apply particularly to clubs supported by British miners. Supporters from the Newcastle region in New South Wales were considered by some to be the most rabid. This was difficult for the more relaxed Australian sporting supporter to understand.

The later migrants from the Continent, not inhibited by the yoke of Anglo-Saxon reserve, were often more demonstrative in both a vocal, and at times, a physical sense.

Reporting of such incidents was often exaggerated by a compliant media. With a vested interest in furthering competing codes, there was concurrent lack of publicity regarding similar incidents in the 'more Australian' sports. This was vexing for administrators, players and fans with the wider health and promotion of the game at heart.

Cycles of 'boom and bust' have continued to the present. Followers have been, at varying times, overly optimistic or pessimistic about the progress of the sport within Australia.

Soccer is, has been, and will continue to be a significant contributor to the complex and unique jigsaw of Australia's footballing landscape. It is also the code with the greatest capacity for growth.

What is historically evident and important to record is that the sport of soccer has shown remarkable resilience to survive and ultimately prosper. This is despite continual adversity and periodic stasis in the most competitive 'footballing' nation and marketplace in the world.

What follows is the chronicle of the 'birth and childhood' years of a sport which is yet to savour full maturity in the Great Southern Land.

Chapter 2

The Case for the Code 1859-1879

Evidence that forms of soccer have been played in the Australian colonies dates back to the 1820s. It would barely have resembled modern soccer, but would have been a hybrid sport based on the football games which were played over large fields in early 19th century Britain. Such games were played on Shrove Tuesdays between Ashburton and Derbyshire or in the various prestigious public schools such as Eton, Rugby, Charterhouse, Westminster and Harrow under varying rules.

In 1859 the Hobart press reported that there would be St Patrick's Day celebrations at Richmond, Tasmania on Friday 18 March which would involve various sports including:

> A grand football match between two elevens, selected by G. Gregson and John Stockell, esquires for 10 pounds.[1]

Judging by the number of players selected, this was almost certain to have been advance publicity for a soccer match. Early rugby was played by 20 players and Australian Rules was not played in Tasmania until 1864.

In 1866 a soccer match was played in Brisbane by the Brisbane Football Club. This could be considered the first documented soccer match in Australia. During this era the number of players on each team was not stipulated and players could handle the ball as a 'catch' until 1870:

About thirty members of the Brisbane Football Club mustered in the Queen's Park in the afternoon, and a game was got up. Though the majority of players were out of practice or unaccustomed to kicking the football, several very exciting contests ensued, and the goals were not kicked without a hard struggle. The rules were not very strictly adhered to, and many of the players used their hands more than their feet.[2]

A subsequent match was played between the Brisbane Football Club and the National Cricket Club in June 1868. On this occasion there were 12 players on each side, only one more per side than modern rules permit:

There were twelve players on each side... The ball was kicked "off" shortly after 3 o'clock, and the Nationals quickly brought it down close to their opponent's goal, and in spite of all the efforts of the Brisbane Club player, managed to keep it there for some little time. At length a lucky kick and a rush sent it back, and before the Nationals could retreat in sufficient force to defend their goal, the ball was kicked through by Mr Hill.[3]

Depending on which state attempted to stage a 'pure' soccer game, the matches were often influenced by rules pertaining to the major code of that state. It can be assumed that in most cases, players or officials were new to soccer and were not completely familiar with the 'London Association Rules'.

In the same year a Mr H. Short had written a letter to the *Express and Telegraph* newspaper advocating the introduction of soccer to Adelaide and a call to challenge a team from Melbourne. His plea was ignored.

In August 1868 another soccer match was played between the Brisbane Football Club and the Police. On this occasion also, the intention was to play a 'pure' soccer match, though at times rules were bent.

Football
Brisbane Football Club v. Police

The football match between the Brisbane Football Club and a team composed of members of the Police Force, and which came off on Saturday afternoon, at the Queen's Park, was a really capital contest ... About 4 o'clock, in compliance with a persuasive kick from the captain of the club, the ball sped on its way up the hill towards the police goal, and the battle commenced... After a plucky struggle Smith sent the "windbag" through the police goal on behalf of the club, in whose favor the umpire decided ... a desire on both sides to discourage un-necessary clutching and violent tripping was observable... Including a number of ladies, who watched the fray at a convenient distance, and appeared to think it excellent fun, there were about 300 spectators present.[4]

The earliest report of a match resembling soccer in Victoria was between the Melbourne Club and the Victoria Police in 1870. The match was based on soccer, though elements of Australian Rules intruded, including passing with the hands. The practice of handling the ball within the soccer rules was only banned in that year, and widespread knowledge of the change in the Australian colonies would have been virtually unknown.

In Victoria in 1873 a gentleman was fired with the desire for Australian Rules to adopt some of the rules of soccer. Writing under the pen name *Trojan*, he wrote a letter to the editor which was published in the *The Argus*:

> Sir - Now that our football season is over or nearly so a review of the matches played prompts me to throw out a few suggestions for the consideration of club committees between this and the next season.
>
> The game, as played here, may perhaps exhibit strength and courage on the part of the players but (to my mind) very little of science, law, or order and is productive of many and serious accidents as the events of the past season testify; ... As played at home (or in London) the game is essentially football, not indiscriminate scrimmage...[5]
>
> I am, &c.
> *TROJAN*

In Queensland, a press report was published about a soccer match played the previous Saturday, on the 19th of August, 1873. The Woogaroo mental asylum and the Brisbane Football Club were the contestants. The match lasted two hours, as at the time 90 minute games were not stipulated in the rules:

> A team of the Brisbane Football Club went up to Woogaroo on Saturday, to play a match with a team composed of the warders and patients of the

Asylum... the result being one goal for Woogaroo, and two for the Brisbane team... At 6 o'clock the two teams met at tea, provided by Dr Jaap, and after satisfying the inner man they all adjourned to the ball-room, and passed a most enjoyable evening in dancing; some of the gentlemen present favouring the company with songs at interval.[6]

This was most likely not the first match to be played at Woogaroo as the *Brisbane Courier* mentioned that 'football' was played at the Asylum in July, 1872. A total of four matches were played between both teams.

During this period proponents of a particular code tried to promote their own at the expense of others. Others suggested alterations to the rules of their favoured or other codes. Some urged all participants to adhere to one set of rules consistent with any of the three codes played in Australia at the time for the sake of consistency.

The first reference to the desire to establish soccer on a consistent basis in Sydney is contained in a letter to the editor of *The Sydney Morning Herald* in 1877.

The letter was signed *Novicrucian,* the pen name of Arthur Savage.

Savage was Australia's first football international of any code. Savage was born in Sydney in 1850, educated in England at the Rugby school and played soccer as a goalkeeper with Crystal Palace. He was selected to play for England in 1876. The following year he returned to Australia and wrote:

> *I have read with a great deal of interest the report of the annual meeting of the Southern Rugby Football Union... The concluding paragraph of the report of the meeting states that upon the subject of an alteration in the rules, so as to abolish scrimmages and running with the ball, the meeting terminated...*
>
> *The first trials of these rules... became the standard code now in use by the Football Association, which was formed the following season... Why not start an Association in New South Wales? The rules are so simple that the youngest of players can easily grapple them, and nervous papas and mamas could watch with pleasure...* [7]
>
> I am Sir, yours &c
> NOVICRUCIAN

There seemed little recognition at the time in Australia that both soccer and rugby codes could exist in tandem. Savage, with experience of playing both codes in England stated what seems obvious; both rugby and soccer could be played simultaneously in New South Wales. His reference to soccer being a sport which 'nervous papas and mamas' could watch their children play more comfortably than rugby still resonates. The relative safety of soccer partially accounts for soccer drawing the largest number of young registrations among the codes played in Australia to this day.

Three days later, a letter in reply was sent to the editor:

Sir,
I read with much pleasure Novicrucian's letter in today's Herald and quite agree with him...
For the last two seasons I have been a member of one of the leading Sydney clubs, and can, therefore, speak from experience that the practice of scrimmages and running with the ball, especially the latter are very damaging to the limbs, and sometimes even the lives of the players... [8]
C. C.

The author of the letter in reply was the pen name of John W. Fletcher an Oxford educated rugby man and school master who had arrived in Australia in 1875. Fletcher adopted the pen name C.C. as an abbreviation of Coreen College, a school which he had established.

A letter was sent in reply by *Old Rugbeian* which said in part:

If there is a strong section of the players here in favour of Association rules, let them form clubs under their rules, and secede from the Union; but I would urge upon those interested not to make themselves a laughing-stock by endeavouring to associate the Association game under FOOTBALL. Should an Association be formed I have no fear but that the Rugby game will be able to hold its own here... [9]

The South Australian *Express and Telegraph* published a letter to the editor. *A Young Colonist* had objected to the conduct of Australian Rules and advocated soccer instead:

> *The South Australian Association might be decidedly altered for the better by adopting the English Association rules. The prevailing feature of the English Association is that no player is allowed to use his hands at all... thus reducing the game of football to football proper; and I maintain that dribbling a ball in and out amongst a lot of players requires a greater degree of skill and is a much prettier sight than the grappling and handling that is practiced at the football matches played in Adelaide.*[10]

What *A Young Colonist* had failed to grasp is that none of the codes in Australia had any intention of departing the field or morphing into another. Australians revelled in the physicality of the other codes and had no intention of making their sports safer for players or less confrontational for spectators. From the earliest times many Australian spectators preferred their football to have an element of blood sport about it.

The fact that soccer has the highest skill factor of all football sports did not implicitly garner admiration. In fact it was often a point of derision. The very skill and lack of contact negated overt physicality, which Australian fans of other codes craved. Soccer, bereft of the worst of codified violence, was to be characterised as a 'sissy' sport by the hardy and hard bitten Australian populace.

The next documented match after the short lived trials in Brisbane was played in Hobart on May 10, 1879. Players from the Cricketers Club formed two teams:

> *The Cricketer's Club made a start for the season with a scratch match... The English Association Rules which have been adopted by this club were played. Chapman's side proved victorious by two goals to one... The club played without goal posts; as Mr Bryant who had promised to bring them, did not do so, coats were used to mark the goal instead.*[11]

Less than a month later soccer in Tasmania had progressed to the degree that the first documented evidence of an organised soccer match between two teams was recorded. This match was played on Mr Marsh's Ground at New Town, Tasmania on Saturday 2 June 1879, between New Town and the City teams.

The *Australian Town and Country Journal* carried a letter to the editor by G.A.F.C. decrying Australian Rules football and championing the game of soccer as played by London Association rules. Such fervent views led to a sense of 'footballing partisanship', a rivalry between codes which has almost certainly become more competitive and bitter than in any other country:

The Game of Football
To The Editor

Sir, - In reading Old Hand's letter in last weeks issue, on the Regeneration of Cricket I find he makes the following assertion, viz, - that Victoria has regenerated football. This I most decidedly deny, and, in my humble opinion, consider football played under the Victorian rules as the greatest abortion of the game it has been my misfortune to see.

If football is to be regenerated at all in this part of the world, it can only be done by adopting the rules of the English Association Union...

Yours, & c, G. A. F. C.

Sydney, June 26, 1879. [12]

Chapter 3

Tentative Roots 1880-1899

After the tentative germination of soccer from 1866 to 1879, the decade from 1880 to 1889 saw the code spread from Sydney to most of the states of Australia.

The rules of the sport evolved over time. Until 1870 players could catch the ball. In 1882 one handed throw-ins were abolished and the use of a crossbar instead of tape was introduced. In 1892 the penalty kick was introduced.

In the same year a referee, who initially had sat on the sidelines and arbitrated between two umpires, was given full control. Goal nets were only widely introduced from the 1890s. By 1893 goalkeepers could not be charged by opponents unless they held the ball. In the early years goalkeepers punched the ball far more than they do now, for fear of being barged. In 1897 it was decreed that soccer teams consist of eleven players and that matches last ninety minutes.

Regular interstate soccer matches were played between New South Wales and Victoria between 1883 and 1888. This series was a way for soccer to progress and gain publicity in the two most populous Australian states.

In 1899 the Wellington Football Association of New Zealand met to discuss the possibility of forming the Australasian Association Football Federation, with the various Australian Associations. It was stated that there had been little progress due to the 'apathetic attitude' of the Australians.

New South Wales

After a lapse of some three years there was no observable sign of any community support to form a soccer side in Sydney.

By 1880 further attempts were being made to foster the code. Notice of a meeting was published in the press. Headed *Football Under English Association Rules* it read:

> *A meeting convened by Messrs J. W. Fletcher and J. A. Todd will take place this evening at Aarons Exchange Hotel to consider and promote the introduction of football under English Association Rules. All football players and others who may be interested in the improvement of the winter pastime are invited to attend.*[1]

Novicrucian wrote a letter to the editor of *The Sydney Morning Herald*, which was published on the same day:

The Game of Football

> *Sir,*
> *I claim the attention and support of Rugby union players in introducing the English Association game in preference to the Victorian Association one, in as much as the former stands purely on its own grounds, and with the exception of the golden rule of off and on side, bears no resemblance to the Rugby union game, while the latter is a hybrid affair, neither fish, flesh, fowl nor good red herring, either to Rugby Union or English Association players, and which, if successfully introduced, would utterly destroy the national characteristic of the game of football in Australia.*[2]
> *NOVICRUCIAN*

A much documented soccer match was played strictly under the English Association Rules on Saturday the 7th of August 1880 on Parramatta Common. Rugby playing students from Sydney's Kings School played a soccer match against the first substantive soccer team in Australia, Wanderers. Wanderers defeated the Kings School side 5-0, in front of a crowd of about 1,000 people:

> *The first match in New South Wales played under English Association rules was played on Saturday last; by the newly formed club against the Kings School Boys, at Parramatta. The visitors had a very fair team, allowing for the fact that hardly one of them had played football for some*

years. The advantage was, however, balanced by the fact that the boys had not played these rules before... The play was remarkably even, particularly after half time, the boys on several occasions only failing to score on account of their want of familiarity with the art of passing and middling the ball.[3]

Reports of the match later misleadingly named it the first match ever played in Australia under English Association rules. It was not the first match. It was the best documented match played up till its time, and was played under soccer rules which were constantly being updated. There can be no doubt that, unlike many previous matches played in Australia, the rules of soccer were strictly adhered to.

Belatedly, *The Sydney Morning Herald* of 24 August 1880 informed readers of the official formation of the first soccer club in New South Wales. It was to be called Wanderers, after the same team which had played Kings School. The uniform the club would wear would be a white jersey and cap, with badge of the Southern Cross, and blue stockings. An account of proceedings was to be sent to England to the Secretary of the English Association, for publication and it was requested that the club be enrolled in the English Association.

It is not clear what enrolment in the English Association would confer an Australian club. It was a futile attempt to interest English authorities in the progress of soccer in the Antipodes. Australian officials hoped that financial assistance, exchange of knowledge or even future matches could flow from enrolment. Such hope was more redolent of an unrequited romance. The Wanderers team failed to become 'enrolled' in the English Association.

English indifference at the official level to the development of soccer in Australia was to last for many decades and only bear limited fruit by the 1920s. In general, such relations proved to be long on talk and short on practical support or action over the next forty years. Australian soccer fans had to wait until 1925 to see an English FA team play Australia at home.

Whether serious assistance from the 1880s by English authorities or clubs to Australian soccer authorities to develop the 'grand old British winter pastime' could have progressed the game here is hardly a moot point. It would have greatly helped an infant sport struggling for life in hostile soil.

An evocative pen picture of soccer in 1880 on the sixtieth anniversary of the first match was rather florid:

As you read this during the progress of to-days game can you visualise just 60 years ago, when the only playing area was at Moore Park, just near Mount Rennie. Young players of that day, dressed in frock coats and tall top hats, and sporting moustaches and even side whiskers 'hoofed' it each Saturday to participate in triangular contests between Arcadians, Wanderers and Caledonians... [4]

A letter by soccer evangelist J.W. Fletcher in 1880, was published in England. It conveyed the modest but historically significant genesis of soccer in New South Wales:

We have, of course an uphill game to fight, but you will see we have made a splendid commencement, and feel sanguine of success in spite of the Victorian game. The ice has been broken for next season, when we intend to be early in the field. Will you kindly introduce us to the Football Association? I fancy our modest commencement is only the introduction to a brilliant future for Association football here, and we wish to work in concert with the English Association...
Yours etc.
(Sgd.) J.W. Fletcher
Hon Sec. N.S.W. Wanderers [5]

In 1882 the New South Wales English Football Association was formed to foster soccer in New South Wales. The first secretary of the Association was Andrew J. Macauley. Two year later this body was replaced by the South British Football Soccer Association. The secretary of the Association was Neville Stephens.

A geographic characteristic of the development of soccer in New South Wales from inception was the formation of clubs in three distinct areas. These were the Sydney metropolitan area, the South Coast and the Newcastle region.

The bedrock of the sport were to be Scottish and English migrants. Players from the Newcastle region and the South Coast were usually Scottish miners or residents of mining towns, while players and supporters in Sydney were often Englishmen who worked in factories.

In Sydney soccer gained particular popularity in the working class suburbs of Granville and Pyrmont. The game developed in Granville when Hudson

Brothers Engineering Works of Redfern signed up a group of Scottish blacksmiths at Kilmarnock and Glasgow in 1882. The firm won a contract to build rolling stock for the NSW Government Railways and moved to Granville, later becoming known as the Clyde Steel Works:

> *The eighteen men who signed contracts in Scotland, arrived in Sydney in June 1882. They included John Nielson, who would become captain of the new club and 18 year old William Baillie, who would become the club's second captain. Packed in Baillie's bags when he left Scotland, was a brand new soccer ball and shortly after they reached Granville he produced the ball and shouted to his mates 'Come on boys, let's have a kick!'* [6]

In Maitland, Minmi Rangers became the first soccer club formed in the area. The team was established by Scottish migrant miners in 1884. In the same year, the Northern New South Wales British Football Association was inaugurated. The Lambton Thistles and Glebe Blackwatch clubs were formed in 1885. Wallsend, Greta Bluebells and Carrington Blackwatch first played in the Newcastle region in 1887.

The Adamstown club played its first match in 1889. Adamstown was formed by Peter Finlayson on Monday, 12 July 1889, when a meeting was held in a cricket shed despite the onslaught of a fierce thunderstorm. It was soon to be known as Adamstown Rosebud.

The story of the formation of Minmi Rangers in the Hunter Valley is picturesque and lyric. Importantly, it epitomises how distant events and Caledonian migrant longings can lead to the formation of a club in Australia:

> *On a certain Spring day in 1884 as the group (of miners) walked along the winding main road the postmistress called Mr Winning with the news 'A newspaper from home for you'... When interviewed some years later Mr Winning said 'Sure, I remember the day. The departing sun left its crimson reflections on the western sky'...* [7]

Mr Winning had scanned the newspapers for a month for news of the 1884 Scottish Cup Final between Queens Park and Vale of Leven. The latest newspaper announced that Vale of Leven was unable to play the Cup final on the appointed date and the trophy was awarded without play to Queens Park:

> There was silence till Charlie Kilpatrick said 'Fancy not playing the final. Minmi would have rushed the chance' and that really started the fun... Scones McCroarie chipped in with 'Let's form a football club here to break the monotony otherwise I'll leave for Sydney'...
>
> A deputation comprising Winning, Frame and Wilson saw the Colliery Clerk, Bill Ritchie after work next day...
>
> As the deputation moved off the office verandah, the Pit manager, Mr Gardiner, came out and asked what was going on...he put his hand in his pocket and donated a sovereign, instructing Mr Ritchie to give a similar donation from the cash box.
>
> The next move was a brisk walk down to Gillons shop, also a dour Scot, where three balls were ordered. [8]

Jack Winning was later to die of a heart attack while watching a Weston Homestead soccer match.

Minmi Rangers played their first official match against Hamilton Athletic. A field was laid out at Lambton. Six hundred fans attended to watch a 2-2 draw. Decades later a plaque was erected at the rotunda at Lambton Park to commemorate the first official soccer match in the Newcastle area.

Minmi Rangers went on to win the Gardiner Cup in 1892 against Pyrmont Rangers. At the final goal nets were used for the first time. When players relayed the news to their families they were excited, but realised relatives would be in church at the time the team returned from Sydney. Supporters consulted their ministers who agreed to curtail their sermons so the players could greet the victorious team. Sydney critics stated that 'their machine like combination is the best we have seen in Sydney'. In the first five seasons the team was comprised of former Scottish migrants. Due to a recession in 1911 the team lost senior status in that year.

Minmi became such a hotbed of soccer that it also boasted teams called the Rooks, Starlights, Clippers, Pirates, Wanderers, Gardeners and Squashers. At its zenith the town had about 4000 residents. By the mid 1920s only 400 remained.

The West Wallsend club was formed in May 1891 by Scottish coalminers who had settled in the area to find work in the newly opened mines. That year they participated in a six-team badge series.

The first competitive game occurred on the 30 April 1892 at Johnston Park before a crowd of 1200 against Adamstown Rosebud. The result was a 2-2 draw and the match was celebrated with a banquet at Johnston's Hotel.

Alan Tredinnick reminisced about the development of clubs and players in Northern New South Wales:

> From the outset the average northern footballer worked in a coal mine... A big pit could employ as many as 500 men... The large scale operations had a sprinkling of British migrants; devotees of the round ball game.
> Their sons, nephews and even grandsons worked beside them. Pinning a scrap of paper to a 'prop' at the tunnel entrance was a sure way to recruit a team... or several teams. [9]

Tredinnick described the football kit which the miners wore:

> But there was nothing fancy about the gear they wore! Pit trousers and pit-boots were the go! The gear though was usually modified. You could shorten the legs of a pair of pit trousers for comfort sake and anyway, they were probably already worn through at the knee. You could improve your pit boots by attaching bars to the soles for greater traction... [10]

The first club formed on the New South Wales south coast was Balgownie. Although the actual date of the club's formation is not officially documented, a date as early as 1883 has been posited. Balgownie claim to be the oldest extant soccer club in Australia. The website of the Balgownie Rangers Soccer Club set the club in historical context:

> One of the earliest mining families to settle in Balgownie or Cramsville as it was then called was the Hunters. One of the young members of the family was Peter Hunter who had played junior soccer in Scotland. He brought with him an old football and there is little doubt that this was the first football brought to the South Coast.... By 1883 Peter Hunter's ball was being kicked around the flat ground where William Street joins Lang Street today. [11]

In 1884 a metropolitan Sydney team travelled by steamer to Kiama to play a Broughton Creek combination team, with the Sydney combination gaining a narrow victory. This was the first competitive contact between Sydney and

South Coast teams. The town of Broughton Creek changed its name to Berry in 1889.

The first competition series, called the Badge Competition, was played in Sydney in 1885. The first competition match was played on 6 June 1885 when Caledonians played Arcadians and won 7-1. Caledonians were the winners of the series and were awarded gold medals. Other clubs prominent in the series which ran from 1885 to 1892 were Canterbury, Pyrmont Rangers, Wanderers, Parkgrove and Granville. The Granville team consisted almost exclusively of Scots from Ayreshire. Parkgrove comprised English born players and their matches against Caledonians and Granville were the source of much Anglo-Scottish rivalry.

The Rainsford Cup commenced in 1885. The cup itself named after James H. Rainsford, the licensee of the Cambridge Club Hotel in Oxford Street. The cup failed to be produced and a dummy cup was substituted. At the Sir Joseph Banks Ground, Granville were the first Cup victors, defeating Caledonians 3-2 in extra time.

The Gardiner Cup, however, had a far more illustrious history. It was donated as a challenge cup for perpetuity, becoming the prize of a competition for New South Wales teams played between 1885 and 1928. The silver cup was donated by a soft goods manufacturer named William S. Gardiner. Gardiner was the patron of the Southern British Football Association. In 1888 the first winner of the Gardiner Cup was Caledonians which triumphed over Parkgrove 3-1 at Botany. The Gardiner Cup was succeeded by the State Cup in 1929.

Pyrmont Rangers dominated the early years of the Gardiner Cup. The team appeared in each final from 1889 to 1896, winning four times.

Hamilton Athletic groomed a young 14 year old named James Jackson in 1886. He moved to the Wallsend club. Jackson left Australia to play in Britain with Glasgow Rangers, Newcastle and Woolwich Arsenal. He can rightfully be considered Australia's first successful soccer export to Britain.

In 1887 Fenton Broadwood founded the Thirroul club and introduced soccer boots to the News South Wales south coast. Previously players had worn hob nail boots. Soccer was flourishing in the region. North Illawarra was formed in 1888 and Illawarra Rovers was established the following year.

A team from the southern highlands, the Bowral Rovers, met a team from Mittagong, named Mittagong Rovers. Soccer was to be played in the Bowral-Mittagong area for the next four years before declining until rejuvenation in the twentieth century.

South of Sydney, the Joadja team was formed by Scottish miners who worked the shale deposits for the Australian Kerosene Oil and Mineral Company at Joadja Creek near Moss Vale. The oldest existing soccer trophy in Australia, the Atkinson Price Challenge Cup, was won 2-0 by Joadja against a Granville selection in 1887. Visiting teams to Joadja had to be lowered to the township by flying fox. By contemporary recollection this was a most unsettling experience. The driver of the flying fox would often speed up the descent to frighten visiting teams. In the first three years the Joadja team was undefeated at home. The club was so successful that it came second to Pyrmont Rangers in the badge and cup metropolitan league competition in 1889.

Teams from mining areas often had the advantage over their city factory or office bound cousins. Miners would often finish work early in the day. This enabled players to practice before sunset, an important advantage in a time when floodlighting of fields was unavailable. Miners were also fit and flinty and relished playing the physical form of soccer prevalent in the 19th century.

In 1887 the first North v South matches were played. These were matches between Newcastle and Sydney region clubs and were to be a staple into the 1960s. Newcastle, playing in white shirts, defeated Sydney, which played in blue shirts, by one goal to nil. At times a South Coast team also entered the competition.

The Gardiner Cup Final of 1889 between Pyrmont Rangers and Joadja was redolent of the excitement of cup matches at the time:

> *Pyrmont was rich in the number of her barrackers, who appeared on the scene with large tickets in the front of their hats, upon which was inscribed words of encouragement to the Rangers. Pyrmont did the first piece of scoring, and if the jumping in the air, the waving of hats and handkerchiefs, or the vociferations from all around the boundary lines furnished any criterion, they were the general favourites.*[12]

The first of an inter-district series was played between Newcastle, Sydney and South Coast regions. Newcastle were declared state champions.

The Darlinghurst Skating Rink offered soccer played on ice in a seven aside competition in 1890. The competition, as it were, sank without trace.

New South Wales played Queensland in its first inter-colonial match in

Sydney at Botany in 1890. The match ended 3-1 in favour of the visitors. The Queenslanders played in red and black shirts and socks with blue shorts. It was reported that the result showed that Queensland has nothing to learn from New South Wales. Furthermore, the match, considering the rough uneven nature of the ground, was a splendid exposition of the Southern British Association game and was worth going a long distance to see.

In 1893 a premiership of four clubs from the Illawarra was inaugurated on the NSW South Coast under the South Coast British Football Association. By this time 23 junior teams were involved in competition in the Sydney metropolitan area.

The Balmain club donated the Kerr Cup for competition among schools in 1896. This is considered to be the genesis of organised junior soccer in New South Wales. Balmain was to win the cup three times in succession and were entitled to keep it. Balmain decided to hand it back for further competition.

In 1897 the Southern British Football Association formed a Referees Association. This raised the standard of refereeing to alleviate any conflict caused by inconsistent performances. Player registration rules were made more stringent. Teams playing in cup competitions could not suddenly exploit an administrative loophole and field new players when an important match was looming. Pyrmont Rangers made the final of the Gardiner Cup for the eighth year in succession.

During this era a selection from Sydney played a Newcastle select team each year.

In the 1890s British born players were used to well-tended home grounds with comfortable facilities such as change sheds and even baths. Many of them were deterred from playing in Sydney where unfenced, hard and uneven pitches without facilities were common.

Ex player, Thomas D. Cairns reminisced about the early days of soccer in New South Wales:

> *One great factor in the progress of the game was the sociability which was ever apparent in those days. We were a convivial crowd, we Scotsmen. We entertained visiting teams right royally at our expense. The home team always supplied supper – good and hot... We also provided an entertainment that was, musically, a credit to the sons of Scotia. When Minmi was visited, the principal dish was roast suckling pig with an apple in its mouth.* [13]

In 1898 New South Wales became the first state to drop the word 'British' from their official body. The British Football Association of New South Wales became known as the New South Wales Football Association. At a time when nationalism was high and the Federation of Australia was only three years away officials were already looking for ways to make the sport more appealing to native Australian tastes.

Northern Territory

The only evidence that there was an intention to propagate soccer in the Northern Territory in the 19th century is contained in the following intriguing snippet:

> *We believe steps are being taken to form a football club, under British Association rules. Mr Parsons would be glad to have the names of all those who would be willing to join such club.* [14]

As no subsequent follow up information about teams or matches has been found, it is not clear whether Mr Parsons did gain an adequate response. What seems certain is that no organised competition commenced.

Queensland

During the 1880s many clubs were developing in Queensland. The Rangers team was playing by 1882.

By 1884 the Brisbane competition, run by the Anglo-Queensland Football Association, comprised three teams, with Rangers, Queens Park and St. Andrews competing. A Scottish element was predominant.

The first match played between Queen's Park and St Andrew's under the new association was won 7-0 by St Andrew's:

Anglo-Queensland Association

> *The first match under the auspices of the Anglo-Queensland Football Association took place on the Pineapple ground, Kangaroo Point on Saturday, the contending clubs being the Queen's Park and St Andrew's.*

The clubs played eleven aside, being the usual number in matches under this association. The colours were for St Andrews dark blue and for Queen's Park blue and white... Some good 'heading the ball' was done by the Q. P. team, evoking considerable laughter... and all concerned brought the first Anglo-Queensland football contest to a pleasant conclusion. [15]

Don S. Gemmel was one of the pioneers of soccer in Brisbane and Queensland. He wrote a letter to the editor of *The Courier-Mail* covering the early days in Brisbane:

Sport Lively in the Eighties
Early Vicissitudes of Soccer

Sir,

Mr G. R. Tainton's article in Monday's Courier-Mail reminds me of the primitive days of Queensland Soccer, of which I was one of the pioneers. In the early eighties... some enthusiasts brought footballs in their luggage... We had goal posts and a 3in wide tape, such as Mr Tainton mentions, for a crossbar, and a ball. Coats and hats marked our corner 'flags.' ... ultimately, we secured the ground behind the Pineapple Hotel, in Main Street, Kangaroo Point. Under such conditions Soccer was born in Brisbane ... and (we) decided to form three clubs, named St. Andrews, Queen's Park, and Rangers. [16]

I am sir, &c, DON S. GEMMELL, Gray Street, New Farm.

The three foundation clubs were joined in competition in 1888 by another Brisbane club named Swifts and two teams from Ipswich (30 kilometres southwest of Brisbane), Bundamba Rovers and Queenslanders. In 1887 the Thistle club, which broke away from the original St Andrew's club, joined the competition.

The headquarters of the Association was the Pineapple Hotel. The Pineapple Rovers team was formed circa 1887. Most matches in Brisbane were played on the old pineapple paddock at Kangaroo Point which was owned by the proprietor of the Pineapple Hotel, Ben Clauson.

Fancy dress soccer matches were coming into vogue. Such a match was planned by the Wanderers and Berserker clubs from Rockhampton. A scribe from the local press let his imagination soar:

> *The idea is a novel one... Imagine K.D. Coffin levelling the ground with a gaily bedizened Hungarian peasant, Turk or bull fighter...* [17]

By 1889 Brisbane, Rosebank, Normans, St. Andrews and Thistle had been formed, playing in Brisbane.

Clubs were also founded in Ipswich by English and Welsh miners. Rivalry between Brisbane and Ipswich teams became a feature of Queensland's football culture. The first soccer match in Ipswich was played on North Ipswich Reserve on 26 June 1886.

Other teams formed in Ipswich before the turn of the twentieth century were Blackstone Rovers, Bundamba, Booval and the colourfully named Dinmore Bush Rats from the New Chum area in 1888.

In the suburb of Ebbw Vale (named after a Welsh mining village) soccer was first played in the 1890s. The Whitwood Colliery had created the Whitwood ground so that their predominantly English and Welsh coal mining employees could play soccer. The first soccer game covered by the press was played on 5 July 1892. The home team was a combination of Bush Rats, Dinmore and Whitwood. Soon after, the St Helens team established itself at the ground. The ground was renamed Ebbw Vale Memorial Park and gained distinction as having been continuously used for soccer since the 19th Century.

Matches between Brisbane and Ipswich selections became prominent.

Teams also were developed in the north of the state with clubs in Maryborough and Rockhampton prominent:

Football

> *A meeting was held at the Kelmore Arms on Saturday night, for the purpose of forming a British Association Football club in this town... it was resolved to call the club the Fitzroy Ramblers. The rules of the British Association having been adopted... In the meantime the use of the Gymnasium grounds, North Rockhampton, will he applied for, and a ball having already been secured, a practice will in all probability be arranged for next Saturday.* [18]

In 1889 a new soccer association was formed, named the Queensland British Football Association (QBFA). By the late 1890s soccer displaced Australian rules as the second most popular code in Queensland.

The West Moreton British Football Association (WMBFA) was formed to encompass clubs in the Ipswich region. The inaugural senior teams within the Association were Dinmore Bushrats, Rangers and Rovers. In addition to regular league matches, the WMBA and the QBFA, which represented teams from the Brisbane region selected representative teams to play against each other.

In 1892 the North Queensland British Football Association (NQBFA) was formed in Charters Towers. Most of the committee were players and officials of Scottish heritage.

Concurrently, a Charity Cup competition was established with a trophy to the value of 50 guineas being awarded to a metropolitan Brisbane club. The competition was based on the Scottish Glasgow Cup competition. A number of local hospitals were to be the recipients of funds raised.

Junior soccer was boosted when the first official competition was arranged by the QBFA in 1896. Five teams took part including junior teams from the Dinmore Bushrats and Thistle clubs.

The QBFA reported that 12 clubs played under their jurisdiction in 1898. The Association ran one senior and two junior competitions with 810 players registered.

In 1899 the WMBFA changed name to the Ipswich and West Moreton British Football Association (IWMBFA). Three Ipswich region based teams, Dinmore Bush Rats, Ipswich Rovers and Bundamba Rangers, played regular competition matches with two Brisbane clubs, Norman and Rosebank.

South Australia

In South Australia, E.O.W. Roeder initiated soccer matches in Adelaide in 1893.

A meeting was held in Adelaide to form a new body to develop the sport. A short time later a match was played on 5 July, 1893 between a scratch team and sailors from the ship HMS *Ringarooma*. Manila rope was used for goal crossbars, which at times confused officials, as to when a goal was scored. This may be considered the first organised soccer match held in Adelaide and South Australia.

Many doubted that soccer would supplant Australian Rules:

> *The unassuming football match played last Wednesday on the ground of Prince Alfred College between representatives of HMS Ringarooma and a local scratch team may possibly prove to be the opening of a new era in the record of the game in this colony. The encounter in question was regulated by the laws of the English 'Association' game, and it seems to be understood that two clubs will be formed in Adelaide under these rules... Whether the Association code is likely to supplant it (Australian Rules) may be doubted. Established institutions have a great advantage...* [19]

It should be noted that the participation of teams representing British sailors and soldiers was the major impetus provided by Britain towards the development of soccer in Australia in the first 30 years. This contribution though welcome, was one which required little or no effort or input from British authorities in the northern hemisphere.

Soccer players in the armed forces who visited or were garrisoned in Australia naturally desired matches in Australia. In many cases the effect of their presence was ephemeral. Naval or merchant ships would visit an Australian port and an impromptu match would be arranged with locals. Within days the ships would steam out and the match would be reported in the local newspaper, often quite flippantly, as if it was a circus oddity.

However, as will be revealed later, there were a few exceptions. Occasionally, British ships would be included in a local competition on a longer term basis.

A match was played between the Adelaide Rowing Club and the British Association Club. The contest resulted in a 2-0 win for the Adelaide Rowing Club.

Roeder wrote to *The Advertiser* in 1893 that he had communicated with the 'Sydney Football Association' and was hoping to start matches in South Australia.

As a consequence, the first Adelaide league consisted of Pioneers, Rangers and the YMCA clubs. Workers at Holfords Pottery at Norwood also played soccer. The manager of the Potteries, Tom Holford was a pioneer of the sport in South Australia.

Soccer was managing to pique the interest those with an allegiance to Australian Rules:

Association Football
I am, &c. Won Over

Sir—*Last Saturday week I chanced on the old Adelaide's ground behind the zoo, where a football match under the English Association rules now talked about so much took place. I ... must confess the game was more exciting than many good matches I have seen played under our own rules... I thoroughly believe that as there are only 11 men on each side, the English Association game will spread widely in the country districts, where the greater number of men required by our game so far has been to its greater detriment to its success... I must confess I was won over for the good game last Saturday and would now like to see it prosper...*

I am, &c.

WON OVER [20]

By the early 1890s the Depression had reduced the number of British migrants immigrating to South Australia which had been a factor in the growth of soccer. No soccer balls were to be found in Adelaide stores.

In 1895 it was reported that teams of 'British Association' soccer players named 'A' and 'B' had played against each other in numerous matches on North Norwood Oval.

A meeting was held at Jackman's restaurant in King Street to establish a soccer association in 1898 but formal matches had to wait until the 1900s.

Tasmania

A soccer match was documented to have been played near Hobart in 1877. However the code did not progress in a more formal way until near the turn of the twentieth century. It was only in the last two years of the 19th century that soccer was documented to have been played in Hobart again.

In 1898 visiting navy and merchant seamen from HMS *Wallaroo* challenged teams representing the Southern Tasmanian Artillery and Tasmanian Rifle Regiment from Anglesea Barracks, to games on the Queen's Domain, Hobart.

The following year a number of matches were played between a University of Tasmania team and teams with a military background.

No formal competitions were organized until 1900 when an Englishman, the Reverend Frederick Taylor, introduced a league format between three clubs. These were Trinity, representing the University of Tasmania, Gunners, comprising soldiers from Anglesea Barracks and Sandy Bay, who were a team of army volunteers. The competition lasted for three years.

Participation by Tasmanian troops in the Boer War had lured players away from the game by 1899. Some Tasmanians would play British troops in matches during the Boer War.

Soccer would lose momentum until midway through the next decade.

Victoria

In 1881 the Melbourne Rovers, Carlton and Prahran clubs were formed and played impromptu matches against each other. A year later Arthur E. Gibbs made an application for direct affiliation with the English Football Association, which was accepted.

The Anglo-Australian football club was formed on 31 March 1883 after a meeting at Young and Jackson's Hotel on Swanston Street. W. Niven chaired the meeting which attracted 34 attendees.

At a further meeting of the Anglo-Australian Association, it was expected that up to eight clubs would be formed. Soccer's sporting links with the 'Mother Country' would soon be forged:

> *After three season practice here, a strong team will be sent home under the patronage of the English association. It was reported by a gentleman just out from home that the prospect of such an event was causing already no little talk in England and Scotland. Favourable news is expected from England by every mail.* [21]

On 6 April 1883 there was a soccer match on the Civil Service Ground which attracted twenty-five players. It was described as 'football pure and simple'. By August of that year the Anglo-Australian club had eighty members.

On 16 August 1883 a New South Wales team travelled to the East Melbourne Cricket ground to play Victoria. The Victorians appeared in light blue shirts while the New South Welshmen played in dark blue shorts. The matched ended in a 2-2 draw and attracted about 200 spectators. Two days later both teams played a 0-0 draw.

The interstate match resulted from an invitation by the English Football Association for Australia to tour England in 1882. The Australians were in no position in terms of finances or organisation to accept the offer from England. The English made further invitations in 1885 and 1886, but again the Australians were not prepared to accept the offer. [22]

Frustratingly, in the next thirty-five or so years to come, when Australia was in a better position to accept the offer of a visit to England, the invitations ceased.

Almost all players in the interstate matches were British born, most about thirty years of age. Many would have been domiciled in Australia only a few years. They may have had up to a decade of adult experience playing in the competitive environment of either England or Scotland. Almost certainly the standard of soccer played was better than was witnessed at any other time prior to the 1920s.

A year later a Victorian team travelled to Sydney to play two matches against New South Wales. The Victorians lost the first match 0-4 and won the second match 2-1.

The condescending mainstream press in Melbourne rushed to condemn and ostracise soccer in Victoria:

> *The matches which were both drawn were decided failures the attendance not being 5 per cent of an ordinary senior club match under Victorian rules. There appears to be no chance whatever of the English game being popularised in this colony.* [22]

A news report opined that playing soccer was a sign of 'physical degeneracy' as it was not as physical as other codes.

Of all the states or territories, Victoria proved to be the most dismissive in its resistance to the nurturing of soccer:

> *In connection with football, an attempt is being made to introduce the English Association game, but as the popularity of the game as played here has long been established, the effort can only end in failure.* [23]

The South Melbourne, Richmond, East Melbourne, Carlton and Williamstown clubs had been established, playing regular matches in Melbourne for the

George and George Cup. Richmond defeated South Melbourne 3-0 to win the inaugural George and George Cup in 1884 and also won the following year.

In regional Victoria a match was played in Geelong between the Richmond and Carlton clubs on Corio Oval. *The Advertiser* of 2 July1884 carried a lengthy, yet critical, match report. It identified the teams, aspects of the rules, an estimate of crowd numbers and some adverse comment about soccer in comparison to the domestic game. The anonymous correspondent stated that there were around 300 onlookers present at the start but no more than 100 spectators remained at the end.

The Beaney Cup, to be played for by Melbourne clubs, was inaugurated in 1885. The cup was presented by Dr James Beaney, a prominent Melbourne surgeon. The Beaney Cup was won in its first year by Prahran.

By 1887 the Victorian Governor, Sir H.B. Loch, became the patron of a series of inter-colonial matches and attended a match in the company of Lord Carrington and the Mayor of Sydney. Soccer was scarching for support at the highest echelons of society and could periodically claim ephemeral success.

In 1888 the Victorian team travelled to New South Wales to compete against their northern neighbours. The Victorians played in light blue shirts, white shorts and a cap. New South Wales played in a white shirts with a red sash, white shorts and a blue cap. The Victorians won 2-1.

In 1891 Robert Amson, an ex-member of the Carlton Football Club, was sentenced for stealing cups belonging to the British Football Association of Victoria. The two cups were the George and George and Beaney cups. They were worth £55 when stolen, pawned and sold cheaply in Broken Hill. This was an early example of the lamentable history of a lack of care and regard for the preservation of trophies, which was to continue into the 20th century.

By 1895 a single soccer club in Victoria, The British Association Football Club was extant and playing matches among its members.

British miners in the coal mining districts of the Latrobe Valley established clubs, but the sport would not take firm root in Victoria wide until the first decade of the next century.

Western Australia

A club was formed in 1892 after Wilhelm Siebenhaar wrote a letter to *The Western Mail*. A meeting was held on 5 May at Stricklands Hotel when the

English Association and Rugby Union Football Club was formed. Players trained for the English Association game on Monday and Thursday and for rugby on Tuesday and Friday.

The soccer team struggled to find acceptance. Soccer matches were played on The Esplanade, the New Recreation Ground and Weld Square. Some years would pass before soccer was placed on a firmer footing.

On 6 May 1896 Archibald G. Burt wrote a letter to *The West Australian* under the pseudonym 'An Old Reptonian' in the hope of reviving interest in soccer in Perth. Burt and his brother had returned from Repton College in England and were determined to initiate a soccer competition in Western Australia.

Publication of the letter led to the convening of a meeting at the United Services Hotel on 13 May 1896 and the British Football Association was formed.

In May 1896, Perth was the first team mentioned in the press. Initially, however, it seems Perth was more a loose group of individuals of common interest, who gathered to kick a soccer ball around Russell Square than the formal club it was to become months later.

Meanwhile, four substantive clubs named Fremantle Wanderers, Perth, Civil Service and Crusaders played on Loton's Park. After the first year of competition Fremantle Wanderers were crowned inaugural league champions.

A summation of the travails, triumphs and dreams after the first soccer season was recorded:

> *Some considerable difficulty has been experienced by this Association in the matter of obtaining grounds... it appears that the British Association is taking a firm hold on the fields – Coolgardie and Murchison – and is the only game of football played at the Cross. Next season it is expected that there will be at least six clubs in the field, while some hope for more... Why should not this game become the Football of West Australia?* [24]

During the mining boom of 1894 in Coolgardie, Boulder and Kalgoorlie many English and Scottish migrants laid the foundation of what was to become a healthy Goldfields competition. Games were played on red gravel pitches which were uneven and dusty.

The Chairman of the Western Australian Association, W.C. Thomas, introduced the Challenge Cup in 1898, originally contested by the four best senior division sides.

Chapter 4

Fragile Consolidation 1900-1909

The decade from the commencement of the new century to 1909 was a period of fragile consolidation.

In 1901 Arthur E. Gibbs, the treasurer of the New Zealand Football Association visited England and tried to persuade the English to tour the colonies. He was rebuffed when his hosts explained that they would not consider a visit until soccer was better organised in New Zealand and Australia.

The early years saw steady growth of the sport in New South Wales, the rebirth of the sport in Tasmania and encouraging growth in Western Australia. In Queensland the State League persisted intermittently.

In 1904 the first overseas tour by New South Wales occurred when they visited New Zealand. The early years of the decade saw a flurry of momentum and development.

The years between 1905 and 1908 saw lesser progress. During that time interstate matches were not played and interest centred only on local competition. Some of this competition was provided by English opposition, with visiting warships and cricket teams providing sporadic interest. The public and the press usually treated such ephemeral contests as a sporting novelty, rather than matches of lasting consequence.

This led to a certain stagnation in some states. The sport was big enough in New South Wales to maintain an embryonic cocooned momentum. However, in the less developed soccer states a paralysing stasis occurred.

It was only in the last year of this decade that soccer began a renaissance in Victoria, after almost being abandoned between 1900 and 1908.

Discussion continued about the benefit of sending an Australian soccer team to England to play matches in 1908. It was posited that if such a team was sent it would face heavy defeat. A heavy defeat would only ruin the morale of soccer in Australia and lead to the English discouraging further contact with Australian teams.

Some believed, perhaps rightly, that it would be more advantageous to send quality English coaches to Australia to train Australian players in the latest skills and tactics. Some naïve Australian officials asserted that the rich English soccer authorities may voluntarily choose to assist Australia in this way, as a form of footballing charity. They were to be quickly disavowed of such notions.

There is no doubt that the absence of high level British teams touring Australia had a depressing effect on the elevating of standards within Australia soccer. In an era pre-dating actuality sports film and television, there was no way Australian youngsters could view or learn from the best teams in the world at that time.

It is important to realise that British teams would have had to come by ship, making any tour of Australia a near four month event. Top grade or even lower grade teams in England and Scotland did not have this amount of spare time to consider the possibility. The thorny question of which parties would bear costs and handle financial losses, or any profits, was rife for squabbling among officialdom.

Writers to newspapers expressed views that soccer was slipping from public consciousness. The rise of the popularity of rugby in New South Wales was partly being ascribed to an initial tour by the Australian team to England in 1909. Meanwhile, tours by the English amateur Corinthians soccer club to South Africa had elevated soccer in the national consciousness in that nation.

New South Wales

The three major competitions in this decade were centred in Sydney, Newcastle and the South Coast.

The most successful team in the Sydney competition was Pyrmont Rangers which dominated the local competition and won in 1901, 1903, 1905, 1906, 1907 and 1909. Other winners were Pyrmont Volunteers in 1902, Granville in 1904 and Glebe in 1908.

In the Newcastle region Adamstown was the most successful club. It won local titles in 1903, 1905, 1906. West Wallsend Bluebells were victorious in claiming the championship in 1901 and 1902. Wallsend won in 1903 and West Wallsend in 1904. There was no premiership awarded in 1909. On the South Coast the most successful team was Corrimal.

Junior soccer developed from 1900 under the tutelage of Frederick Barlow, who worked as a blacksmith at Hudson Brothers Engineering Works in Sydney. Barlow organised a junior competition between eight schools in the suburb of Granville. His work is one of the earliest examples of the development of junior soccer on a large scale in Australia.

The Kerr Cup was a new juvenile cup competition and in 1900 the finalists were Sirocco and Pyrmont Rangers.

The Volunteer club was one of the pioneers of five-a-side soccer and competed against teams from the South Coast.

The Granville Football Association was formed in 1902. The Association's boundaries stretched from Gladesville in the east to the Nepean River in the west.

The New South Wales Referees Union was revived, with one hundred and three referees becoming members of the Association. There had been a lack of a referees body for two years prior to the Union's formation.

Prior to 1903 soccer clubs were based on individual suburbs or localities. In Sydney, for the first time in Australia, district clubs were initiated. The introduction of district clubs came with the strict rule that only those born or raised within a certain district could play for a particular club. In addition there was no promotion or relegation.

Such a structure was anathema to British migrants who were used to clubs based on smaller localities, free movement of players regardless of birth and the excitement and vagaries of a system of promotion and relegation.

The system as it stood favoured the *status quo* of established clubs. When the British formed their own non district clubs, they discovered that their teams were either barred from promotion to higher levels or barred altogether.

In Australia district based sports teams were part of the sporting landscape. Rugby and cricket were based on the district club system. This worked well, although there were occasional disputes over where boundaries were for abutting districts or suburbs should be drawn.

The South Coast British Association was formed, which was proving to be a landmark year for the development of soccer in New South Wales. Clubs joining the Association were Bulli, Corrimal, Helensburgh, Kembla, Thirroul, Wollongong and Woonona.

In 1904 the Sydney Premiership consisted of the nine clubs of Granville, Rozelle, Balmain, Sydney, Pyrmont, Glebe, South Sydney, Ultimo and Navy.

A Navy League was commenced in Sydney in 1904. In the first match HMS *Phoebe* defeated HMS *Torch* 2-1.

At times a Metropolis team was selected. The team consisting of players from Sydney clubs who would play select teams from the South Coast or the Newcastle regions.

Soccer began in Cessnock in April 1907. A group of fifteen sportsmen met on a vacant allotment just south of the Cessnock railway station. Many of these enthusiasts were recent arrivals from Minmi, West Wallsend, Greta and Stockton.

A report in *The Sydney Morning Herald* on the 1908 Gardiner Cup final in Sydney between Pyrmont Rangers and Glebe focussed on the unusual skills required for the sport, from the point of view of the public more familiar with rugby:

'Soccer' Final
Pyrmont Wins Gardiner Cup
A Fast Game

The Gardiner Cup for British Association football teams was won on Saturday at the Sydney Cricket Ground by Pyrmont, which defeated Glebe by 4 goals to nil... The spectators might have numbered more than 3000...

'This is football proper', the followers of the game say; but it is a moot question whether it is not more entitled to be called head ball. And what sort of heads must these people have, for they will meet the ball from the hardest of kicks on the forehead and return it 30yds or so.

Undoubtedly soccer is a fine game, but it is hardly likely to seriously affect rugby.

At the conclusion his Excellency Sir Harry Rawson presented the Gardiner Cup to Pyrmont, which he congratulated on its victory. [1]

The West Wallsend team was known for its fanatical support. On match days the mining town was virtually deserted as fans packed inside and on top of trams to attend games. During this decade it won the Gardiner Cup in the consecutive years of 1901-02.

Alan Tredinnick recounts the atmosphere which enveloped the game in the Newcastle region coalfields:

> *In the years between 1900 and 1928 when the miners worked the back shift on Saturdays, it was quite common to see these hard working miners arrive at the ground with blackened faces and still in their dirty working clothes, change quickly into their football gear and take the field. After the game a cold shower, change of clothes and the celebrations would begin for both loser and victor, as well as all supporters.* [2]

By 1908 late night shift at mines from 11pm to 7 am was discontinued and work on pay Saturdays ceased. This enabled many competitions in mining areas to be played weekly, instead of fortnightly as had often been the case.

Queensland

The Queensland State League competition ran intermittently during this decade. It was held in all years except for 1903, 1907 and 1908. By 1908 Milton was the only team in Brisbane which was extant. The most successful teams of the decade were Wellington which won in 1905, 1906 and 1909 while Dinmore Bush Rats won in 1900 and 1901.

Royals Football Club had decided to join the Ipswich and West Moreton British Football Association (IWMBFA). Other teams playing in the IWMBFA league in the early 1900s were Ipswich, Blackstone Rovers, Rangers, E Company 4th Regiment, Booval Stars, Bush Rats and Ithica. The League's junior competition was also thriving with teams such as Montes, Rovers, Booval Stars, Bush Rats, Royals and Reliance competing.

Soccer was far healthier at Ipswich than in Brisbane. In April 1901, the IWMBFA President, E.G. Morgan suggested that Ipswich approach the Queensland Association to take over the running of the Challenge and Charity Cups in the absence of regular fixtures in Brisbane.

Queensland is a more decentralised state than any other and soccer was making progress in some of the towns north of the south-east corner of the state. *The Townsville Daily Bulletin* reported:

British Association

> *A meeting of delegates for the purpose of forming a union in connection with the above was held in the Y.M.C.A. Rooms last evening, the following teams being represented— Y.M.C.A., Grammars, Thistles, Souths. A union was formed, and the subscription fee for each club was fixed at 10s 6d for the season...The Charity shield which was presented some time ago by the late Mr Brand (of Messrs Brand and Drybrough) for association football will be placed in one of the windows of Flinders Street in the course of a few days.* [3]

The Toowoomba Downs competition included Newtown, Toowoomba City, Western Suburbs and Oakey.

Social events connected with clubs were an essential part of club activities and helped in the recruitment of players and supporters. In 1903 the Bundaberg Ramblers club organised a moonlight cruise on the SS *Taldora* with a brass band and numerous solo singers providing entertainment for over two hundred guests, a large number from the town at the time.

Soccer was also budding in Charters Towers in central Queensland:

> *British Association football is ousting the Rugby game ...Yesterday Townsville visited Charters Towers, and the local team won by 4 goals to nil. Most of the Charters Towers players learnt the game in Scotland, and the game is likely to make headway here as the alleged selfishness and exclusiveness of the Queensland Rugby Union has disgusted local Rugby players.* [4]

South Australia

In October 1902, a meeting was held in the Adelaide shop of a tailor named Frank Storr. The South Australian British Football Association (SABFA) was formed. A team was created which played in blue shorts with white shorts. This became the separate clubs of Adelaide and South Adelaide. A soccer match between teams representing Adelaide and HMS *Mildura* was played under British Association rules at the Jubilee Oval.

Plans had been laid for the coming season:

A general meeting of the South Adelaide British Association Football Club was held at Bricknell's Cafe on Friday evening. The meeting was well attended, and the programme for the ensuing year was arranged... The ground to be used is the same as that played on last year, at the corner of Hutt Street and South Terrace. It was decided to commence practice at once... [5]

The first regular matches occurred when teams representing North Adelaide, South Adelaide and Woodville competed. The first of these matches, held under the auspices of the SABFA, was played on 25 April 1903 between South Adelaide and Woodville. South Adelaide won 4-1. As a sign of greater maturity within the code a soccer referees association was established in Adelaide.

On 16 March 1904 the visiting English cricketers played against a team from the South Australian British Association Football Club. An inaugural South Australian team was selected to play against sailors from the ship HMAS *Katoomba*. The South Australians won 9-0.

The following year South Australia played its first interstate game against Western Australia. It was part of a three match series with all matches played at Adelaide Oval. South Australia won all matches, 5-1, 5-4 and 1-0 respectively.

It was reported that some clubs had a surfeit of players, ensuring the growth of the game in Adelaide. By 1908 clubs such as Hindmarsh and Cambridge also had a reserve team playing in the premier competition, playing against their first teams.

Adelaide area clubs to be formed in these years included Cambridge, Wallaby (consisting of Australian born players), Loco Club, St Peters and Tramways. Most did not survive the advent of World War I. Competitions at this time were often erratic with games being cancelled due to double booked grounds or a lack of players.

Cambridge won the local Webb-Harris cup in 1907, 1910 and 1911. This cup was originally presented by Charles Webb, a North Terrace dentist. Cambridge presented the 1911 cup to the Association where it became known as the Cambridge Cup.

A junior competition was flourishing in Adelaide by 1909 carrying with it the award of the Fry's Cocoa Challenge Cup for the champions. The competition was won by Cambridge Reserves. Hindmarsh won the League and the Webb-Harris Cup. The club was also fortunate enough to obtain an enclosed oval.

By 1910 South Australia could only boast ten senior clubs. In this respect it was behind Western Australia which could boast three times as many clubs. A South Australian state team visited Perth to play matches against Western Australia.

Tasmania

No formal competitions were organized until 1900 when an Englishman, the Reverend Fred Taylor, introduced a league format between three teams; Trinity (University of Tasmania, Gunners (Anglesea Barracks) and Sandy Bay ('C' company army volunteers). The competition lasted for three years.

In 1901 soccer was demonstrated to interested onlookers in Launceston, northern Tasmania:

Football
British Association Game

An interesting football contest will take place on the Cornwall Cricket Ground commencing at 4 o'clock. The match will be between two teams of man-of- warsmen (sic) from HMS Pylades, who will play the British Association game...The game is a novelty to lovers of the Australian game... and the most amusing part is that playing or touching the ball with the hands is not allowed in the rules of the game. [6]

The involvement of Tasmanian forces in the Boer War (1899-1902) led to abandonment of official soccer competitions in Tasmania between 1903 and 1908 in Hobart and the south of the state.

Challenge matches were played between Cadbury (chocolate factory club), Sandy Bay, North Hobart and South Hobart by 1908. Hobart, YMCA and New Norfolk clubs were formed. Cadbury were probably the first major 'works' or 'company' team in Australia.

The Tasmanian soccer historian Chris Hudson relates the game was largely progressed in Tasmania by the efforts of a retired civil servant, Joseph James Bolding (J.J.B.) Honeysett:

J.J.B. Honeysett and his son Joe settled in Tasmania in the early 1900s, starting a poultry farm on the property 'Hillside' at New Norfolk. They were joined from England in 1906 by their cousin Charles Honeysett, who brought a soccer ball with him. The lads could be seen kicking a soccer ball around the village green... [7]

Honeysett had emigrated from Camberwell, England where he had been a post office clerk. He was determined to reinvigorate the game on the Apple Isle. In 1907 he organised a match between a New Norfolk combination and the SS *Zealandia* and asked players interested in playing soccer to contact him.

Teams representing New Norfolk, SS *Paloona*, SS *Westralia* and YMCA competed in an impromptu competition based in Hobart.

The Tasmanian British Football Association was founded by Honeysett in May 1909. He became the secretary of the Association.

J.J.B. Honeysett's son, Joe, was to play a key role in the development of the sport in the Federal Capital Territory (Australian Capital Territory) in the 1920s.

Victoria

During the first decade of the twentieth century the game in Victoria was almost moribund. The Depression of the 1890s had a great impact on Victoria. Many of the people involved in the organisation of the sport prior to the 20th century had either left the state or the game, and soccer only re-built momentum in the years prior to the First World War.

In the period between 1901 and 1908 there was no premier competition. During this hiatus much of the momentum for the development of soccer in Victoria had dissipated causing the state to play 'catch up' for many decades to come.

This does not mean that soccer was not played at all. In 1903 an exhibition match was played between two teams representing Australian naval vessels between teams from the men of HMS *Royal Arthur* and HMS *Ringarooma*.

Naval crew featured in an exhibition match the following year. On 18 June 1904 the officers and men of HMS *Euryalus* and HMS *Katoomba* played an exhibition soccer game prior to an Australian Rules match. Victorians watched the match with bemusement and could not understand why players would not 'mark' the ball. Players also 'eaded the ball like a bloomin' goat', causing wry amusement.

Teams from British warships again were responsible for injecting a dose of soccer into the sporting diet of Victorians in 1907. HMS *Challenger* and HMS *Powerful* played a match as a curtain raiser to an Australian Rules match between and Port Melbourne and Williamstown.

The era of sporadic exhibition matches was about to change. Harry Dockerty placed a succinct notice in the *Argus* on 21 July 1908 which was to lead to the reinvigoration of soccer in Australia's second most populous state.

Dockerty was born in Scotland in 1880 and founded a successful business as a tailor in Melbourne.

Dockerty was elected the President of the Victorian Association between 1908 and 1919 and also 1922-1924. Astonishingly, he was still President of the Federation in 1965.

Dockerty had been a youth player for the St Kilda team and donated the Dockerty Cup for competition. This was to become Australia's longest running cup competition, running almost without interruption from 1909 to 1996. Others prominent in the formation of the Association included E. Harvey, W.E. Cummings and E.C. Crawford.

The 1908 meeting was held at the Orient Hotel to form an association for the organising of the sport in Victoria. The British Association Football League was formed with hopes to create up to eight clubs. In July some sixty players assembled at Middle Park to play scratch matches. The intention was to commence formal competition the following year.

On 15 August 1908 a neophyte Victorian selection played against the visiting British team from the liner SS *Persic*. A number of other teams also competed among each other. Practice matches played a large part in readying the Melbourne players and public for the start of regular competition the following year.

Shortly after the matches against the sailors from SS *Persic*, the VABFA had arranged matches between six Melbourne teams including Kerr's Eleven and the Dunlop Rubber Company.

In September of 1908 Dockerty organised an 'England v Scotland' match among local players as a further step to more formal competition. Such matches continued into the 1930s.

A correspondent reported on a match between Victoria and the visiting HMS *Powerful* team and summarised the resurgence of soccer in Victoria:

Football
British Association Match

> *The first British Association football match played in Victoria for many years took place on the Richmond Cricket-ground yesterday. A Victorian team met the footballers of the Powerful, now in port. ...The final result was - Victoria, 4 goals. Powerful, 1 goal...The Victorian team is comprised entirely of British born players. The association has been in existence five weeks and there is a membership roll of 152 players. It is intended to form eight teams next year, and compete for a cup already offered for competition.*[8]

By 1909, Lord Dudley was installed as the new patron of the Victorian Amateur British Football Association. Competition commenced, and ended with Carlton winning the newly created first division championship and the inaugural Dockerty Cup. The six teams playing in the new competition were St Kilda, Prahran, Fitzroy, Melbourne, Carlton and Williamstown.

In June 1909 the touring Western Australian team which was returning home after playing matches in New South Wales competed against a Victorian selection and won 3-0.

In Victoria, as in all the predominantly Australian Rules playing states, it was often difficult to find rectangular grounds to play soccer on. The travails of attempting to establish a new club and facilities were highlighted when a local, Mr Roberts wished to form a team based on a Williamstown factory and establish a ground where it can play. The issue was debated at a local Council meeting:

Football Notes:
British Association Football

> *There appears to be a genuine desire to try and establish the British Association game of football at Williamstown by Mr J. M. Roberts, who is prominently associated with a newly establish local firm. This gentleman, writing to the Council Tuesday night, stated they were desirous of securing*

a ground... Cr Liston in seconding pointed out that a copy of the rules should be forwarded to the committee in order to ascertain if the width of the ground was sufficient. After Cr. Crockford had referred to the presence of the Lux-Light establishment as likely to prove a barrier, the motion was carried. [9]

Western Australia

Soccer in Western Australia was probably more dominant than in any other state of Australia, except for New South Wales, in the early twentieth century. Coverage of the game in newspapers was almost as extensive as Australian Rules. By 1910, Western Australia could claim thirty soccer clubs, which, considering the Western Australian population of 271,000 people, was a creditable result.

Soccer had however, its familiar detractors. These opponents were more than keen to vent their spleen via the generously supplied oxygen of the entrenched sporting press. One of them was *Spectator*:

> *Last Saturday was an off-day with the exponents of Australian football, and the afternoon was, in consequence, very dull in Perth and Fremantle. An exhibition of the British Association game was given at the local oval but the followers of that pastime were not very strong in evidence.*
>
> *The British Association game is not, it must be said, a favourite with the Fremantle public. The latter are perhaps somewhat conservative (or patriotic) in their inclinations, and they look upon the alleged true football as a foreign matter.* [10]

A match was arranged between the visiting English cricketers and a local Association side in 1902. The Englishmen had arrived early on the liner S.S. *Omrah* so match arrangements had to be expedited.

The game was described by the press as 'the first international match ever played in Australia'. The match was won 4-0 by the English cricketers. The West Australian team wore gold shirts with a black swan adorning the pocket. Some 4,000 spectators witnessed the match.

A second match was played which was won 3-0 by the Englishmen. However, the visiting cricketers were gracious enough to admit that with a bit more luck from their West Australian opponents, the result could have been quite different.

A long running Charity Cup was inaugurated in 1902. A striking three foot tall trophy, it had originally been ordered by the Western Australia Amateur Athletics Association. However when the cup arrived from the makers, Henry Wilkinson of Sheffield, England, the Association could not pay the 100 guineas for it. It was bought for 110 guineas by the Burt family who donated it for a soccer competition with the proviso that the proceeds of games were to benefit charities. The first winners were Olympic FC which defeated Civil service 2-0 in front of some 2,000 people.

Country clubs Cue and Day Dawn were formed in the mid-Western Australian Murchison region. The clubs which were separated by four miles, played regular matches against each other.

Some matches were planned to be played under lights. In the event, bad weather ensured only one match between Casuals and Civil Service was played on 3 September 1903. Arc lamps were set up to light the ground and a white ball was used.

Kalgoorlie saluted the birth of soccer in the mining outpost:

British Association Football

Lovers of the British Association game of football will be pleased to hear that efforts are being made to start a club in Kalgoorlie. There are already two clubs at the Boulder, one at Coolgardie, and one at Kanowna and should one be formed at Kalgoorlie it will bring this really scientific game into prominence. [11]

Most of the players in the Goldfields came from towns such as Leonora, Menzies, Kanowna, Kalgoorlie, Boulder and Coolgardie. In 1900, visiting teams from Southern Cross, based in Fremantle, and a combined Coolgardie and Kalgoorlie team from the goldfields played a Perth select team in a triangular tournament. The Goldfields British Football Association was formed in 1900.

At this time a feature of Western Australian soccer were frequent 'Coast v Goldfields' contests. The first of these occurred in July 1900 when a select team from the Coast played a select team from the Goldfields.

There was keen interest in soccer in Collie, south-west of Perth and a team from Collie played a composite Perth team in Fremantle in 1903. Organisation of soccer became more professional when, concurrently, the first Western Australian association of referees was formed.

The following year soccer spread to Bunbury and there were sporadic matches between Bunbury and clubs from Perth and various ships visiting the maritime town until 1910.

In 1905 the soccer journalist *Referee* noted the growth of the game. He replied to criticism from Australian Rules sources that soccer officials were attempting to convert schoolboys to soccer by providing trophies:

> ...*the game on the goldfields is looking very healthy this year, and there has never before been so much enthusiasm shown for soccer. Mr. Hahn of Boulder City has given them a splendid Challenge Cup... The proposal to give medals to the winners of the two school competitions will, no doubt, bring out the old cry of bribery from our opponents, for the Association has never done more than present trophies for competition among the scholars.* [12]

Tommy Nisbet, a former Scottish Queens Park player, who later became secretary of the West Australia Soccer Association, reminisced about his first involvement in the game in Perth in 1906:

(By *Eight-Half*)

> '*I was pottering round at the Perth Esplanade with the usual crowd that kicks at the ball prior to a match. The City United team were one man short, and Alec McDowall asked me to fill the vacancy. I agreed, and as I was without a football strip, I simply peeled off my coat and went to it.*' [13]

In 1905 the Young Australian Football League (YAFL) was established by senior Australian Rules authorities to promote the spread of Australian Rules in schools. The YAFL had become alarmed at the number of youngsters choosing to play soccer. The YAFL accused British born teachers of promoting the playing of soccer and rugby at the expense of the indigenous game. The YAFL motto was 'An Australian Rules Club in every school'. This ginger group had no intention of co-existing with soccer or rugby. It wanted other codes to be starved of attention in the schoolyard. Despite opposition from entrenched sporting circles fourteen junior clubs existed in Western Australia by 1906.

Prominent West Australian club teams in the decade of 1901-1910 were Civil Service, Perth City, Rangers and Fremantle Rovers.

There were eighteen clubs playing senior soccer in Western Australia in three divisions of the British Football League by 1907. Additionally, fifteen schools were fielding teams. At this time a lack of enclosed grounds made it difficult for top clubs to charge admission to matches and help balance their books.

Soccer has always had its detractors. Sometimes their dislike took physical form. Vandals, with no love for soccer, destroyed a set of goalposts at a city ground in 1908.

Training College won the League Championship for the first time in 1909. Many of their players pursued careers as teachers on the Goldfields while spreading the popularity of soccer beyond the metropolitan area.

A select team from Western Australia comprised mainly of working class English and Scottish workers toured the eastern states in 1909. Western Australia played matches in New South Wales, Victoria and South Australia. Their best result in New South Wales was a 2-2 draw with the home team. Western Australia moved on to defeat Victoria 4-0.

When the Western Australians played in Sydney in early May 1909 they were welcomed warmly by New South Wales officials. The Western Australians had expected to win because half their team were teetotallers. The New South Wales Football Association president, John Nobbs, replied that all the New South Wales team were teetotallers.

The 'Sandgroper' tourists defeated a combined coalfields team at Maitland, 2-0. The Novocastrians laid on a fine welcome with a trip to Morpeth, a visit to Glebe Colliery, viewing of cranes in the harbour and an evening vaudeville show.

In 1910 Claremont won the Metropolitan Premiership and the Challenge Cup.

First Tour by an Australian Soccer Team

In 1904 the New South Wales team became the first Australian team to travel overseas when they visited New Zealand. An Australian team was initially invited by the New Zealanders. However as there was no national system of control at the time, a New South Wales team accepted the invitation.

A party of 15 players left Sydney on the SS *Maranoa* on 22 June 1904. Of the players, all bar two came from Sydney with the exception of one from Newcastle and one from the South Coast. Ten of the players were Australian born. The first international match played was against North Island and resulted in a 1-1 draw. Matches were played throughout New Zealand in Auckland, Palmerston, Masterton, Wellington, Christchurch, Otago, Dunedin, Invercargill and Canterbury. In total nine matches were played including two matches against New Zealand, which resulted in a 1-0 win to New South Wales and 3-3 draw.

On return, the touring team played a 'welcome home' match against the Rest of NSW, winning 3-1.

A report on the first match victory by the tourists (1-0) against New Zealand, combined congratulations with candour:

> *The New South Wales team have put the first intercolonial match played against New Zealand to their credit. It is the highest point which has been reached by Association football in this State.*
>
> *The New South Wales forwards excelled in combined play but it has to be again recorded that their efforts in front of goal were miserably weak. It is hard to understand that they have failed so miserably in this department of the game, as before the departure of the team this was looked upon as one of the team's strongest points.* [14]

On their return the team was treated to a 'smoke concert'. Mr Robinson, the team manager, favoured the public with his summation of the tour:

> *The team was delighted with the hospitality extended them... At Invercargill the men amused and tried to keep themselves warm by running around 'the southernmost lamp in the world'. The first test match against New Zealand at Dunedin was splendidly contested, though NSW were the better eleven ... Medcalfe and Harrison have not returned to Sydney. They stopped in Wellington, where they hope to settle down...* [15]

Robinson concluded that the Australians were not used to the wet and soft grounds in New Zealand and tried to play the ball too swiftly. He also praised the skill of New Zealand goalkeepers, whom he ranked above their Australian opponents.

Chapter 5

Growth and Contraction 1910-1918

The pre-World War One period saw the sport take its first steps in the two Territories of Australia, the Australian Capital Territory (known as the Federal Capital Territory) and the Northern Territory.

Arthur E. Gibbs was elected to a position as a colonial representative within the English Football Association in 1912. Gibbs had played in England and had been secretary of the Anglo-Australian club in Melbourne. He moved to New Zealand and arranged tours and returned to England in 1906. This led to expectations that Gibbs would enable sporting contact between England and Australia. In general his exertions were to prove fruitless in the short term.

In 1912 tentative preparations were made for an Australian team to tour North America in 1913. An Australian Rugby League official had visited the USA and was asked if Australia could send a 'soccer team'. The Australians would play in various cities including Vancouver, Toronto, San Francisco, Salt Lake City, Chicago, New York and Washington. The North Americans would pay expenses. The possibility of extending the tour to Great Britain was also envisaged. This so called 'world tour' foundered.

As the broken decade unfolded the outbreak of the World War I in 1914 was to stymie the momentum of growth.

A planned Australian tour of New Zealand was cancelled. Players were called up to serve and many were to pay the ultimate sacrifice on the battlefields of Europe.

In one state only, that of New South Wales, was competition to continue unbroken though the years of war at the highest level.

Australian Capital Territory

The first soccer match recorded in the Federal Capital Territory (Australian Capital Territory) was played in the village of Ginninderra on Friday 19 August 1910, as part of the Ginninderra Agricultural and Pastoral Show. Ginninderra played a visiting team from the settlement of Yarralumla, which the Yarralumla team won 1-0. Later that year there was a return match played at Yarralumla.

In 1911 a club of army cadets from Duntroon replaced the Yarralumla team. They were joined in 1912 by the Canberra club which comprised members of the Department of Home Affairs. Acton club was founded in 1913 and powerhouse workers formed the Jerrabomberra Football Club in 1914.

Duntroon and The Department of Home Affairs played a match in the town of Queanbeyan, which is just within the NSW border on the boundary of the ACT. A reporter previewed the match:

Soccer Football

In the park to-morrow afternoon teams representing the Royal Military College and Department of Home Affairs will play an exhibition match of British Association Rules. This is the first time this fast becoming popular game will be played in Queanbeyan... The proceeds are in aid of the hospital... a large number of people from Acton and Duntroon are coming in to witness the match. The small charge of 6d will be made for admittance to the ground. [1]

The match was won 3-1 by Canberra (Department of Home Affairs) team. A columnist was sceptical about the soccer making local impact:

Many of the spectators in Saturday's Soccer football match were a little nonplussed regarding the manoeuvres of the players. They could not understand butting the ball with the head or the goalkeeper giving it an upper-cut with his closed fist. There is no doubt about it being a scientific game, but writer, like the canny Scot, 'has his doots' about the game catching on locally. [2]

With the impetus of the development of Canberra as the National Capital, construction workers were the backbone of many teams in the ACT from this date onwards. The Canberra District British Football Association was formed in 1914. The initial teams were Jerrabomberra, Ginninderra, Duntroon and Canberra.

New South Wales

British sailors from HMS *Powerful* won the State Cup in Sydney in 1910. A curiosity of the Sydney metropolitan competition is that HMS *Powerful* was designated to represent the Australian navy. The navy was designated as a *district* on 'terra firma' which is quite different from a naval vessel.

The inclusion of teams from naval ships in a soccer competition was complex:

> *Two teams from the Navy are entered in First Grade – viz. HMS Powerful and HMS Prometheus. The Powerful team will, however, not be able to take part in the competition until sometime in June, when the ship returns to port... This is inevitable in the case of Navy teams, but the Council is always anxious to accommodate them, for they are good sportsmen, and their ground at Lyne Park is generously placed, as frequently as possible, at the disposal of the Association.* [3]

When HMS *Powerful* left Australian waters in 1911 a number of their soccer players decided to stay in Australia.

HMS *Powerful* played matches where the ship berthed. A match was played in Fiji against a district selection made up of social club sides from Rewa and Levuka.

It was later reported that another ship's compliment (HMS *Encounter*) had jumped into the breach of HMS *Powerful* in regular competition.

In 1910 the New South Wales Football Association celebrated twenty-five years since its founding in 1885. The Association President John Nobbs was a local MLA for Granville and had been a major influence in the game for twenty-seven years. Nobbs stated that when the Association commenced it had about

100 members (i.e. players), whereas by 1910 there were nearly 3,500 members.

In New South Wales the Nurse Cup was becoming a significant competition for junior teams. Additionally, a State Schools Championship commenced. Representative teams from regions such as Newcastle, South Coast and the Sydney Metropolitan area competed.

A first grade soccer match was provided for the inhabitants of Manly, who had hitherto been denied the sport:

> *At Manly Oval Glebe and Rozelle furnished an interesting game before a very fair sized crowd including many ladies who in the early part of the match shrieked whenever a player butted the ball. Later however they took it as a matter of course, being apparently satisfied that the impact was not injurious.* [4]

Members of the New South Wales Referees Association went on strike seeking more recompense for their work in 1911. In the same year Mr H.H. Nurse initiated a South Coast Challenge Cup to be competed for by teams from the South Coast and outside the region. All matches would be played in Wollongong.

In the 19th century the Lever brothers had formed the Sunlight Soap company factory at a site named Port Sunlight on the Mersey River near Liverpool, England. The company created housing and amenities both sporting and social which were, at the time, novel in Britain. A Sunlight soap factory was subsequently opened in the Sydney suburb of Balmain. By 1915 the Sunlight soccer club had formed. The company donated the Sunlight Cup to be presented to winners of a knock-out competition.

Company based or sponsored clubs and teams spread to other states. However, the majority of them were based in New South Wales and predominantly in Sydney, Newcastle and Wollongong.

Soccer can be a dangerous game at times, but usually not fatal. In 1912 a player named Patrick Doyle died while playing for his British naval ship team HMS *Fantome* at Garden Island. He fell into an adjacent dry dock.

In the same year the Balmain club swept all before them winning the League title, the Gardiner Cup the second league and junior competitions. The NSW Junior Soccer Association was formed and the NSW Football Association celebrated twenty years since its formation.

The Annandale club became the first club in Australia to provide numbers for their shirts.

A local hotbed of soccer was the Sydney suburb of Granville. Many players were employees of the 1,400 strong Clyde Engineering Company (CEC) which by 1915 covered over twenty acres. CEC built four locomotives per month and also constructed bridges and iron and malleable castings.

In 1912 the sport was gaining traction among miners in Broken Hill. The following year the Barrier Association was formed with five clubs competing. Matches were played against South Australian sides from Terowie, Orroroo and Petersburg. Players were keen, as they were conducting practice matches in February when temperatures reached 104 degrees Fahrenheit.

The important issue of nurturing soccer in schools was bearing fruit in NSW. Teams accredited to the Granville and District Association included Granville North, Granville South, Granville Superior, Auburn North, Auburn South, Carlingford, Dundas and Parramatta North, Holroyd and Merry Farmers. The total number of senior teams in the Association numbered twenty-eight, with ten school teams and six juvenile teams. Such a listing underscores the importance of the Granville and Auburn suburbs as hotbeds of soccer in the Sydney metropolitan area.

The refined sensibilities of a newspaper correspondent from were offended when he observed the kit standards of some senior Balmain players:

> *The Balmain executive should insist on all their players taking the field in proper attire. One player looks anything but decent, and week after week he turns out without the recognised stockings, leaving two beefy and fat legs to the vulgar gaze. A couple of other players get on one's nerves. They wear caps and are unable to do anything unless these caps are in their hands while either running or kicking.* [5]

The professionalism of the sport on the south coast of New South Wales was enhanced when the South Coast Referees Association was formed.

By 1913 the Western District Association included teams from Katoomba and Harden. Further west five teams named Brokens, Y.M.C.A., Umberumberka, Norths and Cockburn engaged in competition within the area of Broken Hill. Progress of the game in Broken Hill was hindered by a lack of finance:

Soccer Football Notes

> *The soccer code has had a struggle for existence in Broken Hill for the last four years ... From the referees' point of view goal nets are a very desirable, but an absent item. This I learn is, however, a matter of money. A little more financial support is badly wanted for the soccer game in Broken Hill...*
>
> *In connection with the soccer code the example set in the Australian game of having a timekeeper might well be followed. A referee has enough to do to watch for infringements without having at the same time, to keep the toll of the minutes.* [6]

The growing popularity of soccer in the Sydney metropolitan public schools was observed with A, B, and C grade competitions commencing in 1913.

A new rift developed between those favouring the existence of district or club teams. This was a problem which would bedevil the organisation of soccer in the various states of Australia over the following fifty years of the twentieth century.

In 1914 the Kerr Cup was presented to the Northern District British Football Association for competition. The cup was first won by Merewether Advance in that year.

A breakaway group was formed in 1914 with the formation of the Metropolitan Soccer League. The fight was over by 1916 as the demands of war led to the abandonment of the district system. It was not until the 1920s that the district system was reinstated.

Non-district clubs, most of which had Anglo or Scottish origins, favoured the club rather than district system. Their officials considered that their clubs should have the have right to attract the best players, regardless of where they resided. They believed that the payment of players in a professional or semi-professional capacity would attract the best players to their teams. This measure would encourage the growth and professionalism of the sport in the wider sense. Such preferences reflected the organisation of soccer in Britain.

District clubs, which grew in number, were favoured by Australian officials and as such mimicked the way the other codes in Australia were largely organised. They adhered to an amateur code of conduct.

In 1913 the interstate match between New South Wales and Victoria was reinstated.

The New South Wales Football Association agreed to reintroduce the Gardiner Cup competition, which garnered only ten entries, after it was discontinued in 1916 due to the exigencies of war. The Corrimal club was formed on the New South Wales south coast.

By 1917 the South Coast and Granville District Referee Associations had to cease supplying referees for matches, due to a lack of manpower. Only the Northern Referees Association from the Newcastle region could continue to officiate.

The Whitburn Stars team could claim the record for the number of brothers playing in a club team simultaneously. From 1917 nine of the Hodge brothers created a record which has probably not been bettered since.

It was decided that the Sydney competition would revert to the club rather than the district system in 1918. Three clubs (Balmain, Newtown and Drummoyne) which had participated in the top echelon called the First League withdrew. Royal Navy and YMCA were represented in the First League and Balmain Kia-Ora, a company club of a cordial manufacturer was a debutant in the top echelon. The second echelon or Second League included the soap manufacturer Sunlight and Gladesville, which included patients or staff from the Gladesville Mental Asylum.

The centralising of all northern New South Wales soccer to Newcastle was abandoned when the Maitland British Football Association was established and gained control of 32 teams. The Newcastle Association reverted to overseeing the progress of soccer in Newcastle and its suburbs.

Junior soccer was extremely popular in Newcastle in 1918 with sixty-four primary school teams playing as well as twenty-three high school teams. In the Newcastle region it was estimated that 1,000 players were signed up to play in all competitions.

Northern Territory

The first soccer match to be held in the Northern Territory between a scratch team from Darwin and the crew of the Royal Navy ship HMS *Prometheus* was played on 30 December, 1911:

A football match was played on the sports ground last Saturday evening between a team representing Darwin and the visiting sailors. The Prometheus team won by two goals to one, after some hard and fast play...
We believe this is the first time football has been played in the N.T.- certainly the British Association game has not been played before... [7]

This match seemed to have been unique. There is no evidence of matches being played in the following years, until there was mention of a match after World War I had finished.

Queensland

Dinmore was a hotbed of soccer in Queensland. It had four teams named Reliance, Bush Rats and two Whitewood teams. At this time Ipswich teams played in two different leagues. Bundamba, Montes and Booval Stars competed in the IWMBFA and Dinmore Rats, Rovers and Reliance played in the QBFA.

In 1912 a team comprising players from the IWMBFA Ipswich and East Moreton defeated New South Wales 4-2. The Queensland Referees Association was formed, with Mr J. Kendall elected as the first honorary secretary.

A schools competition was initiated in Brisbane with twelve teams. The winner of the competition was East Brisbane A.

Boys were also playing the game in Toowoomba. Four teams competed for the Fortescue Cup in 'the garden city'. The cup had been provided by the local jeweller.

In 1913 a correspondent, possibly of Scottish origin, wrote to the local newspaper about a visit to a senior match at Toowoomba. He noted the lack of facilities, including nets on the goal, a dressing shed and the lack of a 'water closet'. A lack of facilities at grounds in Australia was often to be remarked upon, especially by British immigrants.

Interest in soccer in Cairns was reported in a rather cryptic fashion. The local press stated that 'it is expected there will be many followers of the sphere'. Later matters had progressed somewhat and three teams, Railway Rovers, Rangers and Sawmills were in competition.

Matches were also played in Townsville. At the conclusion of a four team competition in 1913, three teams were tied on points. This caused much consternation among officials from the Townsville British Football Association.

Teams playing in Cairns at this time included Cairns United, Alligator Creek, SS *Wyreema* and Cairns Rangers. There were also three teams playing at Gordonvale.

By 1919, with many soldiers returning from the Great War, the sport, as it would in all capital cities, was set for a revival in Brisbane.

South Australia

In 1910 the South Australian state team journeyed to Western Australia and played three matches against the home state. Western Australia won the first two matches 2-0 and 4-1 and the last match ended in a 1-1 draw.

At this time a match was played in Port Pirie when the steamer *Port Phillip* played a local eleven.

In order for a sport to gain popularity it must be available to all sectors of society. To that end Mr Holiday, secretary of the British Football Association wrote to the Adelaide press expressing his hope that Adelaide University would field a Varsity soccer team stating:

> *That if any game of football is destined to become the Empire game, that game is 'Soccer' and if the University of Adelaide is to be represented in contests at football against other seats of learning from more distant parts of the Empire it is inadvisable of them to dismiss the claims The British Association has upon them...* [8]

Soccer was the subject of debate among the boy scouting fraternity. At a Baden Powell Camp a referendum was successfully held to decide whether soccer or Australian Rules would be adopted as the winter football sport of South Australian scouts. Boy scouts were finally being taught the finer points of soccer. One wag stated with sarcasm 'I trust there is nothing in the constitution that will make them liable to a charge of treason'.

The death of King Edward VII on 20 January 1910 was marked by the cessation of matches on a weekend in May as a sign of respect. The local sporting press described the King as a 'keen soccer man' noting that he had attended English Football Association cup finals and matches between the British army and the navy.

The Port Adelaide club went through the season undefeated in 1911.

Cambridge Club also won the Webb-Harris Cup outright.

In many states cup competitions often predated league competitions. Confusingly, teams in many states played a league style competition which was often called a cup competition. There were however numerous other cup competitions in the early years including the Fry's Cocoa Challenge Cup, Cambridge Basse Challenge Cup and the Moulden Challenge Cup.

By 1911 the competition in Adelaide was generally well run. However, the local press complained that teams which were not in the running for major trophies (Webb-Harris, Basse Challenge or Fry's Cocoa Cup) were guilty of starting games late or not fielding their best teams when playing away from home. A team named as being guilty of this behaviour was Norths.

The following year the Cambridge club changed its name to Tandanya, which means *place of the red kangaroo* in the local Aboriginal language. This was an early example of a club changing its Anglo based name to one of an indigenous origin. South Australia could boast eighteen local clubs fielding 404 players.

Teams from South Australia such as Petersburg regularly played teams from Broken Hill in New South Wales. This was a cross border relationship that was to endure many decades. Broken Hill Clubs were closer to some South Australian clubs than other clubs in New South Wales. The town of Petersburg changed its name to Peterborough in 1917 as a result of anti-German sentiment. The Petersburg club would also regularly play Adelaide teams at home. In 1913 the South Adelaide team left Adelaide station on a Friday night for a six hour train trip to Petersburg. They were met at the Petersburg platform at 1.30 am. Players and officials then viewed the locomotive workshop late on the Saturday morning and played a match that afternoon. Not surprisingly the 'city slickers' lost the match.

In April 1914 a representative team from Broken Hill travelled to Adelaide to play two matches against the South Australian team. The season was marred by the resignation of the SABFA treasurer and animosity between some executive members and officials from affiliated clubs. In the same year, Alderman Moulden, the chairman of the SABFA donated a handsome cup to be competed for by Association clubs.

A hint of the crowd sizes of the era can be ascertained from a match report. In 1914 North Adelaide played Adelaide at McKinnon Parade and a crowd of 600 was reported.

Players were answering the call to arms. On 11 September 1914 the SABFA held a social evening with dinner and music to farewell twenty-three players who had chosen to join the Expeditionary Force overseas.

A case of theft rocked the South Australian Soccer Association in 1915. The Treasurer left Australia taking all the Association's money with him along with the Association's records. This would not be the only occasion that a club Treasurer would abscond with funds.

In 1915, the winner of the last league championship during the war period was Cheltenham. The season was recalled for the difficulty of its completion. Players left clubs through the year to join the military. The South Adelaide club was particularly affected, losing ten players during the season.

Between 1916 and 1918 there was no organised competition, as most of the clubs had disbanded due to the War. Over thirty players had enlisted from the Port Adelaide club alone.

It was reported that just after World War I there were only seven teams in South Australia.

Competition recommenced in 1919 when five clubs (Hindmarsh, Sturt, Cheltenham, Tramways and North Adelaide) nominated for the senior competition. Tramways, however, left the competition before the 1919 season had finished.

Tasmania

The Tasmanian British Football Association (TBFA) was formed in 1910. The first southern championship commenced in 1910 with the winner being Hobart. In that year the South Hobart club was formed. Apart from Hobart and South Hobart two ships took part; SS *Westralia* and SS *Paloona*.

Soccer did not gain traction in the north of Tasmania State until 1911. Norman Vincent was instrumental in forming teams in Launceston in that year while the St George team was formed in Hobart.

Teams were also established in the north of the state at Burnie and Devonport. Although matches with interstate teams were infrequent, a fierce rivalry built up as the intrastate North v South matches became established as a regular fixture.

South Hobart, which is one of the oldest clubs in Australia with an unbroken history was founded in 1910 by J.J.B Honeysett. The home ground at Washington Street is still used by the club today.

State champion clubs from 1910 to 1914 were Hobart, SS *Westralia*, St George and Corinthians in consecutive years.

The vessels, SS *Westralia* and SS *Paloona* competed in the southern championship in 1910. Due to maritime duty the ships could only compete on alternate weeks of the season.

In 1911 Tasmania hosted New South Wales in its first interstate game. The match drew 2,000 spectators and was won 5-3 by the visitors. Concurrently, an official association was formed in northern Tasmania to manage and promote the sport.

The formation of the Northern Tasmanian British Football Association in 1912 included the clubs of Elphin, Tamar and Launceston United.

This paved the way for regular matches between select teams from the north and south of the state. The first of these matches was played at York Park in Launceston on 22 June 1912 with South winning 2-0.

At the same time Captain W. Cottrell-Dormer presented a cup for competition by senior Tasmanian clubs. The Cottrell-Dormer Cup was donated for the winners of a competition to decide the champion team of the state. The first victors were Corinthians from Hobart which defeated North Esk from Launceston.

Cup competitions were proliferating on the Apple Isle. H.H. Nurse, team manager of a New South Wales team which played in Hobart in 1911, donated a cup in his name the following year, to be contested by reserve teams.

In July 1912 the Tasmanian team made its first visit to the mainland. It visited New South Wales where they played a number of matches. When the team played New South Wales at the Sydney Cricket Ground they were outclassed 11-0. The team also played in Melbourne on the way home, losing 8-1 to Victoria.

In 1912 Ernest Storr, who had previously been a motive force in establishing soccer in South Australia, along with his brother Frank, moved to Tasmania. He played for Corinthian and later became a state selector in the 1920s.

In a sport of which official recognition from upper echelons of society was wanting, it was a coup to have the Governor of Tasmania, Sir Harry Barron, accept the title of patron of the Tasmanian British Football Association

As in New South Wales, (although it was a different competition), juniors played for the Nurse Cup. In 1912 six schools in Hobart had received soccer balls donated by the Association as a means of popularising the code.

In 1913 a former referee and a member of the TBFA, C. Falkinder also presented a cup for a state wide competition as a knock out cup. It was named the Falkinder Charity Cup.

The local association was keen to grow the sport in schools. Six soccer balls were donated to Hobart schools by the Association. The Tasmanian Junior British Football Association was formed in 1913 and shields were presented for state and secondary school competition. Teams such as Macquarie Street and St Luke's were the most prominent.

A Referees Association was established. The local association had just received the latest rules from the football authorities in England and noted that a goalkeeper can only handle the ball within his penalty area, not to half way as had previously been the rule. In Tasmania, as elsewhere in Australia, it took time for the latest rules to be adopted nation-wide.

The soccer world was growing globally and tangential international links were being established in unexpected ways. Nevertheless, in 1913, the Tasmanian Association was surprised to receive a request from the Netherlands Football Association for any information about soccer on the island.

Links with overseas may have been welcome but interstate links seemed harder to strengthen. The Commonwealth Football Association held a meeting in Melbourne and admonished the Tasmanian association for only attempting to send a proxy member, which was deemed outside the regulations.

The 1914 season kicked off with high anticipation. One correspondent named 'Hotspur' noted that some players had come from English clubs such as Aston Villa and West Bromwich Albion. One hundred and twenty-one players had registered to play with clubs controlled by the southern association. The Corinthians club were southern premiers in 1914.

By that year the Tasmanian state team had improved, and in hosting Victoria, lost only 2-0. Concurrently, the British Football Association changed name to the Tasmanian British Football Association.

The Cameron Shield was initiated for a state school premiership winners in 1915.

Senior football was played in Tasmania until midway through the season of 1915 when the competition of that year was declared void:

> *As far as could be ascertained, the number of the association's members on active service totalled nearly 100... to the great mass of the British people, the most popular code of football was Association, and the keenness displayed by the British Tommy in his beloved game must logically find a*

response in the mind of his Australian brother-in-arms... Early in August it was decided to close the season immediately.⁹

With three-quarters of senior players enlisting for the front, the Association turned its attention to the propagation of the junior competition. The McClymont Cup was inaugurated in the north of the state for junior competitors.

Joe, J.J.B. Honeysett's son, became the honorary secretary of the Tasmanian British Football Association. He had also been a player captain, secretary and treasurer of the South Hobart club. In 1916 he enlisted for World War I as a lieutenant. Joe Honeysett was captured by the Germans and became a prisoner of war. After his return to Australia, Joe was to contribute much to the development of soccer in the Federal Capital Territory (ACT).

In 1917 J.J.B. Honeysett, who had done much to establish the game in Tasmania, returned to England as an invalid and died at the age of 61.

Victoria

The Governor-General Lord Dudley and the State Governor Sir Thomas Carmichael were patrons of the Victorian British Football Association at the commencement of the decade. This may seem to be a coup. However as both dignitaries were British, the first English and the second Scottish, the impression was enforced that soccer was a 'foreign and British' sport. As if to reinforce this notion, England v Scotland matches between teams of locals with respective British roots were the most popular matches in Victoria at this time. By 1911 these 'country' matches were drawing over 4,000 spectators.

Seven clubs played senior grade soccer in Melbourne in 1910. This was short of the numbers playing the game in smaller states such as Western Australia which had eight clubs. Victoria, being the locus of Australian Rules, was always going to struggle to establish soccer widely. One notable new applicant to the Association was the Dunlop Rubber Company. After the Cadbury company in Tasmania, it was perhaps the second major company team to take part in organised competition in Australia.

After a junior association was formed, five teams played junior soccer in Melbourne in 1910.

Carlton defeated Prahran 1-0 to win the inaugural Dockerty Challenge Cup in 1910 in front of a 'large crowd'. The term 'large crowd' was often quoted in reports of Melbourne matches in this decade, as in most cases an actual figure was not provided.

The British Football Association sent teams to two rural areas of the state to promote the game. A team visited Powlett River to play Wonthaggi Rangers while another expedition was made to Bendigo for matches.

By 1911 thirteen clubs representing one hundred and sixty-one players were represented in competition in Melbourne. The Burns club was formed in this year. In September 1911 an 'Australia' v 'Great Britain' junior match was staged to promote junior soccer. The 1911 season ended with Williamstown winning the premiership shield. St. Kilda won the Dockerty Challenge Cup and Wallabies won the junior league cup competition.

Meanwhile the game was developing in the country with exhibition matches being held in Mildura.

Five new clubs were formed in 1912. They were Footscray, Melbourne Thistle, Sunshine, Birmingham Victoria and Moorabbin. Moorabbin were formerly Sandringham City.

Harry Dockerty suggested that soccer supporters could form a social and political ginger group to assist British migrants assimilate in Australia. This suggestion, which may not have assisted the cause of popularising soccer in the wider Australian community, did not come to fruition.

As in New South Wales, British sailors were instrumental in the game and many players came from a British fleet stationed at Flinders Naval Depot. At that time the British players were more experienced than the locals. In 1913 a team from Flinders Naval Depot scored 13 goals against South Melbourne.

By 1913 there was an eight team league. Teams included Carlton, Williamstown, Yarraville and Melbourne Thistle. The most successful teams of the era were Williamstown which were First Division Champions in 1911 and 1912 and Melbourne Thistle which were victorious in 1914 and 1915. Competition matches were not held between 1916 and 1918 as it is estimated that 75% of players enlisted in the forces and saw active service abroad.

There were a number of teams formed outside metropolitan Melbourne in rural Victoria prior to the First World War. Mildura fielded two clubs named Mildura FC and Irymple FC.

In 1913 New South Wales ventured to Melbourne to play Victoria. This was the first state clash between the two great rivals since 1888 when Victoria won 2-1 in Sydney. On this occasion two matches were played, resulting in a

3-2 win to Victoria and a 2-2 draw.

The following year the annual meeting of the Victorian Amateur British Football Association was informed by Mr Dockerty that 597 players had been registered during the season just concluded. Twenty-two clubs were affiliated with the VABFA.

The VABFA also congratulated a new journal named *The Winner* which gave ample space to the sport of soccer. In the same year Victorian teams toured both New South Wales and Tasmania. Footscray Thistle won the Division I trophy and became joint holders of the Dockerty Challenge Cup with Northumberland and Durham after playing a 0-0 draw. The Junior Cup was won by Sandringham.

Enlistments in the army and navy had sapped the metropolitan competition by 1915. Only nineteen clubs were affiliated with the metropolitan competition compared to twenty-two the previous year, despite the addition of two new clubs, HMAS *Cerberus* and Windsor. Melbourne Thistle defeated Albert Park in the final of the Dockerty Cup.

The 1916 senior season in Melbourne was abandoned though a few matches were played among those who had not left for the front. In June a team representing the VABFA played a team from the Royal Naval Depot in a match at Middle Park.

Western Australia

In Western Australia the Edwardian period saw the supremacy of Australian Rules challenged by soccer in a battle which was more hard fought than in other states.

The most successful clubs of the decade were Claremont which won the competition 1910 and 1912 and Thistle which won in 1914 and 1915.

There was a stigma associated with soccer in Western Australia, which in the eyes of mainstream Australians was blighted by class and ethnic prejudice. Most players were of working class origins from Britain.

Western Australia played five matches in Adelaide in 1905. Games were poorly attended partly due to a tram strike and the South Australian Association made a loss of 50 pounds.

The senior league competition accepted four new clubs in 1910. They were Ex-Students, Locos, Midland Junction and Subiaco. This extended the senior league in Western Australia to nine teams. This totalled one more team than was playing at the highest echelons of Australian Rules in Perth.

In 1911 the metropolitan Association could point to an explosion of interest in soccer. Twenty-seven clubs were affiliated with the Association, an increase of ten compared to the previous year. The Association managed to clear itself of debt prior to the season opening. The competition cup was won by Albion.

At this time senior matches were played on The Esplanade No. 1 ground and Wellington Square Nos. 2 and 3 grounds. The Association had twelve senior teams, twenty junior teams and a dozen school teams in 1912. Junior school players competed for the Armstrong Cup.

The soccer correspondent for *The Golden Gate* newspaper 'Crossbar' lamented the standard of field preparation. He was satisfied to note that penalty areas and goal lines had been marked which 'represented progress.' 'Crossbar' implored the Association to invest in goal nets which were £5 5/- each and pressed the case for enclosed grounds with turnstiles.

A Referees Association was formed and the whistle blowers were finally paid. 'Crossbar' spoke for all referees up to the present day when he lamented:

> *Honesty and duty must be ever their motto, and their task is often unpleasant... Where can he look for friends? I know of at least three referees in W.A. who are almost heartbroken at the treatment they have received...* [10]

A newspaper correspondent, 'Penalty', wrote in defence of soccer playing migrants from Britain:

> *It is unreasonable to expect these 'new chums' to cast aside a game they have known all their lives for a handling game... You might just as well ask them to drop playing cricket in summer and ask them to take on throwing boomerangs.... Do not treat the game with contempt, as if it was loathsome and despicable, for it is a game which probably has the most exponents and followers the world over.* [10]

The Collie British Football Association was established in 1912. Participating clubs were Westralian, West Collie, Collie Town, Wallsend and Collie Burns. Paddy King provided a Challenge Cup to be played for during the season.

During this year there was a match played between Perth District and

Fremantle District selections. Another representative fixture was the Coast versus Kalgoorlie match.

The dominant Perth newspaper gave a picturesque description of a visit by the Fremantle club to play Wellington Mill near Bunbury:

> *The Port club had a most pleasant three day outing to the vast forest regions near Bunbury...The gigantic trees, the wild bush scenery, the hills and dales through which the quaint little train wriggles...render this journey most interesting and educative. The game itself was played on a pitch cut absolutely from the virgin bush and a crowd of some three or four hundred sitting around on tree stumps...* [11]

One positive feature of the game in the West Australian press of the time was the allocation of space given to the programme and results of junior matches. The coverage exceeded that of any other state.

In 1913 the Geraldton Association was formed by E.G. Farrington. It consisted of three teams. The teams were Geraldton Town, Civil Service and Geraldton Thistle. Geraldton Town and Civil Service were joint winners of the 1913 Premiership. The Caledonian club, which grew from the members of the Fremantle Caledonian Society was founded by George Brown. Brown was to have an association with the club for over twenty years. The team would initially play in distinctive primrose and pink striped shirts, which were the first national colours worn by the Scottish team.

Soccer was prominent in the Kalgoorlie area by 1914. Boulder, Mines, Cambrian and Kalgoorlie were the competing clubs. There was consternation in Australian Rules circles when it was noted that the Perth Modern School and Claremont State School had decided to only field soccer teams. Headmasters came under pressure to explain their stance.

Tommy Nisbett was a veteran of early soccer in Western Australia and the secretary of the Western Australian Soccer Association (WASA). Nisbett wrote a history of soccer entitled *British Association Football in Western Australia*. He estimated that eighty-six teams were playing the game in 1914. Thirteen clubs were playing in the metropolitan competition while twenty-four clubs were playing junior soccer and twenty-nine clubs were playing in the schools.

In the senior ranks Fremantle Thistle dominated the metropolitan competition. The club won the League as well as the Challenge and Wanderers

Cup. The Wanderers Cup had been donated by the now defunct Wanderers club and was played between the champions of the first and second Leagues.

Their success was mirrored in the junior competition when Rangers Glebe won three competitions; the League, Challenge and Glick Cup. Towards the end of the 1914 season clubs were already losing players to the war effort.

Very few grounds were enclosed and equipped with turnstiles, which would have enabled effective ticketing of top grade matches. This inhibited the development of clubs in the higher echelons. Claremont Oval was an exception.

By 1915 it was getting hard to complete the season. The Claremont club had lost 75% of their players to active service and similar figures pertained to other clubs. Eight first team players of the Caledonian club made the supreme sacrifice out of twenty-five players and officials who served. Another seven players were wounded.

Special matches were played in order to raise money for the Red Cross Fund, with teams of local players representing 'Australia' and 'England' playing each other. By the end of the season Fremantle Thistle had won the Charity Cup and Wanderers Cup.

The war had taken its toll of West Australian referees. By the end of 1915 two referees had lost their lives in battle, another was seriously wounded, while another two were at the front.

Eloquent yet sombre words were written by a soccer correspondent when talking of the 1915 season:

> *On looking back on the past year the uppermost feeling of the soccer community must be sadness with a measure of pride. Pride in the knowledge of the self - sacrifice made by many of our comrades in answering the appeal of our nation and regret at the pitiless loss of life. A number of those who were with us this time a year ago will no longer play the game. They fill honoured graves on the heights of Gallipoli...* [12]

Due to the exigencies of war there was no local competition from 1916 to 1918 except for the continuation of juvenile competitions.

Commonwealth Football Association

On 15 December 1911, representatives of the state associations and New

Zealand met at the Sports Club, Hunter Street, Sydney. They formed a national soccer body, the Commonwealth Football Association (CFA) to organise the sport at a national level.

The CFA was to include representatives from all Australian states and would be the body which organised intra-state matches, and arrange international matches and in particular a match with England. Tasmania was concerned about joining the new body as the state had an affiliation with the English Football Association, a concern which was only be resolved in 1914. Among the 'smaller' states, there was also a perception that the CFA would favour the dominant soccer states of New South Wales and Queensland, assigning lesser status to their own needs and views.

Although the New Zealanders had been a motive force behind the Conference, they demurred when asked to join a Board of Control of the Association. The finances of New Zealand soccer was in better health than Australia and the Australians were disappointed by the rebuff. The Australians realised that if both countries worked together, they would have a better chance of attracting tours from Britain and Europe.

By the 1920s the relationship between Australian and New Zealand authorities had soured and was not to be repaired until the 1930s. One practical impact of the rift was that any efforts to package a tour for European sides which would include both Australia and New Zealand was doomed. This in turn lessened any profits which could be made by all parties when a tour came to Australia.

The initial conference focussed on endeavours to bring a British team to Australia, although some delegates had mixed feelings about a visit. They welcomed the idea of a tour, but feared that an Australian team may be heavily defeated by English visitors. Such defeat may engender negative publicity about the local game, which would damage the fragile integrity of soccer, rather than progress it.

The first president of the CFA was Jack Logan and the first secretary was Stephen Lynch from New South Wales. Logan had played club football in Sydney, but had subsequently left for Queensland and was in fact the Queensland delegate at the conference.

The conference debated diverse topics. Amateur and professional status, players' apparel, interpretation of the laws of the game, promotion of the game amongst boys, initiation of Inter State matches and the nurturing of the code in schools were discussed.

The initial conference also received communication from the French club Bordeaux requesting a tour and an invitation from William Taft, President of the United States of America welcoming an amateur team to tour the USA. Neither of these offers were seriously considered.

In 1913 a second conference was held in Melbourne. The Association discussed sending an Australian team to the Panama Exhibition at the San Francisco Exhibition and playing in New York.

Efforts were made to organise for an Australian team to compete at the next Olympic Games which had been set down for Berlin in 1916. The Olympics were held under the auspices of FIFA. Australia and England were not FIFA members, but the English gave Australia permission to compete under 'its own name'. At that time Australia and New Zealand competed at the Olympics together as Australasia, although Australia wished to compete on an individual basis. Perhaps, with all these bureaucratic obstacles, it was fortunate that the Olympics were not held in Berlin in 1916, due to the outbreak of World War I two years earlier. The Conference decided to concentrate on intra-state matches.

A third conference was held in Brisbane in 1914. After overtures to New Zealand to join the CFA were rebuffed, it was decided that the body would represent the Australian Commonwealth exclusively. It was also decided that players had to have two years residency in Australia in order to play for an Australian national team and that the CFA should remain affiliated with the English Football association and not join FIFA.

The following conference of the CFA due to be held in Hobart in 1915 was postponed. It would be six years before another conference was held.

Chapter 6

Servicemen and soccer during the First World War

The outbreak of World War I almost led to the cessation of organised football within Australia. With the exception of the Sydney and Newcastle areas, first class soccer competitions ceased to be played in Australia between 1916 and 1918.

The number of soccer players who answered the call to arms was large. It is estimated that 50% of players in Victoria volunteered and 70% in South Australia. In New South Wales all 15 members of a Balmain team volunteered, but two were rejected because they only had one arm. 250 Brisbane players had registered for enlistment by 1915. By the same year 241 Western Australian players had enlisted from thirteen clubs; thirty-three had been killed and thirty-two had been wounded.

Games were spreading to army camps such as Dubbo. Other camps, such as Morphettville in South Australia indulged in the sport:

> 5 o'clock in the afternoon finds several impromptu football matches in progress. It is interesting to note how the post and rail fence divides the football codes of the two contingents. On one side the Imperial reservists are engaged in a rough and ready exhibition of 'soccer,' and on the other the men of the infantry battalions were taking in the more familiar Australian game.[1]

Official farewells to camps or service overseas were to become a regular event as for example among South Australian players. A contemporary article reported:

> *The South Australian British Football Association tendered a farewell social to the members who are included in the Expeditionary Force at the King of Hanover Hotel on Wednesday evening. Mr R. J. Holiday, chairman of the association, welcomed the members and wished them God-speed... He said that all those Britishers be they soccerites or not, who were included in the Expeditionary Force, would have the satisfaction of knowing that they carried with them the good will of all Australian Britishers.* [2]

The Victorian Amateur British Football Association estimated that up to 40% of its members had enlisted to fight in World War I by 1915. Almost 1,500 soccer players were training at the Broadmeadows army camp.

The Mercury of Hobart reporting on the sacrifice made by Tasmanian players swelled with patriotic fervour:

> *It is gratifying to note that Soccer footballers in Tasmania have... responded to the call of empire in splendid fashion. Considering the comparatively short time that British football has been in Tasmania, followers of the game in this State, must, indeed, be proud of the number of players who have joined the Expeditionary Force.* [3]

Off Western Australia, Rottnest Island hosted 1,300 German and Austrian internees. A vigorous soccer competition existed on the island during the First World War.

Australian troops relaxed by playing soccer. However, for many it was a sport they lacked familiarity with. A West Australian, farrier Bob Anderson, based in Heliopolis near Cairo wrote:

> *I am still in the land of Moses... However we could be in a worse place. We have plenty of football (soccer). We have formed a team out of this company, but it is the same old story, only about half of us know the game.* [4]

Australian soldiers who took a liking to soccer found that their interpretation of the sport was a little more robust than their English opponents.

One Anzac wrote a letter about witnessing the 'Tommies' play soccer in France, just behind the front trenches. He noticed that the referee blew his whistle more than an Australian referee would.

An article was written about a match played between Australian and English allies in Mesopotamia, what is now modern day Iraq. To the chagrin of the 'Tommies' there seemed to be confusion over which code rules would be observed:

Soccer In Mesopotamia

Try and picture the scene at the match, the 6-inch guns were booming in Baghdad, the most the players wore were pants, and some had not even a fig leaf on.... The ground was strewn with bombs, cartridges and paraphernalia the Turks had left behind in their hurried retreat... the Aussies got going dinkum and scored a goal... then one of the Aussies made a low tackle and brought a Tommy down and in the thud the Tommy's leg snapped with a noise like the crack of a rifle. The final score was 14-0 in favour of the Aussies, and the Tommies vowed they would never play the Anzacs again as they did not know how to play the game. [5]

The game continued as part of the social activities of members of the Australian armed forces serving overseas. With the cessation of hostilities in 1918 many military personnel were waiting for months in Britain and Europe to return to Australia. Competitions in a variety of sports were organised to provide recreation for those waiting to be repatriated. Lieutenant G.H. Goddard wrote about competitions between Australian troops held in France and Belgium:

Association football has always had its band of enthusiastic followers. It found them in Corps Competition... The relative merits of rugby, Australian Rules and association football were as keenly debated on the battlefields and in the back areas of France and Belgium as they ever were under the sunny skies of Australia. It was possible to make a good guess at the State from which a man hailed by the vehemence with which he supported a certain brand of football. The argument with the Kaiser was more easily settled than this one. [6]

C.M Wrench wrote in his book *Campaigning with the Fighting 9th* about his sporting experiences with the A.I.F. 9th battalion, prior to the return of the battalion to Australia. At Chatelet in southern Belgium in the early months of 1919, his team was organised by Lieutenant Leo Alcock. Matches were played with other Australian battalions and local civilian teams. The team won 6 and drew 2 matches with the 1st, 3rd, 5th, 10th, and 11th Australian battalions as well as the 1st Australian Tunnelling Company:

> *The battalion was able to produce a strong and enthusiastic soccer team... The Chatelet civilians however were not content to be mere spectators when soccer matches were being played as with Rugby Union games, but formed a team themselves which became the battalion team's chief competitor. These matches with the Belgians were played mostly on Sunday afternoons and were very popular with civilians as well as with unit supporters.* [7]

Chapter 7

Friction and External Contact 1919-1929

The decade saw the resumption of football after the dislocation of World War I.

This was an era during which the Australian national team played its first matches. For the first time administrators harnessed the global nature of the world game to engage in competition within and beyond Australian shores.

The 'district' versus 'non district' dispute was to rear its head again, leading to further antagonisms among administrators and turmoil which retarded the game. Only the states of Tasmania, Western Australia and both Territories were spared this vicious debate and acrimony.

The 1919 season was marred by the fact that many players were ill from contracting the global Spanish Flu. When a Newcastle selection played Maitland in 1919 all spectators wore masks and there were frequent team changes. Clubs found they had to replenish squads throughout the season.

At this time the Protestant Churches Soccer Association was initiated in Sydney. By 1928 over eighty clubs would become affiliated.

The Australian Soccer Association was formed with headquarters in Sydney in 1921. Ernest (Ern) Lukeman was elected as secretary. This body was a successor to the Commonwealth Football Association which had been inactive since 1916. Harry Dockerty was elected the first President of the post war Association. The New Zealanders were courted again when it was proposed that the CFA should change its name to the Australasian Football Association. The New Zealanders wary of being let down again, declined the invitation.

The following year Arthur E. Gibbs, the Australian representative on the English Football Association Council, expressed his desire to have an English team visit Australia.

Gibbs admitted that a professional team was unlikely to tour as the trip would take about six months, which interrupted the professional season. A tour of amateurs would be problematic, as amateurs were required to work for a living and could not spare the luxury of so much time off to travel. Gibbs's solution was to invite a team of university students who had completed their studies. Yet to embark on their careers, a visit Australia would not impinge upon their professions. They would provide a fair test of local teams without the too stern test which Australians playing English professionals would endure. Australian officials, at least in theory, welcomed a visit by foreign national teams or clubs.

In order to build capital, a motion was carried at the 1922 ASA conference. It stipulated that 2.5% of gross takings of all inter-state matches were to become the property of the ASA. This tax was to be a significant form of income for the ASA. At the conference a list of states strongest in soccer participation were tabled. The ranking, from strongest to weakest comprised New South Wales, Queensland, Victoria, Western Australia, South Australia and Tasmania.

The 1923 conference decided that the ASA would become a Limited Liability Company. The ASA became the Australian Football Association Limited (AFAL). This company was successful in garnering enough funding to accommodate the rash of international matches between 1922 and the 1925 English FA tour.

By the mid 1920s the other codes in Australia cast nervous glances over their shoulders at any advances made by the round ball game. Larger sporting venues were controlled by these codes. Their officials became anxious about the rise of soccer, and literally shut the gates in the faces of soccer officials.

Crowds at soccer matches were growing. Stimulated in part by the regular visit of foreign touring teams from New Zealand, Canada, England, Hong Kong and Czechoslovakia, it became urgent for top level clubs in each state to find major enclosed grounds to play matches on.

Enclosed pitches were of the best quality and were within a venue which had the best facilities. They usually came equipped with turnstiles which enabled clubs, state and national associations to maximise gate returns from matches and retain accurate information about crowd figures. In this respect, clubs from New South Wales were in the most advanced position.

A correspondent to *The Mail* in Adelaide expressed his alarm at the growth of soccer and the supposed threat it posed to Australian Rules:

What are Football League authorities to do something definite in

checking the growth of soccer here? If soccer is allowed to grow in favour it can result only in weakening our own game and rob us many players.... They boast that they will this season have three leagues... In addition, they will have national, international and interstate home and away matches during this season... What are we going to do about it? Let us all get together, with one idea (and I don't think it one-eyed), to push the game of soccer clean off the map of Australia.
   I am etc. TED SANDERS
   Balham Avenue, Kingswood. [1]

Despite the ructions within the game and the constraints put upon the code by external competitors, the general future for the sport seemed bright. As is often the case with human nature, such optimism led to inflated expectations. Expectations have often run ahead of reality as exemplified by an article by J.F Black:

Look back ten or 15 years and the progress of the code, not only in New South Wales, but in Australia, is easily discernible. Now endeavour to look 10 years ahead and forecast the progress that will be made! Soccer advancement is so good that there is no reason to limit hopes in respect of the future. It is simply a matter of organisation, patience, coaching, and a steady application to the task in hand that will place the code in the premier position so far as winter sport is concerned. [2]

The formation of a team representing the Sunlight Soap Company and its sponsorship of a cup competition in the 1920s led to other company and factory soccer teams being established in New South Wales.

In 1922, Fred Barlow, the president of the New South Wales Soccer Football Association, celebrated forty years of involvement with soccer. He had been one of the pioneers of the development of the Granville District club.

The growth of soccer in schools and among juniors continued. Junior teams were formed, including Lilyfield, Lakemba, Pyrmont, Annandale, Bondi, Lithgow, Avoca and Caledonians. The Protestant Churches competition was already a force at this time and included teams and denominations such as St. Marks, Baptists, Congregational, (Congs), Thistles, City Mission and Presbyterians.

Confrontation and discontent however would come from among the ranks of football followers, with breakaway leagues the talk in New South Wales. Added to the mix were the perennial state jealousies engendered by blinkered officials of each state. They often failed to see the higher need for the universal development of the game across the nation, and the importance of the success of the national team in building the image of the sport.

A sporting editorial in 1923 exposed the web of failed alliances and cooperation among those governing the sport in New South Wales and liberally admonished all:

> *Ever since the beginning of the season the different associations controlling Soccer Football... have been fighting... First the Granville Association had a difference with the Metropolitan Senior Association; then the Protestant Churches were protesting at the action of Granville in accepting Church teams and running a Church competition; then the junior football world was at sixes and sevens... Then there was the greatest dispute of all in which the N.D.B.F.A. (Northern District British Football Association) were fighting the S.M.D.F.A. (South Maitland District Football Association) for control of certain teams...* [3]

The twin forces of pressure and confrontation both from those outside the code and tensions within the code would do much to mould, retard and develop football over the next 60 years.

The four football codes met in Sydney in 1923 to see if they could make the hiring of Sydney metropolitan grounds cheaper and better coordinate the use of grounds among the codes. Joint tenders for ground hire were discussed.

In 1924 Granville appointed the Scotsman David Christie as their coach. Astonishingly, five years later, he was the only coach in the top echelons of the Sydney Metropolitan competition. Most clubs did not have coaches but relied on team captains to devise tactics and to convey on field instructions. It was no wonder that overall progression of the Australian soccer player's technique and tactics was so slow to improve. Even when it did improve as in the 1930s, it did so unevenly, without an overall plan or the latest knowledge from overseas.

This was compounded at national level where an official committee of selectors from various states, rather than a single national coach, selected players to be 'capped'. National team players, especially those from different states, were often only introduced to each other in the dressing room prior to a match, with no previous training as a unit being possible. This parlous situation at national level would only be comprehensively addressed by the mid 1960s, with the first national coach appointed.

In 1925 ructions appeared among the clubs from Sydney and Illawarra. Some Sydney players were playing on the South Coast, which flouted residency rules. Illawarra clubs ignored the rules and withdrew affiliation from the Metropolitan Soccer Association.

The South Coast professional league comprised teams from Woonona, Thirroul, Helensburgh, Coledale, Metters and St. George. Neither Balgownie nor Corrimal joined as they were anxious to compete in the Gardiner Cup, from which the dissenting clubs were barred.

By 1926 officialdom decided that most bodies playing association football have the word 'soccer' in their title. The Australian Soccer Association noted that a priority was the need for coaches with credentials and the ASA would request British authorities to send two coaches to Australia.

For many players the cost of playing the game was a contributing factor. Players often had to pay a club joining fee as well as weekly fees and pay for a team uniform.

It is interesting to note the commercial associations connected with the rise of soccer accoutrements. In the 1920s, among others, Spalding, Barlow, CBB, Albion, Ford's and Sykes soccer balls were advertised. The Spalding balls were manufactured in Leeds, England. The Barlow balls were manufactured in Sydney.

In the 1920s the Mick Simmons sporting store in Sydney (which still exists today) offered goal nets with ropes and guys for 130/-. The Sykes soccer ball was the most expensive at 42/6-. The store also supplied soccer boots. The most expensive was the M.S. White Chrome boots which were described as having a 'blocked toe and outside ankle pad, with strap over instep, fitted with toe bar and studs for 21/-'. Soccer pumps, referee's whistles, laces, screw in studs, lacing awls and soccer ball bladders were also available.

W. Considine, an apparel importer in Sydney, offered imported English soccer jerseys for 80/- per dozen, shorts at 4/6 a pair and 'stockings' at 4/3 a pair. The Farmers department store advertised Australian made jerseys at 12/6 each. Available in club colours, the jerseys were described as having 'elastic weave', button fronts and linen collars.

Possessing the correct apparel was one thing but displaying it with elan was quite another. An article appeared *from a women's point of view* about the clothing and style of the players. The woman, rather coyly unnamed, was obviously a connoisseur of the aesthetics of the participants:

> In my opinion many players do not do themselves justice in the way they take the field. Men of splendid physique, whose muscular development is a thing to be proud of, hide themselves very often in ill-fitting garments, which not only shows the individual to disadvantage, ... it is ridiculous to see tight fitting trousers on a centre-forward... and to see wing men flying along in flapping pants, which flutter gaily round the speedy wearers knees. There is a certain plump referee, whose wide and highly respectable trousers always cause the ladies amusement.[4]

The general sports newspaper *The Referee* presented a handsome shield to the Australian Soccer Association for presentation to the winners of a national schoolboy soccer carnival in Adelaide in 1926.

The rules of soccer were changing in subtle ways. International rules now permitted an attacking player to have only two opponents, not three, in front of him and the opposing goal to remain onside.

Teams from Bowral, Berrima and Moss Vale decided to play for the Southern Highlands Districts Soccer Association and compete for the Burchell Cup by 1928.

In Sydney, in 1929, there was an interstate soccer series among teams with players of the Jewish faith. The Sydney Judean League team defeated Melbourne Hakoah. This tournament presaged many other such tournaments in the future.

During the 1920s and into the 1930s the social aspect of belonging to a club entailed certain ceremonies or social events which are less familiar to us today. Female members of clubs would often hold 'whist drives' or 'euchre parties' in order to raise funds for clubs, while baby shows and cooking competitions were also held to raise funds.

End of season club functions, often held in community halls, would usually include diverse toasts to soccer associations, referees, local MLA's, the press and the King. All club teams from juniors to senior players would gather and players who had won competitions would be awarded individual cups. On presentation nights various personalities would sing with performances ranging from the operatic to the humourous.

Often there would also be dancing to a band and an 'ugly man' or 'beauty queen' competition held. Profits from social occasions were often used to purchase the new club kit for a forthcoming season. Supper was prepared by the wives and female acquaintances of players and officials and the evening would often conclude with a rendition by all of 'Auld Lang Syne'.

Australian Capital Territory

The Scottish based Canberra Burns Club, was one of the first Canberra clubs to be established after World War I. On 12 August 1925 the secretary wrote to Sid Story in Sydney requesting matches against New South Wales teams.

A regular soccer competition in the ACT (then called the Federal Capital Territory) was virtually moribund during the years of the Great War.

The arrival of J.H. Honeysett from Tasmania in 1925 was to be the impetus to develop both the sports of cricket and soccer in the Federal Capital Territory. He had accepted a job in Canberra as the private secretary for the Minister for Repatriation.

Honeysett's arrival was greeted with keen anticipation among local sports lovers:

Canberra's gain

A welcome from Canberra cricketing circles is in store for Mr J. H. Honeysett who has assumed the position of Social Service Officer. Judging from comment by The Hobart Mercury, his departure from Tasmania is looked upon as a distinct loss to cricket activities in that State....

Cricket, however, is not the only sport indebted to his enthusiasm, for, with his father, he was responsible for the introduction and establishment of Soccer football in the small State, watching his efforts fructify until sixteen teams developed from an original two. [5]

Joe Honeysett's influence in soccer circles was almost immediate. He was the motivating force behind the formation of the Federal Territory Soccer Football Association at a meeting held in the Eastlake Hall on 21 April 1926.

In 1926 the Federal Territory Soccer Association was formed with five member clubs: Burns, Canberra, Molonglo, Capitol Hill and Northbourne.

One hundred and sixty three players were registered with Federal Capital

Territory clubs. Burns Club won the league and also won the knock out competition.

During this era some Canberra clubs travelled to Wagga to play local teams or welcomed teams from Wagga. In 1927 Burns travelled to Wagga, with Wagga defeating Burns in two fixtures.

There were calls for an enclosed soccer ground, as the code could not take gate money or attract interstate teams while playing on open grounds as existed at Acton.

The Canberra competition was soon to face constriction. With the completion of Parliament House in 1926, development of the Federal Capital Territory began to taper. Many skilled tradesmen of British birth who were the backbone of local soccer teams, left the Territory for guaranteed employment elsewhere.

The Federal Territory Soccer Football Association attempted to join the Australian Soccer Association. However, as none of its members could obtain leave to attend the Congress, affiliation was not granted.

On 7 May 1927, a Federal Capital Territory team played the crew of HMS *Renown* who were in Canberra to take part in ceremonies relating to the opening of Parliament House. It was the first international sporting contest held at Manuka Oval.

In 1928 the season was delayed until May because it was it was not possible to field four teams until then. Later in that year a team from Goulburn joined the competition.

The Federal Territory Soccer Football Association had met to re-invigorate the game in the Federal Capital Territory in 1929.

Four teams competed in the local competition, with Acton, Burns Club, Kingston and Queanbeyan engaged. However, with retrenchment common in Canberra, the four teams were reduced to one combined team before the season ended. A series of matches between the remaining Canberra team and Queanbeyan ensued, with Queanbeyan the victor, taking home the newly awarded Canberra Cup.

The Canberra 'representative' team played two matches in the year. In new colours of a red shirt with white trimmings and white shorts and socks, the team defeated Goulburn, but lost to a team from Chullora.

There was recognition that broadening the competition to encompass rural towns such as Goulburn, Wagga and Bowral may be beneficial.

New South Wales

A club was founded in Granville in 1919 which is still extant. It entered the all age division of the Granville and District Soccer Association. Two names were proposed for the club. One name nominated was The Park Hill Rangers, however the preferred name was Granville Kewpies. A kewpie was a small celluloid doll diggers brought home from France for their girlfriends.

The Granville Kewpies became a great nursery of players in the 1930s, supplying young players to teams such as Granville Magpies, Auburn and Metters. Another great junior team in the Newcastle region was the West Wallsend Woodpeckers, for which the Australian captain Clarrie Coutts played.

The New South Wales Football Association (NSWFA) and the Metropolitan Football Federation (MFF) agreed to end a turf war which had lasted four years. The former body agreed to oversee inter-state and inter-district matches as well as the State Championship (Gardiner Cup). The MFF controlled the highest level Sydney league competitions. This administrative change was also made so the NSWFA could advance the code in rural areas of New South Wales.

The colour of uniforms which soccer referees wore was variable. In 1919 Newcastle referees took a stand and decided to dress in all white. Some clubs played in black shirts. Black shirts were disallowed for teams later in the century when referees changed the colour of their uniforms by officiating in black garb.

Player's uniform colours were also causing confusion. Clubs did not have an 'away' shirt which could be worn during a match which featured a colour clash with another club. The English Football Association had a rule until 1921 which stipulated that home teams change their shirts in the event of a colour clash. Most clubs in Australia played without a change shirt, especially at the lower levels where the expense of a second uniform was a major impediment.

The two bodies involved in soccer in NSW, agreed to redrafted powers in 1919. The NSWFA retained control of State Championships, inter – district contests and interstate contests, while the MFF controlled the Sydney First and Second Leagues. This concord marked the end of a four year battle for administrative supremacy in New South Wales.

The First League included newcomers, Cockatoo Naval Dockyard, Granville and Balmain Caledonians. In the Second League, Glebe United, Orange Grove and Balmain Gladstone were newcomers.

The Junior Association reported that forty-five teams were playing in Sydney over three grades.

Visits by British ships, both merchant and military, provided an opportunity for locals to test themselves against officers, sailors and passengers from the 'mother country'. A warship entered Sydney Harbour with a royal visitor, Edward, The Prince of Wales. The Prince later became King Edward VIII. George K. Martin, the Secretary of the Metropolitan League, leapt from a launch to the deck of the warship to seal a match with the British mariners:

> *Sydney supporters are looking forward to the visit of HMS* Renown *with pleasure. Mr Martin, secretary of the Metropolitan Soccer FA, has received word from the committee arranging the festivities that the officers and ratings of the* Renown *have much pleasure in accepting the challenge of a game at soccer issued by the Metropolitan Association on June 10 at Wentworth Park Oval. An effort is being made for his Royal Highness to kick off...* [6]

H.M.S *Renown* played 13 matches in Australia against state, club and naval ship teams. *Renown* won eight, drew three and lost two matches.

In 1921, the congestion of grounds in the Sydney metropolitan area was eased somewhat by the lease of Wentworth Park by the NSW Association. The First League expanded greatly to sixteen teams, which were split into two divisions. The Second League also included teams such as Burns Anniversary Club and NSW Fire Brigade.

There were further changes in the First League with the entry of Granville and Campsie Thistle, Dulwich Hill and Pyrmont Rangers. In the first weekend of the season it was reported that 1,520 players played senior and junior soccer in the Sydney metropolitan area.

Soccer was spreading through rural New South Wales after the difficulties engendered by the World War I.

The Waverley Soccer Club and the West British Association Football Club were established in Broken Hill with vacant land opposite the Allendale Hotel being chosen as a training ground.

Wintry Goulburn also welcomed the novelty of an invigorating match of soccer when the local club met the Waverley Tramway team at North Goulburn Park.

A club was established at Katoomba in 1923 after a meeting at the local School of Arts. This was decades after James Fletcher first organised the sport in the Blue Mountains town as headmaster at Coreen College. Membership fees were 5/- and the club colours were black and white.

In no other state was the sport of soccer so steeped in history as that of the New South Wales mining areas. When twenty-one miners and their horses were killed at Bellbird in an underground explosion and fire on 1 September 1923 supporters grieved:

The Bellbird Tragedy

> *The tragedy of Bellbird has shocked the community... There is between the Soccer Code and Coalfields a stronger bond than any which exists between them and any other branch of sport. Our finest players are miners and teams such as West Wallsend, Weston, Cessnock and Wallsend in the Northern Districts and Coaldale, Woonona, Thirroul and Balgownie on the South Coast, have won laurels for themselves in the Soccer world. Masters of Balgownie and Creighton of Weston have both captained Australian teams...* [7]

There were twenty-one high school teams and eighty-four primary school teams competing in the Kerr Cup school competition. Schools in the metropolitan Sydney area formed 119 teams. The number of rugby league teams in schools was 120.

By 1924 it was decided to introduce eight district clubs. Players had to reside within the district they represented. The clubs were Balmain, Annandale-Leichhardt, Pyrmont, Eastern Suburbs, Canterbury, St. George, Gladesville-Ryde and Granville.

6,000 players were registered as playing soccer in New South Wales. The Protestant Churches Association fielded forty teams and formed its own Protestant Churches Referees Association which had sixteen members in 1923. With numbers booming, the Ryde Soccer Association was formed, playing out of Ryde Park.

The Northern Suburbs Association (NSA) was formed to control soccer on the north shore. Teams representing North Sydney Rangers, Hornsby District, Sydney Harbour Bridge, Roseville, Lane Cove and Crows Nest competed in its first division.

In 1925 some within the game pinned their hopes on the formation of a state league. Due to the residency requirements which disallowed some Illawarra players from residing in Sydney, six Illawarra clubs joined two Sydney clubs in starting a new breakaway league. The league however failed to materialise when clubs from the Hunter Valley failed to join them.

By 1926 the Wagga Wagga and District Football Association was formed. Wagga, Wagga Experimental Farm, Newtown and Hardy's Ltd comprised the clubs. The teams competed for the Maples Charity and Hardy's Cups. Wagga teams also matched themselves with teams from Temora in New South Wales and Leeton from Victoria.

The top Sydney competition could bring in respectable crowd numbers. In 1927 the Gladesville club spent £3000 on developing their ground and was rewarded with 4,000 spectators on their opening game against Balgownie.

Prior to the 1928 State League the most prominent Sydney clubs were Pyrmont which won the Championship in 1921 and 1922 and Granville which won for three straight years from 1923 to 1925.

In New South Wales there are 450 adult teams with a total of 7,000 players. The game was well established at Katoomba, Lithgow, Cootamundra, Goulburn, Wagga Wagga, Armidale, Harden, Lismore and many other country areas. In the Sydney region there were 123 schoolboy teams, 33 in Newcastle, 10 in Illawarra District, 14 in South Maitland and 20 at Granville, a total of 200 teams.

Soccer in Newcastle boomed during the 1920s. In 1921 the premiership final between West Wallsend and Cessnock attracted gate takings of £286 and 5,270 spectators.

From 1920 to 1926 the most important matches were played at the Tramway ground in Hamilton. The Northern District British Football Association moved their headquarters to Hobart Park in New Lambton in that year.

Many minor clubs played soccer in and around Newcastle. Weston had clubs named Advance, United and Albions, while Charlestown boasted the Gamblers and Waratahs. Wallsend provided six teams called Nations, Ricketts, Gumleaves, Ghosters and Ballarat Rovers.

The Newcastle Soccer Association decided to revert to 'club' rather than 'district' teams in 1927 after fifteen years of working under a 'district' model. This put them in conflict with the New South Wales Soccer Association.

In the Newcastle competition West Wallsend was the most prominent team.

It won the Newcastle title from 1919-1921, 1925 and 1926. Near neighbours Wallsend won the title in 1922, 1923 and 1924. With the formation of the State League, Cessnock from the Newcastle region won the title in the consecutive years of 1928 and 1929.

By 1928 a successful attempt was made to form a state league. Eleven teams joined a new league known as the New South Wales State Soccer League: Aberdare, Cessnock, Kurri Kurri, Wallsend and Weston from the Newcastle region, Annandale-Leichhardt, Gladesville-Ryde, Granville, Metters and St George from Sydney and Woonona from Illawarra. Many of the people supporting the breakaway league were of British origin, and fell out with Australian officials of the New South Wales administration. The officials sought to enforce the district system. The League lost affiliation with the Australian Soccer Association which was to last four years.

The establishment of the New South Wales State League led to the discontinuation of the Gardiner Challenge Cup after 1928. The Cup had been contested by New South Wales clubs since 1888.

In 1928 a new State Cup was played for by clubs playing under the newly formed NSW Soccer Football Association. The cup was donated by Mr Jim Pringle, the proprietor of the Chelmsford Hotel in Kurri Kurri.

In the State Cup two teams shared the gate takings while the Association took one third of the gate in the semi-finals and finals. Visiting clubs were to be paid fourteen fares and the referee was to be paid out of gross gate takings. The first club to win the State Cup was Aberdare which defeated Cessnock 2-0 at Cessnock Pit Paddock.

In 1928 teams from the Newcastle region first played a combined Sydney and South Coast team. The winners were given the McWilliam Cup. This 'north v south' competition lasted until 1940.

In 1929 the Northern District British Football Association which controlled junior soccer in the Newcastle region was succeeded by the Newcastle Soccer Association.

State level matches were ongoing, if not frequent fixtures. In 1923 the New South Wales team met Victoria for the first time in nine years and soundly defeated their southern rivals 5-1. New South Wales played a team from China in 1923, the Canadian team the following year and the English team in 1925. They played the Czech club AFK Vršovice (Bohemia) as well as the second visiting team from China in 1927. Of these matches notable victories were a 5-2 defeat of Canada, a 5-4 victory over Bohemians and a 6-3 victory over China. A self-confessed *rugby league convert* viewed the New South Wales v English MCC team match in Sydney:

> *That the Englishmen are fine exponents of the round-ball game has by this time no doubt firmly implanted itself in the minds of the Sydney public... Since giving up the Rugby League game, mainly owing to its official action in refusing to allow the Englishmen to play on the Sydney Cricket ground, I am delighted with the excellence of the round-ball game. It certainly surpasses the Rugby game for team work and provides sufficient thrills to satisfy the most exacting...* [8]

Northern Territory

In 1919 a soccer match in The Northern Territory took place when at Parap there was a match between a G. Ducketto XI and a Ryder-Bailey XI.

Soccer in the Northern Territory was in a tenuous condition in this era. As in other areas of Australia, it was often left to crews of ships to organise local matches. In 1922 the crew of HMS *Hollyhock* played a match against a local eleven. The match was described as being a 'rare display of soccer in the Territory'.

In the years from 1922 to 1927 soccer in the Northern Territory was kept alive by the participation of Northern Territorians of Chinese extraction.

The local Chinese played matches among members of their own club by 1923.

The novelty surrounding the pioneering ethnic Chinese soccer team from Darwin was noted. A report of their match against a team of Anglo-Australians named the *Europeans*, the first of a series played that year, on 1 January 1924 concluded:

> *The Darwin Chinese Soccer Football Team is probably the first of the kind in Australia. Other than the team from China which paid a flying visit to Australia recently, no Chinese team has even taken the field in a football match in Australia....The Chinese wore picturesque blue uniforms, and while they put a great amount of energy into the game, appeared to be nervous...* [10]

In the next two years the Chinese and Europeans played among each other and visiting teams of sailors from the coal steamer *Michigan,* HMAS *Sydney*, HMS *Concord* and HMAS *Geranium.* Such interaction was enjoyed greatly by both visitors and locals.

In 1927 a meeting was held at the Chinese Recreation Club to form a Soccer Football Association. The Association comprised clubs named Chinese Recreation Club, Oil Tankers and Darwin.

By the end of the 1920s however, racial tensions were causing problems in all codes of football in the Northern Territory. Following the refusal of white Australian Rules teams to play against Aboriginal players, the newly formed Darwin Soccer Association which coalesced around the Darwin Chinese Recreation Club, applied to use the town oval. This was refused by the Town Council on racial grounds.

Competition must have largely broken down in 1928 although it was re-established in 1929. Team selections were made along racial lines:

Soccer - Practice was held on the Oval

> *The Chinese Club may possibly place two teams in the field. It is suggested that one team should consist of Chinese only, another of exclusively Malays and Philipinos, another of whites... If the Chinese were allowed to fortify their team with half castes a fourth team could be put in the field.* [11]

Between the years 1927 and 1929 players of Chinese descent were also prevented from playing Australian Rules. This ruling in part explained the high proportion of Chinese playing soccer, although the fact is that many were more partial to playing the sport.

Queensland

The Brisbane Premiership competition included clubs from Brisbane and Ipswich. The Brisbane club Pineapple Rovers and Ipswich club Bundamba Rangers were the most prominent clubs in the 1920s. Pineapple Rovers won the metropolitan Premiership three consecutive years from 1924 to 1926. Bundamba Rangers won in 1922, 1927 and 1928.

There were three grades of junior clubs competing for three separate cup competitions in 1920. The Mildura Cup was competed for by school teams. The Queensland schoolboy team also played the New South Wales team in 1920.

The Queensland delegate to the Commonwealth Football Association, meeting in Melbourne, reported that Queensland had fifteen senior clubs, thirty-eight junior clubs, twelve juvenile clubs and two school clubs. There were Associations at Ipswich, Oakey, Rockhampton, North Coast and Toowoomba with a total playing strength of 2,500 players.

The QBFA secured the Brisbane Cricket Ground as its playing headquarters and venue for its most prestigious competition matches.

In 1921 the senior teams from Ipswich played in the Brisbane Metropolitan competition. The growth of the sport was causing a shortage of referees, so the Referees Union sent out an urgent call for additional members. By 1922, twenty senior clubs took the field in Brisbane, an increase of five from the previous year.

A combined Queensland and New South Wales team visited New Zealand for matches. It was the first time that Queensland players had played overseas.

The 1923 season opened with Brisbane City playing Pineapple Rovers in front of a 3,000 crowd at the Brisbane Cricket Ground. A Queensland select junior team played matches against New South Wales juniors in Sydney. Players had to be under twenty-one on 1 January 1923. In today's terms, this is considered too old to be a junior player.

A soccer paper named *Soccer Record* was published in Brisbane in 1924.

By 1925 Queensland possessed three hundred clubs. One hundred and twenty-five were in the metropolitan area and one hundred and seventy-five were located in the country. Four thousand players took the field each Saturday afternoon.

Queensland was also tarnished by administrative strife. Dinmore Bush Rats, Blackstone Rovers and Bundamba Rangers withdrew from the Queensland Football Association competition. They objected to not being given enough home matches in the West Moreton region. The clubs were fined £5 each and the Wynnum, Dinmore Wanderers and Shafston Rovers clubs were promoted to take the place of the dissenting clubs. In a fractured competition Pineapple Rovers won the premiership and Latrobe won the Charity Cup.

In the same year the visiting English FA team played Queensland and comprehensively defeated the locals 11-0.

In 1925 the head of the Soccer Referees Association informed the QFA that his two sons, who had enrolled in Brisbane Grammar School, had been forbidden from bringing a soccer ball to school. They were given the option of playing rugby league or giving up soccer. The BGS headmaster had described soccer as 'that larrikin game'.

In Queensland a plethora of cup competitions were available to teams all over the state. There was an inter-city cup final competition in which the winner of the Brisbane competition played the winner of the Ipswich competition. In 1926, Thistle, from Brisbane, defeated Dinmore Bush Rats. In the early 1920s a Brisbane select team played other regional teams for the honour of winning the James Pike Cup. In 1924 Brisbane defeated a Mackay select team to win the trophy.

Queensland, a state with a more diversified population outside the capital city than any other Australian state, assiduously created more rural clubs. By 1921 a Toowoomba senior competition consisted of three clubs named Cawdor, Casuals and Rangers. The Atherton Tablelands Football Association was formed in 1926 with clubs from Malanda, Kairi, North Johnstone and Glen Allyn.

The 1925 metropolitan season saw gate receipts of the Federation increase dramatically. In some instances they reached £100. Only a few years before gates of £5 were common. Pineapple Rovers were premiers and Latrobe won the Tristram Shield.

The Queensland Referees Association placed a set of demands before the QFA the following year. It demanded an increase in fees for referees in first grade matches above the 7/- 6d paid and also payment for linesmen who had hitherto been unpaid. This year also saw Ipswich clubs return to the Brisbane competition. In this year Blackstone Rovers won the QFA Premiership and Tristram Shield. It was the first club to obtain the double.

By 1927 Brisbane metropolitan soccer was governed by a newly formed body, the Brisbane and District Soccer Association (BDSA). This caused tension with the parent body, the Queensland Football Association (QFA). The premiership was won by Bundamba Rangers and the Tristram Shield and Charity Cup were won by Latrobe.

In 1928 the BDSA took over control of all league matches which previously had been run by the QFA. The QFA only had control of interstate and international fixtures held in Queensland. The metropolitan first division was enlarged from eight to ten teams. The Premiership was won by Bundamba Rangers and the Tristram Shield by Dinmore Bush Rats. In the same year

84 schools in Brisbane were playing soccer.

Flouting of customs regarding equipment or facilities was at this time common. However, the nadir of basic convention was established in 1928 when a top level match between Brisbane City and Blackstone Rovers had to be abandoned, when neither the home team nor the visiting team could supply a ball...

In 1929 there was animosity between clubs playing in the Ipswich area and Brisbane clubs. The genesis of the problem was the proposed non allocation of a share of gate takings to three Ipswich clubs. These clubs had reached a semi-final to be played at the Brisbane Cricket Ground, colloquially named 'The Gabba'. In an era when gate takings were the most substantial way for clubs to gain revenue, this decision had a severe impact on the finances of the Ipswich clubs.

The dispute resulted in clubs in both regions establishing their own competitions. 'The Gabba' was lost to soccer and gained by rugby league. Many players retired and the standard of football declined. Latrobe won the Brisbane Cup, Challenge Cup and Tristram Shield.

Queenslanders are renowned for their informal hospitality. When the Czech team AFK Vršovice (known as Bohemians) played Queensland in 1927 the government of Queensland presented two wallabies to the first president of independent Czechoslovakia, T.G. Masaryk. During the long journey to Czechoslovakia a Bohemians player named Havlín cared for them. President Masaryk donated the marsupials to Prague Zoo.

South Australia

During this decade the most successful teams were Cheltenham and West Torrens. Cheltenham won metropolitan senior championships in 1920, 1921 and 1923, while West Torrens which won in 1925, 1928 and 1929.

The 1920 season opened with correspondents lamenting former players who had perished in World War I. During the year HMS *Renown* and HMAS *Melbourne* played matches against local teams. HMS *Renown* featured The Prince of Wales (later Edward VIII) among their complement. Mr T.T. Thompson was elected chairman of the South Australian British Football Association. This was notable, as Thompson was the first Australian born chairman, after a succession of British born predecessors.

The Basse Cup was won by Prospect, the Moulden Cup (Championship) by Cheltenham and the Cambridge Cup by South Adelaide in 1921. Adelaide had nine clubs with one hundred and fifty players.

In 1922 a Referees Association was formed which obviated a rather casual approach to the appointment of officials. In the same year a junior league competition for those from 15 to 19 years of age was established. A schools league competition consisted of ten teams.

The first international match was played in South Australia in 1923 when Australia played China in the 5th test at Jubilee Oval. Over 20,000 people attended the match which ended in a 2-2 draw. Concurrently, a state select schoolboy team visited New South Wales to play matches against other juniors.

Antagonism towards the code in South Australian schools was rife. An Adelaide headmaster complained that the 'British Association' game had lured schoolboys to play the sport with the inducement of trophies and trips. He described soccer as a 'foreign' sport and urged Australian Rules authorities to redouble their efforts to entice children to play the indigenous code. However, the junior game would not be contained by malevolent forces. In 1923 a select South Australian school team travelled interstate for the first time to play matches, with the opponents being NSW schoolboy select teams in Sydney and Newcastle.

In 1924, the South Australian British Soccer Football Association (SABSFA) was re-named the South Australian Soccer Football Association (SASFA). The top division was to be named the Metropolitan League consisting of eight teams with an eight team second division. It was also agreed that a scheme based on district football was to be implemented.

Top level club names for the 1925 season would be North Adelaide, South Adelaide, West Adelaide, Port Adelaide, East Torrens, West Torrens, Sturt and Glenelg.

It was reported that Adelaide has 66 soccer clubs, with 11 more in country centres. Nearly 2,000 players played soccer in South Australia each Saturday. This marked a huge increase in playing strength in the state since 1921.

In 1925 with the impending visit of the English FA team to Adelaide, the Australian Rules League prevented Adelaide Oval from being used for an exhibition match against an Australian XI:

I commend the delegates to the Football League for their attitude towards relinquishing the Adelaide Oval to Soccer Association, who are trying by every means to supplant our national game. The last soccer match I saw cost me 6/- or more for entrance fees, for I took my wife to see Chinamen play on the Jubilee Oval. Of course, it was not profiteering. Next month, I hope to see a good Australian game on the Adelaide Oval for half that amount. For sheer audacity these Pommies beat all I have seen. [13]

An irate female reader of *The Advertiser* had a letter published in response the following Monday. She was critical of the attitude of 'Australian':

Perhaps a mere woman should not attempt to express her opinion on sportsmanship, but after reading the comments in Friday's paper, I feel compelled to do so. Are our League officials' ideals of sportsmanship governed by £ s. d.?... it is only natural that soccer enthusiasts should want such an important game staged on a city oval... I am sure Australian is mistaken in thinking soccer players want to supplant our national game? 'Australian' must remember that soccer is played all over the world, and our game in Australia only, is he jealous? Now is the time for us to give of our very best to this first visiting team of English footballers. [14]

The exhibition match featuring the Australian XI against the visiting English F.A. team was eventually played at Thebarton Oval, with the English winning 4-1.

The game was growing in rural South Australia. The Upper Murray Soccer Association was formed in 1925 with teams from Renmark, Berri and Lock 5.

The Pelaco Cup was established in 1926 although it was not played for in 1942 and between 1947 and 1949.

There was a split in the Association by 1927. A breakaway body which called itself the Adelaide and Suburban Soccer Football League (ASSFL) was formed. It comprised the clubs of Kingswood, Lancashire, West United, Railways, Osborne Athletic, Ascot Park, Unley United and Cheltenham. These clubs feared that the introduction of the district system could mean the extinction of their own clubs.

Players in the ASSFL were not recognised by the SASF and deemed ineligible to represent South Australia in state matches.

The two leagues were finally brought together as the South Australian Soccer League (SASL) over three divisions for the 1929 season. Automatic promotion and relegation was initiated and no district qualification of players was required. This enabled some players to join weaker clubs and make for a more even competition.

Tasmania

By 1920 the annual general meeting of the Tasmanian Soccer Association (TSA) reported that the sport was still recovering from having sent players to World War I. Over 100 men had volunteered for service.

The Hobart based A Grade season commenced as it did pre-World War I, with four teams competing. The teams were Corinthians, Hobart, St George, and South Hobart. A Referees Association was formed to control all matches.

In the north of the state the competition comprised the clubs of Elphin, North Esk and Tamar.

The state of the game in the Apple Isle was seen to be healthy with no less than fifteen teams engaged in three competitions conducted by the Soccer Association. A Referees Association was formed after a meeting at the YMCA headquarters in Hobart.

The senior competition in Tasmania at this time was split into northern and southern championships. Winners of both competitions played each other to be crowned the State Champion team and be rewarded by winning the Cottrell-Dormer Cup.

From 1919 to 1923 the South Hobart club was the state and southern championship winners.

The Linney-Barber cup was inaugurated for Northern teams in 1922 by Captain H.C. Linney-Barber. It was presented to the winners of the Northern League.

A year later the Ewing Cup was created as a trophy to be given to the winners of a North v South representative fixture.

The TSA obtained its first enclosed oval at South Hobart in 1923, which allowed for ticketed matches.

There were senior matches played on the west coast. The Pioneer Football Club was formed in Queenstown and another club represented Gormanston in 1923.

From this time onwards northern teams were in the ascendant. The clubs of North Esk, Elphin and Patons and Baldwins dominated. North Esk won the northern championship in 1922, Elphin were victors in the years 1923, 1924, 1927 and 1928. Patons and Baldwins, (a factory club based on its British cotton mill employees) won the northern title in 1925 and 1926 and for the first time won the State Championship final over South Hobart 2-1 in 1926.

On the island maritime state of Tasmania, (more so than other states) visits by ships, whether military or commercial, provided an opportunity for soccer matches with locals. In 1924 a British naval squadron visited Hobart and Launceston. There was a naval presence at the unlikely venue of the Launceston City Abattoir which had been transformed into a 'fantasyland' when the Tamar Soccer Club hosted the Hobart City United club at a banquet and social night.

The Seamen's Mission in Hobart organised matches between the crews of visiting British and Australian ships in 1925. School soccer had also advanced in the Launceston area, with three divisions of junior teams competing.

In 1925 the South Hobart Wanderers junior team commenced a tour of Sydney and Newcastle. This was a rare and ambitious endeavour for a junior team in this era.

A meeting of the Southern Tasmanian Soccer Football Association the following year noted that Association finances had barely progressed in 20 years. It was decided that senior players would pay a yearly registration fee of 10s and junior players 5s with half the fee being recompensed to clubs.

The Northern Association ran a 5 a side competition by 1927 with thirteen teams competing, in addition to the traditional game while in Hobart the Governor, Sir James O'Grady, had the honour of kicking off the State Premiership match between Sandy Bay and Elphin.

In 1928 it was decided that takings from the southern Charity Cup final between Sandy Bay and South Hobart would be donated to the Kennerley Boys Home. The local press stated that 'fence jumping pests' and 'dead-heads' would be identified and removed. Players who passed on their free tickets to others were also warned, as well as a number of people who identified as 'officials' in order to gain free admission. These problems can be traced back to less than effective enclosed grounds in this era.

In 1929 a new cup was presented for competition in the north. The jeweller

Morris Joseph was the donor. The cup was won three times by the Tamar club and in the early 1930s kept by them.

In 1928 a new force emerged in the game. Hobart Athletic won the southern and state titles, despite only being formed four years earlier.

By the end of the decade soccer in Tasmania was in relatively rude health with three senior divisions competing in the north of the state. Twelve clubs comprised the Junior Soccer Association in Hobart. Three of the teams were from local clubs and four were formed by schools.

The Tasmanian state team had the opportunity to play foreign opposition. It played the first of four matches against a visiting Chinese Universities team (from the South China Football Association) in 1923.

The team from Hong Kong drew 4,000 spectators in North Hobart. Many of those attending had never seen a soccer match before and there was an eerie quietness in the crowd as spectators followed the match intently. The locals won 2-1 after the Chinese player, Chan So had deliberately blasted a penalty kick over the bar. The Chinese player explained that it would be ungentlemanly to score a goal against the hosts in such a manner.

Victoria

In Victoria, the cessation of football during the First World War ensured that the code had to re-build from 1919. Pivotal to the regrowth of the game was the arrival of many British migrants in the first half of the 1920's. More than any other state, apart from Western Australia, soccer relied on British migrants to contribute to its development. To be precise, within Victoria, it was the Scots who would have a disproportionate influence in the development of soccer.

There was strong opposition to the sport from the media and the premier Australian Rules competition, the Victorian Football League (VFL). The VFL (more so than the New South Wales Rugby League) went out of its way to cast football as a 'foreign' code. The VFL disallowed the playing of soccer at larger Melbourne venues, thus hampering its development.

The Victorian team which last played in 1914 (with the exception of the odd game against Tasmania) did not play interstate again until the 1920s. The Victorian Association faced financial difficulties which made the playing of state team matches tenuous. When the Tasmanian games took place all expenses were paid by the players, who were not reimbursed for time taken off work.

H.M.S *Renown* played the Victorian state team at the Melbourne Cricket Ground in front of 44,000 spectators in 1920.

When Australia first played its inaugural international matches in New Zealand in 1922, no Victorians were selected for the squad. Victoria had not played a match since 1914 and they were considered underdeveloped for international representation.

At this time there were twenty-two teams engaged in competition and players in the region of 600. Two grades were formed known as First and Second League, while a Reserve League was comprised of the second teams of the senior grade.

Northumberland and Durham won the Metropolitan championships in 1920 and 1922. Much of their success was due to the goalkeeping exploits of English born goalkeeper Jim Robertson.

In 1922 *The Herald* published an article on the growth of soccer in Victoria. It praised the founding officials, such as H.J. Dockerty who were imbued with the spirit of the 'seemingly hopeless project of establishing soccer in Victoria'. *The Herald* acknowledged that soccer had gained a foothold and raised the vexing issue of soccer being unable to obtain enough enclosed grounds for top grade paying fixtures. The article, unsurprisingly, failed to mention the reluctance of councils and Australian Rules authorities to contribute to the solving of the problem.

Footscray Thistle won premierships in 1924, 1925 and 1929. Footscray's most influential player was the Scottish born forward Johnny Orr, who was to play well into the 1930s.

Other competing clubs were Heidelberg, Box Hill, Brighton, South Yarra, Coburg and South Melbourne.

By 1925, 1,250 players were taking the field each Saturday in six divisions, representing forty-six clubs.

Junior soccer was officially, albeit grudgingly admitted into schools in Victoria in 1925. This late adoption helps explain the relatively retarded situation soccer found itself in until after World War II, especially in relation to the other major states of New South Wales and Queensland.

There were eleven teams playing in four divisions of the Metropolitan Soccer Association by the following year. Footscray Thistle won the Division One Championship that year in an eight team competition which included teams such as Navy and Melbourne Welsh. The three other divisions boasted teams such as Werribee, Box Hill, Union Jack, Austral and Air Force.

Competitions were also held in rural towns. Clubs and associations were established in Wangaratta, Wonthaggi, Yallourn, Bendigo and Colac.

During 1927 Hakoah, one of the first clubs with an 'ethnic' connection was formed in Melbourne:

> *A group of Jewish migrants mainly from Poland inspired by the tremendous success of Vienna Hakoah, decided to form a Jewish soccer club in Melbourne. Several meetings were held by a very enthusiastic group of Jewish football players at the Polish Club in Neil Street, Carlton...* [15]

Hakoah fielded a team from 1928 in the metropolitan 3rd Division. One of Hakoah's most prominent players from the inaugural year onwards was Aku Roth. He was born in Warsaw, raised in Germany and became captain of the Hakoah team. He would still be playing in 1945 and in his later years would captain Victoria and play one match for Australia against the visiting Indians in 1938.

The club needed to play on Saturdays, causing some angst among the more conservative Jewish supporters and members.

In 1927 Victoria hosted a schoolboy tournament for state teams from Queensland, New South Wales, and South Australia. It was named the Interstate Technical Schools Soccer Championship.

There was a split in Victorian soccer circles in 1927 and 1928 when the debate about whether to have suburban or district clubs was discussed. The Melbourne Metropolitan District Association (MMDA) were at loggerheads with the Melbourne and District Association (MDA). The MMDA was disbanded in 1928 and came under the control of the Victorian Soccer Football Association (VSFA). Players and referees were also divided. Sanity prevailed in March 1929 when both parties made peace.

Soccer was making progress in Geelong. The second largest city of Victoria staged a demonstration charity match on Monday, 26 April 1920 on Geelong Oval, between a team from the crews of the visiting warship HMAS *Platypus* and the Victorian amateur and British Football Association team, Windsor.

The Geelong United Soccer Club was formed in 1923 and entered Division Two of the Metropolitan competition in 1924. In 1926 a Geelong league was formed. It eventually comprised the teams Geelong City, Ford, Valley Mills,

Overseas, Queenscliff and the Commonwealth Woollen Mills. The navy and the military were represented by HMAS *Brisbane* and the Queenscliff Garrison.

As Roy Hay and Ian Syson noted, migrants benefitted from the sense of community and solace which soccer played in development of their lives:

> *Whatever its later image, soccer was an extremely convivial game between the wars. Hardly a match which involved travelling for one of the teams passed without a meal or a dance or both, interrupted by numerous toasts and self-congratulatory speeches... The predominantly British migrants probably had less of a cultural gap to bridge than many who came later, but there is no doubt that soccer helped them on their way - providing contacts, support networks, boosting business, helping support local industries, e.g., the domestic manufacture of soccer boots and balls.* [16]

Western Australia

Teams competing in the Perth metropolitan competition in 1920 comprised Perth City United, Claremont, Thistle, Rangers, Casuals, Claremont-Glebe, Training College, Perth, HFI and Fremantle Caledonian. By 1921 sixteen teams competed in two divisions.

Claremont won the metropolitan First Division in 1919 and 1923, Perth City United won in 1920 and 1922. Thistle were winners in 1921 and 1925 and Fremantle Caledonian were victors in 1926 and 1927.

Soccer in Western Australia was developing throughout the state. Albany, Denmark, Gnowangerup, Bunbury, Narrojin and Geraldton were running competitions.

The game developed strongly in the regional towns. In the coal mining town of Collie, 200 kilometres south of Perth, the growth of teams was expedited by the formation of the Collie British Football Association in 1921. Soccer had been played in Collie since 1902. At least four teams were playing in Collie in the 1920s. By 1928 players signed for teams representing their working mines; Bullfinch, Cardiff, Ewington and West-ton.

In 1922 a tradition was established which was to last until 1939, and was particular to Western Australia. Country clubs or associations would visit Perth annually to compete for the title of Country Week champion.

The teams competing in the first year were Collie, Geraldton, Gnowangerup and Katanning.

The WABFA changed its name to the Western Australian Soccer Football Association (WASFA) in 1925. There was discussion over whether teams should be composed of players from districts in which they lived rather than from any locality or club. Many WASFA officials were against any change to a district system, as they represented teams with players of a wide geographic spread. Many of those favouring the club system hailed from the British Isles.

In 1925 the Western Australian champions Thistle United travelled to Adelaide to play the South Australian metropolitan champions, West Torrens.

The Denmark Association near Albany fielded four clubs by 1928, while the Augusta-Margaret River Association ran six clubs the following year.

Gaining suitable grounds to play soccer on was a constant battle, not aided by the fact that local councils usually favoured the dominant football code. In Albany the local club had difficulty persuading the local Council to prepare the ground properly for soccer matches, although the Council had no qualms in assisting the local Australian Rules officials.

Centre Back wrote in the press pinpointing a lack of publicity for soccer as a factor which held back the growth of the sport. His comments would equally apply to all states and territories of the Commonwealth for many decades to come:

Soccer
A Popular Winter Game

By Centre Back

Soccer has never become very popular in Western Australia. The game was first started here about 27 years ago... Now, when so many immigrants are pouring over this way, the English leavening is becoming greater, and the day of the British Association game is bound to come... Every paper has for years written columns about the Australian game, but in the majority of them there is seldom a line about soccer... [17]

F. F. wrote a hyperbolic report about his visit to a local soccer match:

A Football Fracas
The Subtleties of Soccer

By FF

If you are dull and the world seems out of joint, go to a soccer football match... You will hear a dozen dialects, from Cockney to pure Doric, jumbled together, in times of excitement, into a linguistic hotchpotch that could hardly have been bettered, or worsened, at the Tower of Babel. A soccer crowd at an exciting match is a fearsome thing, especially if you are very small and insignificant, as I am, and are jammed on the touchline amidst a rampaging mob of excited barrackers, none of whom are strictly sober... [18]

By the end of the decade there was a thriving schools competition of seven clubs. In 1929 Perth Boys' School won both the 'Captain White' and *Soccer News* trophies. Archibald Burt, who had established soccer in Western Australia donated the Burt Centenary Challenge Cup to be contested by school teams.

Australian respect for the quality of Asian opposition was somewhat lacking. When a team from a Japanese warship expressed the wish to play a local Western Australian team their offer was politely declined. It was suggested that the mariners watch a match between two Perth teams instead.

If the powers that be did not consider it fair to play against Japanese soccer players they relished the chance to play the English cricket team at soccer. Perhaps, in retrospect, they may have wished they hadn't pandered to British colonial vanity. Western Australia played against the English MCC team in 1925, losing all four matches. The state team also played a Chinese University team in three matches. It won one and lost two matches. In 1927 the Czech club Bohemians visited, winning all three matches.

Chapter 8

Australian International Matches 1922-1926

In 1922 the first Australian representative team was selected to play three international matches in New Zealand as part of an 'ashes' tour. In addition, the team played eleven matches against local or city teams.

The team left Australia on 22 May on the ship *Ulimaroa* and arrived in Wellington. On the night of their arrival they were treated to an opera performance of *Mikado*, before travelling to Wanganui.

The squad consisted of G. Cartwright, J. Cumberford, W. Maunder, W. Bratten, D. Cumberford, W. McBrile, C. Shenton, J.B. Bryant, D. Ward, G.W. Brown, A. Gibb (Captain), A. Fisher (Vice Captain), S.A. Story, W. Dane, T. Thompson. The Australian team played in light blue shirts with a maroon 'A' on the left breast.

The veteran, Alex Gibb became the first Australian captain. He played for Queensland clubs, among them Bundamba Rangers and South Brisbane Scottish. He would captain Australia on six occasions. The tour was also distinguished by that fact that Scottish born brothers, Jock and Dave Cumberford, would play together for Australia against the New Zealanders.

The first match of three 'Tests' was played against New Zealand in Dunedin on 17 June 1922 and resulted in a victory by the home side by 3-1 with W. Maunder gaining the distinction of scoring Australia's first international goal.

A report about this historic first match stated in part:

> The first test match between Australia and New Zealand drew a crowd which mounted from 3,000 at the outset to about 10,000. The usually green surroundings of Carisbrook were dulled by a curtain of mist, and a slight drizzle was falling just as the teams entered the field... That a

fairly big percentage of the onlookers were followers of the rival code of Rugby was clear from the comments and the amusement expressed at the back and forth 'heading' tactics...[1]

Alex Gibb had a tenuous link to Dunedin. As a schoolboy in Scotland he had help despatch a flag to a school in Dunedin. He was invited back to the school, as students lined a drive to welcome him while 'his' flag gaily fluttered. Suitably impressed, Gibb diplomatically granted the scholars a half a day off and a promise of no homework that evening.

Australia went on to draw 1-1 with New Zealand a week later in Wellington. 12,000 spectators viewed the match, which was a record soccer attendance in New Zealand. This was the first point Australia had won in an international match. The Australian team then lost 3-1 to New Zealand in their last match in Auckland.

Australia played fourteen matches. Nine were won, four were lost and one was drawn.

The team returned to Sydney in July and were accorded a home coming reception at the Great Southern Hotel at The Haymarket. A peevish Alex Gibb, suddenly bereft of diplomacy, commented that the New Zealanders were worthy, yet inferior opponents, and blamed Australia's losses on 'sloppy grounds and bitterly cold weather'.

The annual conference of the Commonwealth Football Association in 1923 was preoccupied with arranging a visit of the English national team, noting that it would cost £12,000 to cover the visit. This was the 'holy grail' of team visits. It was considered by many to be the tour which could propel soccer in Australia to rightful, yet unseen heights. This tour would have to gestate for two years.

The New Zealanders toured Australia in 1923. The first match was in Brisbane on 9 June 1923. This match was memorable for two historic reasons. It was the first international match played in Australia and the first time Australia had chalked up a win against another national team with a 2-1 victory. William (Bill) Maunder scored the winning goal in the last minute of play and 7,000 spectators witnessed this historic match. The gate takings were £370 and the tour was considered a financial success.

New Zealand improved in their two last matches in Sydney and Newcastle by winning 3-2 and 4-1 against the hosts.

The New Zealanders attracted over 10,000 spectators when playing New

South Wales at Wentworth Park, which was a record crowd.

At the conclusion of the series, Queensland Football Association secretary W. Fisher, presented the manager of the winning New Zealand team with a small razor case. He had taken the case to Gallipoli, when a member of the AIF. The box had been restored by Harry G. Meyer, the manager of the New Zealand team and contained the ashes of cigars smoked by the captains of the Australian (Alex Gibb) and New Zealand (George Campbell) teams:

> *The razor case was restored to new condition, and the lid permanently soldered on. This has been mounted in a beautiful casket of Australian and New Zealand timbers, made by Mr J.S Koan, a New Zealand artist at this class of work.*
>
> *The base on which the casket stands, and also the lid of the casket are of New Zealand honeysuckle... and the body of the casket is of Australian maple, all polished to perfection with plated hinges and key. The top of the lid is surmounted by a Soccer ball, while the front panel bears a silver kangaroo in the centre, with a silver fern leaf on each side bearing the letters N.Z. in blue enamel.* [2]

It was anticipated that the 'ashes' razor case would travel across the Tasman Sea, depending on which Australasian nation won the 'ashes'. It was provided with the thought that the casket would carry more sentiment than a 'mere' cup would provide. Unfortunately, this 'sacred soccer reliquary', designed with such care, was to suffer the fate of many historic Australian soccer trophies and become lost, perhaps a victim of 'Trans-Tasman transition'.

In the same year a Hong Kong based universities team toured Australia and over 40,000 people saw them play at the Sydney Cricket Ground as part of a 23 match series. This was the first time three soccer balls were used during a match.

The soccer tour was an unintentional result of plans laid by a former army officer, Harry A. Millard. Millard had been impressed by the physiques and mentality of the Chinese and recognised an opportunity for sporting entrepreneurship. He had been commissioned by the Rugby Association to travel to China in 1921 to engage a rugby team to visit Australia. However, a rude shock was in store for Millard.

The rugby authorities was prepared to spend a large amount of money on the venture. Millard presumed that the Chinese played rugby, when in fact they played soccer. Millard cabled Australia stating that it would be impossible to send a rugby team to Australia. A disappointed Millard set about to find out just what kind of soccer the Chinese could play.

Eventually the Chinese soccer team arrived to Australian shores. Millard's original plan was to select seven players from Central China and four players from northern China. However, after witnessing the performance of the Hong Kong team at the Far Eastern Games he selected the island team from the British colony.

The visit had strong political overtones. The tourists represented the Nationalist Government, which was involved with a long struggle with the Communist Party for control of China. Additionally, the entry of the team from China raised issues relating to Australia's White Australia Policy, which at the time excluded non-whites from coming to Australia.

The Commonwealth Football Association approached the Prime Minister, Stanley Melbourne Bruce, to obtain the view of the Federal Government concerning the proposal to invite a soccer team from China to visit. The Australian soccer authorities were querying whether there would be any objections to the visit, on the grounds of racial exclusivity.

Bureaucratic objections were soothed and the visit of the Chinese universities team commenced. As the Hong Kong based team arrived in Queensland a newspaper correspondent noted the arrival of the Chinese team with equal amounts of curiosity, chauvinism and wonderment, common to contact with the populace of the 'exotic' east:

Chinese Soccer Team

Of the 17 members of the team, 14 belong to the South China Soccer Club, which has latterly been formed into the South China Athletic Association, which comprises all branches of athletics in Hong Kong...

Thick set, muscular chaps, every one of them, in rather striking contrast to the diminutive Chinaman we are accustomed to seeing in Brisbane, these sons of the orient are every inch of them athletes of the first water...

Their guernseys are picturesque. A dark blue in the main, a flag of their country is displayed across the breast, with the light coloured, badge of the South China Athletic Association on either side... [3]

Not all locals were as welcoming to the team from China. The Mayor of Newcastle, sceptical about the benefits of the tour, refused to hold a civic reception for the team calling the visit 'a stunt'.

In South Australia the local Soccer Association contacted the South Australian Football League (SAFL) which governed Australian Rules. It requested that the SAFL postpone its games so the soccer match against the Chinese team could be played on Adelaide Oval. The request was refused.

Meanwhile, H.A. Millard, ensconced in Shanghai, could hardly contain his enthusiasm while communicating with Sid Storey, the Secretary of the New South Wales Soccer Association:

> *Once I had decided on Soccer I left no stone unturned...Unlimited possibilities have been opened...On your Association the honour will rest as being the sponsors of the first team of Chinese Athletes to branch into a new sphere of the sport. This will be the first team of Chinese Athletes to leave their country to appear in a European country and play before Europeans...Already I have been interviewed by representatives of Chicago and New York papers...* [4]

The local soccer press took the opportunity to enlighten locals about culture and customs in China. They were informed that there are eight languages in China. All people bearing the same name are considered cousins and therefore cannot marry. Furthermore, a Chinese gentleman does not remove his hat indoors as it is considered poor taste.

It is somewhat ironic that in the days of the White Australia policy the visit of a Chinese team could have proved so popular. However, as in all parts of the world the lure of the exotic (the definition of which varies depending on geography) always has its cachet.

Scribes were moved to write in epic terms, unwittingly confusing Chinese and Japanese cultures:

> *Now there came unto Australia a Tribe of Men called Chinese, and they were mighty of Sinew and Muscle, and soft of voice; they came from the Land of the Orient, the Far East, the land of Kimono and Rice, where almond eyed maidens stitch blossoms onto Raiment of Silk...* [5]

The press praised the deportment of the 'celestial' Chinese players, their sportsmanship and the ease at which they 'conformed to western standards of ethics'.

For the fourth 'test match' against Australia in Sydney the publicity stated 'the Chinese cannot play on the rougher grounds, but on Sydney grounds you can expect a scientific exhibition and a glorious display of footwork'.

The Chinese team played twenty-four matches including five 'tests' against Australia. Australia won four matches and drew one match with the visitors. A profit of 20% was made from the visit by the organisers, some £1,500 which was re-invested into the sport.

The popularity of the Chinese student team had repercussions. Firstly, the visit encouraged further visits by teams of Chinese origin, although none had the novelty value and hence popularity of the 1923 visitors. Secondly, the success of the tour caused consternation in the rugby league community. When the Chinese team played in Sydney, the New South Wales Rugby League was so astonished by the size of the 47,000 crowd at the Sydney Showground that it became reluctant to allow soccer to be played freely at the large grounds in Sydney.

The Canadian national team had the distinction of being only the second national team to tour Australia, during a thirteen week tour. They were considered to have a doughty midfield and to possess crafty passing skills. All but one of the players were under 30. The tour lasted five months and players ranged from all over Canada with British Columbia having the largest representation, with four players. They were considered 'fellow Britons'. This fraternal Empire friendship was to be severely tested on the field. Matches degenerated into physical battles with many players injured on both sides.

At least three Canadian players were badly injured. Harry Mosher, the star Canadian goalkeeper, was the worst casualty. He broke a leg in two places while playing against Victoria, Two hours elapsed before he arrived at hospital. He could not leave by ship with his teammates when the tour concluded. He was so disillusioned that he decided to play ice hockey instead of soccer on return to Canada.

Over six matches Australia won 3-2 in Brisbane, lost 0-1 in Sydney, won 4-1 in Sydney eight days later, drew 1-1 in Newcastle, lost 1-4 in Adelaide and won 1-0 in a third match played in Sydney. The Canadians did not tour Tasmania or Western Australia.

The Canadian matches marked the Australian international debut of an inside-right, Alec Cameron. The English born Cameron went on to play sixteen matches for Australia. Cameron played for Adamstown Rosebud, and when twenty-three years old was offered a contract with the English club Bolton Wanderers which he declined.

The first 'test' match was held in Brisbane and there was controversy in the Australian camp before kick-off. Firstly, no New South Wales based players travelled to the Queensland capital to take part, so the team selected could have been said to be less than ideal. Secondly, the Australian team refused to take the field when the Australian outside right player Edwards was dropped in favour of Mitchell, even though Edwards had initially been selected in the first eleven. After a vote among the team Edwards took the field and the match commenced. Despite these obstacles the Australians defeated the 'Maple Leafs' 3-2.

The second 'test' at the Agricultural Ground in Sydney marked the first occasion the Australian team wore shirts of myrtle green with gold and the Australian coat of arms. An element of farce was introduced when the Canadian team were required to dutifully stand to attention to the tune of *For They Are Jolly Good Fellows*. This tune was played in lieu of the official Canadian national anthem. Perhaps this diplomatic *faux pas* stirred the Canadians, who reverted to a tough tackling style of soccer to graft a 1-0 victory.

When the Canadians played a Newcastle Eleven at the Newcastle Sports Ground, in was the first soccer match played at the venue. The 'Maple Leafs' played in blue shirts and Newcastle in the select colours of black and white stripes. A crowd of 6,000 watched a 1-1 draw.

In the fourth 'test' in Newcastle the referee commenced the match only to be told by the Canadian captain that his white shirt matched the Canadian team shirts. The referee had to approach a ball boy, who wore a black and white striped shirt, and swap his shirt with him. The referee was the subject of mirth as he wriggled impatiently to make the youth's shirt fit him in front of the grandstand.

The final match was added to the five match series after the Adelaide match to recoup some of the money that had been lost on the tour. Until the Adelaide match, the Canadian tour had lost £1,148. Another Sydney match to decide the series was scheduled. The match was billed as the decider but the organisers were somewhat disappointed that only 8,000 spectators turned up to see the game.

The Canadians was farewelled from Sydney by soccer officials concerned about fiscal matters. The manager of the 'Maple Leafs' admitted his charges had 'an almost too good a time in Australia'.

A battered Canadian side left Australia by ship, minus their wounded first choice goalkeeper. Some tearful young women at the pier possibly agreed with the manager. All apparently was fair in love, war, sport and British Empire relations...

A soccer writer (AJB) wrote in the sports newspaper, *The Arrow*, that he did not favour sending an Australian team to England in 1924. He compared it to a scenario where 'A man dining at an Ambassadors restaurant would not thank you if you handed him a scone or a sandwich'. The English, who he stated 'play to perfection', would not pay to watch an Australian side getting thrashed every week. His prediction may have been accurate, but if you can only become the best by playing the best and learning, avoiding the best was certainly no long term solution.

The Australian soccer team was being treated by its own guardians as a weak, sickly and illegitimate youth with low self-esteem. Like the offspring of an English aristocrat and an Australian servant girl, it was a colonial embarrassment to be sequestered in the Antipodes. Most emphatically it was unfit, unskilled and ill equipped to achieve anything other than to sully the shores of Albion. Australian officials agreed that it would be preferable if the English were to tour Australia. Harsh lessons, administered by our betters, were best digested on Australian soccer fields, far from the pitiless gaze and derision of English terrace spectators, officials and the press.

In 1925, after years of negotiation and imploring by Australian officials, an English Football Association (FA) representative team toured Australia. The team was variously described in pessimistic or optimistic tones by the English press. At one moment it was of third division standard or on another occasion full of promising youngsters. Such descriptions denigrated Australian playing standards while perhaps making 'early excuses' in case the team fared poorly.

New Zealand officials had been asked if they wanted the English tour extended to their islands. The reply was negative, a decision they subsequently regretted. If New Zealand had taken part the Australians would have found that the tour costs would have been cheaper.

The Australian *Arrow* sports paper described the English visitors as 'virile'. It stated that it would have been 'an easy matter for the FA to select a side composed of men whose names appear on cigarette cards'. Instead, implied the paper, the English FA had taken a more courageous decision. It chose lesser known fit young men to combat the rigours of Australian conditions.

Like an abstract painting, the touring English team represented whatever qualities each individual could discern from their own perspective. Nevertheless, regardless of pedigree, the visitors were to give Australian teams some harsh lessons.

The manager of the 1925 English tour was John Lewis. Over 70 years of age, John Lewis had been the founder and chairman of Blackburn Rovers and described as a 'prince of referees'. He also represented Lancashire at the English Football Association. He was a lifetime bureaucratic English soccer insider and variously described as a 'hard-headed unflinching Britisher' and 'the greatest authority on soccer in the world'.

The English FA team played a total of 26 matches against both the Australian team and State and regional selections and won all matches. In 'test' matches against Australia, the English team won 5-1 in Brisbane, 2-1 in Sydney, 8-2 in Maitland, 5-0 in Sydney and 2-0 in Melbourne. The schedule of matches ranged from Western Australia to Bundaberg. The tour did much to give the game a higher profile at the time, yet also highlighted the gulf in quality between players in Australia and England.

When the English amateur team arrived in Fremantle the local press was eager to boost their credentials. Players were described as if they were matinee idols. Reportedly, they were big, hefty, good tempered and jolly, with colour in their cheeks and a sparkle in their eyes. Furthermore, they had well cut features and musical voices. The team demonstrated deft footwork by juggling a penny among a group of players without it touching the ground. A team manager was eager to tell locals that the amateur team had defeated an English professional selection 3-1 in the year.

When the players practiced at Claremont in preparation for the 24 match tour, a local reporter was impressed by the crisp uniform of the players with a white shirt bearing the crest of three lions and dark blue shorts. Players had the name of their club written on the tops of their socks. The Englishmen shot on goal with great power and precision, while their goalkeepers, though not tall, were extremely agile.

With publicity of that calibre, interest in the longed for visitors from the 'mother country' was intense, and the tour released a pent up desire among local fans.

In Newcastle, NSW, the English played a local selection and there was pandemonium in the ground. 15,000 fans overcrowded the stands and burst onto the sidelines, with police helpless to intervene. Press tables were overturned, people stood on roofs of stands and two people were hospitalised after falls.

The English team played a NSW south coast selection at Bode's Ground, winning with ease. The scenes of pandemonium witnessed at Newcastle were not repeated and on a rest day the English tourists were shown the local sights including the famous blow hole at Kiama, which was at its most tempestuous, and therefore seen to advantage.

Australian officials, though enthusiastic about the tour, could have been more professional. During the first international match in Sydney £182 in takings was stolen from a box in an unguarded room with an open window.

On a comic note, a local journalist indulged in colonial chauvinism when it printed what it termed *Diary of an English Visitor*. This was without doubt a fictitious anonymous extracts from the 'diary' of a team member of the 1925 touring English squad:

> *Arrived in Australia.... came to Melbourne, where the populace did greatly amuse me. All they speak about is the width of the thoroughfares and the narrowness of the flappers skirts. Have not met the Prime Minister but expect to... To Sydney by train ...So far no cannibals, no alligators, no cowboys... Am greatly offended to learn we are called 'Pommies' out here, some do not mind at all, but it hurts my dignity and I feel it my duty to report the matter to King George upon my return home...* [6]

At the conclusion of the tour John Lewis's assessment of the Australian soccer scene was sobering. It mixed the acuity of a foreigner used to premium conditions back home, with the arrogance of a touring Englishman from the Football Association.

Australia, he stated, quite rightly, should have better soccer pitches. Soccer should not be played on oval fields where spectators were too far from the action. He also correctly criticised the lack of cooperation between state bodies and a considered that a paid secretary of the national association was required. He conceded the difficulty of administrating soccer efficiently on such a vast continent.

Lewis named the Australian player, Roy McNaughton, as Australia's best. He stated that McNaughton would have no trouble playing for a Division 1 club in England.

Some of his players, Lewis claimed, had been charged (fouled) unfairly to the extent that 'one many never play first class soccer again'. His players were expected to play too many matches compared to the Australian team and he regretted that he did not bring a larger squad than the 18 he brought to Australian shores.

Like a baleful schoolmaster who would only reveal his full assessment of an indolent student in an end of year report, he stated that he would reserve most of his opinions and conclusions until an official report was proffered to the English Football Association. At press conferences and in his official report Lewis was most critical that Australian players were flouting the rules of amateurism by being paid more than bare expenses, which the English players were provided. His opinions carried weight in the official halls of British soccer and most probably retarded Australia's attempt to compete in Olympic and World Cup tournaments for decades to come.

Most damningly of all, the manager saw no immediate prospect of an Australian team being invited to tour Britain. Australians it seemed, simply were not worthy. The 'assessment' of John Lewis would be served long, hard and cold. Australians would wait until 2003 before they would witness an Australian team play England on its own soil, and above all defeat it.

One long lasting benefit of the English tour was the donation by the Football Association of England of a silver trophy valued at 250 Guineas for competition between the states.

> *The trophy represented a player throwing the ball in, with the British and Oz coats-of-arms on either side. It was generally referred to as the BFA (British Football Association) Trophy... Four teams took part in the first interstate competition played in 1928...Victoria won the match in Melbourne 3-1... to become the first holders of the BFA trophy.* [7]

Those contemplating a future English tour were provided information on the financial demands of the English visitors during the 1925 tour:

Few people outside the movement will conceive readily that it cost £10,000 to land John Lewis and his band of Soccer stars to Australia. All players had to be paid £8 per week wages during the currency of the entire tour... The whole enterprise cost nearly £20,000, and when the venture showed a profit of several hundred Pounds, it can be seen that good teams in Soccer will surely attract the public. [8]

It was anticipated that the Australian team would tour New Zealand in 1926. This trip did not occur because the two Associations could not agree on terms. When the New Zealanders toured Australia in 1923 the Australian Association pocketed all the gate money. The New Zealanders offered to host the visit of the Australians in 1926 and pay Australian players 10/- per day. However the Australian Association also asked for a cut of the gate takings to which the New Zealanders could not agree.

1927 was a busy year for touring soccer teams to Australia. The first professional continental side, AFK Vršovice (Bohemians), from the Czech capital of Prague, were the initial visitors.

AFK Vršovice toured Australia after offers to the Czech National team and the Sparta Prague club were turned down. The club name was a problem. Australian officials demanded a name corresponding with the country of origin. The Vršovice team adopted the name Bohemians, which means Czechs, since Bohemia is the historical name of the western part of Czechoslovakia. The tour initially cost Australian authorities £2,750.

Famously, the Czech team changed its name officially to Bohemians FC after the tour and adopted the badge of a kangaroo, which they retain to this day. They are known as the *klokani* (kangaroos).

When the Bohemians played a match against New South Wales in Sydney language difficulties hindered official proceedings:

Last Saturday the manager of the visitors intended to present a flag of his country to the N.S.W. Association President, but only had the opportunity to present a cut glass vase, the referee whistling for the start of the game... Even in the tossing for ends referee Wright had to arrange for the captain of the visitors to nominate before the toss his call, otherwise, neither the referee nor the N.S. Wales captain (Judy Masters) would have known when Pinc, captain of the Czechs, had called heads or tails. [9]

Prior to the first 'test' against the Czech team, locals considered no details about the forthcoming encounter too trifling. Fans were told that the ball to be used was the product of Stokes, McGowan Ltd., of Sydney and was made of the finest Australian waterproof leather.

When the Czechs took on a Newcastle select side they refused to wear shirts with numbers on them, as they claimed that numbers were not needed at home. Australia, backward in so many facets when rules changed, was actually an early adopter of numbered shirts.

Reporters praised the Czechs for their cool and measured style of play. Unlike the Australia teams which played a 'kick and rush' style, the Central Europeans kept the ball low with a minimum amount of heading and high lobs to forwards.

Virtually concurrently, a team of Chinese students from Shanghai toured Australia playing twenty-seven matches. During the tour the Chinese players went on strike. Australia beat the Chinese on two occasions and drew the third match. The tour was managed and financed by the Chinese, and the organiser, Professor Kwong, was liable for £1,400 of the £2,300 incurred as a loss.

Statistics reveal that this second visiting Chinese team was more successful than their earlier compatriots. They defeated an Australian XI 3-0 in Adelaide and defeated Victoria 4-0. Critics noted that their players exhibited speed with precise dribbling, though their short passes were often astray.

A report was published on the strength of the numbering visiting soccer teams to Australia that year focussing on what was seen as a British export coup:

Spread Of Football
A British Export
Supremacy Of Soccer

(BY BCM.)

Although it does not figure in the Board of Trade returns, football Soccer is a notable British export... The presence in Australia and New Zealand at the moment of teams representing such widely separated countries as Canada, China, and Czecho-Slovakia affords most striking evidence of the spread of the game. Quite clearly, Soccer, more than any other sport, is the universal game. [9]

The Australian team played against teams from the Dutch East Indies (now Indonesia) and also visited Singapore in 1928. The best players were unavailable for the tour due to a ban on their participation by the New South Wales State League. A team representing players from New South Wales, Victoria, Queensland and South Australia played twenty-three matches. This tour was historic. It was the first foray into Asia by an Australian side. The local association trumpeted the pedigree of soccer in Java hoping the Australians would send a competitive team.

The team engaged teams from Surabaya, Semarang, Bandiong, Macassar and Singapore, winning seventeen, drawing four and losing two matches.

For the Australian team, soccer was taking them to a nearby country, albeit an exotic area of the world few Australians had visited. One Balgownie player named 'Titchy' Thompson wrote of his impressions.

Macassar had hundreds of 'funny little boats' in the harbour and huts nestled among bamboo and coconut palms. Surabaya was attractive though the Australians had trouble getting accustomed to the food. An 'Australian lady' was concurrently visiting the Surabaya hotel. She was requested to ensure that 'the meal was cooked to suit the Australians'. The hill roads of Semerang reminded Thompson of NSW south coast roads, while Djoka was so dirty that if it was in Australia 'the whole of the people would be run in, and most likely the town burnt down'. The team visited the Borobudur temples and were captivated by a gamelan band. In Batavia the team had to share a cargo boat with hundreds of 'stinking' pigs. Life became more opulent on the last leg in Singapore. The team visited the Governor's Residence, played tennis and billiards and were royally entertained by a British military garrison 'which included members of the British nobility'.

The Java tour attracted the ire of some Australian officials. They lamented the loss of club players to a tour which many officials did not value, because it was to an Asian nation.

Although matches were played mainly between Australia and her near neighbours, some dreamed of an Australian team touring the world:

It needs but little imagination to visualise the excellent advertisement Australia would receive if the organisation of a team were accomplished... Of course it would be suicidal for an Australian team, at the present juncture, to undertake a world tour, as it is readily conceded by competent judges that the standard of our players is not yet parallel with that of either Great Britain or some parts of the Continent. [10]

Yet again, Australian officials refused to acknowledge an unpalatable truth about sporting progression. For the Australian national team to play lesser teams was no panacea. To improve, teams must test their aptitude against the very best opponents available.

It would take over forty years for dreams of regular world touring to become a reality.

During the 1920s the possibility of Australia competing at the Olympic Games was canvassed. Plans were not realised as the Australian Olympic Federation adhered to the narrow definition of amateurism. This disallowed any sportsman earning income from their sport, however small, from competing in the Olympic Games. At this time participation in the Olympic Games was greatly desired. It represented the pinnacle of international soccer, as the inaugural World Cup did not commence until 1930.

The hopes of Olympian participation were aired in the press:

John U. Storr... started the round ball rolling in Adelaide... Storr says it is pretty certain that the Australian Soccer Council will send a team to the Olympic Games, and reckons that will be the start of regular Australian participation in international soccer. [11]

The Commonwealth Football Association contacted authorities in Belgium with the hope of arranging matches and participating in the 1924 Paris Olympics. The Belgians replied in the affirmative, but contact was too late to allow for proper arrangements to be made.

Australian officials set their sights on the 1928 Amsterdam Olympics. Mindful that all players participating in the Olympics had to be amateurs, local soccer officials harboured reservations tinged with guilt. Some Australian players had accepted £5 in match payment when the English team toured and it was not unknown for Newcastle region players to divvy up their portion of gate takings. How could they approach the Australian Olympic Committee with a clean conscience and ask for such players to be included in an Olympic team?

At a meeting of the Commonwealth Soccer Football Conference in 1927 officials were undecided about pursuing Olympic Games participation. Officials were nervous about the effect severe defeats in Olympic matches would have upon the local and global reputation of Australian soccer. Delegates also had feared repercussions concerning the best Australian players breaching the strict rules regarding Olympic amateurism.

Mercifully, for all concerned, hopes were fading of Olympic glory for a soccer team from the Antipodes:

> *When the Czechoslovakian team were in Sydney (1926), their managers undertook to endeavour to arrange an itinerary of at least 24 matches in Europe for an Australian team in Soccer at the Olympic Games... There seems, however, very little prospect of the tour this year, which is as well, in view of the unsettled position regarding the Olympic amateur definition.* [12]

Chapter 9

The Women's Game

Women started playing soccer in England in the 1890s. By 1895 the British Ladies Association Football Club was formed with fifty members.

Soccer played by women was regarded as a novelty, one which intrigued some and appalled others. In the same year a London newspaper editor exclaimed 'Feminine Football – A Revolting Exhibition' as a headline after a report of a match between two women's teams.

Regardless, there were frequent matches in England which were popular. Most notable were some matches between the famous English factory team of Dick, Kerr Ladies F.C. and French teams which occurred in 1920. In 1921 the English FA would ban women's matches for the next fifty years.

It would be a long road to worldwide acceptance and respect for the women's game.

An early mention of women's soccer occurred when a schoolgirl's match was reported on in the local press in Queensland. The game was played in the Toowoomba suburb of Harlaxton in 1917.

By 1921 the Metropolitan Soccer Football Association in Sydney, noting the relative success of women's soccer in England, met and asked for interest among the public of starting a women's Association:

> *A meeting was held under the auspices of the Metropolitan (Soccer) Football Association, at the Sports Club, Hunter Street, last night to consider the formation of a 'Women's Soccer Football Association'. There were over 30 ladies present.*
>
> *The ladies watched the proceedings with interest and were keen for the formation of an association. Some of them had played in Canada, New*

Zealand, Great Britain and Melbourne. It was decided to form an association called the Sydney Ladies Soccer Football Association.[1]

Within weeks one hundred and twenty women had expressed interest. Reports clung to old stereotypes, stating that the officers selected had been chosen 'based on their appearance'. The women lived in such diverse suburbs as Parramatta, Hornsby, Manly, Glebe and Helensburgh.

Female players met to practice at Wentworth Park. Despatches from training sessions obsessed on an atmosphere of not just novelty, but frivolity. It was stated that many of the girls were wearing bathing costumes and chewing gum. They were described as 'belles on the ball'. Few were wearing boots applicable for playing soccer and the 'kick and giggle' school of playing was apparently 'most evident'.

Some of the earliest women's teams to be formed were on the South Coast at Woonona and Balgownie.

A month later interested parties met to form the Queensland Ladies Soccer Football Association. Brisbane women's teams included Brisbane Ladies, South Brisbane and Latrobe. The secretary of the QLSFA stated that although the players are keen 'the girls are scared of public opinion'.

By July 1921 there were two women's clubs in Toowoomba name Rovers and Cities.

'*Right Half*', writing in Brisbane's *Telegraph* supported the women's endeavours. However, he was concerned about the ability of the physiques of young women in his city to adapt to playing soccer:

> *The question has been raised whether the Australian girls are of a sufficient physique to play football. I was talking the matter over with an official of the QFA, the other day and he pointed out that the average Brisbane girl was not so big, strong and well developed as the Lancashire girls.*[2]

The Brisbane women were invited to play a curtain raiser before an Australian Rules match in Brisbane in September 1921. They felt unprepared and as one player stated 'making asses of ourselves'.

However, some weeks later, after further training, a women's match was played. North and South Brisbane teams competed at the Brisbane Cricket

Ground. North Brisbane won 2-0 and gate takings were estimated at £90. The crowd was estimated at 10,000. The women's team also played at Bundamba Racecourse.

The local paper devoted attention to the feminine soccer contest:

Further attention is drawn to the forthcoming visit to this city of the team of metropolitan ladies who will contest a Soccer football match next Saturday afternoon on the Bundamba Racecourse. A great deal of local interest is centred on this novel display by the ladies...It is whispered that a local lady, prominent in social life, will supply the initial kick which will put the leathern sphere into motion... [12]

At the time there were no female referees. A Brisbane newspaper, keen to exploit any prurience which could attributed to women playing soccer, scrutinised a voyeuristic vignette prior to a match at Bowman Park, Paddington in 1921. When one of the Brisbane female teams formed a circle to allow a player to change jerseys they attracted the attention of the male referee who went closer to enquire what the holdup was. When he was in their vicinity 'he stopped, blushed and beat a hasty retreat. There was a loud guffaw from the spectators'

By the end of the year there were three women's clubs in Brisbane with sixty players.

When the Brisbane women's teams planned to commence the season in 1922, the location of their match was kept secret. 'The girls want to get into good nick before they are made the object of public gaze', explained the QLSFA secretary, Miss Verna Neil.

In the Queensland capital a women's team practiced in the moonlight by kicking a ball which had been illuminated by aluminium paint, so as not to arouse immodest interest. The press was invited to witness Brisbane Ladies play Brisbane City but were warned that if the game aroused too much public curiosity or ridicule the match would be abandoned. The local press, as if observing exotic fauna, reported:

It was sometime after 3 o'clock before the Cities attired in smart maroon caps and jerseys, black shorts, stockings and boots emerged from their dressing room... They were in general healthy, well-built young women with a pleasing absence of such coarseness of features as the uninitiated or

predicted might be apt to associate with female footballers.
The Brisbanes (sic) whose colours were cream, white, and blue, came out from behind huge clumps of lantana... ³

The Queensland Ladies Football Association was formed in 1926. A Brisbane City club was formed and played two clubs from Kedron called Kangaroos and Wallabies. Newspaper reports of matches in Queensland seem to cease after 1926 indicating that this brief flowering of the women's game was temporary.

Women's soccer in New South Wales was more resilient. In 1928 a match was played in Maitland between Weston and Kurri North End teams. A year later a match was played in Newcastle between Speers Point-Teralba and Weston-Kurri Kurri. This was a charity match in aid of the Wallsend Combined Mining Unions relief fund raising £40. Described as 'speedy soccer Amazons' one astounded male spectator opined that the match was a demonstration of the 'virile tendencies' of young women.

Evidence of women's soccer played in any sustained or organised way in the 1920s was restricted to the states of New South Wales and Queensland.

In 1929 Weston and Speers Point women's teams played a night match at the Sydney Sports Ground. A report of the match described the players as 'twenty-two bare-kneed Amazons'.

By the 1930s women's soccer was making strides, particularly in the Lithgow region. In 1931 more than fifty women and girls met and decided to form a Women's Soccer Football Association.

The Zig Zag and Blue Birds clubs were formed, with the intention of playing matches against Sydney and northern coalfields sides. The meeting was described in condescending tones as 'keenness personified' and 'a plot to displace man from his fast disappearing places of privilege'. In the same year women's teams at Coledale and Scarborough played matches on the New South Wales south coast.

In 1932 the Lithgow area clubs of State Mine and Vale of Clwydd were playing matches.

Women's soccer at this time was only played spasmodically and any news about the game as played by women was scarce. At Broken Hill in 1936 it was decided that a women's soccer team would be formed. The game would be played with amended soccer rules and called *soccerette*:

Women Will Play Soccer
Four Clubs Will Affiliate

Definite steps towards the formation of a soccer association for women were made at a meeting at the Southern Cross Hotel on Monday night when representatives of four clubs, affiliated with the Broken Hill Ladies Cricket Association, attended.

Those present realised that the rules of soccer could not be interfered with and decided that the game to be played by the Broken Hill women would be named 'Soccerette,' the rules of play being amended rules of soccer. The rules will be revised in such a way to minimise all risk to the participants...

Mode Of Uniform

The association decided that it would not bind the clubs to a set uniform, but would make it optional. This will enable the clubs to decide whether they will play in shorts or slacks, but each member will have to wear the same dress. [4]

Ten days later the paper announced that four teams had been formed representing Brewer's Arms, Southern Cross, Wests and Railway Town. Unfortunately interest among the females of the city abated and many prospective *Soccerettes* decided to play basketball instead. With only Railway Town able to form a team the *Soccerette* competition was abandoned before it could begin.

Women's teams from Deepwater and Yagoona were photographed for Sydney's *Daily Telegraph* in 1939.

Clubs from Centrals and Granville, Cumberland District, Lysaghts and Western Suburbs also competed in the early 1940s.

In 1942 women's teams from Granville and Granville Central played matches at Redfern Oval in Sydney in aid of Boy's Town.

However acceptance of women's soccer was slow to gain general acceptance. In 1943 a 'married women's burlesque soccer match' to be held at Guildford Park was called off after it was described by clergymen as 'grossly indecent'.

Regardless, women's soccer seemed to gain some momentum during the war years. In 1943 a match was played between the Guildford Black Cats team and a team from Wollongong at the Sydney Sports Ground. The Guildford team also played a team of male jockeys at soccer, winning 3-1.

Women's soccer was played sporadically north of Sydney after 1945. A match was played between women's clubs from Lake Macquarie and Charlestown at Speers Point in 1947.

In 1948 female soccer players were still treated with condescension. In Queensland, a women's curtain raiser match was played before the final of the Charity Cup final at North Cairns Reserve. The teams were name the 'Dills' and the 'Dopes'.

Prejudice against women playing soccer was common. In New South Wales, a young woman described as a 'Tomboy' wrote to a Sydney paper. 'Tomboy' stated that she would like to see a women's club formed. A waspish journalist with the pen name "Old Maid" replied 'where is your sense of decency. You would do a lot better if you were bottling pickles than playing men's games'.

A team of local female players took on a North Perth male team in 1949. This was considered unusual enough for the match to be covered by photographs in *The Western Mail*. The women were yet again described as 'amazons'.

Women's soccer was establishing an imprint in the NSW Illawarra region at this time. Bellambi, Coledale, Thirroul and Scarborough clubs fielded teams. Kurri Kurri hosted a women's match which, according to press reports, attracted 'a large crowd.'

Chapter 10

High Hopes And Reality
1930-1939

By the early 1930s the Great Depression had affected soccer's fortunes.

Many clubs, especially in rural areas disbanded as young men left the land to find work in the cities. Conversely, some clubs were formed by unemployed workers.

In 1931 the Corrimal club on the New South Wales south coast gave unemployed people free entrance to their matches after fifteen minutes had elapsed, so as not to confuse gate keeping records. North of Sydney, the Cessnock and Aberdare clubs agreed to give away twenty-five free tickets to see their matches to the unemployed in 1934.

In 1936 Australian authorities were hoping that English Football Association would agree to send coaches to Australia and help pay their salaries. This was yet another plea which was disregarded, with only a few wealthy clubs being in a position to lure coaches to Australia on an individual basis.

Meanwhile, most prominent senior clubs still selected teams on the basis of the opinions of numerous club 'selectors'. On the field of play team captains had the responsibility of directing colleagues during a match.

In the mid 1930s soccer was starting to develop deeper roots with improved economic conditions stimulating the sport. Players were being paid more money and the number of foreign teams visiting increased, which aided the development of the national team. All this was almost to come to a virtual halt with Australia's participation in World War II in 1939.

New trends in this decade are worthy of note. In New South Wales the elevation of company or factory (sometimes called 'works') based sides such as Goodyear and Metters into the highest level of competition was to usher in a level of professionalism which had hitherto rarely been experienced.

In Victoria, clubs such as Hakoah and Savoia were among the earliest of the 'ethnic' clubs to play at a high level and taste success. This was a feature that would work its way through all the Australian states after World War II.

The Australian team played three matches in New Zealand, winning them all comfortably. The visit of the English Amateur team in 1937 garnered much enthusiasm and publicity. In a notable first the Australian team beat the English team 5-4 in Sydney. In 1938 the Indian team visited and drew a lot of media interest as they played in bare feet. The visit of the team from Palestine in 1939, which featured a team of Jewish players, was a portent of the influence that area of the world and the Israeli national team was to play in Australian soccer from the 1960s to the 1970s.

Australian Capital Territory

In 1930 the Canberra club played Queanbeyan, which lay across the Federal Capital Territory border in New South Wales, in a ten game series. The York Park Ground, opposite the Hotel Wellington was secured as a home ground.

With forty-two players, the Canberra club commenced a sub-competition in June 1930 with three teams, Rangers, Rovers and Thistle from their club roster. All matches were played at York Park. Only one set of shirts was available for the teams, which would have caused difficulties.

A junior competition included the teams of Federal Rovers, Kookaburras, West Queanbeyan and Duntroon.

The Canberra club raised funds by arranging social dances accompanied by the Ambassador's Orchestra at the Capitol Theatre in Manuka. On one occasion, the event had be postponed due to the installation of cinema equipment permitting the screening of 'talkies'. The club would hold weekly meetings at Mr Beaver's shop in Kingston.

In July 1930 a fancy dress soccer match was played in order to raise funds for the Unemployed Relief Fund in Canberra, followed by a smoke concert in Eastlake.

The Depression led to a slowing of construction in Canberra and many workers who had played soccer left the Capital. The Canberra club lost many players and the three club competition of Rangers, Rovers and Thistle established in 1930 was discontinued. Early in the season the Canberra club played a match against the unemployed at Kingston Oval.

The Canberra Club then spawned a two team competition featuring the Canberra Blues and Federal Magpies. The two teams competed for the Federal Capital Soccer Shield which was won by Federal Magpies. In the same year a Canberra XI team played the powerful Sydney club Metters at Manuka Oval. The local selection was defeated 1-6 by the company team from Sydney.

By 1932, despite the gloom surrounding the game, regeneration was in order when the Federal Monaro District Soccer Association was formed:

Soccer Association Formed In Canberra Four Clubs In Competition

The soccer clubs of Queanbeyan and Canberra have decided to form a soccer association known as the Federal Monaro and District Association... It was decided to run two competitions, one for the Canberra Cup and one for the Adelaide Tailoring Co.'s Shield, with permission of the donors. The competitions will consist of eighteen matches, and the first round will commence on Saturday, May 14. Four clubs - the Canberra Blues, Federal Magpies, West Queanbeyan and Queanbeyan Caledonians - will take part. [1]

The Federal Monaro District Football Association added Burns Club and Gundaroo to the local competition in 1933. The Canberra club fielded a team and Queanbeyan had two teams in the competition which made for a five team league. Five teams played in a junior competition.

Organised soccer was discontinued in 1934. A failed attempt was made to re-initiate the game in Canberra in 1937. Soccer was not to re-establish itself with a league competition until after World War II.

New South Wales

The most successful club in New South Wales during the 1930s was Goodyear. Goodyear won the metropolitan senior championship three times in consecutive years from 1937 to 1939. The Newcastle region based teams of Wallsend and Adamstown both won two championships. Wallsend were victorious in the consecutive years of 1931 and 1932 and Adamstown in 1934 and 1935.

By 1931 the St George, Gladesville and Annandale-Leichhardt clubs had become companies. They issued shares, in order to better finance their operations. West Wallsend won the State League Cup in this year.

Enthusiastic readers of the New South Wales publication *Soccer World* could order hard bound editions of all issues for 1s/9d.

In 1930 the Robinson Cup was inaugurated as a knock out cup competition for Newcastle area teams. Adamstown won the trophy for the first two years.

In 1931 the State league competition was divided into northern and southern sections, which alleviated some costs and travelling times. Cup competitions continued to be run on a state wide basis.

A club called LGT Rovers was formed in Wallsend in 1932. LGT was a club 'patron' or sponsor and the name was worn on their red shirts. This may have been one of the earliest examples of club sponsorship on a shirt. North of Sydney, the 1932 season opened with optimism. Kurri Kurri, Gladesville and Wallsend clubs had built new grandstands.

As usual bureaucratic jealousies were simmering. This time the instigators were referees. A split developed between referees north of Sydney and their Sydney metropolitan cousins. Consequently, a Newcastle centred Northern Referees State League Referees Association was formed in the Newcastle region as an angry response to Sydney referees being appointed to Newcastle area matches.

Wallsend won the State Soccer Premiership in 1933. It's most famous player and servant was their forward, Alec Cameron. He devoted fifty years to the club and played fifty international matches for Australia. Wallsend was also a pioneer in arranging long distance club excursions by train for members. The trains were dubbed 'Red Terrors'. During the off season in November up to 3,000 Wallsend people took a day excursion to Sydney's Taronga Park Zoo from the Newcastle region.

In the same year seven members of the first NSW soccer team, which played in 1883, were honoured at a jubilee dinner.

Bureaucratic infighting ensured there was a contentious meeting of the NSW Soccer League. The committee recommended a return to State League proper and that metropolitan, Maitland, Newcastle and south coast clubs should all play in competition matches on the home and away principle.

The State League was reduced to fifteen clubs, a reduction of three, by 1934. The State League headquarters moved to Sydney from Maitland. Adamstown were Premiership winners in 1934.

The New South Wales Football Association explicitly stated that no player will receive payment for playing matches under its jurisdiction. Clubs would be responsible for providing playing kit and travel expenses.

That year was one notable for the formation of amalgamated clubs. Among them was Balgownie-Corrimal, Bulli-Woonona, Myocum-Mullumbimby, and Boolaroo - Speers Point. With the economic Depression still active, some clubs envisaged that amalgamation was a way to ensure a robust future and compete with the 'factory' clubs.

At this time authorities became aware that certain clubs in the New South Wales State League were paying inducements to players to switch clubs and paying a player's weekly wages. Players were only meant to be recompensed for expenses. This action was condemned and banned by the League management.

In Sydney the 1930s saw big business invest in soccer clubs and teams. Metters, a manufacturer of stoves and white goods entered the top level of the Sydney soccer echelons with championship intent:

Association Rules
Metters Club's Enterprise

Metters by taking over the Arlington Recreation Ground Dulwich Hill has pleased many enthusiasts who welcome the opportunity of seeing first grade football played in their suburb. The club distributes 72 free passes to schoolboys of the district for every home game.

Formerly a disused brick pit, which has been filled in and completed by relief workers under the control of Petersham Council the Arlington Recreation ground with its terraced banks and up-to date dressing rooms and appointments promises to become a leading Soccer ground. Although not entirely finished, it will hold four thousand spectators in comfort... [2]

Metters, which boasted seven Australian international players, flouted rules about amateurism by giving each team member a £35 cash bonus at the completion of the 1938 season. The club secretary made no pretence of the payment and called for open professionalism.

Metters (nicknamed *The Stoveies*) was always looking to play quality opposition and in 1931 played a match against naval trainees from the *General Baquedano,* a Chilean naval ship. This was a rare visit by South American soccer players to Australian shores during this era.

The Goodyear Rubber Company was to become a leading 'factory' team and a worthy sporting rival of Metters:

Goodyear Sports Ground

> *The Goodyear sporting ground at Camellia, near Granville, will be officially opened tomorrow afternoon. The Goodyear Tyre and Rubber Co. (Australia), Ltd., has displayed considerable interest in developing sporting facilities for about 800 employees, and has concentrated particularly upon baseball, Rugby and Soccer football. The teams have participated in the various divisions of the City Houses competitions, and the area which has been made available for the games is splendidly equipped... At 3.15 a game is scheduled between Goodyear Soccer football team and Gladesville-Ryde.* [3]

Goodyear first played in the Premiership of the newly named New South Wales State League Soccer Association competition in 1935 and featured the well-known player Alf Quill. Quill would go on the following season to score fifty-six goals for 'The Tyre Boys' that year.

The success of the work's team engendered envy from other clubs. In 1936 the Weston and St George clubs tried to institute a local regulation that all works teams should only field players who worked for their team's employers. Metters, Clyde Engineering, Goodyear and Wollongong Steel Works threatened to leave the State League and the suggested regulation was rescinded.

The so called 'company' or 'factory' clubs such as Metters and Goodyear were the subject of criticism by suburban clubs. These clubs claimed that Metters and Goodyear signed players for three years (a longer period than usual) even if they had no use for them.

In 1939, suburban clubs, such as Granville, claimed that they spent time and money developing young players, only to have them lured to Metters or Goodyear with the promise of employment in their factories. No recompense was paid to the suburban clubs. The irony in Granville's claim was that for a period of two years previously the Granville club had the 'industrial' name of Clyde Engineering.

At a New South Wales Association meeting in 1939 the 'factory' clubs survived a motion to have their names changed. Regulations were changed to allow unwanted players to transfer to another club more expeditiously if a club was in dire need of a player.

In the late 1930s company teams of prominent shopping retailers entered the lower levels of the Sydney competition. The Hordernian Soccer Football Club was formed by members of the Anthony Hordern department store. The team was nicknamed the 'counter jumpers', a colloquial term for a shop assistant. Another retailer, Grace Brothers, nicknamed 'the boys from Broadway' also fielded a team.

Globe Worsted Mills which had a factory in Sydenham played in the Sydney and District Soccer League, while Kia-Ora played in the Granville District Football Association. Kia-Ora was a cordial manufacturer founded in 1903 and its name came from the Maori meaning 'be well/healthy'.

Aviation manufacturer De Havilland, which was located at Mascot Aerodrome, fielded a team in the second division of the Sydney and District Soccer League.

The City Houses Association competition included Australian Wine Glass, Arnotts, Hordernians, Clifford Love, Austral Bronze, Lustre Hosiery, Woolworths, Bradford Kendall and Smith Son and Rees. An identically named competition was also centred among Newcastle businesses.

Other teams of note which played senior soccer in the 1930s in NSW include two teams with Scottish roots. Concord Scottish and Rockdale Scottish played in the Sydney and District 1st Division. This was the second tier of soccer in NSW. Invicta was the club of a company which made clothing and fasteners and the NSW Police played in the third tier of NSW soccer in the Sydney and District competition 2nd Division in 1935.

An interstate carnival was held in New South Wales in 1932. All states except Western Australia took part and a league system was used. Each state played each other once and the top two teams playing off. Round robin matches were played in Sydney and Newcastle. New South Wales dominated all the other states and defeated South Australia 6-1 in the final to the delight of about 5,000 local fans.

In 1932 a Wallsend goalkeeper called Archie Dellaway found himself representing Queensland. The regular Queensland goalkeeper had been injured during their tour to New South Wales. Dellaway was drafted to play for the Sunshine State against a Northern New South Wales side, despite having never visited Queensland. This was made possible when he was transferred to the Queensland club Bundamba for two days. After the match the Queensland authorities wanted him to keep playing for them and offered him a job in Ipswich, which he declined.

In 1933 sailors from the touring German naval cadet light cruiser *Köln* arranged a soccer match against the Royal Australian Navy at Lyne Park. The Germans, playing in white shirts with blue shorts, won the match 8-3 against a team which mainly comprised players from the HMAS *Penguin* naval base club.

In 1934 the Adamstown club played seventeen matches without defeat, a record at the time.

Sidney (Sid) J. Grant was appointed the President of the New South Wales State Soccer League in 1935. A schoolmaster, he had risen through the Kurri Kurri club. He became a soccer historian and statistician in the late 1920s and would later be a respected soccer archivist and historian, publishing a history of soccer in Australia in the early 1970s.

When teams from the Hunter region had to play a team from the south coast there would often be a trip of nine hours involved. Players would leave the north at about 6 am in the morning to board a slow bus. Often the bus would break down or be slowed on one lane roads. Most cafes would close about 6 pm, making getting a dinner or any food on the slow trip home precarious. Exhausted players would reach home past midnight.

In 1936 the State League clubs initiated an 80/20 match day takings split. The home team club would keep 80% of gate takings and the visiting side would receive 20% of the takings. This marked a change from previous seasons when the home team kept all takings. In the case of cup ties, as in previous years, the takings would be split evenly between competing clubs.

The New South Wales Referees Association was revived in 1936. This body succeeded the State Referees Association which had split into northern, Sydney and southern sections. At this time the interpretation of the laws was not uniform, nor widely disseminated within the soccer community. Officials, clubs and players were soon brought up to date with the latest laws and interpretations.

A Southern Miners Association competition was established by 1937 on the south coast, so that miners could compete on weekends. In the same year Alf

Quill scored a record seventy-eight goals for Wallsend in competition.

The metropolitan first division was reduced by four teams in 1938. The three northern teams of Aberdare, Kurri Kurri and West Wallsend and the southern team, Wollongong, were excised from the competition. The stipulated reason was to reduce the number of uncompetitive matches.

Clubs were also asking high transfer fees. Until 1938 the highest transfer fee requested was £12. The Wallsend club was asking £150 for the transfer of Alf Quill to Adamstown, a fee which many thought would stymie the transfer. The Cessnock Caledonians offered Adamstown £350 for the transfer of William Coolihan, which was an Australian record offer.

The Protestant churches competitions in New South Wales were burgeoning. The Newcastle Association alone comprised thirty-four clubs and over 500 players in 1939. In total 104 clubs, comprising 1,000 players were enrolled in competition in NSW. Consequently, the Churches competition was well funded. In 1939, a record 335 trophies to the value of £225 were awarded to victorious teams.

All matches need referees and in that year 38 referees offered their services to the Newcastle Referees Association. In 1939, Fred Daniels of Newcastle donated a cup in his honour for the winners of a soccer competition among junior players in the local area. The Daniels Cup was played for until 1970.

The ex-Australian international player James 'Judy' Masters celebrated 20 years as the secretary of the Balgownie club in 1939. His service to Balgownie, his one club, was probably unsurpassed. Masters coached most of their players and first played for Balgownie in 1904. He played over 400 club matches and was never cautioned. Masters earned a living as a miner in Corrimal. Balgownie had a reputation for only signing local players.

Employees formed amateur teams playing in a midweek competition. These included Teachers' College, Tramways, Motor Transports Section S. Corps, HMAS *Penguin* and Public Service.

The economics behind the running of the game by the NSW Soccer Football Association was exposed. Clubs did not pay competition entrance fees, however, every home gate was levied £8 and 5/- which amounted to £66 to the head body. This amount was levied regardless of the crowd or gate takings and some coalfield clubs had difficulty paying the fee. The head body took all revenue, less expenses from representative fixtures and also took money from semi-finals and finals of premierships and cup competitions. Expenses paid by the Association included travel cost for players and managers, as well as meals and accommodation.

One issue which aroused disquiet among the most talented players in NSW was that representative players were not paid for matches played from 1932 till at least 1935, due to restricted finances.

Prejudice against soccer was still prevalent. A letter by the head of North Sydney Boy's High School, J.W. Thompson was published in *The Soccer Weekly* of 10 April 1938, stating that soccer was banned by the headmaster of Newcastle High School. The headmaster claimed that as rugby league was the most popular game in the district, it was a better game for character building than soccer.

In 1939 Gladesville-Ryde became the second club in Australia to employ a professional coach from Britain.

The Robinson Cup became the permanent property of Wallsend. Wallsend won the cup three times in succession from 1937 to 1939. The Daniels Cup became the replacement to be contested and Wallsend won the inaugural competition.

With war having commenced in that year, New South Wales clubs were made aware that refugee players may be coming to Australia to boost the stocks of players. This call was a portent of what was to occur post 1945 with the mass arrival of more than 100,000 displaced persons from Europe.

Northern Territory

In the early 1930s there were reports on a match between 'white' players and a team of 'coloured' players. The 'coloured' players represented the Chinese community which were a mainstay of the game in Darwin throughout the decade.

Such matches were the prelude to regular competition. In 1933 the British Football Association was formed and three clubs named Magpies, Kookaburras and Chinese Recreation Club formed a competition.

An evocative report of the end of season social dance was published. The event was both a fundraiser for the Association and a chance for players and supporters to relax after the season. The event characterises the deep social ties which soccer engendered in times when anything like true professionalism was beyond state or local associations:

Soccer Dance

What can be termed as an extremely successful, happy-go-lucky and enjoyable dance was held in the Star Theatre on Friday last under the auspices of the Soccer Association. It was by far the largest crowd seen at a dance for quite a while... During the evening balloons, streamers and confetti were made full use of and I was asked by some if the balloon bursting competition was arranged just to advertise the Soccer code; at least the committee should have issued shin guards to the ladies. [4]

The local competition was revamped in 1934 and three clubs were formed in Darwin. The clubs were Darwin, Garrison (which represented the local military base) and Rovers.

By 1936 local club matches had been abandoned or relegated to a level which did not warrant reporting in the local press. From this time on reported matches were impromptu games played between visiting pearlers and locals.

A match was played between pearlers from the remote Aru Islands (Dutch East Indies) and Singapore in Darwin:

Soccer
Singapore v Aru Islands

The attendance at the soccer match on Saturday was somewhat disappointing, but the players were energetic and enthusiastic, though the long grass militated against much good play, for it checked the speed of the players, as well as the progress of the ball, which was slowed down considerably in passing. The game was won by the Aru Island team... Play lasted an hour, so that the game ended all too soon for the spectators.

The teams...hope to have other matches in the future, when they return from their season on the Aru Island pearling grounds. [5]

Darwin locals and another team of foreign pearl fishermen played a match. Some of the locals had difficulty in adapting to the rules of soccer. This underscores the decline of the standard of soccer as the 1930s drew to a close in the Northern Territory:

> The international soccer football match last Sunday, between a team from the pearling fleets and locals had quite an appreciative audience and it was full of interest to the spectators, and of incidents to the players... One or two were handicapped because of their association with the Australian game of hand ball, and could not resist the temptation to grab a fistful of the ball when it came within reach of them.
>
> The little Koepangers played pretty football, and did very well to hold the heavy Australian team to one goal. It is estimated that, they were giving away about 30 cwt. in weight... [6]

Queensland

The powerhouse team of the 1930s in the Brisbane area was Latrobe. The Milton based club won four consecutive State League championships from 1930 to 1933 and again in 1935. Latrobe's key player was the forward Eric Gorring, who was part of six premiership winning teams from the late 1920s.

The second most successful team of the 1930s was Y.M.C.A. which won in 1934 and 1936.

In 1930 the turmoil in the first division in Brisbane continued. The first division of Brisbane Soccer comprised Latrobe, Thistle, Norman Park, Pineapple Rovers, Toombul, Wynnum, Toowong and YMCA.

The James Stewart Shield was competed for by junior clubs from 1930. The trophy was described as being a good publicity for the state's resources as it contained Queensland metals, timber and minerals.

The Mourilyan soccer club, near Innisfail, held a concert to raise funds. This was common practice at the time, especially in country towns when it became an opportunity for local stars and starlets to shine. The acts covered a wide gamut from comic songs (*Me ain wee hoose*), a saxaphone solo, orchestral pieces, conjuring tricks, an accordion duet, a violin solo and juvenile acrobatics from 'Miss Murgatroyd'.

The first division of Queensland Soccer Football Association (QFA) comprised of only two teams, Toombul and Thistle by 1931. All other teams played in a breakaway competition run by Code Ltd, which featured Norman Park, Wynnum, YMCA, Pineapple Rovers, Toowong and Latrobe clubs.

The split between the Brisbane and Ipswich competitions continued until well into the 1930s. Oxley and Brisbane Thistle competed in the Ipswich competition, which was organised by the Ipswich and West Moreton British Football Association.

The newly renovated Wembley Oval in Burke Street, Coorparoo became the new headquarters of Brisbane soccer in 1931. The venue included seating and comprehensively equipped dressing rooms. Soccer was previously headquartered at the Brisbane Cricket Ground but had been displaced by the Queensland Rugby Union.

By 1932 the Queensland Soccer Council had jurisdiction over the six distinct Associations of Brisbane, Ipswich and West Moreton, Toowoomba and Darling Downs, Wide Bay and Burnett, Central Queensland and Northern Queensland.

The Latrobe club was dissatisfied with the decision to play matches at Wembley. The club threatened to play with the Ipswich and West Moreton competition in the following year. Consequently, the Brisbane and District Football Association (BDFA) was formed which led to the eventual integration of Brisbane and Ipswich clubs.

The Tableland Soccer Football Association was formed at Atherton with clubs from Atherton, East Barron and Yargin competing.

Soccer was thriving in Rockhampton. Four senior clubs competed for three trophies and four junior teams competed for two trophies. There were also four 'minor grade' teams with players up to 15 years of age.

Soccer in North Queensland was thriving by the late 1930s with teams in Tully, Innisfail, Ravenshoe, Ingham, Townsville, Ayr, Bowen, Mossman and Cairns. The Fishery Falls team, south of Cairns was almost entirely composed of Italians who, presumably worked on the cane fields.

Dinner dances with raffles and 'smoke socials' were a way for clubs to raise funds prior to World War II. The Wanderers Soccer Club in Cairns was no exception:

Night in a Grocers Shop

The Wanderers Soccer Club successfully ran the 'Night in the Grocers Shop' at the Trocadero last Monday night: The hall was decorated to represent a grocer's store...

In the place of honour was Mr W Ward's old-time dance band, who kept the dancers moving to the best of dance music on a really fast floor. The patrons were kept cool by the Troc punkas. Mr R Lewis and Mr J Steele obliged the company with a specialty novelty tumbling act and Mr T Doherty obliged with a song... a special cash prize for fancy dress was paid to Miss Enid Svendsen. The £1/1/- hamper was won by Miss Flo Hitch... [7]

In 1935 the Queensland team played at home against New South Wales for the first time at night under electric lights. Queensland had gained Clarrie Coutts the the ex-Australian international, as the state coach. However he caused consternation in Queensland soccer circles when he returned to Wallsend in New South Wales after only a few months.

By 1937 the Queensland Soccer Council (QSC) was planning to attract senior players to coach juniors for a small payment. Details of control over the running of the scheme was disputed by various soccer associations in the state, and progress was slow, with plans being made for implementation in 1940.

Mackay had a four club commercial league consisting of teams of various local businesses by this time. The competition was named the Warehouse League.

Ructions within soccer mean that Queensland and New South Wales would threaten to split from the Australian Soccer Football Association. Ostensibly the two most influential soccer states claimed they had been denied rights under the umbrella of the ASFA:

Football

A threat, that unless the Australian Soccer Football Association calls a meeting before the end of January the State controlling bodies in New South Wales and Queensland would withdraw from that organisation and set up a new Australian council, was made last week after a conference between representatives of the New South Wales Soccer Football Association and the Queensland Soccer Council...

The statement added that under the constitution of the Australian Soccer Football Association administrative and financial control had meant a complete denial of the rights of the two most powerful soccer States. [8]

South Australia

The most successful teams of the 1930s were Port Thistle and West Torrens. 'Port' won the South Australian League Championship in 1934, 1935 and 1937 and West Torrens which won in 1932, 1936 and 1939.

The main cup competitions were the Pelaco Cup and the Pozza Cup.

A prominent soccer family of the era were the Sharp brothers. Five of them played in South Australia at senior level, the best known being Vic Sharp, who was capped for Australia in 1936 against New Zealand.

In 1930 there were thirty-two senior teams competing in Adelaide, including Port Thistle in its inaugural year. In 1933 the Birkalla Rovers club was formed and in 1935 the North Adelaide side changed its name to Prospect United. Hindmarsh Stadium replaced Jubilee Oval as the main ground for soccer matches in Adelaide.

The Australian rules player, W. Scott, commented on the growth of soccer and rugby in South Australia in 1932:

> *Supporters of the 'national' code must view with concern the increasing number of soccer grounds in our parklands, and the revival of Rugby in Adelaide might easily result in that style of football gaining a hold as strong as that already obtained by Soccer. I was appalled last week to read in one of Australia's leading sporting papers the headline, 'Australian born players make good at Soccer.' Surely the governors of our game realise the danger which besets them by reason of Soccer being played in our schools, and Rugby and soccer teams coming here to play what to every Australian should be a foreign code.* [9]

Paranoia was vented at soccer officials later the same year when it was claimed officials barracked for England during a cricket tour:

Soccer Delegates Cheer Australia's Downfall

> *News of the downfall of the Australian batsmen was greeted with tremendous bursts of cheering and applause at the annual general meeting of the South Australian Soccer Association this afternoon. Most of the*

members of the association were originally from Britain. The chairman gave out the scores from time to time. [10]

The subtext of the article was that soccer was played by, officiated by and supported by people who were 'un Australian'.

Nevertheless the sport was gaining in popularity among the young in metropolitan Adelaide. There was a Schools Association of sixty-five teams and a two division scout league as well as nine teams in a junior weekend association competition. By 1932 the Kingswood club could field six junior teams. The Metropolitan Association secured Jubilee Oval as its headquarters.

In 1934 the Pozza Cup, donated by local tailor Ugo (Hugh) Pozza, was introduced and vied for by the top four teams in the league. The Pozza family was to be a force behind the Kingswood club and later the Juventus club which was formed in 1946.

Two years later South Australia hosted New South Wales and Victoria as part of its centenary celebrations. Matches were played at Hindmarsh Stadium and New South Wales dominated the other states. New South Wales obliterated Victoria 10-0 and comfortably beat South Australia 6-0 to win a special Centenary Cup.

There was a superficially amusing story about a horse invading a soccer field. The serious conclusion to draw from the incident made a compelling and mandatory case for clubs at a senior level throughout Australia to play within enclosed grounds:

Horse Holds Up Soccer

A horse obstinately stood in the middle of the field, delayed the start of the Kingswood-South Adelaide first division soccer match at Hutt Street, in the South Park lands, this afternoon. Richardson, a Kingswood forward, seated himself jockey-fashion on the horse, and tickled its ribs, without result. Players of both teams crowded round, patted the horse, called it names, and tagged at its ears. The horse blinked placidly, spread its feet more firmly, and stayed where it was. The referee bounced the ball off the horse's ribs. Presently the horse languidly strolled towards the side line, stopped again, responded to encouraging tongue clickings and removed itself from the playing area. [11]

The Soccer Association bought its own ground in 1938. This led to temporary financial difficulties. Due to the efforts of Ted Rowley the ground was named Rowley Park. The purchase of Rowley Park forced the Association to relinquished control over Hindmarsh Oval.

By 1939 the Referees Association reported that it had presided over 540 matches with thirty-six referees involved.

At the close of the decade an unusual melding of various sports interests occurred. Birkalla Rovers soccer club, the South Plympton Australian Rules club and the Plympton Park Girl's Hockey club announced that they would form a loose 'association'. This seemed mostly to have taken the form of social dances, although Birkalla Rovers challenged the South Plympton Australian Rules team to a match played under the 'national code'.

Tasmania

Two Tasmanian teams dominated the State Championship in the 1930s, with Cascades and Sandy Bay winning four Championships each. Cascades were victorious in 1931, 1932, 1934 and 1935 and Sandy Bay won in 1933, 1936, 1938 and 1939.

The Break O'Day Association was formed in the Fingal Valley on the north east coast in 1930. The first soccer match in the north-east was played at St. Marys in August 1930. The three clubs were St Marys, Cornwall and Fingal. The teams competed for the Hood Cup. Most players were Welsh or Scottish miners. This association was to have a short life. By 1933 many miners had left for the mainland cities of Newcastle and Wollongong for employment. By the end of 1932 the Break O' Day Association comprised one club, Black Diamonds. By 1933 the Break O' Day Association had disbanded.

Clubs were formed at Devonport and Burnie in 1930. The following year a Referees Association was initiated with 14 referees officiating in its inaugural year. The referees agreed to hold meetings twice a year that the Tasmanian British Football Association headquarters at Tunbridge.

In the same year the southern competition gained use of the Moonah ground for matches.

In 1933 Southern Tasmania hosted a match against a team from the touring German cruiser *Köln* at South Hobart winning 2-0.

Chris Hudson noted that hard economic times had affected soccer in

Tasmania during the 1930s:

> *During the 1930s Tasmania could only afford to send two representative state teams over to the mainland for the annual Australian interstate carnival due to the Depression... This factor alone stemmed the tide of skill within the state, resulting in the mainland states moving in leaps and bounds relative to Tasmania, which was missing out on new techniques and styles being played elsewhere. Also due to the Depression, people were leaving Tasmania for employment on the mainland, which adversely affected the player pool situation.* [12]

The 1930s saw the rise of factory or company clubs throughout Australia and Tasmania was no different. In 1931 the formation of the Cascade Brewery team was announced, playing in the colours of the Cascade ale brews of red and green. With a factory team representing a brewer and another representing the confectioner, Cadbury, many tastes were catered for...

By 1931 the south of the state could boast four hundred players and twenty-seven teams. A Referee's Association had been formed which would meet to hear complaints about decisions made by clubs.

In 1932 an intra-state series comprised teams from the North, South and East Coast. The East Coast team was dissolved in 1933.

A series of matches were played in the north between players of English, Scottish, and Tasmanian heritage in 1934. The Scottish team were the victors.

The Tasmanian British Football Association gained the lease of the South Hobart ground in 1936.

The visiting South Australian side played three matches in 1937. South Australia defeated Tasmania 5-3 and 3-2 victories were recorded over South and North Tasmania selections. The Australian Soccer Football Association donated a trophy to be contested between school teams from the north and south of the state.

In 1939 the Northern League was in disarray. Invermay and North Launceston were disqualified from the league due to failing to pay fines. The only remaining club was Patons and Baldwins, which was declared champions.

South Australia returned to play Tasmania in 1939. Before the Governor, Sir Ernest Clark, the South Australians won 4-2 on a waterlogged pitch. South

Australia went on to draw with a South selection 1-1. The North Launceston and Invermay teams were ejected from the northern competition mid-season for refusing to pay increased affiliation fees to the Northern Association.

With the outbreak of war in 1939 all senior competition in Tasmania ceased, with only junior matches being played.

Victoria

The Victorian Soccer Association obtained the use of the Motordrome for enclosed matches in 1930.

The most successful teams during the 1930s were Hakoah, which became First Division Champions in the years 1934, 1935 and 1938, and Moreland which won in 1936 and 1937. The victories by the Hakoah team are significant, as they represent the first major trophies won by a non-Anglo based club in Australia.

In 1930 cup match preparations throughout the state and a carnival of Jewish based teams were of public interest. The contest was among the earliest of the ethnic or religious based tournaments which were to become increasingly popular after the immigration of displaced persons from Europe after World War II.

A soccer team was formed in Morwell in 1933. It joined the Gippsland Association which already fielded clubs from the mining areas of Yallourn.

The Hakoah club was promoted to the First Division of the State League. The following year it was the first club to play a match against a club from another state. Hakoah brought the champion Kingswood club from Adelaide who were the local champions to play a match in Melbourne.

An article was published which ruminated on the disadvantage soccer faced in Victoria in particular and Australia in general:

> *Mr Minor, one of the Vice-Presidents of the Central Gippsland Soccer Club gave a short address on 'The Future Outlook of Soccer in Australia.' Soccer, he said was international... and could not be called foreign as some Victorian delegates of Australian rules called it.*
>
> *This is the code that is to be kept out of certain grounds in Melbourne. These men call themselves sportsmen and gentlemen. They would never stop it... We had sat quiet for years but forces were now at work to combat the only opposition in the world and that from a state with two million*

people... Where you meet an educated and much travelled Australian he had an open mind on the matter. There is plenty of room for all the codes. All we ask is for an open field and an even chance. [14]

By the middle of the decade the St Kilda club withdrew from competition after 25 years.

There were eight clubs in Division One and nine clubs in Division Two in the Metropolitan Melbourne competition by 1936. A schools competition included a competition for the Dunkling Cup.

The Italian based Savoia club often played matches against an Italian fascist club named Gino Lisa at Royal Park, Carlton. Both teams met in 1937 to play for the Coppa Florentino, won by Savoia, which was presented by the Italian consul in Melbourne. By 1939 the Gino Lisa organisation was under surveillance by Australian authorities and subsequently banned.

In this era the Apollo Athletic Club, representing players of Greek heritage, commenced playing matches in Division III.

During this decade there were numerous articles in Victorian papers about the rise of soccer, and to a lesser extent rugby. Such articles focussed on the negative effect this would have on the development of Australian Rules. One way in which the Australian Rules authorities maintained control was by controlling the leases of enclosed grounds in Melbourne. The 'lesser' codes struggled to obtain enclosed grounds to play top class matches on.

Another method of ensuring the dominance of Australian Rules in Victoria was banning rugby and soccer from being introduced in public schools:

Rival Codes
Fears in Victoria

Fears that the introduction of Rugby Union football into public schools might seriously affect Australian Rules football were expressed by delegates at a meeting of the Victorian Football League on Friday night. The discussion arose during consideration of a letter which was read from the Victorian State Schools Amateur Athletic Association intimating that it had rejected a proposal to introduce Soccer into State schools.

It was agreed that the State Schools Amateur Athletic Association should be thanked for its rejection of the introduction of Soccer into schools, and also that headmasters of Victorian Public schools should be written to directing attention to the protest of the League against the introduction of Rugby into schools, and asking the reason why football under Australian Rules should be rejected. [15]

In 1938 the Melbourne press reported that soccer authorities were offering schools £50 if they would switch allegiance to soccer from Australian Rules. Schools would be provided with soccer uniforms, balls and coaching. Whether this was true or not, it seems many school headmasters were using the story as a means of leveraging more money from the Victorian Football League so they could prove their faith to the indigenous Australian Rules code.

Western Australia

In the west the most successful club during the 1930s was Victoria Park. The senior team won the Division 1 Championship in consecutive years from 1934 to 1939. Northern Casuals were the next most successful team winning in 1930 and 1932.

At this time a team named Maccabean, supported by the Jewish community started playing in the Second League of the Metropolitan Suburban League in Perth. The club later changed its name to Maccabi.

Teams from Kalgoorlie and Boulder played many matches against each other:

Soccer Football

A very good and interesting game of this code of football was played on Sunday on the Commonwealth Park when Boulder met Kalgoorlie. This season Boulder seemed to have the stronger team, but were rather weak when it came to shooting the ball through the goal. Whatever Kalgoorlie lacked in strength they made up for in tenacity and determination... When the whistle closed the game, Boulder (was) winning by 2 goals to 1. It is rumoured that it is the intention of the Mayor to set the ball rolling at Boulder. [16]

By 1931 the Depression was biting hard in Western Australia as elsewhere. An immigrant's home formed a soccer team but struggled to supplying kit for the team. A Mr Nye formed the team to:

> *Counter-act the demoralising effect of hours of enforced idleness. A soccer team had been formed among the men, and in matches, against teams from visiting boats, it had given a good account of itself. Football clothes however could not be provided out of the committee's funds and he appealed to any club or person who had any disused clothes of that nature to send them to the home...* [17]

A small league of three clubs named Thistle, Town and Rangers were competing in the coastal town of Geraldton by 1931. The inland town of Wiluna also formed a club.

In April 1932 the Western Australian team played a match against officers of two visiting Japanese cruisers HIJMS *Asama* and HIJMS *Yakumo*.

The West Australian reported on a one sided match won 10-2 by the locals:

Soccer International Match
State Team Victorious

> *An international match was played at Perth Oval yesterday afternoon between a team representing Western Australia and an eleven selected from the visiting Japanese cruisers...*
>
> *Lack of combination and weak shooting was particularly noticeable in the Japanese forward line, and resulted in many fine opportunities of scoring being missed. Although outclassed, the Japanese revealed themselves to be keen sportsmen and contested the game in true international spirit.* [18]

The Victoria Park forward Jack Conduit signed for the English second tier soccer team Blackpool in 1934. He became one of the few players to sign for a high level soccer club in England before World War II. Conduit's play was described as being similar to the Newcastle and Arsenal star Charles Buchan. Conduit returned to Perth in 1935.

A schoolboy team from Kalgoorlie were the first country junior team to visit Perth and play matches in 1935. Most of the boys were under 14 years of age and came from school teams from the rural mining city which had been established for up to five years.

The metropolitan senior completion was divided into three divisions with promotion and relegation instituted. A match was played with teams representing England and Scotland with players from respective places of heritage.

In the 1930s matches between a select team of players of English and Scottish origins were popular. Teams met at Leederville Oval and contested the Boan Trophy.

The Boulder City club arranged a tour of South Australia and New South Wales in 1938. The club performed creditably, defeating the Tasmanian and South Australian teams in Adelaide. They succumbed to New South Wales opposition in the form of Granville, a Goodyear and Granville combination and Wallsend. This was a major undertaking for a regional club from Western Australia.

In the same year Western Australia played against the visiting Indian team, winning 5-1 in the first match.

The following year the state team also played Palestine, drawing 4-4 and losing 7-3.

Chapter 11

Australian International Matches 1930s

In 1931 an Australian team returned to the East Indies for the first time since 1928. Australia played matches against teams representing Celebes, Surabaya, Batavia, Bandeong, Java Chinese, Macassar and Singapore. News of this tour was relatively scant.

As usual, the selection of the Australian team was subject to interstate rivalry and rancour from clubs, displeased to have to release players for the tour.

State League players were included in the squad even though the State League was not affiliated with the Australian Soccer Football Association (ASFA). The ASFA reluctantly agreed to this because it had promised the Netherlands East Indies authorities the best team possible. If the team had not been strong the promoter would have possibly lost money and this was not something the ASFA wanted.

Five Queenslanders were in the squad. The manager was Ernest Lukeman. The team played 13 matches of which nine were won, three lost and one drawn. The highest Australian scorers were Dick James of Queensland and P. Lewis of Victoria. On return, the Australian team management said that the tour was valuable but that it should have started earlier in the year to avoid high humidity.

The public was informed by the press that the tourists were 'the unhappiest soccer party to leave these shores' and many complaints about the trip were aired.

Some Australian players complained to Javanese authorities about financial conditions which centred upon the exchange rate of pounds to guilders.

This was not behaviour which had been approved by team management. Consequently, on return to Australia they were reprimanded.

Players argued among themselves, stating that some in the squad were mere 'passengers'. Grounds were 'bad' and refereeing 'weak'.

Queensland players complained that they were not fully aware of some official functions. On the return trip to Australia a team member had a 'native chair' he had purchased in Java thrown overboard by another player. He threatened legal action.

Officials returned complaining about a lack of hospitality from the hosts. However, they admitted that the play of the locals had improved since the 1928 tour to the islands by Australia.

An old foe, the New Zealand soccer team played Australia on 5 June 1933 in Brisbane. The introduction in the match programme stressed the ability of soccer to connect the Empire in an article entitled *The Leathern sphere links the empire*:

> Once again is demonstrated the value of sport as an Empire binding factor, for to-day the representatives of two great Dominions meet in a trial of strength on the football field... Look where you will, you will find that football and especially Association football – is playing no small part in keeping the British Empire united. [1]

Such Trans-Tasman bonhomie promptly evaporated. The Australian Association discovered that the tour by the New Zealanders made a financial loss of £550. The Australians blamed the financial loss on the poor quality of the opposition, while the New Zealanders replied that poor tour publicity and the economic conditions were to blame. This led to the Australians asking the New Zealanders to bridge some of the loss. The Australians even asked the Kiwis to cover the cost of a £32 laundry bill which the New Zealanders described as 'trivial and in bad taste'.

The New Zealand series marked the international debut of two prominent Australian players. One was Roy Crowhurst, the Metters forward. He scored two goals against the New Zealanders. George Smith who became a record goals scorer for his country, also made his first appearance, scoring seven goals in the series. Both became mainstays of the Australian team throughout the 1930s.

The ASFA negotiated a tour of New Caledonia in August 1933. It was agreed that the hosts would incur all expenses. The team to tour New Caledonia included seven players from New South Wales, two from Queensland and two from South Australia. It was proposed that the Australian team play five matches in New Caledonia. It is interesting to note that the touring party consisted only of thirteen players. Presumably the officials were relying on all involved staying fit and healthy.

Ceremonial aspects of the first international match between Australia and New Caledonia were of importance:

> *The first Test match between the Australian Soccer team and New Caledonia was played at Noumea on August 15, in ideal weather. It was a holiday, and the crowd numbered one third the population. A band played God Save the King, The Marseilles, and Advance Australia Fair, the Governor shook hands with the players, and the captain of the home team presented an honour flag to the Australian captain (Smith). A great game delighted the crowd, Australia winning by two goals to one.* [2]

The Australian team played three matches against New Caledonia, winning all matches, with the scores being 2-1, 4-2 and 7-3. The team also defeated a New Caledonia XI 8-1 and the local champion team named Impassible 6-1.

An Australian proposal for a three cornered tournament in Australia comprising matches between the national teams of Australia, England and Scotland, was refused by both the English and Scottish Football Associations. Germany was also invited to tour but the German Football Association declined the offer. Australian officials were told the travel exertions would be too great and would interrupt their domestic season.

The Secretary General of the Czech Chamber of Commerce in Sydney, Mr L. Vazek, served on the board of the St George club. In 1934 he liaised with the Czechoslovakian Football Association in an attempt to arrange an Australian team tour of Europe. The plan was for Australia to play national sides from England, Czechoslovakia, Hungary, Austria, Italy and Germany. This was yet another touring plan which never eventuated.

There was tension between the 'upstart from the Empire' and the 'mother country':

Proposed English Tour
Definite News Early

Very soon now it will be known whether the proposed tour of England, Ireland, Scotland and possibly Europe and America will eventuate or not... Ever since taking office, Mr Druery has been aspiring to the passage of an Australian team to England, and spent much time in writing to the English Association. But Sir Frederick Wall was not a scrap sympathetic, and as Mr Druery aptly put it, 'stunted our Soccer growth'.

However with the accession of Mr Rouse to the throne vacated by Sir Frederick, Mr Druery immediately secured a hearing and received a reply that although the English FA regretted its inability for 1934, they hoped for success of Australia's application for 1935. [3]

Unfortunately such hopes of a British or Continental tour turned out to be another mirage. It was not until 1970 that Australia would play a European team on their home soil when Australia defeated Greece 3-1 in Athens in an historic victory. In 1934 the officials would never have believed it would take 89 prior internationals to reach that milestone.

In 1935 the Australian Government expressed concern when the Russian team showed interest in touring Australia. The visiting team would be required to lodge bonds:

Russian Soccer Team Wants To Visit Australia Government Demands Bond

CANBERRA, Tuesday.

An application had been made for the admittance of a Russian soccer football team to Australia in 1936. The Minister for the Interior (Mr Paterson) had informed the Australian Football Association that it must lodge a guarantee of £100 for every member of the team entering the country. A guarantee of £100 had been charged for each member of the Chinese soccer team when it visited Australia. The Czechoslovakian team had been admitted in 1927 under a guarantee furnished by the Australian Soccer Football Association, but without a monetary bond, there having been no general restriction on white alien migration at that time as there was at present. [4]

The visit of the Russian team failed to occur.

Efforts were being made to develop the game in the dominions of the British Empire. The New Zealand Soccer Association decided to support an Australian suggestion that the English Football Association should convene a meeting of dominion associations in London to discuss the furtherance of the game in the British dominions. It was suggested that the conference in London should consist of a representative from each of Canada, South Africa, New Zealand, India, and Australia. It was speculated that there had been a grant of £500 to Australia, and another of £1,000 to Canada to pursue international matches and co-operation.

In 1936 the Australian team played three matches in New Zealand, winning all of them in comfort. Australia defeated New Zealand 7-1 in Dunedin, 10-0 in Wellington and 4-1 in Auckland.

A match report highlighted the ease with which the Australians dominated their near neighbours during the tour:

> *The superiority of soccer in Australia over the standard in New Zealand was again demonstrated when the Australians scored a runaway win in the second test. The scores were 10 to nil, Australia scoring five goals in each half...*
>
> *Throughout the second half the Australians played less strenuously, but provided the crowd with a splendid exhibition of scientific foot-ball, adding two further goals in the first eight minutes... New Zealand attacked strongly, but owing to deplorably bad shooting did not look like scoring...* [5]

Although a visit by the English professional team was an impossibility, the English Amateur team visited Australia in 1937 to play matches against Australia. The matches were regarded by Australian officials as full international matches.

The first match was played in Sydney in front of over 30,000 spectators, which was a record crowd. Australian officials were criticised for only allowing the Australian team to assemble and practice three days before the match. Despite this, the Australians won the match 5-4. Australia distinguished itself as being the first dominion nation to defeat an English team, albeit amateurs.

Over £3,000 was raised in gate takings, ensuring the match was a financial success. Any debt incurred with the tour was cleared and from then on all takings were profit.

The match program for the 'Second Test' at the Exhibition Grounds in Brisbane on 17 July 1937 exuded a warm welcome stating that 'the representatives of the 'Motherland' will find a genuine love of England and the English'.

In total the English Amateur team played three matches against Australia, losing two matches (5-4, 4-3) and winning one (4-0). The efforts of the Australians were credible, when it is considered how badly the locals had been defeated by a slightly more high calibre English team in 1925.

The tour marked the international debut for Australia of the defender, Bill Coolahan. Coolahan first played for West Wallsend as a 16 year old and played twelve matches for Australia. Despite being a defender, Coolahan also managed to score over one hundred goals in his club career.

The English tour made a profit for Australian authorities and £100 was disbursed to each state soccer association.

English players expressed a point of view on whether Australia would benefit from training from English coaches. Some said that Australian players may not suit a rigid English system which would destroy the 'dash and originality' of Australian players.

The next team to visit Australia after the Englishmen was the Indian national team in 1938. The team sailed from Colombo in Ceylon during August of that year, arriving in Fremantle in September.

In the eyes of Australian soccer reporters and the public the timing of the visit placed the Indians in a pressured situation. The English Amateur visit had made a profit of £3,000. Two questions occupied the minds of Australians. Would the Indian team be of quality and interest? Would the visit generate a profit? To a degree the two questions were linked. A poor quality team would be unlikely to generate either interest or profit, while a quality team, generating healthy gates, would be more likely to induce a profit.

Decisions were made which curtailed anticipated costs. Referees and linesmen were paid half of what they received when officiating at the English amateur matches. Matches were insured for wash outs. However, all turned out modestly well, as a £200 profit was made.

The Indian manager, Mr Gupta, explained that soccer was 'almost a religion', especially in Bengal, with Calcutta boasting four hundred clubs. He was quick to shower Australia with compliments such as 'the Indian sunshine bites but the Australian sunshine kisses'. If India had toured during an Australian summer instead of winter his comment may not have been so benign...

An Australian paper stated that 'the team includes two university graduates and a medical doctor besides three customs officials, so that it becomes obvious that the team are by no means barbarians'.

The Indian side was reputed to be fast and nippy with agile forwards. Full backs would reputably 'amaze the Australian public by the manner of their clearances'. The Indian's style of play was described as 'scientific' and their ball control and passing flair was a highlight.

The Indians were also stoic. They played domestic matches in monsoonal conditions and when offered a light ball to practice with in Sydney, preferred another ball which was heavier when wet.

Many of the Indian side, with the exception of five players, played in bare feet, often wrapped with bandages. Mr Gupta explained that it was possible and preferable to play in bare feet in the wet and lush fields of India. Playing in bare feet enhanced a player's feel for the game, ensuring superior ball control. Mr Gupta further explained that playing in bare feet enabled players to pull the ball backwards with their toes and change direction quickly, something which a player with boots could not do. He did not think it was likely that opponents with boots would bruise the feet of the Indian players because they were so fleet footed.

The fact that the Indians played in bare feet was a great talking point in the press months before the commencement of the tour. That fact alone generated great curiosity and publicity.

However, on some Australian grounds which were hard and uneven, such as the Melbourne Cricket Ground, some Indian players were to suffer from cut feet.

The tourists were praised for the manner in which their players refused to object to refereeing decisions or get annoyed with opponents. Local reporters cited their behaviour as an object lesson to Australian players.

The Indians had a forward named K. Prasad who was ranked as highly as any player in Australia. 5 ft 3 in tall and weighing 8 stone, he was extremely fast and was nicknamed *Mickey the Mouse*.

History was made for Australia when Lex Gibb was capped for Australia. His father, Alex, a team selector, had been the historic first cap for Australia, against New Zealand in 1922. This made them the first father-son duo to play soccer for Australia. Australia's leading goal scorer against the Indian team was Jack Hughes, the Metters forward. He scored nine goals for Australia against the Indians.

The Indian team played and defeated an Illawarra selection 6-4 on 20 September 1938. The match attracted some 3,000 spectators with gate receipts of £162. Prior to the match the Indian team were taken by coach to view Bulli Pass the panorama of which the tourists described as 'absolutely wonderful'. Additionally, the Indian team management were given the privilege of opening ground improvements at Ball's Paddock, Woonona, home of the local Woonona club.

Indian stoicism had its limits. Players became tired when travelling on slow and uncomfortable trains. In Queensland, the Indian team which had hitherto travelled 2nd class, upgraded to 1st class with sleepers, paying the supplement from their own pockets.

The Indians played sixteen matches. Matches were played against all state teams except for Tasmania. Australia played India in five test matches, winning 5-3 in Sydney, drawing 4-4 in Brisbane, losing 1-4 in Newcastle, winning 5-4 in Sydney and 3-1 in Melbourne.

With the Indian tour almost concluded, the souvenir program for the fourth test between Australia and India, played on 24 September 1938 at the Sydney Showground, provided an assessment of the visitors:

> *It is many a day since an overseas team has created so much interest and pleasure as the Indian side... The play of the Indian team is new and novel, without doubt better than the Chinese team of 1923. The ball control and accurate passing of the visitors is similar to that of the Scottish professional. Our grounds (other than the ground played on to-day) do not come up to the standard of those in India and it is reasonable to assume that the Indians are playing under difficulties...*[6]

It seems that reviews of the touring Indian side had been mixed. In 1939 a soccer writer named 'Northern Soccer Correspondent' writing for *The Sydney Morning Herald* opined that the quality of the Indian tourists was not good enough to excite officials and the public. In his view the 'well-intentioned' visit of the Indians had 'undone the good' the English amateur touring team of 1937 had done.

He damned with faint praise 'able' Central European teams and feared that a visit from Continental clubs could be a public relations problem. If a touring club side was poor and easily defeated by Australia, the tourists would be criticised. To the contrary, if a touring side was to dominate an Australian team, this would represent a greater embarrassment to Australian soccer. 'Northern Soccer Correspondent' cautioned that waiting a year or two for English or Scottish teams to visit would be more prudent.

One complaint 'Northern Soccer Correspondent' made was logical. He griped that many of the tours extended over too many matches. This had the effect of causing visiting teams to lose their stamina or competitive interest when playing more minor tour matches. Furthermore, such tours took the spotlight away from the yearly domestic metropolitan league matches, which often were played without club 'stars' who were on national or state duty. This led to lower gates at local matches. Such laments have been a constant in our game. During this era some tours by foreign teams would encompass up to 17 matches and last for over two months.

Nevertheless, soccer officials were keen for international visits to continue with regularity. By 1939 it was rumoured that the Hungarian national team would tour Australia. It was, however, the Palestinian side which toured Australia over a period of two months. Critics, without knowledge of the standard of soccer in Palestine, were sceptical about whether the visitors from the Middle East were of the 'quality' to play Australians.

The tour was masterminded by Josef Skolnik, a foundation official of the Hakoah club of Melbourne and a former vice-president of the Victorian Soccer Association. He persuaded the Jewish community to help fund the tour.

The Palestinian team consisted of Jewish players. Most of the players were from the Maccabi-Tel Aviv club. Eight were born in Palestine, with the others coming from Austria, Poland and Hungary.

The press was eager to inform readers of the attributes of the party. The Austrian coach, Egon Pollak, was described as having the 'physique of a boxer, courtesy of a cavalier and the charm of a diplomat'. He also was a concert quality baritone opera singer, giving two recitals while in Australia.

Isaac Viner, a 'half back' was a speedster holding a Tel Aviv sprinting record, while the towering full back Abraham Halevi reputedly could kick the ball from goal mouth to goal mouth and could jump the height of an average man.

Hyperbole threatened fact when the Palestinian player named Zvi Fuchs was described as having lungs like the Finnish runner Paavo Nurmi and the ability to play for 'six hours non-stop'. The team manager, Mr R.S. Arizi, could say 'shoot laddie' in eight languages.

The Palestinian players were allowed to drink 'now and again' and most smoked, although smoking was discouraged on the afternoon prior to a match.

The Palestinians, in an almost comical error of stylistic and tactical attribution, were described as playing 'like a Scottish soccer team'. Australian spectators, when told of some of the player's names, would, as in the case of the Indian team, adopt nicknames, thus obviating the tiresome need to enhance their linguistic abilities. The public were informed that 'Palestinian' names would be a 'nightmare' for soccer scribes, whose journalistic professional dignity would prevent them from using nicknames. A trawl through contemporary newspaper articles proves that the names of the players were constantly mis-spelt.

The Sun newspaper from Sydney succeeded in blending blatent anti-Semitism with crude sexual insinuation in a 'humour piece' describing a fictitious Palestinian player:

> *A Palestinian soccer player named Moshyechezekiel Schnaidermirmovitch explains to us:-*
> *We play it good, the Soccer, because we get it very active mit kicking mit the feet, it isn't only one all we play it mit, but we train it mit three balls at once, and all of them is gilt ones.* [7]

The Palestinian team took two months to reach Australia from Port Said and two months to tour. That may have given more adroit Australians time to perfect their pronunciation skills...

Australia recorded a 7-5 victory in Sydney (with a team comprising New South Wales based players) a 2-1 win in Brisbane, a 1-2 loss in Sydney, a 4-1 victory in Newcastle and a 4-4 draw in Melbourne. The schedule for the touring team verged on the masochistic. In total, 17 matches would be played with the team travelling over 2,000 miles in the first month, mainly by 2nd class train without sleeping accommodation while playing weekend and mid-week matches.

The Palestine visit marked the sunset of the Australian international career of the prolific goalscorer, George Smith. Smith mainly played for NSW south coast clubs, and in particular, Corrimal. In his long career, Smith scored a record 66 goals for Australia in 26 matches.

On a trip between Melbourne and Sydney some Palestinian players were so tired they tried to sleep on luggage racks, until being forbidden by a train guard. Mr Arizi stated that Victorian trains were bearable, but that New South Wales trains were of 'Rumanian or Bulgarian standards'. Sid Story, chairman of the Australian Soccer Association, replied to a request by the Palestinian team to travel first class. Untainted by diplomacy and with withering candour he stated that 'when we entered into the contract (2nd class fares) we did not even know if the team could play football. Now we know they can'.

As usual, there was concern about scheduling and suitable ground allocation for the touring side, based on the demands of other sports. The Wigan Rugby League team would also be in Sydney and Brisbane at the time of the Palestinian visit and this caused tensions between the soccer and Rugby League authorities. Humdrum Australian scheduling difficulties turned to obscure sporting farce when the Brisbane 'test' between Australia and Palestine had to be advanced by a week because the Brisbane Exhibition Ground was booked for an 'All Australian Lacrosse Carnival' on the preferred date of soccer officials. Officials from the Victorian Football League in Melbourne, not to be outdone in any competition to deny hospitality to the world game, refused to allocate any of their grounds to the visiting Palestinian team.

The financial details of the tour by Palestine were divulged:

Football

> *The touring party will consist of 17 players and a manager. The Jewish community of Melbourne is providing £1000 towards financing the tour. In the event of a profit, one third will go to the Jewish players as an added allowance, and two-thirds to the Australian Soccer Football Association, with the maximum profit to the Jewish players of £333.* [8]

While touring, the team was warmly welcomed by the Jewish-Australian community which hosted players and officials at many functions. The most prominent was the Jewish Bachelors' Ball in Melbourne which was held at the Palais de Dance. The gala event featured 1,300 attendees with the guests of honour being the Jewish Australian Governor-General Sir Isaac Isaacs and Lady Isaacs.

The Palestinians toured in blue and white striped shirts, which prompted the New South Wales team to change from their light blue shirts to red to avoid a clash of colours, for the first time in fifty years. Journalists were fascinated by the boots the Palestinian players wore, which did not cover the ankles as traditional English style boots of the time did. They were described as a mixture of a running shoe and a soccer boot, but in fact presaged the style of boots to be worn post World War II.

The visitors were praised for their effective teamwork and skills. Although they only defeated the Australian team once, the Palestinians had comfortable victories over the state sides of Victoria, Queensland, South Australia and Western Australia. Only the New South Wales team and regional teams of New South Wales such as the South Coast and the Newcastle region could compete with them. These results highlighted how much more soccer had progressed in New South Wales compared to the other states.

The last match of the Palestine tour was played on 5 August, in the shadows of World War II. Six Palestinian players or officials, including the coach Egon Pollak, applied for and were granted permission to remain in Australia. Two players subsequently signed to play for Melbourne's Hakoah club.

Less than a month later on 4 September, Prime Minister Robert Menzies declared that Australia was at war with Germany.

Chapter 12

Soccer in the Shadow of War

During the war years the only state competitions which endured throughout were played in New South Wales, South Australia and Victoria. Young adult men joined the forces or performed other essential work or study. The soccer careers of many senior players withered on the vine. Discovering that they were too old when war ended, sporting careers were abbreviated.

For some, service in the armed forces enabled them to play soccer in overseas locations such as the sands of Tobruk, the fields of France and the jungle clearings of New Guinea, a thought which seemed unimaginable and perhaps exotic in early 1939.

In what seems a bizarre local event, soldiers at the Enoggera army base in Queensland trained by playing soccer in gas masks. This was done in order for the men to experience moving freely with the masks on.

'Enemy aliens' who were housed at camps such as Hay in New South Wales and Tatura in Victoria created soccer competitions to pass the time. Some of the players were the famous 'Dunera Boys'. These were Jewish youths and young men from Germany and Austria who had been shipped from England to Australia on the ship HMT *Dunera*, arriving in 1942. Many were to play a significant part in the intellectual life of Australia after World War II. Other teams were formed in prisoner of war camps, consisting of mainly German and Italian nationals. A 'Juventus' team was formed at the Hay camp by Italians while the 'Dunera Boys' formed a team called 'Arsenal' in Tatura.

Junior soccer continued without a pause. However, older youths had no senior competition of any note to graduate to. As with Australians in all other areas of life, the hopes, ambitions, and careers of soccer players, young or old, would alter forever in the vortex of war.

Australian Capital Territory

Soccer in the Second World War years was almost moribund in the ACT, although a match was played by visiting British servicemen representing teams from the Royal Air Force and the Royal Navy in 1945:

> Football under two codes attracted a big crowd to the Manuka Oval on Saturday for a carnival in aid of the Australian Comforts Fund.
> Soccer, revived after an interval of thirteen years was seen to advantage in a game between British service teams in which R.A.F. (Sydney) defeated Royal Navy (Canberra) by four goals to two...
> A lithe side against more stockily built seamen, the R.A.F. wore black armbands in memory of comrades killed in recent air accidents. Both teams observed a minute's silence in midfield for the same purpose. [1]

At a peace carnival in September of that year teams from the Royal Navy played a match at Manuka Oval in aid of repatriation funds.

New South Wales

1940 was considered the diamond jubilee of soccer in Australia. This milestone was based on the Wanderers v Kings School match of 1880 being counted as the first game.

On the field the milestone was celebrated when Metters played Wallsend at Arlington Oval. Metters won a high scoring Jubilee Cup game 10-7 against Wallsend. A week later a gala dinner and smoke concert was held in Sydney at Sargent's on Market Street to commemorate players who had played soccer for Sydney teams in the period from 1886 to 1891. Two players from the first NSW club, Wanderers, and three NSW players from the first Victoria v NSW interstate match of 1883 attended.

Promotion of soccer matches in Australia has often drifted between the bizarre, exotic and chaotic. In 1940, the Metters club succeeded in the near impossible, by combining all three attributes. It announced that a 'North American Indian' named Chief Thunderbird would attend a home match at Arlington Oval, when Metters played Wallsend. The chief would commence the match with a 'war whoop' and support Metters, the team in light blue. Unfortunately Thunderbird started barracking for the red shirted opposition team in error. When Alf Quill scored for Wallsend he commenced his elaborate war dance celebration in front of the stand. This was too much for the near apoplectic Metters chairman, Bill Douglas, who stepped in to remind the Native American of his fleeting guest obligations. At the conclusion of the match Thunderbird met the players and critiqued 'You boys would be lost playing gridiron, but can you toe that ball!'

Metters won the State Championship that year after twelve years, so maybe Chief Thunderbird did bring the *Stovies* good luck… The Metters team dominated the premier Sydney competition winning the State Cup and various minor cups. Over £600 was distributed to the winning first team squad, with each player receiving £45, which at the time was a record.

Meanwhile, the great 'industrial derby' opponents of Metters, the Goodyear Tyre Company club, was facing a crisis in 1940. Due to a dramatic downturn in tyre sales caused by wartime restrictions on vehicle use, tyre production had fallen greatly. All but one of its international players had been released from work. The club withdrew from competition in that year.

Many other clubs faced closure due to the exigencies of the war. In 1940 the Wollongong club, which had only been admitted to the State League a year before, disbanded and pledged £60 to the construction of the new HMAS *Sydney* warship.

Communication of match scores was not always the most up to date. The Coledale club on the NSW South Coast had a solution and sent off carrier pigeons to convey the half time and full time winning score against North Wollongong to its distant fans.

In 1940 the *Newcastle Sun* printed news under the heading of 'soccer vandalism'. It was reported that the Secretary of the Australian Football Association, F.R. Druery, had suggested that the cup given to Australia by the English FA for competition among the states in 1924 be melted down. The value of the melted down trophy would be distributed among the state soccer federations. Druery complained about paying insurance for the Cup which was 'littering-up his home'. The trophy had not been competed for since 1935. Fortunately further discussion scotched the proposal.

Meanwhile, efforts were made to find the missing Gardiner Cup in 1941. It was discovered that it had been in possession of Mr S.H. Stack who was

President of the New South Wales Association in 1929. The Cup had been in his possession for 12 years. Sid Storey, the Trustee of the New South Wales Soccer Association said he planned to re-introduce the Gardiner Cup competition when the time was appropriate.

Metters again won the premiership in 1941. The Leichhardt-Annandale team also had a rarity at the time, a Chinese winger named Shui Yick Yeung. He was the only player from the 1941 touring Chinese selection to stay in Australia to play club soccer. In that year the Leichhardt club, winners of the State Cup, also paid players a record bonus for the year of £38 10s and they each received a sports coat.

Two top grade teams played various matches in Sydney to aid the Comforts Fund Appeal in 1942, which enabled food parcels to be sent to servicemen at the front. The Protestant Churches Association decided to discontinue competition until the war ended. Clubs promoted to the State League were having problems signing former players from other clubs. They claimed that the powerful and established clubs did not want to even up the competition by relinquishing players. The Lake Macquarie club was most vocal, threatening to leave the State League if the situation was not resolved.

Wallsend were State League premiers and State Cup winners in 1942. In a stellar season Wallsend also won the northern premiership, the Daniels and the Northern War Cup. In many instances the coalfields clubs north of Sydney had an advantage over Sydney clubs in that employment of miners remained constant in order to satisfy the war effort.

In Sydney, clubs had a manpower shortage as men went to war. Those in employment often worked longer shifts which gave them less time to recuperate and play soccer. There was also an acute shortage of referees in the north as inductee examinations had not been conducted for eighteen months, although the Sydney region was also affected.

Some families devoted their lives to a favourite club. In Sydney the Leichhardt-Annandale Club had six members of the Hankins family on the Committee. The family had been members for 32 years, ever since the club was founded in 1910. Two of the family members were women, making them the only female life members of a soccer club in Sydney.

The Merewether club sought to initiate the latest training measures by increasing training to two days per week and introducing blackboard tactical lectures which were considered a novel training aid recently used by successful overseas clubs.

The Metters club, the most successful in Sydney, threatened to withdraw from the League if they could not secure Arlington Oval at Dulwich Hill as their long term home ground. Fortunately, the Petersham council sealed a deal which reduced Metters rental of the facility.

Shortages were affecting clubs in other ways. They found that sports retailers had few new shirts and that the range of colours and designs were limited. North Shore initially registered as wearing blue shirts, but had to change to red and black halved shirts as a consequence. Players lacking shorts were advised to make them out of linen sheets, while bullock's bladders were suggested as inserts in soccer balls.

Special matches were played in Sydney and Newcastle to aid the Comforts Fund Appeal. Money raised contributed to many food parcels being sent to troops overseas.

In 1942 P. Docherty scored ten goals for Lysaght-Orb against Kearsley in a State League match. This was a record for the time.

Bill Coolahan, who had played 331 first grade matches and skippered Australia against the English amateurs, India, Palestine and China announced his retirement in 1943. The historian, Sid Grant, dubbed him 'Bill the Lionhearted' for his never-say-die attitude and named him the most influential player of the previous twenty years.

On the field, Wallsend again won the State championship.

The most disruptive story of the war years in New South Wales was a breakaway movement in 1943. The dispute started when Metters and Wallsend played a match against each other on Easter Saturday, 24 April 1943 in contravention of Association sanction:

Breakaway of Clubs
New League Formed

Wallsend, Metters, Leichhardt Annandale, and Adamstown clubs have withdrawn from the N.S.W. Soccer Football Association. Action which was taken... yesterday followed a decision to fine Metters and Wallsend £10 each for playing a challenge game on Easter Saturday in defiance of a ban placed on the match by the council...

Leichhardt-Annandale and Adamstown delegates withdrew their clubs affiliation in sympathy with Metters and Wallsend. The clubs immediately formed a new association which they will call the New South Wales State Soccer League...

The game had become stagnant... schoolboys and other junior bodies receiving no consideration...[2]

The effects of yet another bureaucratic fracas took its toll on the soccer scene. In 1943 it was announced that *The Soccer Weekly*, the official organ of the NSW Soccer Football Association (NSWSFA) was to cease publication for the season, with clubs being left to publish their own programmes. The net gate proceeds from the Grand Challenge Match between Metters (undefeated southern leaders) and Wallsend (undefeated northern leaders) on 24 April 1943 was invested in Commonwealth War Bonds in aid of the National War Effort. In Sydney the proportion of junior players to seniors was 5,000 to 200.

In 1943 the Ogilvie Cup was instituted. It pitted a team from the Newcastle region against a combined Sydney and South Coast team. It replaced the McWilliam Cup which was discontinued in 1940. The Ogilvie Cup ran until 1962.

War shortages provoked a warning from the NSWSFA. Clubs needed to take special care of their sporting kit. If not they were informed that they may have to shed club colours and make shorts out of sheets. Woollen shirts could not be bought and the choice in linen shirt 'colours' were black or white only.

There were two separate champion clubs in New South Wales. The winners were Corrimal Rangers and Wallsend. Corrimal won under the auspices of the NSWSFA. Corrimal only lost one match in that year and won the Sheahan, Hickey and Gibson Cups. Wallsend won under the banner of the New South Wales State Soccer League (NSWSSL) The northern club possessed the star forward Reg Date who scored nine goals in one match.

Newcastle soccer referees decided to play with white shirts, rather than the dark shirts they had worn previously.

Paradoxically, the 1943 metropolitan season was considered quite a success. So much so that some officials broached the subject of full-time professionalism, a subject which would be shelved until after the war ended.

Clubs which had formed a break away competition were given till March 1944 to re-join the established State League competition or be disqualified from playing for three years by the Australian Soccer Control Council.

In the midst of the war an Englishman named Fred Gribble who had played for Brighton in England established a 'bureau' to look for soccer talent in Sydney. Any players selected would be screened by senior clubs. This came at a time when many junior clubs were going into recess.

By 1944 the breakaway and old league joined forces:

Dispute Ends

The dual control which has existed in soccer administration since May, 1943 has ended with a decision made yesterday under which the State association for all practical purposes will disappear.

All its assets will be transferred to the State League when the association affiliates with it. At a meeting in Newcastle yesterday the Northern League delegates agreed to accept the offer of the State League...[3]

With unity came calls for the regionalisation of an expanded competition. Players had difficulty gaining time off to attend far flung matches. Clubs also saw such an arrangement as a way of lessening travelling costs and time.

Wallsend won the State Cup and Metters won the First Division Premiership.

The Woonona club secretary initiated what was a novel scheme for the era. Mr Molloy instituted a smoking ban among players. The campaign, he claimed, reduced the number of smoking players from four to one, and led the team to a ten match winning streak.

Some interesting teams with foreign roots played in the NSW Minor League by 1944. Chung Wha was a team of Chinese players led by S.Y. Yeung who was part of the 1941 Chinese tour team. Yeung stayed in Australia to pursue his career as an engineer. A Dutch East Indies team played in the same league. Players were described as having played in Europe, as many players were of Dutch origin.

A new league system was unveiled in New South Wales for the 1945 season. This replaced the unified New South Wales Soccer League with separate competitions in the northern and southern areas of New South Wales.

Many British servicemen applied to join local soccer clubs. Some untruthfully stated that their experience was in the higher levels of the sport in England. When trialled, many were failing to reach the reserve grade standard. This made many clubs wary of signing British servicemen.

The State League launched a soccer company, in which six directors would lodge a £100 fee to join in 1945. This move was opposed by some of the northern clubs in the Newcastle region. The fee was dropped. The New South Wales Soccer League consisted of northern and southern clubs from the Newcastle, Wollongong and Sydney region. Among them was a Royal Navy team from HMS *Golden Hind*. This was the first time a Royal Navy team had been represented in the top echelon of New South Wales soccer since HMS *Powerful* in 1910. Weston, Kurri Kurri and Cessnock clubs returned to the top echelon of competition after several years.

The Protestant Churches competition resumed in Sydney after a break of some years with eighty-five teams participating.

An article appeared about a rather spoilt senior Wallsend player named Jimmy Cuthbert. His Scottish mother was described as the 'best soccer barracker'. During the season she would cook him a special chicken soup with ingredients she kept secret. She would hand him a marrow bone with a spoon at half time which Jimmy claimed enhanced his performances. She would polish his boots with special dubbin and pack two types of boots, one with stubs for wet grounds, the other with bars for dry grounds. She would cheer him on shouting 'come on awd man' Perhaps his mother would also run his bath when he returned home...

In 1945 the Australian soccer goalkeeper Norman 'Norm' Conquest announced his retirement after having been the Australian goalkeeper since 1941.

A scheme was initiated in Newcastle to train soccer coaches. In an era when many amateur teams did not have knowledgeable or qualified coaches, a program of lectures about the rules and tactics of soccer was given to school sport masters and senior and junior club officials.

Northern Territory

Much of the soccer that was played in the Northern Territory during the war years was played by the three services.

At the Larrakeyah Barracks servicemen played officers and sergeants played kitchen staff in impromptu matches in 1940.

By 1941 Navy, Field Ambulance, East Point, D.I.B. (Darwin Infantry Battalion) and headquarters teams were engaging in a competition which was organised by the 7th M.D. Soccer Association.

There was a Northern Territory Forces competition with teams such as Fortress, L of C, Navy and Infantry competing in 1944.

There was a determination for a competition to be formalised:

> *An inaugural general meeting to make plans for the Darwin Soccer Competition will be held at the Parap Hotel Civil Drome, at 1930 hours on Wednesday, January 10. This competition is open to any Army, Navy, and Air Force teams and all units interested in entering teams in this Association are asked to attend.* [4]

The first division comprised ten teams, while eight teams formed the second division.

The RAAF organised a zonal competition for their servicemen in 1945 which comprised four teams at the Batchelor aerodrome, south of Darwin.

Queensland

In January 1940 the four Ipswich clubs of Bundamba, Blackstone Rovers, Booval Stars and St Helens declined to join up with the new Queensland soccer body, the Queensland Soccer Football Association (QSFA).

Officials from the Ipswich clubs claimed that they were not consulted about a new constitution and the appointment of officers. By March of that year problems had been resolved and an eight team first division was formulated.

Tommy Duck scored four goals for Bundamba Rovers causing scribes to give him the temporary world spotlight over the Disney 'cousin' Donald...

At this time twenty-two junior clubs were affiliated to the Association which represented over three hundred players.

In June 1940 the Queensland Association granted free entry to matches for servicemen and in July club teams played special matches, the proceeds of which were donated to the Patriotic Fund. The YMCA club won the Tristram Shield over Blackstone Rovers in that year while Corinthians won their first senior metropolitan soccer premiership.

In the country soccer went on much as usual. The Ayr District Soccer Association had a successful season. Ingham won the Noora Cup from Ayr and Townsville. In Townsville four senior clubs competed in a competition which a local scribe praised for its maturity:

> *Townsville soccer enthusiasts are determined to carry on the sport although a large number of their players are on military service. The modern desire for speed and excitement is reflected in the tactics of Soccer football in North Queensland. A team which knows the art of ball control will always outplay a team which hunts the ball like a pack of wolves...* [5]

In 1941 confidence was expressed in soccer in the Maryborough region. Due to the war effort the city was expecting many British migrants to join the local ship building industry. The metropolitan championship consisted of four clubs.

The Brisbane championship was won by Blackstone Rovers, while Bundamba Rangers won the Hilton Shield.

By 1943 only Ipswich provided a competition as before. Matches in Brisbane were cancelled with the exception of those played between military or essential service teams.

An Australian Army Services Corp team played an exhibition match against a United States Services team. Sides representing various area of the Australian army formed teams such as Army Medical, Searchlights, Armoured Unit, Army Employment, Army Engineers, Army Service and Dockers.

In 1944 competition continued at Ipswich with a six team competition. Two Dutchmen from the Netherlands East Indies Air Force played for the YMCA team in a competition which also included Corinthians, Bundamba, St Helens, Blackstone and Eastern Suburbs.

A ten team Brisbane league commenced in 1945. This competition included two teams from the Navy.

Naval, army and air force teams were prominent in towns on the Queensland coast. Many naval teams visited Maryborough in 1945, providing welcome competition.

In August 1945 Townsville hosted the Miss Australia Soccer Carnival which mainly featured British military teams.

Junior soccer was reviving in Ipswich. By the last year of the war fifteen teams were registered with the junior association.

Times were hard for many local clubs. Booval Stars from Ipswich were on the verge of selling their ground on account of having rates in arrears. This account was settled by a generous benefactor just before the proposed sale. Nevertheless, better times were around the corner and one of the signs of resurgence was the renewal of Tristram Shield matches in the Brisbane locality.

In August 1945 the Kruger Cup final was played for the first time. Created as a cup competition matching selections from Brisbane and Ipswich, Ipswich ran out victors in a high scoring match, 6 goals to 5.

South Australia

Graham Russell of Hyde Park highlighted issues which stymied the sport in South Australia:

Call for Action to Revive Soccer

> *What is wrong with soccer football in South Australia? During my last nine months' enforced residence in Adelaide I have noted a lamentable deterioration in the game... One reason for the deterioration in standard is the poor display of the referees... Soccer should hold its own in South Australia — there is no need to look with hatred on the national game, as some of the 'leaders' do. They can live side by side, contentedly and harmoniously, just as soccer and rugby do in the Old Land...* [6]

Two ethnic teams played in the lower leagues in South Australia. Savoia represented the Italian community, while Hellenic represented the Greek born community.

Both clubs withdrew from competition after Italy joined Germany as Axis partners in the Second World War. Nevertheless, this marked the nascence of the influence of two of Australia's most prominent ethnic contributors to the sport in Australia.

The soccer association was pro-active at this time. In 1940 it gained control over eight acres of land at Brompton which it converted into playing fields called Brompton Recreation Ground over many years.

Sturt won the metropolitan premiership in 1940, although some teams were short of players due to the war effort. West Torrens won the Pozza Cup for the third time, thus keeping the trophy, while it also won the Pelaco Cup.

Registrations for the 1941 season were half of what they were for the previous six seasons. West Torrens became the metropolitan First Division premiers while Sturt won the Pelaco Cup. Junior registrations were still buoyant with ten teams competing in a Scouts League, which carried prizes of the Charles Moore Shield and Pelham Cup.

The visiting Chinese (Nationalist China) team made social goodwill visits in concert with their match in Adelaide:

> *Members of the Chinese Soccer team and officials visited the State War Memorial yesterday and a wreath was placed on the shrine by the captain of the team (Mr Tsui Ah Fai). At midday the visitors attended at the Keswick military hospital. They entered every ward, and to each patient presented a small gift in token of the goodwill of China.*[7]

With only five of the 1941 twelve team league teams able to muster squads the metropolitan senior league competition did not continue in 1942. However, there were some impromptu matches against military teams. The Association decided to concentrate on running junior competitions. A feature of the year were matches between locals and naval and air force teams from the Dutch East Indies.

In the steel town of Whyalla, where workers were required for the war effort, matches continued into 1942.

By 1943, twelve teams played each other in the Adelaide region and sometimes against various military teams. Supplies were getting scarce and the Association had difficulty obtaining soccer balls. The Referees Association went into recess. Clubs named Javanese, British Tube Mills and Perry Engineering played for the first time. The Javanese team could not find regular employment and disbanded mid-season. Northumberland and Durham won the 1943 metropolitan premiership and the Pelaco Cup.

The next year the same number of teams took part in the metropolitan league. Clubs were asked to observe a minutes silence before kick off in memory of fallen comrades. Soccer balls were so scarce that the Association asked for defunct clubs to sell unwanted balls to them. Birkalla Rovers were Premiers and also won the Pelaco Cup.

The sobering effects of the War had influenced all areas and people of Australian society by 1945. However, soccer continued to be played in Adelaide. The West Torrens and Park Albion clubs and the Referees Association were re-formed and six clubs played at the highest level in the metropolitan competition. Players who had played for various services clubs became contracted to the suburban clubs. Birkalla Rovers repeated their feat of the year before by winning the metropolitan premiership while Port Adelaide won the Pelaco Cup.

Robert Telfer, the influential Secretary of the South Australian Soccer Football Association and referee, noted how the soccer fraternity in South Australia acknowledged those who had fallen:

> The SA Soccer Football Association, like all other sporting bodies, had many members who have made the supreme sacrifice... at all soccer games the referee calls the players to the centre of the field before the start of the game, and all stand in silence for one minute. The observance of a minute's silence, while paying respect to the fallen, should bring to mind the horrors of war and with it the realisation that, as our fallen comrades gave their lives so that we should have a better world to live in... [8]

Tasmania

In 1940 Hobart's West End club disbanded and changed name to Corinthian Rovers. South Hobart won the STBFA championship while the Northern League lost players to the war effort and the senior roster fixtures were abandoned by August.

The following year eleven teams took part in the Hobart senior competition over three divisions. Sandy Bay became Division One Premiers, won the Falkinder Cup and also the state championship. Enlistments for war were increasing and it was reported that seventy-five Hobart soccer players had joined the Navy and a complete team from Launceston had joined the forces.

South Hobart won the Ralph Falkinder Cup in 1942. The club decided not to field an 'A' grade team and instead concentrated on fielding younger players. This approach was mirrored by other clubs in Hobart. An Army and Association team participated in senior competition. There was no senior competition in the north of the state.

Satisfaction regarding the maintenance of soccer activity under war conditions, and confidence in the prospects of the code, were expressed by the chairman (J. H. Storr) and others at the annual meeting of the Tasmanian British Football Association.

Reviewing the season, the annual report emphasised junior matches. In the absence of many senior players on war service, activities were restricted to 'B' and 'C' grade competitions. Proceeds of matches had been donated to the Comforts Fund, VAD and St. John Ambulance Association.

School teams competed for the Druery Cup for the premiership competition and the Downey Cup in a knock-out competition. Elizabeth Street School won both trophies in 1943.

The death of Revered F.S. Hay was a sad blow to the Tasmanian soccer community. Hay had done much for the sport of soccer in Tasmania:

> *The Reverend was born at Bishop Auckland, Durham, in September, 1867.*
>
> *Coming to Australia in 1897, he began a ministry in Queensland. His association with Tasmania began in 1916… As a young man he represented his country at soccer, and did much to foster the game in Australia wherever he was stationed. He was president of the British Football Association in Tasmania, and was a leading spirit in the game.* [9]

The 1944 and 1945 seasons followed the 1942 pattern with a sprinkling of senior players augmenting teams of junior players. Occasionally, a senior team was formed to play a special match. On one occasion, in 1945, a southern Tasmanian senior selection competed against the teams of two Royal Navy submarines which were visiting Hobart, winning both matches.

The South Hobart team had the rare opportunity to play a team of Europeans from a Norwegian ship named the *Sjobris*, which was visiting Tasmania in 1945. The British destroyer HMS *Urchin* weighed anchor in the north of the state and Devonport locals were treated to a match between the crew.

The development and reward of Hobart juniors continued. Seventy-six schoolboy players attended a function in which they were served cordial, sandwiches and cakes. The Druery Cup was presented to the dominant Elizabeth Street School, winners of the premiership.

Victoria

In 1940 the metropolitan First Division competition consisted of eight clubs. Clubs such as Brighton, Collingwood and South Melbourne were having to field juniors in their senior teams. The Premiers of that year were Nobels who swept all before them. The club also won the Dockerty Cup for the third year in a row.

Meanwhile, a junior side was also developing a fearsome reputation. The Albion Schoolboy's club cleared all before them, winning a premiership and three extra cup trophies available. They won all competition from senior boys to under 14 years.

The metropolitan season in Melbourne began with an eight team competition in 1941. University High School Old Boys played in the senior division replacing Collingwood. Navy and RAAF teams were prominent in the lower division. Moreland were premiership winners and I.C.I. won the Dockerty Cup. Amid criticism about playing a sporting competition in a time of war it was pointed out that the development of team harmony, fighting for a unified cause, fitness and good health were all attributes required in a combat environment.

The development of junior teams came under greater stress. The problem, as elsewhere in the Australian wartime economy, was lack of manpower. Promising juniors were promoted to fill positions in senior teams, vacated by adult players:

> *Junior players are being sacrificed and lost to the game through senior clubs including them in first and second teams and cancelling junior games. This means that players who do not find a place in senior games are being left without a game and are naturally drifting from the code...*
>
> *Chief offenders so far have been Nobels and Moreland ... Half of Nobels team on Saturday were juniors, and Moreland had some in their reserve team.*
>
> *Hakoah and Prahran have not entered junior teams and are failing in their obligations for the future...*[10]

A year later the season began with the RAAF team being promoted to the first division. Brighton and South Yarra did not field sides and Moreland and Hakoah amalgamated. There was only one division of senior competition instead of four, as had existed in the previous year. The first division championship was won by the Prahran club. Prahran also won the Dockerty Cup for the first time.

In 1942 Bill Cumming was elected chairman of the Victorian Soccer Association. This marked the high point of his long involvement in soccer in Victoria. He arrived in Australia in 1908 from Scotland and played for Carlton United and subsequently held various administrative positions. Cumming was to be involved in the sport until 1948.

Nobels and South Melbourne United dropped out of the 1943 competition.

Two teams of Netherlands East Indies servicemen took their place under the name Netherlands.

The 1943 premiership victory by Moreland-Hakoah was significant as it was the first championship victory by a club with non-Anglo influence. This victory would presage similar victories by many ethnic clubs in the 1950s in Australia. The Dockerty Cup was won by Brighton.

News of rural soccer teams playing during the war period was scarce. Clubs from West Sale and Yallourn played each other in 1943 and teams in Morwell were also playing matches. During this era the Salmon Cup was competed for between junior clubs.

A Sporting Clubs Patriotic Ball was held in Melbourne by the United juniors to raise funds for the Patriotic Fund. The United Juniors also staged a match against a Javanese team, during which a collection was taken up for the war effort.

In 1944 the Netherland East Indies, AIF and Nobels clubs withdrew from competition. South Melbourne United and Sunshine filled their places. Middle Park became the locus of many matches as three grounds were set aside for soccer. Prahran won the First Division in 1944 and Brighton won the Dockerty Cup.

The senior metropolitan championship was boosted by teams from the services in 1945. The senior competition comprised teams from the RAAF (Ascot and Laverton), a British warship (HMS *Beaconsfield*) and a team representing the 8th AEC (Australian Employment Corp). AEC were mainly youths from the SS *Dunera*. The young men had been interned at the Hay and Tatura camps. They were released from the camps to join the Australian Employment Corp to assist the Allied cause within Australia. When this team withdrew from competition mid-season they were replaced by a 6th AEC team.

The senior league was split into two sections which prevented too many lop sided games. Prahran won the first division premiership in 1945 and Moreland-Hakoah won the Dockerty Cup.

Western Australia

In the first full year of war matches were played in Perth at Leederville Oval in support of the Patriotic Fund. East Claremont won the WASA premiership.

The First League in Perth consisted of only Caledonians, East Claremont, Maccabean and Spearwood by 1941. Enlistments for the war were having their impact on soccer playing numbers. There were many matches forfeited which suggests an inability of clubs to hold players from enlistment or other activities which precluded playing matches. Swan Valley, a team of Yugoslav players from second division, won the metropolitan football association cup.

In 1942 the metropolitan league competition was suspended indefinitely and did not recommence until 1944. In that year four teams from Perth played matches in aid of war charities.

By 1945 the soccer code was reviving in the west. Ten teams played in the metropolitan first division. A Royal Naval team named Jolly Rogers won the metropolitan competition.

Soccer in the goldfields ceased after the completion of the 1940 season. Boulder City won the Nicholson and Casey Cups of the Eastern Goldfields Soccer Association in that year, although the Sparta Club, which was formed as part of the Slavonic Association, lingered into 1941.

A prisoner of war camp was established at Marinup, about sixty miles from Perth. The camps consisted mainly of Italian and German internees and soccer matches were organised by the prisoners.

Chapter 13

Australian International Matches 1941-1945

At the Federal Conference of the Australian Soccer Association in Adelaide in May of 1939 plans were made for the Islington Corinthians from London and the South African national team to tour Australia in 1940. It was further proposed that the Australian team would play reciprocal matches in South Africa in 1941 prior to visiting England and Europe. However, the outbreak of World War II scuppered those plans.

At the same conference Australian authorities decided to ask the English Football Association if they would donate £6000 to purchase sporting grounds. This latest request to England from their familiar colonial outpost of soccer mendicants was to fall on deaf ears.

The only team to tour Australia during the war years was a team representing Nationalist China in 1941. Due to the Japanese occupation of China, the team was restricted principally to thirteen players from Hong Kong and three from Shanghai. They were also described as the Sing Tao-Eastern Combination. The team was comprised of members from three Hong Kong teams which had filled the first three places in the 1940-1941 competition in Hong Kong. In previous years some players had been part of the Chinese Olympic team.

There had been some criticism of the previous Chinese team to visit. It had been skilled, although it had lacked as the press termed it, 'some virility'. Team manager, Mr Peter Woo, assured the local press that the players would possess 'plenty of fire'. The Nationalist China team wore yellow shirts with red and black sleeves and white shorts.

Until the 1960s international players were chosen to play for Australia by a committee of selectors. Differences of opinion within a committee could make selection protracted. State and regional jealousies and other geo-politics considerations often ensured that a national team of less than optimum talent was selected.

For the series against China, there were six selectors. The selectors were S.A. Storey, F.R. Druery, D. Johnson, J.O. Wilshaw, E.P. Rowley and J. Peebles. The selectors hailed from a variety of states including New South Wales, Victoria, Queensland and South Australia.

The midfielder from Metters, Jimmy Osborne, was to finish a distinguished 24 game Australian team career against the visiting Chinese team. The series also marked the last international soccer match for the Wallsend forward, Alf Quill. Conversely, the Chinese visit enabled Reg Date, the prolific Australian forward and club mate of Alf Quill, to make his debut for Australia.

The paucity of Chinese food was said to affect the performance of the Chinese tourists in Newcastle:

Chinese Soccer Players Miss Their Vitamins

Twenty members of the Chinese (Hong Kong) soccer team reached Brisbane today 'starving' for a full-course Chinese meal.

'We lost the fourth test at Newcastle on Saturday because we could not find a Chinese restaurant in the city,' said the team manager, Woo Lal Tin.

'The boys had lost so much weight in the previous 6 days from eating foreign food that they had no vitamins left for the match'...

Brisbane soccer officials took the team to a hotel. The team manager said if they could not get Chinese food at this hotel they would have to call at a Chinese restaurant while in Brisbane. [10]

A reception for the Chinese team was held at Leichhardt Town Hall on 12 July 1941. Dance music was provided by Ern Tribe's Footwarmers who performed such numbers as The Nankin Waltz, a Canadian three step called The Wagga Wobble and a barn dance named China Blue(s).

In the souvenir programme published for the match between China and Queensland at the exhibitions Grounds on 26 July 1941, Chun-Jien Pao, the Consul-General for the Republic of China anchored the visit of the team firmly in a political context:

The motive behind the visit of the Chinese Soccer Football Team to this great smiling land is not only to test their art of playing Soccer with the Australian players of the game, nor merely for the interest of promoting sportsmanship internationally, but also to bring to Australia goodwill from the people of my country...

Long live the British Empire! Long live the Republic of China! May the relations between our two countries and two peoples be closer and closer, and, with the co-operation of the United States of America and other friendly Powers, our bond be the cornerstone of a Peace with Justice in the Pacific. [11]

All of the players applied to stay in Australia after the tour. The team stated that the players would like to play in the Sydney competition as a Chinese team. The team manager stated that if the players could not obtain jobs, they would become self-employed. However, only one player, Yik Yeung was permitted to stay, signing for Annandale-Leichhardt in Sydney.

A financial loss was reported on this tour. Peter Woo blamed the loss on a lack of interest in the tour by spectators from the states of Victoria and South Australia.

Chapter 14

Servicemen and Soccer during the Second World War

Australian servicemen were keen to play soccer even before they embarked for overseas.

In 1940 Australian about 60 enlistments at Puckapunyal army camp in Victoria published an appeal in Melbourne's *Sporting Globe* newspaper for soccer equipment. They called themselves the first soccer team in the A.I.F, and were named the Australian Army Supply Corp Patrol Company soccer team. The team was playing in army boots on rock hard ground. They asked soccer clubs and the public to donate boots, shinpads, shirts, shorts, goalposts and nets. A week later the *Sporting Globe* reported that a fishing net manufacturer had supplied two goal nets.

Soccer was also played at the army camp at Kapooka in New South Wales. In 1942 there was an army inter-unit competition held at Cairns in Queensland which comprised of five teams.

Australians played English army teams at training camps in England. Not surprisingly, the English took the encounter seriously:

> *To-night an Australian and English team met for the first time in a game of soccer.*
>
> *The opposing team arrived clad in a uniform kit of blue shorts, sweaters, socks and stopped boots while our fellows turned out in the wildest assortment of gear imaginable. When the time the bell went the Tommies had piled up what looked like a cricket score but our chaps were well satisfied at the goal someone had managed to secure... 'What oother game doo ye play choom' I heard a Tommy ask. 'Ever played two up' asked his companion...* [13]

'Fitchett', the Acting official Correspondent with the AIF provided a report on match played in Palestine by Australian troops:

> *Football with an international flavour has been added to the sporting activities of the AIF, the first match of the kind being played by a scratch soccer team from an infantry battalion and the Rishon Maccabi team at Rishon le Zion...*
>
> *Local style refreshments and produce were prominent and did much to lend cheer to the occasion. Perhaps it should be explained that a large brewery is situated at Rishon...*
>
> *The Australian team had never played together before...*
>
> *The final score was 3-1 against them. Their uniforms were varied and ragged, but this is soon to be remedied as soon as the Comforts Fund can obtain suitable sweaters and trousers in the appropriate colours. Football boots are also scarce. For this game a 30 mile trip had to be made to a famous Scottish regiment to borrow them...there are a good number of Soccer men in the force, especially among the units from the coalfields...*[14]

The Maccabi soccer team from Jerusalem, some of whose members had toured Australia, offered a soccer ball to a battalion of Australian soldiers in Palestine to encourage the playing of soccer.

The Australian army soccer teams played a match in Lebanon in 1941. Due to a lack of flat ground the match had to be played on the grounds of the American University.

In Papua a light hearted match organised by Australian troops of the 15th Battalion. Troops wore respirators which caused amusement.

Gifts of soccer balls by Australian troops to the natives of New Guinea were received with glee:

'Fuzzy Wuzzies' Like All-In Soccer

Lae

> *Soccer footballs have proved the best morale builder to New Guinea natives in the 'recaptured' territory... An officer said that the natives forgot their troubles and local arguments at the sight of a football. The officer stated he had asked for 500 footballs for the Allied return to Rabaul and 250 each for New Ireland and the Solomons.*[15]

Two members of the Palestinian team which toured Australia in 1939 fought for the Australian army in New Guinea, paying the ultimate price. Beth-Halevy was killed at Lae and Mirmovitch was buried at Wewak.

On the island of Bougainville matches were played between a RAAF team and teams representing New Zealanders and Fijians.

Chapter 15

Enter the Immigrant 1946-1949

The post-World War II years ushered in an era of relative peace in the world. As with most routines and rituals in society soccer resumed a path which generally mirrored its pre-war organisation.

Many clubs were able to survive the war years and re-form, however tenuously. One example was the North Lidcombe Methodist soccer team. 16 men enlisted for the war in 1940. They pledged that they would take the field again. They honoured that promise in 1946 when their team again took to the field, minus three players who had been killed during the conflict.

Clubs which had been less active due to war time exigencies were free to invest in players and facilities and garner war weary supporters. New clubs also emerged, serving the leisure needs of repatriated troops, an increasing population and shifting demographics.

The post-war period saw the eclipse and exit of most factory or commercial teams from the upper levels of soccer. Goodyear did not compete after the war and Metters receded in 1947, leaving district teams to fill the sporting vacuum and dominate the soccer landscape.

At a time when television had not been introduced to Australia, attendance at matches of all codes played was very popular. Watching team sport was a relatively cheap form of winter weekend entertainment for family and friends.

With only the newspapers and intermittent radio reports to keep fans informed, the only way to experience play in full was to attend a match.

In 1948 L. H. Pike was an Australian representative to the Football Association in England. He criticised British authorities for not making a tour to Australia, a priority. When told that British clubs had prior commitments to the Continent, Pike replied that British football authorities should be more active in developing ties with Empire nations.

Fortunately, the tide was to turn in the long running and lopsided relationship between Australia and British soccer authorities. Australian soccer officials, too often spurned, were to discover that other, mostly Continental nations, were keen to visit Antipodean shores. Furthermore, these visiting teams would attract a growing cohort of avid spectators. This in turn was to spur more British sides to tour from the 1950s.

The biggest change to the sport, which would echo through the decades, was the mass arrival of European continental migrants.

These migrants, from whichever nation, possessed certain attributes. They were young, fit, optimistic, determined and risk taking. They had the resilience to adapt to new environments.

Continental and British migrants came from the area of the world where soccer was the predominant or only footballing code. Soccer, pre-eminent on their sporting landscape was of high quality and possessed glamour, economic clout and mass support.

The most active, talented and gifted of these migrants were to imbue the Australian soccer scene with a much needed injection of ambition and increasing excellence.

Whether they participated as players, coaches, administrators, journalists, sponsors or avid supporters, migrants were to infuse a sense of devotion, gravitas and a restless drive for perfection to the sport. Like the sport, migrants were yearning for success and ultimately affection in the broader community.

Crucially, migrants came to Australia without an inferiority complex about the worlds' most popular sport, which had been incubated within the souls of so many local followers.

Many relished the opportunity to 'prove the knockers wrong' and show the world that Australian clubs and the Australian national team could match it with the best. Some transferred their allegiance to Australia so entirely that they looked forward to the day that Australian national or club teams would match or defeat the corresponding teams of their former homeland.

It was as if the migrants had a secret compact. If they were to be rewarded with a peaceful and prosperous life in Australia, they would, as a favour in return, develop and present to the world from the Antipodes, soccer teams which the world would treat with respect.

What cannot be debated was that the genesis of this ambition was to be held in the hearts of these migrants who embarked from migrant ships arriving in the Southern Hemisphere from 1946.

Like many worthwhile projects the fruits their labour were decades in the making.

Australian Capital Territory

In 1947 a large number of British migrants were recruited to come to Canberra and construct the capital. They provided an instant impetus for the formation of soccer teams. One such team was Canberra Wanderers which was formed in the same year.

A contemporary report stated that six British builders in Canberra had been approached by a Sydney soccer club. Some of the British migrants were willing to travel from Canberra to Sydney to play matches for Sydney clubs, if they could not be guaranteed work in Sydney. The Sydney based Metters club interviewed players in Canberra with the offer of employment in their factory, although this was officially denied by Metters.

An article hinted at the slow re-invigoration of soccer in Canberra and surrounding regions. The growth was to be spurred on by residents of the migrant hostels, who had come to Canberra after the war either to work for the Commonwealth Public Service or in the private sector:

Soccer team in Canberra

A soccer team with an 'international' flavour, the Canberra Wanderers, has been entered in the Goulburn Soccer League competition to commence shortly.

Comprised mainly of members of the Eastlake and Riverside Hostels, players include Australians, Welsh, Scotch and Irishmen.

Trainer-manager J. L. Porter, ex-professional member of the London

Hotspurs team, said he was arranging matches with teams from Wollongong and Newcastle, as well as knock-out matches in Sydney. [1]

A Southern League team from Sydney played Canberra Wanderers at Manuka Oval in front of almost one thousand spectators in 1949.

A match between English and Maltese migrants on Griffith Oval was held up when a fox terrier chased a hare onto the pitch. This caused much amusement for the one hundred and fifty Maltese fans. The more salient fact to arise was that this match marked the nascence of European impact in Canberra soccer circles. It was noted that Polish and Italian teams were being prepared from among the migrants at the Eastlake and Riverside Hostels.

Canberra juniors and seniors played tournaments in Goulburn and Wagga at this time.

As a consequence of migration, it was reported that there were enough migrants from certain ethnic groups to form their own mono-cultural teams:

Soccer Matches at Goulburn

A Canberra Soccer team will enter a knock-out competition for the Southern District Cup at Goulburn in September. Other teams are expected from Wagga, Goulburn, Bowral, Junee and Mundaroo... A challenge match between Canberra Wanderers and a Maltese team will be held at the new Griffith Oval on Sunday.

Maltese, Polish and Italian teams and sides from Riverside and Eastlake Hostels are expected to take part in a local competition. [2]

The first post-war ACT Premiership would not start until 1950.

New South Wales

New South Wales is known as the Premier State, This label also applies to its place in the soccer hierarchy in Australia. No other state approached or even now approaches the numbers playing the sport. Soccer was entrenched in Sydney, the Illawarra and the Hunter Valley and numerous other rural locations. The period from 1945 to 1949 was to see the code harvest the benefit of the return to peace. Returning servicemen signed up with clubs and the added influx of refugees from Europe and British migration.

Nevertheless, feuding within soccer ranks was again to overshadow events on the field. It was agreed by Newcastle clubs that a public company be formed to run the elite levels of the sport in New South Wales. The company would have directors.

The Newcastle representatives had a change of heart and wanted the decision rescinded, as they feared domination by clubs in Sydney and the Illawarra. Eventually three directors were nominated from Sydney, three from Newcastle and one from the South Coast. All seven directors who had to lodge a £100 company fee were from Sydney or Illawarra areas.

Clubs would play in northern and southern divisions. This was to replace the planned inter-city competition which would have intermixed northern and southern clubs in competition.

Wallsend, Lake Macquarie and Swansea clubs declined to take part in the new 1945 competition. Merewether, Dudley and Lysaghts Orb were initially replaced in the northern competition by Cessnock, Weston and Kurri Kurri.

The Royal Navy, represented by players from HMS *Golden Hind* and Corrimal were the new clubs accepted into the southern Sydney and Wollongong based division.

The Sydney clubs of St George, Gladesville-Ryde and Drummoyne initially failed to gain re-admission. It was decided that all clubs in Sydney and Newcastle which had failed re-admission to the First Division would form a new Second Division competition.

The competition was set to boom. By August 1945 attendance gate takings were 33% higher than in 1944 with more of the season to be completed.

Compared to today these were simpler times and pastimes of almost Victorian tastes were still popular. In 1945 the Aberdare soccer club held a picnic and sports competitions in the summer. Events include an egg and spoon race, a sack race, a needle and cotton race and a throwing the cricket bat competition. There were separate events for single men and women as well as married men and women.

The Newcastle Referees Association reported thirty active members by 1945 and stated that it was well pleased with the efforts of its members from the previous season. In the same year West Wallsend celebrated their 50th anniversary by winning the State Cup.

With the war ended, HMS *Golden Hind* sailed beyond the horizon and back to Britain with its complement of marines in 1946.

Lysaght-Orb applied and was given the right to play in the State League, thus being the only amateur club to participate. Players were only paid meal and travelling expenses, and no bonus for playing.

An unusual match was played between Eureka Youth Club and Bulli on the south coast. Eureka chose to field a mixed team, with five women and six men being selected in the team.

In the same region, a soccer match was in progress at Woonona during Anzac Day in 1947. The players were excoriated by a Reverend at a service nearby. He stated that the young men at play had no idea what Anzac Day stood for and had no appreciation of the sacrifices of Australians at war. The ill-informed stereotype that soccer players had never sacrificed themselves at war for Australia, or were unappreciative of those who had, was to die hard...

Plans for the Sydney metropolitan season to commence in 1947 were made public:

Soccer's Four New Clubs

There will be 20 teams in next season's Soccer competitions-an increase of four on last season...

The separate southern and northern competitions have been retained, but will each have 10 teams instead of eight as in the 1946 season. New southern clubs are St. George and Pyrmont-Balmain. In the north, the new clubs are Dudley and New Lambton... [3]

Poaching of prominent players was alleged to have taken place that season:

Soccer Poaching Inquiry Ordered

The Board of Soccer directors has ordered an inquiry into the methods adopted by clubs in obtaining players transfers...

Protests against the poaching of players have been made to the board by the Swansea-Belmont and Canterbury-Bankstown clubs.

Canterbury-Bankstown centre forward Reg Date withdrew his appeal for transfer just before the director's meeting began.

Date has made repeated requests to his club for transfer to Lysaghts Orb.

> These have all been refused. Canterbury officials are alleged to have accused Lysaghts Orb of making a monetary offer to Date ...[4]

Reg Date was both a match winner and a money spinner for any club which could afford his services:

> Date has been instrumental in the rise of Canterbury, a leading Sydney club, from obscurity to one of the best drawing clubs in Soccer. Canterbury officials had thoughts of disbanding in 1944, their pay-off for the season being 18 Pounds.
> Officials poached players in a last effort (Date coming from Newcastle) and they won the 1945 premiership and 'cut up' more than £600. Last season Canterbury won most Cup games, and 'chopped up' nearly £1000 and a fund to foster juniors.[5]

Reg Date had been a prolific goal scorer at a young age. At 12, he played for Plattsburg school. His grandfather promised him 3d. for every goal scored. Reg never scored less than seven goals in a junior match and once scored 21 goals. His grandfather had to forego tobacco for a year and walk to work to pay his grandson's debt.

Date scored 1,616 goals in junior and senior fixtures. 664 of these goals were scored in senior matches. He scored nine goals in one game, seven goals in two games and six goals in three matches. It was rumoured that Date was offered a signing on fee of £100 by the Lysaghts Orb club plus a £5 per game playing fee and a secure job to transfer from Canterbury. At the time signing on fees and weekly payments were forbidden.

Date was not the only prolific scorer in 1947. Frank Parsons scored seventy-three goals for Leichhardt-Annandale. ABC radio broadcast what was claimed to be the first live soccer radio match, when Frank Parson's Leichhardt-Annandale played North Shore at Lambert Park in March.

Adding to his precocious goal scoring feats, Parsons scored seventy-eight goals in 1948 and was called up to represent Australia in a career of 16 matches.

In Sydney, a team named Ex-Imperials consisted of players from the upper echelons of English and Scottish soccer. They played in the second tier and were interviewed about Australian soccer. The centre forward, Pat Cassidy, expressed his views:

> *Cassidy says Australian grounds are rough. For that he blames the aluminium studs and crashing tackles of Rugby players. Separate ground should be provided, he claims... After their matches the Ex-Imperial players, who shout 'shoot laddie' in many dialects, give a few wrinkles to opponents. Then they go back to their club-room in the city to play billiards.* [6]

In 1948 the northern and southern metropolitan divisions introduced promotion and relegation for the first time in an Australian major league competition.

Another view on the hesitant progress of Australian soccer was provided by Alf Jennings, who had played in England and Australia offered his views on how the sport in Australia could improve. Talking to *Sporting Life* in May 1949, he stated that there was too little competition with too few teams. He said that the custom of playing early matches before a main match (unknown in England) sapped the enthusiasm of spectators for the main match. Too few clubs owned their own grounds and Jennings criticised the uneven state of the pitches, which he claimed adversely affected cultured soccer and the adequacy of the seating for spectators.

One significant player hanging up his boots in 1949 was Alf Quill. Born in 1910 in Sydney, Quill was renowned for his speed and was a gifted sprinter. His club career commenced with Pyrmont in 1928. He played for Wallsend, North and South inter-district squads, New South Wales and Australia. Quill scored 868 goals in senior competition. The next highest scorer in his era was George Smith with 521 goals. Quill represented Australia eight times.

There was an appeal to young referees to join or continue in the game and further their education. With news of the Olympic Games being held in Australia in 1956, the NSW Referees secretary J. Nies offered the following incentive to potential novices:

> *Here is a great opportunity for the young man wishing to take up refereeing. Any young man between the ages of 20 and 25 should contact me immediately. By starting now he would have the experience to handle this type of game by the time the games series commenced. What an honour to referee a game in the Olympic series! Think it over, you young chaps, you will never get this opportunity again.* [7]

The stringencies of World War II were to have an effect for many years. When the Cootamundra club was re-formed in 1949 it used old wartime camouflage nets on its goal posts.

The migrant community was already forming teams in the migrant camps. One such example was Greta Austral, which was formed at the Greta camp in 1949.

Migrants were also joining soccer clubs in rural areas. In Cootamundra the local paper extolled the virtues of two recent European recruits:

> *Officials have secured the services of a star player as goalkeeper for Saturday's match. He is Antoni Dutkiewicz, a Polish ex-serviceman who is presently working at Galong... Another migrant Jan Rosner, Cootamundrea's centre-forward is also a Polish ex-serviceman. Previously Rosner had been referred to as a Balt.* [8]

Northern Territory

In the Northern Territory soccer took some years to take root after the years of war. A soccer field was secured on the corner of Gilruth Neck and Mindil Beach Road. Padre Irving was a leading figure in the re-invigoration of soccer. He chaired many meetings which led to teams being formed.

In 1949 officials in Darwin placed an order for a supply of rule books and referees' whistles from the Queensland Soccer Football Association. The code in the Northern Territory was very much rebuilding from its foundations prior to World War II.

Players of Chinese heritage continued to play a role in the sport. As they had in the previous decades, the Darwin Chinese Recreation Club players were prepared to lace up their boots in the tropics.

The Northern Standard reported on an initial post World War soccer match as late as 14 April 1949 which involved Civilians playing a Services team. A curtain raiser was played by a state school team and a team from a Catholic school.

Just over a week later moves were afoot to establish a league in Darwin:

> *It is believed that many individuals in Darwin are ex soccer players but feel out of it because they are not in any official team. Persons handing in*

their names to the secretary or other committeemen will be allotted to suitable teams. If groups would like to play but are not sufficient for a team on their own, they should contact the Secretary who will help them out of their difficulties... All European, native and mixed race players are equally welcome in the Association... [9]

Teams which eventually formed a competition were Francis Camp (comprised partly of Displaced Persons European immigrants), Stubbs, DCRC (Darwin Chinese Recreation Club), Coonawarra, Civil Service, Stuart Park, Navy, Qantas and RAAF.

Throughout the year the competition was blighted by teams suddenly forfeiting matches due to lack of players. The Stubbs and Coonawarra clubs were dissolved within the season.

As the season progressed matches moved to the Francis Camp Ground. An unusual request from referees was that leather bars be used on boots rather than studs.

Despite all obstacles the 1949 season muddled through and an enjoyable social event was organised to celebrate the culmination of the season:

Successful Ball Winds Up Soccer Season

Parap Parish Hall presented a gay scene on Tuesday night on the occasion of the first annual Presentation Ball of the Soccer Association. Herman Pon's orchestra was given little rest between dances and the celebrations continued until 2 a.m.

Highlight of the evening was the presentation of trophies won during the soccer season...

Lion's share of the trophies was taken by the Stuart Park team which won both the Administrator's Cup and the McNab Perpetual Shield...

A banquet supper delightfully prepared and served in pleasant coolness in the open air set the seal upon an excellent evening's entertainment. [10]

Queensland

The year of 1946 included an expanded Brisbane metropolitan competition:

Big Programme In Senior Soccer

Thirty-one senior Soccer teams will play in the 1946 season, which opens to-morrow. Many interesting duels are expected...

During last season only eight senior teams competed, but the return of servicemen and keener interest in the code generally has resulted in many new teams being formed. Latrobe and Booval, inactive during the war years, have been readmitted to the first division...New clubs to senior ranks are Wattles, Caledonians, Judinns, Raceview, Redbank, Oxley, and Norman United should do well. [11]

The Tristram Shield, which is the premiership of the Brisbane metropolitan area, was won by St Helens which had star players, centre-half Lex Gibb and the centre-forward Gordon Nunn in their team.

After the strictures of the war years the green shoots of soccer was cautiously evident in Queensland, including Townsville:

Soccer

After having been defunct for a period of four years, the Townsville Soccer Association has been re-formed. Due to the presence of the R.A.F. and the RAN in Australia during the war, soccer gained immense popularity, especially In New South Wales and Queensland...

Anticipating a major revival in the code, the Townsville Soccer Association has re-formed, and has bright prospects of regaining one field in Victoria Park and one in National Park. So far, five senior teams, Tigers, Waterside Workers, Rovers, Estates and Trojans have nominated for the fixtures, and two junior teams have been entered also... [12]

The Queensland soccer team was lacking in practice after the war years and in an interstate fixture the New South Wales team, spearheaded by the prolific scorer, Reg Date, put their northern neighbours to the sword:

NSW Overwhelms Q'ld at Soccer

BRISBANE, *June 17. The New South Wales soccer team completely overwhelmed Queensland at Bundamba today. The visitors gave a brilliant exhibition and won 10-0. Not since 1933, when they went down 12-2 to New South Wales in Brisbane, has Queensland suffered such a defeat.*

R. Date, centre forward for New South Wales, played brilliantly and scored eight goals. [13]

By 1947 there was a stable six club competition in Townsville and Rockhampton had a three club premiership.

The code was flourishing in the Brisbane metropolitan area by 1949. The senior GSFA competition was spread over five divisions and encompassed forty-six clubs. Sixteen clubs were represented in junior grade competitions. Corinthians won the Brisbane premiership at Heath Park, defeating St Helens with five thousand spectators in attendance.

In Cairns the growth of soccer was aided by the arrival of Greek, Italian, Yugoslav and Baltic migrants.

South Australia

Adelaide readers were informed that decisions had to be made about the composition of the first division competition following renewed interest from many clubs:

Soccer Clubs to Re-Form

By PIVOT

The executive council of the SA Soccer Association...will have an unenviable task in deciding which teams shall constitute the first division of the league. It is unlikely that the First Division will consist of more than eight teams. Former first division clubs which have been in recess for several years and will re-form this season are Kingswood, Sturt, West Adelaide and Northumberland and Durham club... These clubs will doubtless expect to be included in the top division. [14]

As a harbinger of the future, two ethnic clubs representing the Italian and Greek and communities were formed. Juventus made their debut in 1946 while Olympic was formed a year later. Supporters of these clubs comprised those who had supported Savoia and Hellenic before World War II, as well as swelling numbers of post war migrants. The Premiership champions of 1946 were Kingswood. Birkalla Rovers won the Hugh Pozza Cup and West Torrens won the Pelaco Cup.

The Juventus club played in the highest division in Adelaide by 1947. In this year Rowley Park at Brompton was finally opened for play after seven years of development.

Club soccer was booming with forty-two clubs affiliating with the Soccer Association, the most since 1939. Birkalla Rovers won its third championship in four years when it defeated Juventus. Cumberland won the Pelaco Cup final. The junior game was also thriving with six hundred youngsters playing in the metropolitan area.

In 1946 Ugo (Hugh) Pozza, who had been associated with the Kingswood club for over 20 years, presented a new Cup for competition. His original Pozza Cup had been retained in perpetuity by West Torrens after the club had won it three times. The new Pozza Cup, described as the most valuable in Australia was said to be worth £200. The trophy was 3ft high and weighed 120 pounds. Small replicas were provided for the next eleven years. Ugo Pozza was to be awarded life membership of the Federation.

By 1948, the need for retaining and increasing referees was so pressing, that Division One referee wages were doubled and those in charge of Division Two matches were increased by 50 per cent. Twenty-eight matches in both divisions were refereed by only twenty referees. Fifty-five clubs were affiliated with the South Australian Soccer Association.

Maltese migrants came to support the short lived Melita Eagles which was formed in 1949, while Serbs founded the Beograd club. The Railway club in Adelaide consisted mainly of Baltic migrants by 1949.

Further migrant influence was exerted by players from the displaced persons Woodside camp near Adelaide. The club created was Woodside United, formed in 1949 with a £10 loan from a camp supervisor. Forty truckloads of dirt were levelled at the camp to form a ground and extra money was raised from concerts and amusements.

Woodside United players were from many nations such as Latvia, Serbia,

Lithuania, Czechoslovakia and Hungary. The team also featured J. Sloma who was a schoolboy goalkeeping international for Poland. In July of 1949 a first division match between Kingswood and Cumberland was played at the camp to show the migrants the standard of local soccer.

The Woodside United team was becoming formidable. In August 1949 it defeated the South Adelaide state team 4-2. The migrants were described as 'craftsmen who played as a unit'.

The effect of the migration boom was also seen in regional South Australia by 1949. At Port Pirie the team named Centrals had Australian players. British players competed for Wanderers, Italians for Savoy and a Greek migrant team was being formed.

Woomera, the site of a rocket range, could also boast six casual teams in 1949. Some players were migrants and the town was about to institute its own league.

It was stated that the admission of Australian teams to the British Soccer Pools competition was luring British migrants to Australia. Migrants were studying maps of Australia to locate the teams and were felt encouraged to immigrate.

Many in the game viewed the arrival of the European and British migrants as a massive boost to the code in Australia. A South Australian reporter stated that 'these wanderers are just the blood transfusion the doctor ordered'.

Tasmania

Senior soccer did not recommence in Tasmania until 1946. The southern league consisted of seventeen teams in three divisions. The northern league only consisted of Patons and Baldwins, Invermay and South Launceston.

The first North v South match played that year resulted in the South having a comprehensive 9-0 win.

In 1947 the number of teams in the south increased by three, while the number in the north stayed at three.

The Patons and Baldwin club of Launceston played a match against Bradford Mills of Victoria in 1947. This marked a rare visit by a club team to Tasmania.

South Hobart became state champions for three consecutive years from 1946 to 1948, while the northern team Invermay were the victors in 1949.

The effect of post war migration was also being felt on the island state of Tasmania. In an interview George Pearson discussed the formation of an early post war ethnic team in the north of the state:

> The Black Bears around this time were an interesting side. They were the first of the Austrian/German displaced persons to arrive in Tasmania after the war and didn't come into town much – maybe they were still frightened of retribution I don't know. They all worked on the hydro schemes in the highlands. They were immaculate in their strip, nobody had quite see the like! When we lined up before kick-off we each received a small bunch of flowers from our opposite number as a token of goodwill and friendship.[15]

A former Australian Rules player named Max Burke raised an alarm. Interviewed by the press, he stated that in some schools three-quarters of all boys have no interest in Australian Rules. He was quoted as saying that rugby was making advances in Hobart and soccer in the north of Tasmania. He called on concerted action by Australian Rules and school athletics bodies to arrest the waning interest in the Australian code.

In the same year displaced persons made their presence felt on a southern Tasmanian soccer ground. A match was played between DP's mainly of Yugoslav, Czech and Hungarian origin and the Norfolk team. The result was a 2-2 draw.

Victoria

After World War II, British migrants to Victoria boosted the ranks of players and spectators among Melbourne clubs.

Sunshine United re-formed with the help of a British migrant base and a team called Park Rangers also had British support. The influx of British players who were familiar with professionalism threatened the status quo of organised amateur soccer. Such players expected payment to play, often in excess of what was considered adequate. Many British players would eventually be lured to the newly forming ethnic clubs which would, by the 1950s, have the financial muscle to pay more than the Anglo-British regional or suburban clubs.

At the conclusion of World War II there were thirty clubs competing in the Victorian Amateur Soccer Football Association. A number of country teams flourished, especially in the Latrobe Valley, where mining communities gave staunch support.

By 1946 there were forty-six teams in the competition and Bradford Cotton Mills, Olympic, Park Rangers, Ringwood, South Yarra United, and Western Suburbs had joined the senior competition. Service teams which had previously populated the competition such as RAAF and HMS *Beaconsfield* withdrew from competition.

Hakoah benefitted from the immigration of Jewish migrants. It dissolved its amalgamation with the Moreland club, dropped divisions and reassumed its Jewish identity.

In 1948 the Italian Juventus Club was formed:

> *Father Galanti, (Catholic Church) who worked for the Archiepiscopal Committee, has been credited with suggesting the idea of forming an Italian-backed soccer club in post-war period and eventually convinced members of the Italian community of establishing a soccer team in 1948. Soccer had already been a feature of Italian community life in Melbourne during the 1930s through the agency of the Savoia club, though it disbanded at the outbreak of the Second World War.* [16]

The influx of migrants to Victoria had an expansionary effect on the number of teams playing senior soccer by 1948. In that year four senior divisions replaced the two divisions formed the previous year.

Chauvinistic 'code sectarianism' within Australian society was alive and flourishing. Soccer was not mentioned when the Australian National Football Council (Australian Rules) adopted 'a war footing'. The militaristic tone of their manifesto seemed dramatic. However it was obvious that the aim of the ANFB was to obliterate all footballing diversity found in its path:

> *A five year plan to subject the Rugby States of NSW and Queensland... Blueprint for the conquest aims at a full-scale invasion of what Council calls the 'underprivileged football States' of NSW and Queensland to rescue their benighted citizens from the dominance of Rugby... They have plotted a five phase attack to force the enemy Rugby back beyond even the Brisbane line: Soften up the enemy by showing propaganda films illustrating the advantages of Australian Rules football. Infiltrate and dig in across the border, in the Riverina (formerly the sole duty of Victorian forces). Send commando teams to NSW and Queensland*

to give exhibitions... Outflank Rugby by bidding for their grounds for lease to new Australian Rules clubs, even obtaining freehold of ovals if possible... [17]

In 1949 the three senior metropolitan league divisions had expanded from eight to ten teams to cater for new clubs and players. The Victorian Soccer Football Association found itself with responsibility for one hundred teams. It had plans to spread the game to country schools and districts and groom amateur players so that they could compete in the 1956 Australian Olympic team in Melbourne.

Shermans, the British soccer pools operator, announced that it would include Australian club teams results during the three month lay-off of the northern season being offered in Australia. This would result in 'thousands of Britons hearing of South Yarra, Prahran and Box Hill.' The company was investigating the legality of their gambling game being made available for Australian based punters.

In the last year of the decade Victorian soccer authorities, spurred on by the rising number of migrant players and the prospect of hosting the 1956 Olympics in Melbourne, launched ambitious development plans. Schools in the country and the city would be encouraged to create teams and senior clubs would be encouraged to mentor junior clubs. Interstate and exhibition games in the country would also be increased. Gifted amateurs would be nurtured to form a nucleus of a 1956 Olympic team squad.

With the game growing rapidly the Association faced the problem of not having enough grounds to play soccer on. Clubs were levied £25 as a contribution to a grounds trust development fund.

Western Australia

The season in Western Australia re-commenced in 1946 with an association of fifteen clubs. Ten teams were in Division One of the capital city competition. The Division One champion was the Caledonian club, which also won in the following year of 1947.

Western Australian soccer celebrated a fifty year Jubilee with a grand dinner in Perth. Some players from the first year of the Association in 1896 were in attendance.

There were 649 players registered in Western Australia by 1948. The metropolitan First Division was split into East and West section boundaries with ten teams each.

The first major ethnic club formed in Western Australia was Azzuri, which represented the Italian community, and was formed in 1948.

The West Australian side returned victorious from the Southern States Carnival which was held in Adelaide. The Championship featured South Australia, Tasmania and Western Australia, which defeated Tasmania 6-2 in the final.

In 1949 the arrival of European immigrants was evident on the playing fields. The Italian club Azzuri joined the third division, as did a club named Macedonians. The League gained four divisions. In the Northam migrant camp Czech and Hungarian migrants had formed teams.

The State selection faced the stern reality of European opposition by suffering crushing losses to the touring Yugoslav side (Hajduk Split) by 1-14 and 1-13 in consecutive matches.

The *WA Soccer Football Journal* made its debut, commenting on both local and foreign soccer news, results and events.

Chapter 16

Australian International Matches 1945-1949

In 1945 Frank Druery, secretary of the Commonwealth Soccer Football Association, had plans to reinvigorate foreign team contact after the War.

Druery approached the USSR to send a team to Australia without success. He then tried to negotiate a dominions soccer series with the home countries (England, Scotland, Wales and Northern Ireland). This would include Australia in a round robin competition in which the Australian team would visit Britain every third year. Druery also approached the British authorities for seeding money. This request was also denied.

The public and the press were eager for possible visits to become a reality:

Move For Soccer Visit Next Year

> *The end of the war in Europe has caused Australian Soccer authorities to speed up negotiations for the visit of an international side in 1946.*
>
> *Negotiations with several countries are in a more advanced stage than has been generally supposed, and it is no secret that leading Soccer authorities of the countries concerned are anxious to accept an invitation to tour the Commonwealth...and it is anticipated that arrangements for the visit to Australia of at least one international side in 1946 will be announced.* [1]

Hopes of a visit by a foreign team in 1946 faded. A request by a Singapore national team to tour in 1947 also did not transpire.

The international calendar recommenced with a tour by the South African national team in May and June of that year. The South African team had been due to visit Australia in 1939, however the tour was cancelled as war intervened. A shortage of shipping berths from South Africa loomed to threaten the 1947 tour but eventually a ship was found. An Egyptian ship, *Ismar*, left Durban for Perth on 1 April with the tourists.

This was the first contest for the Australian team since the visit of India in 1938.

Remuneration to be received by the Australian players was scant compared to the present:

> *The players will receive an allowance of £1 a day. Australian Soccer Association officials have decided to pay players £2 each when chosen for minor matches against the South Africans.*
>
> *Players chosen to represent N.S.W. and Australia against the tourists will each receive £4.* [2]

Sid Grant, statistician of the NSW Soccer Football Association, welcomed the South African team with the characteristic amity forged among Commonwealth nations in the Association's *Handbook for 1947*:

Hail the Springboks

> *Welcome! Ambassadors of South African sport from across the Indian Ocean.*
>
> *It is a great honour and pleasure to welcome you to another outpost of the British Empire- a land of sunshine and sport...*
>
> *We herald you as a band of pioneers, who have come to help popularise here the world's greatest code of football.*
>
> *It is a worthy mission, and may our game be richer by your coming.*
>
> *We hope to be worthy opponents on the green swards of the Commonwealth...* [3]

With the echoes of World War II still reverberating, locals were informed that fourteen of the South African players had served in the War. Two of them were decorated for gallantry and four of them were made prisoners of war. Many players post war were clerks, miners and tradesmen. Three of the tourists had played against England in 1939. The South African team were sponsored by a tobacco company and all players were granted free cigarettes.

The South African team, possessing the whiff of glamour, were busy off the pitch. They attended a Lord Mayor's reception in Melbourne. When they stepped out on a balcony they were 'enthusiastically greeted by girls in the opposite building'. In the evening they attended a performance at the Princess Theatre of 'Life with Father'. They were also attended an Anzac Day march in Adelaide.

Five matches were played, with the South Africans winning three matches, Australia one and there was one draw. Australia fielded well known players including Reg Date on his international debut. Cec Drummond, Joe Marston and the goalkeeper, Norman Conquest were also star Australian players. In the five matches Reg Date memorably scored seven of the eleven goals scored by the Australians in the series. The Novocastrian, Alec Heaney made his debut against South Africa at a late age of twenty-nine. He captained Australia twice against South Africa.

When Australia played South Africa in Adelaide in April, the match was refereed by Robert Telfer, who had been the secretary of the South Australian Soccer Association for a decade.

For the first time the Australian team played in white shirts with a gold and green 'V' and black shorts, so their colours would not clash with the Springbok's green shirt.

The tour was generally good natured on the pitch. However, the South African manager, J. Barbour was less happy away from the sidelines. He objected to the minimum sized pitches which were used at most venues. Barbour also complained about accommodation, which left some players to share beds. He opined that 'because of the way we have been hearded (sic) around Australia officials must have thought we were a lot of Zulus'. Like almost all officials of visiting teams, he found long train trips exhausting and he also found fault with Australian soccer balls, which he claimed were of inferior leather quality, and prone to lose shape.

At the completion of the tour the South African team was farewelled from Australia with a *Grand Soccer Ball* at the Trocadero dance hall in Sydney on 9 June 1947.

The South African team left Australian shores with an invitation for Australia to tour their homeland in 1949. This tour did not occur.

In August 1948 the Australian team travelled across the Tasman for the third time to play New Zealand.

There was, however, drama mid-flight. After the team's Sunderland flying boat had left Rose Bay in Sydney and were 250 miles into their journey, smoke and flames came out of the engine and the plane had to return. The team subsequently left on a Constellation airliner.

In Auckland, the Australian team manager had all his clothes stolen from his hotel. As he had a fifty inch waist measurement, ready to wear clothes were difficult to procure...

Undeterred, the Australians completed a whitewash of players from the 'Land of the Long White Cloud' winning all four matches by handsome margins, scoring twenty-five goals and conceding only one goal. Despite the whitewash the tour was barely covered by the Australian press.

Frank Parsons had a memorable tour, scoring 12 of the goals. Parsons scored six goals in one match and recalled the game when interviewed by Greg Stock:

> *Frank Parsons: That was in Wellington and I had an uncle who lived over there and I was most anxious to do something to please him (laughing). That was how I got some of the stuff that's in my scrapbook. Uncle Tom used to get the papers and send them to mum and mum would cut out the bits and stick them up.* [4]

Frank Parsons continued to describe the rather amateur and directionless organisation of the Australian soccer team in those times.

> *Greg Stock: Most of the Australian team of the 40s and 50s didn't even have one training session before their matches?*
>
> *Frank Parsons: Never. Well the team that went to New Zealand (1948) we had players from Queensland, South Australia, a goalkeeper and one other and I hadn't seen them before in my life. One was a little fella who could play on the wing and the goalkeeper who I guess was selected to introduce someone from that part of the world to an Australian side.*
>
> *Greg Stock: On tour did you train together and develop a combination?*
>
> *Frank Parsons: You did everything together alright but there was no*

method about it because we didn't have a coach who could present us with a method...The only time we planned anything as players was on the South African tour but in New Zealand there was absolutely nothing. Cec Drummond was our captain and with all due respect to Cec he was not really able and talk to anyone about football because he did not have a great capacity for conversation. Our managers over there were unhelpful. Neither of them were soccer players and neither of them would have known anything more than the fundamentals they had picked up from being spectators.

Greg Stock: So there was not even a coach appointed?

Frank Parsons: When we were playing we didn't ever have a coach... We had two managers who couldn't have said anything about how to pick a team or deciding on a playing method against a team over there they might have seen, nobody knew anything. It was pathetic... [5]

The next team to tour Australia, in 1949, was described as Yugoslavia. They were also described as the Olympic team. However this was erroneous as only some touring players represented the Olympic team, which was the runner-up at the 1948 London Olympics, and all players were from the Croatian Hajduk club from Split. The broader name given was a ploy to get more spectators through the turnstiles and to soothe political tensions.

Initially the tour was not welcomed by the Australians who were told that £16,000 pounds was demanded by the tourists. Sid Story, secretary of the Australian Soccer Association reiterated familiar suspicions. He was wary about the quality of the Yugoslavs, and considered the demands too great. Further negotiations resulted in a compromise whereby the Yugoslavs would pay travelling expenses and take 60% of the gate.

One Newcastle reporter feared that the international visit would threaten to interrupt the coverage of the soccer pools from England which featured Australian matches in the English summer. Furthermore, he opined that Australian players would be better served reserving their international form for a mooted tour of Australia by England in 1950.

The ignorance of Australian officials concerning the quality of most continental European and Asian opponents before 1950 was vast and widespread. The exception were national sides from the British Empire, which seemed to have been accepted at face value and with a fraternal lack of distrust.

By June 1949 local authorities and journalists were more relaxed about the standards of the Yugoslavs as they realised they 'were well up with the standards of Scottish or English representative teams'. By July the description was upgraded to 'near world class.' It was anticipated that the visitors would incorporate the novel 'third back' tactical formation. The star player was rated as the goalkeeper Vladimar Beara, who was dubbed 'as quick as a cat'.

Articles soon appeared listing the visiting players, with Australians assured that the pronunciation of their names 'would be a headache at receptions and elsewhere'. However, not all Australians were so bashful as to not give the visitor's language an airing. The Victorian Premier was amazed when the Vice-President of the Victorian Soccer Association, Mr Dawnay-Mould and a local MP upstaged the Premier. Addressing the visitors in their language with a written address Mr Dawnay-Mould airily stated that he knew German and that 'anyone who can speak German can read Yugoslav'!

The Yugoslav team arrived in Australia well drilled from an unbeaten tour of France and Belgium and gave Australian teams a lesson in the quality and sophistication of eastern European soccer at the time. Locals were informed that the team colours were blue and white with a red star at the breast. All the players, said the team manager, were members of the Yugoslav army and guerrilla fighters.

On arrival the Yugoslavs were out to charm. A coach described the Sydney Cricket Ground as 'God given', despite the fact that hot showers were not available after training in the July winter. At a civic reception in Sydney the Lord Mayor was presented with a brass plaque studded with a map of Yugoslavia with an indented photograph of President Tito.

The charm offensive continued when the team played New South Wales in Sydney. The captain presented flowers to the bemused local captain, Cec Drummond, as a 'European custom'. In return, a local contribution to 'protocol' included the playing of the wrong national anthem prior to the match. Visiting officials desperately gesticulated to the musicians to cease playing. The anthem played was that of pre-war monarchical Yugoslavia under King Peter, entitled 'God the Just One'. The band should have played the communist anthem 'Hail Slavs'. Unperturbed, the Yugoslavs won 3-1 with the consolation local penalty scored by Joe Marston, who would go on to have an illustrious career with Preston North End in England.

The Yugoslavs played with rigorous precision and consummate ball control.

Accurate passing into space or to feet a feature. Players constantly switched positions and made dummy runs. Local journalists, dubbing them 'slick Slavs', were surprised how much the Yugoslav players called for the ball or issued instructions during matches. Such overt vocalisation was not considered within the 'Anglo' norms of playing. Their team work was described as a 'fetish'.

Reporters were keen to note what they considered were 'quaint' Yugoslav customs. It was reported that the tourists had wine for breakfast with the term 'Vin Mrs' being used to order wine from the waitresses at the Olympic hotel in Sydney.

A vaguely prurient article featured an Australian masseuse, Miss Clarice Kennedy. Miss Kennedy, from the Langridge School of Physical Culture, was awarded the task of providing physiotherapy to Yugoslav players, which the visiting players were said to have enjoyed. Miss Kennedy hastened to add that 'I just do their legs, not a full body massage'. Concerned that 'she was making herself cheap', Miss Kennedy consulted a doctor who assured her that work conducted in her professional field was honourable. Under her care, it was said, no muscle had dared to bulge. Women did not customarily massage Australian players.

In further snippets about the culture and manners of the European visitors a local match programme reported with curiosity:

> *Peculiarly enough, although they do not speak English, they sing some songs in the English language with perfection. Their rendition of 'She'll be Comin' Round the Mountain' and 'Tipperary' is as flawless and entertaining as their amazing soccer skill on the field...*
>
> *None of the boys worry about the Australian beer scarcity. In fact they are not really drinkers in that sense at all. Their only inhibitions are those of the average continental diner. – a glass of good quality wine instead of tea or coffee during dinner.* [6]

The Europeans attracted healthy crowds during their 15 match tour. A record south coast crowd of 8,000 spectators watched the Yugoslavs defeat South Coast 4-1. The visitors requested that they be allowed to play substitutes, which was granted. This was not a custom at the time in Australian matches. The visitors also travelled to Broken Hill to play the local combined team. The first ever visit of an international team to Broken Hill had been organised by Rudolph Alagich, who ran the local Dalmatian Croatian team named Napredak. The locals were defeated 5-0.

The team visited the Newcastle steel works and met with 'The Quiz Kids'. 'The Quiz Kids' was a top rating radio show. 'Quiz Kids' were intelligent children who competed in the general knowledge show. One of the female quiz kids asked the soccer players 'Has the introduction of the five-year plan altered the economic life of girls in Yugoslavia'? 'Yes' they said. 'More girls were now undertaking factory employment'. While in Newcastle the Yugoslavs also visited a children's art show.

All tours of Australia by any soccer team included scheduling and accommodation problems together with ground access difficulties created by other codes. This was no exception, with the Queensland Rugby League refusing to release the Exhibition Ground in Brisbane at certain dates, causing an extra £300 Pounds expense for the Yugoslavs. The Yugoslavs stayed at a guesthouse at Redcliffe during their time in Brisbane, as they were unable to get hotel accommodation. Spotlights were erected outside their accommodation, so they could practise at night. Hundreds of Redcliffe residents watched in fascination as they juggled or headed a ball. Their interpreter was a Brisbane dentist.

What the visitors may have lacked in sub-tropical accommodation they made up for in comestibles. A Brisbane *Courier-Mail* journalist wrote an article under headline 'Slavs Take the Cake' listing the amount of food the visitors ate at the local Lord Mayors reception. This included 96 sandwiches, 96 small cakes, 72 sausage rolls, 4 large sponge cakes and over 140 scones and pikelets. To further emphasise the repast, a photo showed the players 'tucking in'. Waiters were 'goggle-eyed'. Furthermore, the team was reputed to have eaten a 'huge Hungarian goulash' at Mt Coot-tha some 75 minutes later.

As the tour wore on the Yugoslavs saw Australia and its soccer culture in a more realistic light. The team refused to play another match on Wollongong Showground against New South Wales, as it had against the South Coast. The unpleasant experience persuaded them that the pitch was too rough, damaged and unsafe to play on.

There were differences of opinion concerning the interpretation of the rules of soccer, depending on whether players had an Anglo or Continental upbringing.

When the Yugoslav goalkeeper, Beara, was knocked out in play when charged by a player from the Sydney Metropolis selection, a riot almost ensued. Beara later left the field in fury, refusing to sign autographs for school children. The coach of the Sydney selection defended the right of players to charge a goalkeeper with the ball. This was acceptable in British Empires countries, but not among Continentals. When goalkeepers of Continental extraction were charged by Australian forwards it always caused offence on the ground and disquiet among spectators, well into the 1960s.

Conversely, Australian crowds were annoyed when Yugoslav players berated or surrounded Australian referees to contest decisions. When the Yugoslavs did this in a 'test' against Australia in Brisbane on the way to winning 6-3, the 17,000 crowd booed the Yugoslavs for three minutes. In Newcastle, a Yugoslav player said to be 'white with rage' when called offside, kicked a ball at a referee, amid boos from the crowd before being sent off. The whole touring team threatened to walk off the field before calm was restored. The habit of the Yugoslav captain of kicking the ball away when placed for a free kick was noted with regret in a final match program.

The tour ended in a financial loss for the Europeans, for which their management blamed, in part, the distribution of free tickets in Brisbane. However the loss can mostly be attributed to Sid Story's crafty financial conditions. All touring costs were paid by the Yugoslavs and many foreign teams failed to realise how expensive it was to travel and stay in Australia. 60% of gates, less tax, due to the visitors, which may at times have been slightly below expectations, would not have made up for costs incurred.

The homesick Yugoslav team left Australia from Fremantle, Western Australia after playing their last match against Western Australia. They were farewelled by compatriots on the liner *Orion*. Most of the local Yugoslavs were market gardeners and there was a shortage of vegetables at the Perth markets because the sellers had decamped to the Fremantle docks.

The Yugoslav captain made no friends in the west when he described Australian Rules as having no features which would appeal to Europeans. 'There is too much knocking and scuffling and very little science', he said.

While in Perth, the team attended a social occasion at Osborne Park where pro and anti Tito supporters scuffled. Team members were accused of assaulting the master of ceremonies. When the players stated that they supported Marshall Tito they were described contemptuously by a Western Australian newspaper as 'soccer commos'.

The team manager, Mr Novak, departed Australia with a volley of criticisms. Australian officials were too keen to make profits from visiting teams. Australian players played the man and not the ball and 60% match profits were not enough to meet expenses. Furthermore, Australian players seemed unwilling to learn the finer points of soccer. Novak complained that his club would receive censure on its return home after being called Yugoslavia, which Australian officials insisted upon, rather than Hadjuk.

A tour which began with such promise and goodwill by a team of gifted players had ended in a tawdry exchange of acrimony and rancour between both parties.

If the Yugoslavs lamented the tour for financial reasons, the Australians also had reasons for regret. Selectors failed to select the best teams which never came close to matching the Europeans on the field of play. Petty state politicking also played its part.

The Soccer Weekly News souvenir programme for the first match between Australia and Yugoslavia of 30 July 1949, highlighted the fundamental problem. Until the 1960s a team of selectors rather than one coach picked the Australian team. After a heavy defeat of the NSW team a sense of dread peppered the editorial of the program:

> *Like the selection of all representative teams from the beginning of time, the choice of the eleven to do battle for Australia in today's first test has brought forth the usual volume of criticism...*
>
> *The selectors went into every angle of a very difficult problem – finding an eleven with the necessary balance and deficiency to best out very clever Yugoslavian visitors... They may not succeed in the earliest stages, but contrary to a general belief amongst soccer fans, I do believe that they will eventually produce an Australian test team which will defeat our clever soccer visitors.* [7]

The local press stated that Australians played 'foot-brawl' against a team of 'artists'. Hopes for Australian teams against Yugoslavia were low.

Despite the machinations of Australian selectors, the fears of the locals were to be largely realised. In five matches against the Australians, the Yugoslavs were to lose only one match, 2-1 to Australia in Newcastle.

Chapter 17

View to the Future

It is fitting that this account of soccer in Australia should conclude with the tour of a European continental side to Australia. The visit of the Yugoslavs can be seen as a future promise of what lay in store for Australian soccer culture. The impact of immigration would alter the predominantly Anglo-Saxon composition of players, referees, administrators and spectators.

Indeed, the period from 1946 to 1949 was the last pocket of time when soccer in Australia was mainly defined by its Anglo-Australian monocultural heritage.

The Anglo-Australian heritage of soccer in Australia was a mixed blessing. For many Australians from the southern states soccer was not 'Australian' enough.

In the southern states the promotion of Australian Rules as the only Indigenous code struck a chord with those of a patriotic nature. Such thoughts were prominent in the first decade of the 20th century when Federation united the various Australian colonies. The second Australian Prime Minister, Alfred Deakin, spoke for many when he passionately promoted the 'Australasian game' in a speech in 1908.

Australian Rules was a hybrid sport. It was played on a cricket oval, with a ball almost identical to that used in rugby and with a style of play similar to Gaelic Football. It was intentionally designed to be a sport which was more physically confronting than soccer, but less so than rugby. This sporting stew, consisting of a concoction of foreign influences, was considered as Indigenous as kangaroo soup.

In the northern states of New South Wales and Queensland the two rugby codes still held sway. Despite the fact that the sport of rugby and indeed cricket was no less or more Anglo in origin than soccer, the round ball code was tarred by its English origins.

Soccer had been cast and stereotyped as the footballing code of the British migrant. He was typically a working class Cockney, northern Englishman or a Scot.

One focal heartland of soccer in Australia were the factories of the industrial areas of our biggest cities, especially Sydney. The other bastions were the mining towns and regions. Scattered throughout Australia, examples included the Illawarra, Newcastle region, Ipswich, or Western Australian goldfields.

Australians however knew also that the sport had worldwide and, in particular, continental interest beyond Britain. For that reason many Australians considered soccer to be a 'wog' sport.

Another stigma which soccer was saddled with was its perception as being a soft or 'sissy' code. Australia was and still is a rugged and harsh landscape. Regard of both men and women was and still is measured in their ability to prevail or attempt to prevail against harsh odds, whether they be extreme temperatures, floods, vast distances and geographic isolation.

A boy adopting soccer as his code often had to fight the perception that his choice reflected a weakness and he would often be teased as a result, sometimes viewed as a coward. This attitude is an almost curiously Australian one.

In Britain, Europe and South America, the playing of soccer has never been cast in this negative light. In particular, soccer in Britain, which was the cradle of the sport, was renowned as fast, direct, and physical. The sport was always regarded as 'manly' and worthy test of physical courage and exertion.

A player from a non-English and even English speaking background would often suffer from racial abuse for simply playing his preferred football code of soccer.

It is an unusual fact that in Australia soccer has historically been the locus of deeply held fears of the 'other', by Australians. Such fears, individually, have always played out in the wider Australian society, but they have combined, perhaps uniquely in the Australian context of sport, in the case of soccer.

Regardless of whether that antipathy was expressed in a hostile or jocular manner, the intent and effect has been to marginalise and inhibit the popularity of the sport to the benefit of other codes.

The effects of World War II were to reverberate in the sport of soccer more than any other sport played in Australia. Australia required labour to re-build its economy and ensure its future defence. The government turned initially to enticing British migrants to Australia from 1946, although it soon became apparent that immigrants from Britain were not numerous enough alone to meet requirements.

A solution to the population deficit was required and from late 1947 until 1952 the Australian government and the International Refugee Organisation co-operated to bring to Australia European post war migrants, most of them refugees or, as they were termed, 'displaced persons'. These people had fled their home country to settle in a refugee camp in another European country. Displaced persons were from nations as diverse as Czechoslovakia, Hungary, Ukraine, Russia, Poland, Croatia, Serbia, Germany, Austria and the Baltic States.

With host European nations keen to move the refugees on and Australia eager to welcome their arrival, the number of refugees determined to make Australia home increased substantially.

Some had applied to emigrate to the USA or Canada and been rejected or stalled, while others knew little about Australia, apart from the fact that it was the home of the kangaroo. It was almost the furthest point from strife torn Europe, which itself was an attraction.

Many were ready to pack their meagre belongings and take their chances in an Australia which for them was a *Terra Incognita*, an unknown land. What they did know and welcome was that Australia was a safe and democratic country with the promise of a good life for those who worked hard.

Most knew little or no English and came with little money and were sent to migrant camps. Many were indentured to the Australian Government for two years which meant that they had to accept work, usually of the low paid manual variety, offered to them in factories or on farms, regardless of their talents or qualifications. After two years they were free to carve out their own careers.

In 1947, the first year in which displaced persons were accepted into Australia, 840 displaced persons arrived. The peak years of displaced persons immigration were the consecutive years of 1949 and 1950 when 75,846 and 70,212 people would immigrate.[1]

The displaced person arrivals were predominantly young and male. They were the very demographic who would be attracted to playing and supporting soccer upon arrival in Australia. For many the highlight of their dreary and often lonely working week was to play or watch soccer with their compatriots. Many Australians opened their arms to the 'New Australians' and many migrant men have fond memories of their early days in Australia. Many married Australian women. Others felt excluded or alienated from the mainstream Anglo-Australian culture.

With no cultural affinity for Australian Rules or the rugby codes they formed community clubs. Within them migrants could play a variety of indoor games such as chess and card games and outdoor sports which had a following on continental Europe.

Diverse sports which had hitherto lacked popularity or success in Australia such as fencing, gymnastics, wrestling, skiing, field athletics, table tennis, water polo and handball all benefitted in Australia with the coming of European migrants.

However, without question the principal sport which many migrants shared a common passion for, regardless of nationality, was soccer.

The migrants quickly formed informal soccer teams and then clubs. In the sanctuary of their nascent clubs, they were removed from the critical gaze and either covert or open disapproval from many Anglo-Australians. Migrants could talk to others in their native tongue and relax, secure in the knowledge that they were among compatriots whose customs and behaviour was implicitly understood.

Local Australian soccer and other sporting officials were later to see and understand, often to their unease and consternation, that the migrants took their soccer and their clubs very seriously.

Vociferous support for their teams and a willingness to invest in their teams and the future of their clubs were to set the migrant clubs on a collision course with the more easy-going existing clubs. Incumbent officials and administrators believed in the ethos of a noble form of British amateurism. It was to be challenged in the 1950s by migrants who had come to love Australia and were ambitious to see the standard and popularity of soccer progress to its limits.

Clubs of Jewish, Italian and Greek origin which had been formed prior to 1950 were already jostling for promotion from lower divisions by the end of the 1940s. They were keen to sign the best players, whether locals or foreigners, and prepared to pay significant wages to attract them.

Many Australian club and national officials in particular, long entrenched in cosy plum positions of authority or favour became openly hostile to the ambitions of the migrant clubs. In return, the migrants and their clubs became hostile to the Anglo-Saxon hierarchy.

For many Anglo-Australians their soccer clubs did not assume such a pivotal place in their affections. Intellectual and cultural support and friendship was provided by their wider Australian community. This was to apply almost as strongly to the British migrant. He or she quickly blended into the mainstream of society, with fluency in English and understanding of the British institutions which underpinned the foundation of Australian society.

In time the numbers of European migrants would be augmented by 'economic migrants'. They would leave their countries of their own free will and official compliance, seeking greater opportunities and an enhanced lifestyle in Australia.

Countries and regions such as the Netherlands, Greece, Italy, Malta, Spain, Portugal, and South America were typical sources which would enhance the rich ethnic mix which would become the staple of Australian soccer culture. All immigrant groups would have a profound effect in broadening Australian attitudes, experiences and tastes in areas as diverse as business, administration, education, the arts and cuisine.

People from individual ethnic groups formed the nucleus of both the players and the spectators by the mid 1950s. The Continentals, as well as the English and Scottish fans, were accustomed to a system of promotion and relegation in the top leagues of their home countries. They could not understand why this system did not always apply in Australia.

Australia does not have a culture of promotion and relegation in other football codes. Why this is so, is not explicitly evident.

However, it almost certainly relates to the fact that Australia, with multiple codes and a relatively small population, was considered to only be able to support a small number of elite teams. If elite teams were to be relegated to a second division they may not survive the financial rigours and loss of spectator support which may come with demotion, and eventually disband.

Teams which played in a league without relegation could plan for the future, safe in the knowledge that a position at the bottom of a league table would still guarantee them a position in their competition the following season. Conversely, the excitement and tension of promotion from a lower division or demotion from a higher division was lacking in Australian footballing competitions.

The promise of promotion to a higher division was not necessarily an unalloyed joy. District or suburban clubs would usually have to cover the costs of greater player salaries upon promotion, and often provide a larger or better equipped home ground with greater spectator seating and amenities. Promotion and the fixed costs were often only accompanied by a minor increase in spectators and gate takings to only partially compensate for the increased outlay.

In Britain and Europe, support for soccer clubs was more passionate, elastic and forgiving. The local populace was more likely to support their club through good and bad times, including relegation, than seemed evident in Australia.

The power of the Australian based district or suburban clubs was on the wane. Local officials often prevented clubs with an ethnic base from gaining promotion through the divisions. This was partly because the officials usually came from a powerbase which included a district club. They were therefore were not inclined to allow 'their' or any other club face relegation.

In the late 1950s some ethnic soccer clubs playing in lower divisions were denied promotion to the top echelon of state soccer competitions. This caused dissatisfaction among club officials, players and supporters and led to yet another split in administrative ranks.

These new clubs, largely composed of European players and supporters, eventually came to dominate the development of senior Australian soccer and its culture in the second half of the twentieth century.

This is a fascinating story in its own right and worthy of further study and elucidation at another time.

Ipswich Bush Rats (Queensland), 1890

Cairns (Queensland), 1893

Adamstown and Broadmeadow (NSW) teams, 1895

Bundamba Rangers (Queensland), 1895

Balgownie Rangers (NSW), c early 1900s

Minmi Squashers (NSW), circa 1906

St Kilda (Victoria), c 1909

Caledonian Club, Fremantle (Western Australia), c 1910

New South Wales state team, 1911

Balgownie Rangers (NSW), 4th Grade Premiers, 1912

Schoolboys' team, Toowoomba (Queensland), 1913

First World War internment Camp, Rottnest Island (Western Australia), 1915

A match at the First World War internment Camp at Trial Bay (New South Wales), 1917

HMAS *Sydney* team, Scotland 1918

Australian Pioneer Battalion soccer team in Britain, 1919

South Hobart (Tasmania) won the Cottrell Dormer Cup in each of 1919, 1920, 1921, 1922 and 1923

Pineapple Rovers (Brisbane, Queensland), 1924

Flinders Naval Depot (Victoria), c 1924

Australian team in Adelaide, 1924. The Australian team played six
A-internationals against Canada in Adelaide, Brisbane, Newcastle and Sydney

Obi Obi, Sunshine Coast (Queensland), 1925

Roy McNaughton played in all five B-international matches against an English FA in 1925

St Helens Club, Ebbw Vale (Queensland), 1926

Unley United (South Australia), 1927

 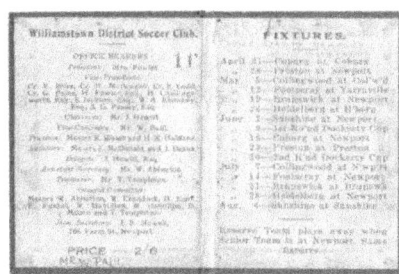

Williamstown (Victoria) season guide, 1928

Hobart Athletic (Tasmania), 1929

HMAS *Canberra* team, 1931 with the Navy House Cup which they won by going undefeated in Fleet Matches

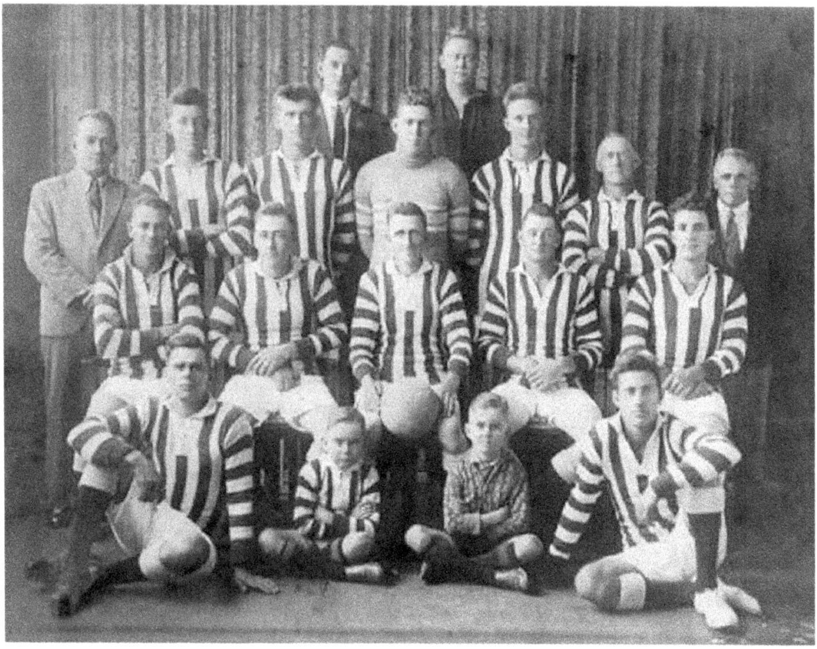

Bundaberg and District Soccer Association team (Queensland), 1932

St. Kilda B.A.A.F.C.

~~Home Telephone M 3664~~ WINDSOR 482

~~Office Telephone Central 1060~~

Dear Sir

You have been selected reserve ~~to play~~ for the ~~second~~ first eleven against Coburg at ~~Home.~~ Away. ~~Albert Ground.~~ Meet at Corner William St and Collins Street East Coburg

at 2-0 o'clock sharp. Telephone me as above at once if not available.

~~W. A. KEMPSON~~, Hon. Sec.

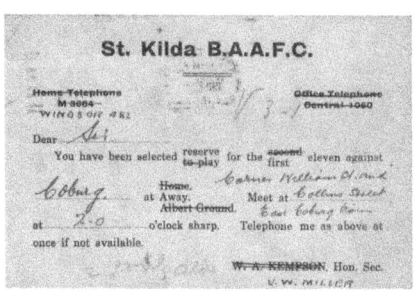

In 1932, local teams such as St Kilda in Victoria advised their players of team selection via a postcard

Wallaby Soccer Football

has been officially adopted by the Australian Soccer Football Association and the Queensland Soccer Council for use in all international and inter-State games in this State.

WHY?

Because after exhaustive trials the "WALLABY" PROVED SUPERIOR for Australian conditions.

MASSEY BICYCLE AND SPORTS DEPOT PTY. LTD.

Opp. ANZAC SQUARE, ADELAIDE STREET.

Queensland Soccer Council.

OFFICIAL PROGRAMME

New Zealand v. Australia

Exhibition Oval, Monday June 5th 1933

FREE EYE TEST

WILSON'S OPTICAL SERVICE

OPTOMETRY HOUSE

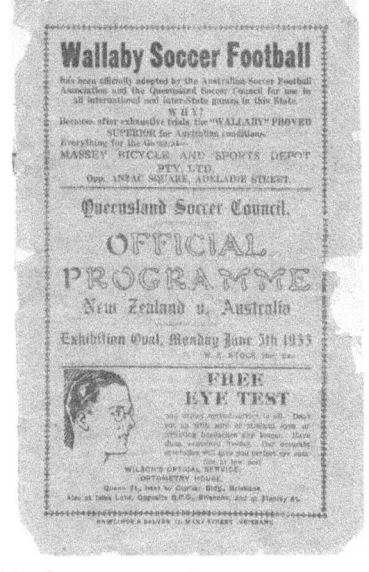

Match programme from an A-international between Australia and New Zealand in Brisbane in 1933 promoting the 'Wallaby Soccer Football'.

News of the SOCCER WORLD

NORTH v. SOUTH - Anzac Day

AT ARLINGTON PARK, 3-15p.m.

You drink the BEST when you order

TOOTH'S

K.B. Lager

A health giving and invigorating drink that fits us for the hardest game.

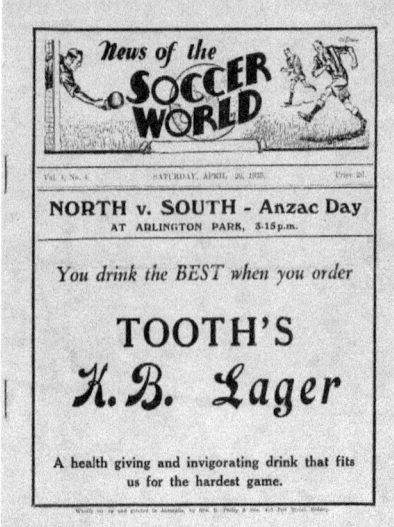

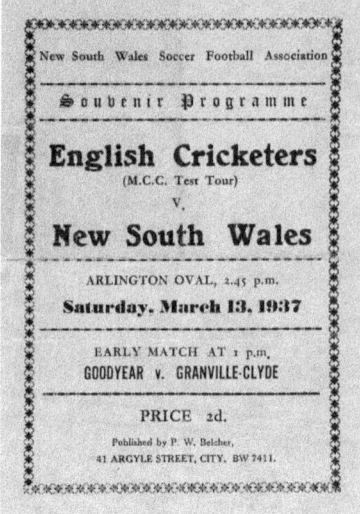

Anzac Day match programme between North and South (Sydney), Arlington Park, 1935

New South Wales Soccer Football Association

Souvenir Programme

English Cricketers

(M.C.C. Test Tour)

v.

New South Wales

ARLINGTON OVAL, 2.45 p.m.

Saturday, March 13, 1937

EARLY MATCH AT 1 p.m.

GOODYEAR v. GRANVILLE-CLYDE

PRICE 2d.

Published by P. W. Belcher,
41 ARGYLE STREET, CITY. BW 7411.

Match programme for an English cricketers side v New South Wales, 1937

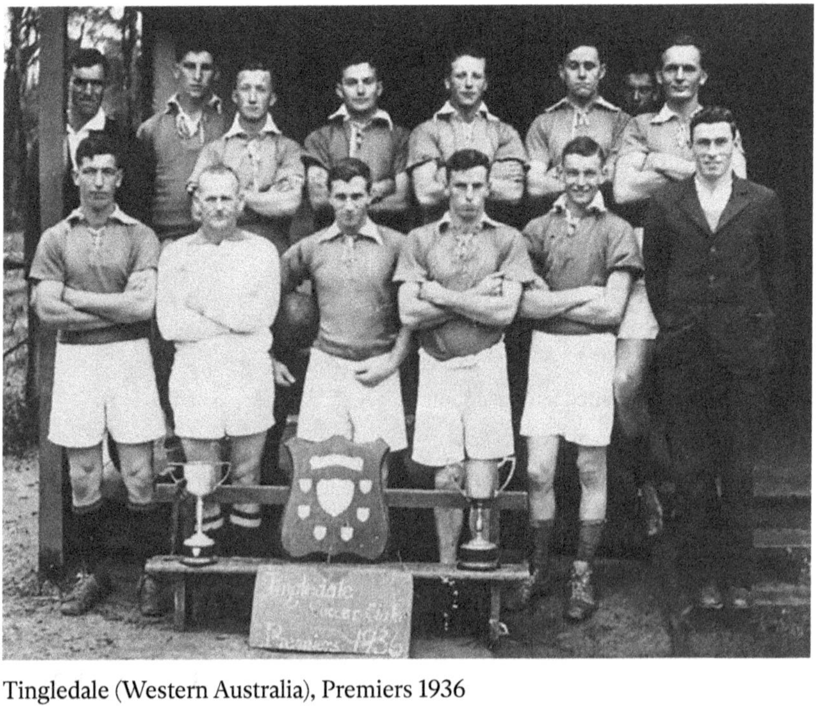

Tingledale (Western Australia), Premiers 1936

Official Dinner programme for the England Amateurs team that toured Australia in 1937

Match programmes from Australia v India in 1938 when five A-internationals were played, and a Queensland v China match in 1941

Australian Army Ordnance Depot team, Tel El Kebir (Egypt) during the Second World War, 1941

Australian troops playing a game at Noonamah (Northern Territory) during the Second World War, 1943

Fifth Signals Division of the Australian Army, Mililat (Papua New Guinea) during the Second World War, 1943

Prisoner of war team comprised of German internees at Murchison (Victoria) during the Second World War, 1943

Acknowledgements

We owe early soccer historians of note a special debt. Among such pioneers were Harry Hetherington and Sid Grant.

More recently, excellent in-depth monographs or articles about the early history of soccer in Australia have been published:

Australian Capital Territory (Nick Guoth)
New South Wales (Philip Mosely)
South Australia (Denis Harlow and Tony Smith)
Tasmania (Chris Hudson and Keith Roberts)
Victoria (Roy Hay)
Western Australia (Richard Kreider)
Australia (Trevor Thompson, Bill Murray, Roy Hay, Ian Syson)
Australian national team (G.E. Olivier-Scerri and Andrew Howe)

For those seeking additional information about soccer in the Australian states and territories I commend their publications.

List of References

Chapter 2 The Case for the Code

1. *Tasmanian Telegraph* 16 March 1859 p.5
2. *Queenslander* 16 June 1866 p.12
3. *Brisbane Courier* 29 June 1868 p. 2
4. *Brisbane Courier* 24 August 1868 p. 2
5. *Argus* 23 September 1873 p. 7
6. *Brisbane Courier* 22 July 1873 p. 2
7. *Sydney Morning Herald* 12 May 1877 p. 5
8. *Sydney Morning Herald* 15 May 1877 p. 6
9. *Sydney Morning Herald* 23 May 1877 p. 6
10. *Express and Telegraph* 4 June 1897 p. 1
11. *Mercury* 12 May 1879 p. 3
12. *Australian Town and Country Journal* 5 July 1879 p. 35

Chapter 3 Tentative Roots

1. *The Sydney Morning Herald* 3 August 1880 p.6
2. *The Sydney Morning Herald* 3 August 1880 p.6
3. *The Sydney Morning Herald* 13 August 1880 p.6
4. *The Soccer Weekly* 5 October 1940
5. *Bells Life in London* 1 January 1881
6. *The Granville Guardian* Vol. 14, No. 6 June 2007
   – Published by the Granville Historical Society
7. Hetherington, Harry – *The Book of Football - History of Soccer in Northern NSW and Sydney and South Coast,* Northern NSW Soccer Council. Newcastle 2003 (microfilm) p.1-71
8. Ibid p. p1-74

9. Tredinnick, Alan *As It Was Then - History of Soccer in Northern New South Wales and Sydney and South Coast,* Northern NSW Soccer Council Newcastle 2003 (microfilm)
10. Ibid
11. Balgownie Rangers web site *www.balgownierangers.com.au*
12. *The Australian Star* 2 September, 1889 p.7
13. *The Soccer News* 30 June 1923 p.4
14. *The Northern Territory Times and Gazette* 28 April 1899 p.3
15. *The Brisbane Courier* 9 June 1884 p.5
16. *The Courier-Mail* 16 July 1937 p.14
17. *Morning Bulletin* 27 August 1887 p.6
18. *The Morning Bulletin* 24 May 1886 p.5
19. *The Advertiser* 8 July 1893 p.4
20. *The Advertiser* 5 August 1893 p.6
21. The *Argus* 29 February 1884 p.7
22. Guoth, Nick, *The British are Coming, Hopefully: Great Expectations and the Two Phases of the Commonwealth Football Association,* Sporting Traditions, Volume 29, No. 1 May 2012
23. *The Argus* 27 October 1883 p.10
24. *Australasian Sketcher with Pen and Pencil* 7 August 1883 p.14
25. *Bells Life in West Australia* 19 September 1896

Chapter 4 Fragile Consolidation

1. *The Sydney Morning Herald* 7 September 1908 p.11
2. *Hetherington* v.1 p.70
3. *The Townsville Daily Bulletin* 30 May 1908 p.7
4. *The Brisbane Courier* 8 September 1908 p.7
5. *The Advertiser* 7 March 1903 p.10
6. *The Examiner* 16 March 1901 p.6
7. Hudson, Chris – *A Century of Soccer, 1888-1988 A Tasmanian History,* Peacock Publications. Hobart 1998 p.11
8. *The Argus* 1 September 1908 p.9
9. *Williamstown Chronicle* 13 March 1909 p.3
10. *The Daily News* 30 June 1900 p.2

11. *The Kalgoorlie Western Argus* 17 May 1900 p.33
12. *The West Australian* 20 May 1905 p.9
13. *The West Australian* 2 July 1935 p.9
14. The *Referee* 27 July 1904 p.8
15. The *Referee* 10 August 1904 p.8

Chapter 5 Growth and Contraction

1. *The Queanbeyan Age* 19 July 1912 p.2
2. *The Queanbeyan Age* 23 July 1912 p.2
3. *The Arrow* 30 April 1910
4. *The Arrow* 1 June 1910 p.12
5. *The Sun* 19 July 1912 p.11
6. *The Barrier Miner* 14 April 1913 p.5
7. *The Northern Territory Times and Gazette* 5 January 1912 p.3
8. *The Register* 25 April 1910 p.5
9. *The Mercury* 7 April 1916 p.8
10. *The Golden Gate* 19 April 1912 p.2
11. *The West Australian* 5 June 1912 p.9
12. *The West Australian* 16 October 1915 p.9

Chapter 6 Servicemen and Soccer during the First World War

1. *The Mail* 25 August 1914 p.3
2. (Ozfootball.net source)
3. Snowdon, Dianne – *South Hobart Soccer Club 1910*-2010 - South Hobart Football Club 2010 p.15
4. *Geraldton Guardian* 7 March 1916 p.4
5. *The Soccer News* 1 July 1922
6. Goddard, G.H. – *Soldiers and Sportsmen - An Account of the Sporting Activities of the Australian Imperial Force during the Period between November 1918, and September 1919, AIF Sports Control Board, 1919* p.17

Chapter 7
Friction and External Contact

1. *The Mail* 14 April 1923 p.7
2. *The Sporting Globe* 25 May 1927 p.9
3. *The Soccer News* 19 May 1923 p.1
4. *The Soccer News* 9 June 1923 p.1
5. *The Canberra Community News* 11 December 1925
6. *The Referee* 26 May 1920 p.11
7. *The Soccer News* 8 September 1923 p.1
8. *The Soccer News* 27 June 1925
9. *The Soccer News* 6 June 1927 p.3
10. *The Northern Territory Times and Gazette* 4 January 1924 p.9
11. *The Northern Territory Times* 17 April 1929 p.3
12. *Queensland Times* 13 October 1921 p.4
13. *The Advertiser* 24 April 1925 p.17
14. *The Advertiser* 27 April 1925 p.13
15. Goldberg, David, *Hakoah Heroes* Carindale, Qld, Independent Ink 2017 p.30-31
16. Hay, Roy and Syson, Ian, *The Story of Football in Victoria,* Football Federation of Victoria , 2009 p.9
17. *The Sunday Times* 24 June 1923 p.5
18. *The Sunday Times* 7 July 1923 p.20

Chapter 8
Australian International Matches 1922-1928

1. *The Soccer News* 1 July 1922
2. *The Soccer News* 4 July 1925
3. *The Longreach Leader* 17 August 1923 p.22

4. *The Soccer News* 21 July 1923
5. *The Soccer News* 15 September 1923
6. *The Soccer News* 19 September 1925
7. *Studs Up* January 1997
8. *The Soccer News* 20 April 1935
9. *The Sydney Morning Herald* 4 June 1927
10. *The Soccer News* 10 May 1924
11. *The Mail* 2 June 1923
12. *The Brisbane Courier* 25 January 1928

Chapter 9
The Women's Game

1. *The Sun* 1 July 1921 p.2
2. *The Telegraph* 23 June 1921 p.5
3. *The Telegraph* 19 June 1922 p.6
4. *The Western Miner* 20 May 1936

Chapter 10
High Hopes and Reality

1. *The Canberra Times* 10 May 1932 p.3
2. *The Sydney Morning Herald* 3 June 1933 p.18
3. *The Sydney Morning Herald* 15 June 1934 p.17
4. *The Northern Standard* 19 September 1933 p.8
5. *The Northern Standard* 9 March 1936 p.8
6. *The Northern Standard* 22 January 1937 p.4
7. *The Cairns Post* 15 May 1935 p.3
8. *The Townsville Daily Bulletin* 3 January 1939 p.9
9. *The Advertiser* 27 May 1932 p.9
10. *The Mail* 19 November 1932 p.10
11. *The Mail* 2 July 1938 p.25

12. Hudson, Chris - *A Century of Soccer – A Tasmanian History* p.33
13. *The Morwell Gazette and Advertiser* 6 September 1934 p.8
14. *The Sydney Morning Herald* 20 June 1932 p.6
15. *The Western Argus* 6 May 1930 p.30
16. *The West Australian* 9 July 1936 p.6
17. *The West Australian* 22 April 1932 p.13

Chapter 11
International Matches 1930s

1. Official Program Australia v New Zealand; Brisbane June 5 1933 p.3
2. *The Brisbane Courier* 24 August 1933 p.16
3. *News of the Soccer World* 20 April 1935 p.2
4. *The Argus* 25 September 1935 p.17
5. *The Sydney Morning Herald* 13 July 1936 p.13
6. Australia v India Program Sydney, 24 September 1938 p.2
7. *The Sun* 20 May 1939 p.4
8. *The Townsville Daily Bulletin* 22 March 1939 p.10

Chapter 12
Soccer in the Shadow of War

1. *The Canberra Times* 30 July 1945 p.3
2. *The Sydney Morning Herald* 3 May 1943 p.7
3. *The Sydney Morning Herald* 6 November 1944 p.7
4. *Army News* 9 January 1945 p.44
5. *Townsville Daily Bulletin* 22 June 1940 p.10
6. *The Mail* 24 May 1940 p.9
7. *The Advertiser* 20 June 1941 p.17
8. *The Advertiser* 5 May 1945 p.8
9. *The Mercury* 4 February 1943 p.2
10. *The Sporting Globe* 14 May 1941 p.10

Chapter 13
Australian International Matches
1941-1945

1. *The Argus* 21 July 1941 p.5
2. Queensland v China Program 26 July 1941

Chapter 14 Servicemen and Soccer in the Second World War

1. *The Argus* 30 September 1940 p.4
2. *The Soccer Weekly* 25 April 1940 p.6
3. *The Telegraph* 28 August 1945 p.4

Chapter 15 Enter the Immigrant

1. *The Canberra Times* 20 April 1948 p.4
2. *The Canberra Times* 24 June 1949 p.6
3. *The Sydney Morning Herald* 17 December 1946 p.9
4. *The Sydney Morning Herald* 14 April 1947 p.10
5. *Sporting Life* April 1947
6. *Sporting Life* July 1948
7. *The Soccer Weekly* 21 May 1949
8. *Cootamundra Herald* 26 July 1949 p.4
9. *The Northern Standard* 22 April 1949 p.12
10. *The Northern Standard* 21 October 1949 p.4
11. *The Townsville Daily Bulletin* 2 April 1946 p.3
12. *Morning Bulletin* 18 July 1946 p.7
13. *The Courier Mail* 5 April 1946 p.3
14. *The Advertiser* 25 January 1946 p.5

15. Hudson, Chris – *A Century of Soccer – 1888-1988 - A Tasmanian History*, Peacock Publications, 1998 p.77
16. Kallinikios, John – *Soccer Boom The Transformation of Victorian Soccer Culture* Walla Walla Press c. 2007 p.23
17. *Sporting Life* April 1949

Chapter 16 Australian International Matches 1946-1949

1. *The Sydney Morning Herald* 12 May 1945 p.9
2. *The Sydney Morning Herald* 14 April 1947 p.10
3. *NSW Soccer Football Association Handbook*, 1947 p.4
4. Studs Up October, November 1998
5. ibid
6. Australian Soccer Football Association - Australia v Yugoslavia Sydney 30 July 1949 p.3
7. ibid p.1

Chapter 17 View to the Future

1. Kunz, Egon F. *Displaced Persons: Calwells' New Australians* Australian National University Press, 1988 p.46

List of Clubs
Notes about the club list

In the following pages is a list of clubs that played senior matches in Australia until December 1949.

The listing is arranged by state or territory boundaries.

Though it is the most comprehensive list yet published, it cannot be considered totally complete.

In compiling the information judgement had to be made regarding conflicting information. For example, newspaper references and contemporary reports often contained varieties of spellings of club names, colours, locations and titles and honours won. In contemporary reports, errors and inconsistent facts are evident.

The information has mainly come from research on the National Library of Australia's Trove newspaper archive, and has been, where possible, cross checked with previously published data from other sources.

The fate of many soccer clubs was tenuous. Many clubs failed to last more than a few years before becoming defunct. In many towns or rural areas a club would become defunct, only to be revived some years later.

Clubs changed name, were absorbed by another club or themselves absorbed another club. Some clubs split, with a splinter group forming a new club.

Dates of club formation are stated if known. A 'circa' date refers to the earliest data found about a club in newspaper reports or other contemporary documents. In some instances, due to a lack of documentary evidence, a club may have been formed prior to a circa date. In many cases it is not known when clubs became defunct.

The physical ground at which a club played is stated, if known. At a minimum a region, city, town, village or suburb is linked to a club. Many clubs in the large state capitals changed venues often.

Club colours, nicknames and titles or honours won are also provided where known.

The notes field contains additional information.

Australian Capital Territory

ACTON
Dates: 1929
Location: Acton Sports Ground
Notes: The club disbanded by the end of the season.

AINSLIE
Dates: 1928
Location: Acton Sports Ground
Notes: The club was in existence for one season and became the renamed Canberra club.

BURNS CLUB
Dates: 1924-1928, 1933
Location: Burns Ground; Capitol Hill; Acton Ground
Colours: Black shirts with white hoops
Nickname: The Scotchmen
Titles/Honours: Premiers 1926-1927; Cup winners 1926

CANBERRA
Dates: 1912
Location: Acton Sports Ground
Colours: Red and white shirts
Notes: Comprised members of the Department of Home Affairs.
The club was renamed Ainslie in 1928.

CANBERRAS BLUES
Dates: 1931
Location: York Park
Colours: Blue shirts
Titles/Honours: Canberra Cup 1932; Glick Shield 1932

CANBERRA WANDERERS
Dates: 1948
Location: Northbourne Oval; Manuka Oval
Notes: Most players were residents of the Eastlake and Riverside hostels.

CAPITOL HILL
Dates: 1926-1927
Location: Capitol Hill: The Causeway
Colours: Royal blue shirts
Nickname: The Hillites

DUNTROON
Dates: 1910-1914
Location: Duntroon, Canberra
Titles/Honours: Canberra and District Champions 1914
Notes: The team comprised non army staff of the Royal Military College, Duntroon.

EASTLAKE
Dates: 1926
Location: Kingston
Notes: Club members were employees of the Government Printing Works. The club was formed too late to take part in the Canberra competition but did play cup and friendly matches.

FEDERAL MAGPIES
Dates: 1931
Location: Acton Racecourse; York Park
Titles/Honours: Adelaide Tailoring Company Canberra Shield 1931

GINNINDERRA
Dates: 1914
Location: Ginninderra Showground, North Canberra

KINGSTON
Dates: 1928-1929
Location: Kingston Sports Ground
Colours: Black and white shirts
Notes: Most players worked at the Government Printing Works at Kingston. The club was previously named Eastlake.

MOLONGLO
Dates: 1926-1927
Location: Acton Ground, Canberra
Colours: Dark and sky blue shirts
Titles/Honours: Premiers 1927; Emslie Cup 1927

NORTHBOURNE
Dates: 1926

Location: North Canberra
Colours: Blue and gold striped shirts
POWER HOUSE
Dates: 1912-1914
Location: Kingston
Notes: Club players built and maintained the Canberra electrical power house.
RANGERS
Dates: 1930
Location: York Park
Colours: White shirts

ROVERS
Dates: 1930
Location: York Park
THISTLE
Dates: 1930
Location: York Park
YARRALUMLA
Dates: 1910
Location: Yarralumla, South Canberra

New South Wales

ABBOTOIRS
Dates: 1939
Location: District Park, Newcastle
Titles/Honours: Second division 'B' section winners 1941
Notes: Played in the Newcastle City Houses and Works Soccer Association.
ABBOTSFORD DISTRICT
Dates: c. 1921
Location: Abbotsford
Colours: Black and white shirts
ABERDARE
Dates: 1925-1937
Location: Cessnock
Colours: Red and black shirts with white shorts
Nickname: The Dares
Titles: State Cup 1928; Stevenson Cup 1930
Notes: Club formed by Scottish miners. Aberdare merged with Cessnock to form Cessnock Caledonian in 1937.
ABERDARE BLOSSOM
Dates: c. 1915
Location: Aberdare
ABERDARE SHAFT
Dates: c. 1931
Location: Cessnock
ABERDEEN
Dates: c. 1945
Location: Aberdeen
ABERMAIN
Dates: 1908 - 1949
Location: Abermain Recreation Reserve
Colours: White shirts with a green sash; blue shirts (1918)
Titles/Honours: Stevenson Cup 1948
ABMAL
Dates: c. 1933

Location: Sydney
ACI
Dates: c. 1940
Location: Sydney
Notes: The works team of Australian Chemical Industries. Competed in the City Houses competition in the early 1940's.
ADAMSTOWN BRICKYARDS
Dates: c. 1930- c. 1936
Location: Hobart Park
ADAMSTOWN CHURCH OF ENGLAND
Dates: c. 1939
Location: Brickyards
Notes: Club played in the Newcastle Protestant Churches competition.
Titles/Honours: 'A' Grade Premiers 1938
ADAMSTOWN ROSEBUD
Dates: 1889
Location: Adamstown Park, Northern New South Wales
Colours: White shirts with a 3" navy blue sash from right to left with dark shorts; red and green shirts with red shorts; light and dark blue shirts (c. 1940); red and green halved shirts with white shorts and green and red socks (1947)
Nickname: The Buds; The Townies
Titles/Trophies: State League Premiers 1930, 1934, 1935, 1948; Ellis Charity Challenge Cup 1894, 1896, 1899-1903, 1905-6, 1908-9, 1912, 1920; Robinson Cup 1930-31, 1934; State Cup 1930, 1934; Gardiner Cup 1909, 1925; Kerr Cup 1925, 1926; Stevenson Cup 1929; Bennett Cup 1938; Sheehan Cup 1940; Daniels Cup 1946
Notes: Club formed by British migrants. Club was named after 'Rosebud' butter.
ADAMSTOWN SHAMROCKS
Dates: 1900-1906

Location: Adamstown
Colours: White shirts with a green sash
ADAMSTOWN SWEETHEARTS
Dates: c. 1906
Location: Adamstown
Colours: White shirts with a red heart
ADELONG
Dates: 1914
Location: Adelong
ADULT DEAF AND DUMB INSTITUTE
Dates: c. 1934
Location: Centennial Park
Notes: Played in the NSW Mid-Week Soccer Association competition.
ADULT DEAF SOCIETY
Dates: c. 1919
Location: Sydney
A.G.E. HOTPOINTS
Dates: 1940
Location: Auburn
Titles/Honours: Cottam Cup 1940
Notes: Works team of the Australian General Electric Company. Played in the Granville and Southern Districts Football Association competition.
A.G. SIMMS
Dates: c. 1940
Location: Sydney
Notes: Played in the City Houses competition in the early 1940's.
ALBION PARK
Dates: 1894; 1936
Location: Raftery's Ground, Albion Park
Nickname: The Parkites
ALBURY
Dates: 1914
Location: Albury
ALEXANDRIA CONGREGATIONAL
Dates: c. 1923
Location: Alexandria
Colours: Red and green shirts
ALEXANDRIA
Dates: c. 1927
Location: Alexandria
ALEXANDRIA ROVERS
Dates: c. 1914
Location: Booralee Park, Bathurst
ALL BLACKS
Dates: c. 1939-1941
Location: Gladstone Ground, Broken Hill
Colours: Black shirts
ALL BLACKS
Dates: c. 1931-1932
Location: Wagga
Titles/Honours: Bourne Shield 1931; Allan McLeish Cup 1931
ALL NATIONS STARS
Dates: 1944; 1947
Location: Gladstone Ground, Broken Hill
Notes: All Nations Stars were formerly called Napredeks. The name was only used in the 1943 season when the club reverted to the Napredeks name. In 1947 the All Nations Stars club re-formed but played only for one season.
ALL SAINTS
Dates: c. 1940
Location: Petersham
ALL SAINTS
Dates: c. 1922
Location: Waterloo Oval
Notes: This club played in the Protestant Churches 'A' Grade competition in 1922.
ALL SOULS
Dates: 1920-1923
Location: Leichhardt
Notes: All Souls laid the foundation of the Protestant Churches Football Association in 1920.
ALLAWAH
Dates: c. 1926
Location: Hurstville
Colours: White shirts with a red 'A'
ALMA
Dates: c. 1939-1944; 1948
Location: Gladstone Ground, Broken Hill
Titles/Honours: Middleton Cup 1944
ALTONA
Dates: c. 1916
Location: Altona
ANGUS ROVERS
Dates: c. 1932
Location: Angus Place
ANNANDALE
Dates: 1913-1922
Location: Federal Park; Ibrox Park
Colours: Red shirt; royal blue and white shirts (1916); blue and white vertically striped shirts (1922); green shirts (1929)
Nickname: The Dales; The Greenlegs
Titles/Honours: State Champions 1913. Metropolitan Premiers and City Championship 1916-1917. Gardiner Cup 1913; City Cup 1916
Notes: Later became the Annandale-Leichhardt club.
ANNANDALE ALBION
Dates: c. 1917
Location: Annandale
Colours: Blue and white striped shirts
ANNANDALE ALTONA
Dates: c. 1917-1921
Location: Annandale
Colours: Blue and white striped shirts
ANNANDALE-LEICHHARDT
Dates: 1925

Location: Ibrox Park, Leichhardt
Colours: Black shirts; maroon shirts
Titles/Honours: Sydney Cup 1930
Notes: Annandale-Leichhardt succeeded the Annandale club.
APSLEY
Dates: 1894-1897
Location: Moore Park
ARCADIANS
Dates: 1885
Location: Glebe
Colours: Navy blue shirts with a Maltese cross and navy blue shorts
Nickname: The Arcs
Notes: Club of St Paul's Church, Redfern and second club formed in NSW. Played first competition match in Sydney on June 6 1885 against Caledonians, losing 1-7. Team consisted of Australian born players.
ARK OF SAFETY
Dates: c. 1922
Location: Sydney
ARMIDALE
Dates: 1914
Location: Armidale
ARMIDALE CITY
Dates: 1920
Location: The Racecourse, Armidale
Colours: White shirts and white shorts; red and white shirts (1921)
ARMIDALE CORINTHIANS
Dates: c. 1921
Location: The Racecourse, Armidale
ARMIDALE ROVERS
Dates: 1922
Location: The Racecourse, Armidale
ARSENAL
Dates: 1942
Location: Sydney
ARMY SERVICE CORP
Dates: c. 1936
Location: Moore Park
Notes: Team played in the Mid-week Sydney Soccer Association competition.
ARNCLIFFE ACES
Dates: c. 1926
Location: Arncliffe
ARNCLIFFE CORINTHIANS
Dates: c. 1922
Location: Arncliffe Park; St George Sportsground
Colours: Black and gold shirts
ARNCLIFFE STARS
Dates: c. 1926
Location: Arncliffe
Colours: Blue and gold shirts
ARNOTTS
Dates: c. 1920

Location: Gees Paddock, Auburn
Colours: Blue and gold shirts
Notes: Works team of the Arnotts biscuit factory
ARSENAL
Dates: 1942
Location: Lambert Park, Sydney
Notes: Players were from the Metters club.
ASHFIELD
Dates: 1916
Location: Ashfield
Notes: Ashfield played in the Metropolitan League in 1916.
ASHFIELD BAPTIST
Date: c. 1923
Location: Ashfield
ASPLEY
Dates c. 1896
Location: Aspley
AUBURN
Dates: c. 1910
Location: Auburn Park; Mona Park, Auburn
Colours: Tangerine shirts with tangerine shorts and tangerine socks; Black and white halved shirts (1922); green shirts (1949)
Titles/Honours: Metropolitan FA Charity Cup 1919; Eastern and Western Suburbs Premiership 1928; B Division Premiers 1948
AUBURN BAPTIST
Dates: c. 1945
Location: Auburn
AUBURN CRESCENT
Dates: c. 1903
Location: Auburn
AUBURN DALLAS
Dates: c. 1903
Location: Granville
Notes: Auburn Dalley played in the Granville competition.
AUBURN DISTRICT
Dates: 1928; 1931
Location: Gees Paddock
Colours: Green and gold shirts
Titles/Honours: Southern Division Cup 1929
AUBURN FEDERALS
Dates: c. 1920
Location: Auburn
AUBURN STARLIGHT
Dates: c. 1946
Location: Auburn
AUBURN UNITED
Dates: c. 1922-1927; c. 1928
Location: Auburn Park
Colours: Black and white halved shirts
Notes: Changed name to Auburn District in 1931.
AUBURN WANDERERS
Dates: 1893

Location: Auburn
AUSTENHAM ROAD METHODIST
Dates: 1920
Location: Annandale
Colours: Red and white shirts
Titles/Honours: PCSFA First Grade champions 1920
Notes: This club played in the Protestant Churches 'A' Grade competition.
AUSTINMER ROVERS
Dates: c. 1949
Location: Clowes Park, Austinmer
AUSTRAL BRONZE
Dates: c. 1937-1943
Location: Sydney
Colours: Sky blue shirts
Titles/Honours: ESSFA Premiers 1938-9; CHSFA Premiers 1940-1
Notes: The team of the Austral Bronze Company which made brass and copper products. Its team played in the A grade City Houses competition in 1938 and the Sydney and District League till 1943.
AUSTRAL WARATAH
Dates: c. 1922
Location: Hurlstone Park
Notes: This club played in the Protestant Churches 'A' Grade competition in 1922.
AUSTRALIAN ARMY MEDICAL CORP (AAMC)
Dates: 1944
Location: Hay
AUSTRALIAN IRON AND STEEL WORKS
Dates: 1930
Location: Port Kembla
AUSTRALIAN ROADS
Dates: 1923
Location: Easton Park
Colours: Black shirts
AUSTRALIAN WINDOW GLASS (AWG)
Dates: c. 1939
Location: Sydney
Nickname: The Glassies
Notes: Played in the City Houses Competition.
AUSTRALIAN WOOLEN MILLS
Dates: c. 1938
Location: Sydney
AVOCA
Dates: c. 1928
Location: Avoca
AWABA
Dates: 1921
Location: Awaba
Colours: Gold shirts with a blue 'V'
A.Y.C.
Dates: c. 1943
Location: Pit Paddock, Cessnock

Colours: Red and black shirts
BABCOCK AND WILCOX
Dates: c.1923
Location: Sydney
Colours: Red shirts
Notes: Babcock and Wilcox was a metal working company located in Regent's Park. The club played in the Sydney and District Division 2 in 1938.
Titles/Honours: SDSA Premiership 1937; Knock-out Cup 1937
BALGOWNIE
Dates: 1883-
Location: Bodes Ground, Wollongong
Colours: Red shirts; black and white shirts with white shorts and black and white socks (1910)
Nickname: The Magpies; The Bals
Titles/Honours: South Coast Premiers 1892, 1895-1896, 1900; South Coast Challenge Cup 1913; Metropolitan Premiers 1926-28; Tooth Cup 1926, 1929, 1932; Moore Cup 1936
Notes: Fifth oldest club in Australia. In the mid 1930's the club merged with Corrimal and was known as Balgownie-Corrimal.
BALGOWNIE ROVERS
Dates: 1914
Location: Balgownie
BALGOWNIE-CORRIMAL
Dates: 1934-1935
Location: Balgownie Park; Prince Edward Park, Carlton
Colours: Black and white shirts
Notes: Short lived amalgamation of Balgownie and Corrimal teams.
BALLARAT ROVERS
Dates: c. 1931
Location: Crystal Palace, Wallsend
Notes: 3rd grade Newcastle club
BALLINA
Dates: 1914
Location: Ballina
Dates: c. 1929
Location: Sydney
BALMAIN
Dates: 1891
Location: Easton Park; Leichhardt Oval (1929)
Colours: Black and gold shirts (1896); Blue and gold.
Nickname: The Balmainiacs; 'Mains
Titles/Honours: Metropolitan Premiers 1895-99, 1911; Gardiner Cup 1895-1897, 1905, 1912, 1916,
BALMAIN ALBERT
Dates: c. 1898
Location: Balmain
BALMAIN ALBION
Dates: 1900

Location: Birchgrove Oval, Balmain
BALMAIN AUSTRAL
Dates: 1897
Location: Birchgrove Oval, Balmain
BALMAIN CALEDONIANS
Dates: c. 1915
Location: Beauchamp Park
Colours: Black and gold shirts
Nickname: The Scotchmen
Titles/Honours: Charity Cup 1915; Dewar Cup 1915
BALMAIN COLLIERY
Dates: c. 1924
Location: Easton Park
BALMAIN CONGREGATIONAL
Dates: c. 1941
Location: Balmain
Nickname: The Congs
Colours: Orange and black shirts
BALMIAN DISTRICT
Dates: 1903
Location: Balmain
BALMAIN ENDEAVOUR
Dates: c. 1896
Location: Balmain
BALMAIN FEDERAL
Dates: c. 1902
Location: Birchgrove Reserve
BALMAIN-FERNLEIGH
Dates: 1914
Location: Epping Racecourse; Easton Park
Colours: Blue and gold vertically striped shirts with white back and front; white 'V' added to blue and gold vertically striped shirt, back and front (1922)
Nickname: The Watersiders
Titles/Honours: Sunlight Cup 1916, 1917; Gardiner Cup 1919, 1920; First League Premiership 1919-20.
BALMAIN GLADSTONE
Dates: 1915-
Location: Lyne Park No. 2; Easton Park
Titles/Honours: Sunlight Cup 1918; Second League Premiers 1919.
Nickname: Mains
Colours: Black shirt with gold 'V' back and front: blue and gold halved shirt (1922)
Notes: Balmain-Gladstone first played senior Second League soccer in 1919.
BALMAIN KIAORA
Dates: 1908 - 1918; 1923; 1940
Location: Birchgrove Oval
Titles/Honours: Second League Champions 1916.
Notes: Kiaora played in the Granville Association competition.
BALMAIN NATIVE ROSE
Dates: c. 1896
Location: Balmain
BALMAIN SCOTTISH
Dates: 1921
Location: Ibrox Park, Leichhardt
Colours: Red and white striped shirts
Titles/Honours: Second Division Premiership 1922
Notes: Debut in Second Division of the Metropolitan First League, 1921.
BALMAIN WORKINGMAN'S INSTITUTE
Dates: 1898
Location: Balmain
BANGALOW RANGERS
Dates: c. 1932
Location: Bangalow Showground, Northern NSW
BANKSMEADOW ROVERS
Dates: c. 1940
Location: Booralee Park
BALMAIN SIROCCO
Dates: 1898
Location: Balmain
BALMAIN UNITED
Dates: 1913
Location: Balmain
BALMAIN WANDERERS
Dates: c. 1910
Location: Balmain
BALMAIN WHITE STAR
Dates: c. 1898
Location: Balmain
BANKSMEADOW
Dates: c. 1940
Location: South Coast
BANKSTOWN
Dates: c. 1923
Location: Bankstown
Colours: Green and gold shirts
Nickname: The 'Town
BANKSTOWN ATHLETIC
Dates: c. 1922
Location: Bankstown
BANKSTOWN JUDEANS
Dates: c. 1928
Location: Bankstown
Colours: Black and white striped shirts
Titles/Honours: Knock-Out Cup 1929
BANKSTOWN PRESBYTERIAN
Dates: c. 1940
Location: Bankstown
BARELLAN
Dates: 1914; 1924
Location: Barellan Recreation Ground
BARMEDMAN
Dates: c. 1928
Location: Barmedman

THE FOUNDATION YEARS 1859-1949

BARNSLEY
Dates: c. 1914; 1924
Location: Barnsley

BATHURST
Dates: 1910; 1922
Location: Railway Oval; Upfold's Flat

BATHURST ALBIONS
Dates: c. 1926
Location: Farm Oval, Bathurst

BATHURST RAILWAY
Dates: c. 1929
Location: Bathurst

BATHURST ROVERS
Dates: 1922
Location: Rovers Ground, Bathurst

BATLOW
Dates: 1914
Location: Batlow

BEAUFORT AIRCRAFT
Dates: c. 1940
Location: Sydney
Notes: Played in the City Houses competition in the early 1940's and then the Sydney and District League by 1943.

BELL AND FRASER
Dates: c. 1928
Location: Sydney
Notes: Bell and Fraser were glass and timber merchants.

BELLAMBI
Dates: 1910-1911
Location: South Coast

BELLBIRD
Dates: c. 1920
Location: Bellbird Park
Nickname: The Birds
Titles/Honours: South Maitland all age champions 1940
Notes: Most players worked for the Hetton Coal Company.

BELMONT
Dates: 1936
Location: Belmont Sports Ground

BELMONT METHODIST
Dates: c. 1939
Location: Belmont
Notes: Club played in the Newcastle Protestant Churches competition.

BELMONT-SWANSEA
Dates: 1935
Location: Blacksmith Sports Ground, North Belmont, Northern New South Wales.
Colours: Orange shirts with green trimmings; white shorts with green socks with orange tops.
Titles/Honours: Daniels Cup 1944-45

BELMORE
Dates: c. 1940
Location: Belmore
Colours: Black shirt with a white 'V'

BELMORE CHURCH OF CHRIST
Dates: c. 1935
Location: Belmore

BERGERS LTD
Dates: 1921
Location: Central Park, Concord
Notes: Debut in the Metropolitan Second League in 1921. Team financed by on the Lewis Berger paint company.

BERRIMA COLLIERY
Dates: c. 1937
Location: Berrima
Titles/Honours: Burchell Cup 1937; Berrima District Soccer Association Premiers 1938, 1940

BEXLEY
Dates: c. 1913
Location: Bexley Park

BEXLEY ROVERS
Dates: c. 1926
Location: Bexley
Colours: Blue and gold shirts

BEXLEY WARATAHS
Dates: c. 1939
Location: Moorefield

BEXLEY WARRIORS
Dates: 1938
Location: Bexley Park
Colours: Green and yellow shirts

BHP
Dates: 1939
Location: District Park, Newcastle
Titles/Honours: Premiership; Sherwin Williams Cup 1939
Notes: Competed in the Newcastle City Houses and Works Soccer Association.

BILBUL
Dates: c. 1924
Location: Bilbul

BINYA
Dates: 1927
Location: Binya

BLACK DIAMOND
Dates: 1907
Location: Lithgow

BLACKHEATH
Dates: 1924
Location: Blackheath
Colours: Maroon shirts
Nickname: The Heath
Notes: Blackheath, Katoomba, Springwood and Springwood Wattles played in the first Blue Mountains competition in 1924.

BLACKMANS FLAT
Dates: c. 1929
Location: Browns Collieries Paddock; State School, Blackmans Flat

BLACKSMITHS
Dates: c. 1936
Location: Blacksmiths
BLACKTOWN
Dates: c. 1928; 1936
Location: Francis Park, Blacktown
BLACKTOWN CENTER OF NATIONAL FITNESS
Dates: 1940
Location: Blacktown
BLACKTRACKERS
Dates: c. 1947
Location: Swansea
Notes: Played in the Swansea Returned Soldiers League.
BLUE CABS
Dates: c. 1924
Location: Cricket Ground
BOGAN GATE
Dates: c. 1928
Location: Bogan Gate
BONDI
Dates: 1931
Location: Canterbury Velodrome
Titles/Honours: Judean League champion 1932-1934
BONDI BEACH
Dates: c. 1925
Location: Centennial Park
Titles/Honours: All age competition winners 1925-6
Notes: Team played in the Eastern Suburbs Association.
BONDI JUDEAN
Dates: c. 1931
Location: Bondi
Titles/Honours: Judean League 1932-1934; Harry Landis Cup 1934
BONDI MARINES
Dates: c. 1940
Colours: Blue and gold shirts
Titles/Honours: Eastern Suburbs Association Premiers 1941-2
BONDI WARATAHS
Dates: c. 1925
Location: Centennial Park
Notes: Team played in the Eastern Suburbs Association.
BONNIE DUNDEE COLLIERY
Dates: c. 1942
Location: Ipswich
BOOK BOOK
Dates: 1928
Location: Book Book, Riverina
BOORALEE ROVERS
Dates: c. 1924
Location: Booralee

BOOLAROO
Dates: c. 1920
Location: Boolaroo
Nickname: The 'Roos
Titles/Honours: Richardson Cup 1922
Notes: Boolaroo amalgamated with Speers Point in 1934.
BOOLAROO CO-OP
Dates: c. 1941
Location: District Park, Newcastle
Notes: Competed in the Newcastle City Houses and Works Soccer Association competition.
BOOLAROO-SPEERS POINT
Dates: 1934
Location: Speers Point
Notes: Speers Point amalgamated with the Boolaroo club in 1934. Amalgamated club known as Boolaroo-Speers Point.
Titles/Honours: Newcastle Soccer Association 2nd Division Premiers 1935
BOOLAROO SWIFTS
Dates: c. 1941
Location: Boolaroo
BOOMERANGS
Dates: 1907-1911
Location: Helensburgh
Titles/Honours: South Coast 3rd grade Premiers 1906
BOTANY METHODIST
Dates: c. 1923
Location: Botany
BOTANY UNITED
Dates: 1912
Location: Botany
BOTANY ALBION
Dates: 1913
Location: Booralee Oval, Botany
Colours: Blue and gold striped shirts (1922)
BOWRAL
Dates: 1914; 1919; 1924
Location: Glebe Park; Bowral Soccer Ground
Colours: Black shirts and white shorts with black socks with white tops.
BOWRAL ALBERTS
Dates: 1896-1898
Location: Mrs Oxley's Paddock, Bowral
BOWRAL MILITIA
Dates: c. 1936
Location: Loseby Park, Bowral
Titles/Honours: Burchell Cup 1936
BOWRAL PIONEERS
Location: Bowral
Dates: 1896-1897
BOWRAL ROVERS
Dates: 1893
Location: Bowral
BOWRAL SCOTTISH ASSOCIATION

THE FOUNDATION YEARS 1859-1949

Dates: 1937
Location: Loseby Park, Bowral
BOWRAL UNITED
Dates: 1948
Location: Bowral
BRADFORD KENDALL
Dates: c. 1940
Location: Lambert Park
Colours: Red and green shirts
Notes: Competed in the City Houses competition in the early 1940's.
BRADWARDINE
Dates: c. 1926
Location: Bathurst
BREAD CARTERS
Dates: c. 1941
Location: District Park, Newcastle
Notes: Competed in the Newcastle City Houses and Works Soccer Association.
BRIGHTON UNITED
Dates: c. 1922
Location: Cook's River Park; St George Sportsground
Colours: Black and white shirts
BRITISH AUSTRALIAN LEAD MANUFACTURERS (B.A.L.M.)
Dates: c. 1929
Location: B.A.L.M. Ground, Cabarita
Notes: BALM was a paint manufacturer.
BROADMEADOW ROYAL ARTHURS
Dates: c. 1907
Location: Broadmeadow
BROADMEADOW
Dates: 1897
Location: Show Ground, Broadmeadow
Colours: Black and gold shirts
Titles/Honours: Newcastle Premiership 1904; Gardiner Cup 1907
BROKEN HILL
Dates: 1912
Location: Goal Reserve; Alma Oval
Notes: Broken Hill were the first winners of the local competition.
BROKEN HILL CALEDONIANS
Dates: 1914
Location: Broken Hill
BROKEN HILL EX-SERVICEMEN
Dates: 1946
Location: Broken Hill
BROKEN HILL ROVERS
Dates: c. 1930
Location: Broken Hill
BROKEN HILL UNITED
Dates: c. 1946
Location: Proprietary Dam, Broken Hill
Titles/Honours: Middleton Cup 1946-1947; De Nicolo Cup 1948

BROUGHTON CREEK
Dates: 1884
Location: Broughton Creek
Notes: The South Coast town of Broughton Creek changed its name to Berry in 1889.
BULLI
Dates: 1887; 1901-1933
Location: Bulli
Colours: Blue shirts
BULLI SURF CLUB
Dates: c. 1940
Location: Bulli
BULLI-WOONONA
Dates: 1934
Location: Floyd's Park, Bulli
Notes: Bulli-Woonona absorbed the former Woonona club.
BURNS ANNIVERSARY
Dates: 1912
Location: Mascot Park
Colours: Navy blue shirts
BURRINGBAR ROVERS
Dates: c. 1914
Location: Burringbar
BURWOOD COLLIERY
Dates: 1944
Location: Charlestown Oval
Colours: Black and gold halved shirts with white shorts.
BURWOOD FORRESTERS
Dates: 1898
Location: Burwood
BURWOOD UNITED
Dates: 1888
Location: Burwood Park, Newcastle
Colours: Dark blue shirts with a red sash and white shorts; white shirts with green stars (1922)
Titles/Honours: Ellis Cup 1891
Notes: Formerly called Glebe Blackwatch.
BUSDRIVERS
Dates: c. 1939
location: Sydney
BYRON BAY
Dates: 1933
Location: Byron Bay
CABARITA
Dates: c. 1924
Location: Cabarita
CABLE MAKERS AUSTRALIA (C.M.A)
Dates: 1948
Location: Woodwood Park, Liverpool
Colours: Green shirts with dark blue shorts and green and white socks
CABRA-VALE
Dates: c. 1920
Location: Cabra-Vale Park
CABRAMATTA

Dates: c. 1928
Location: Cabramatta Park
Nickname: Cabra

CALEDONIANS
Dates: 1885
Location: Moore Park
Colours: Black and white shirts
Nickname: The Scots
Titles/Honours: Badge Series winners 1885-88; Gardiner Cup 1888
Notes: The patron of Caledonians was Lord Carrington, Governor of New South Wales. The team was comprised of Scottish born players only.

CALEDONIAN CELTIC
Dates: 1927
Location: Mortdale
Notes: Changed name to Mortdale Thistle in 1928

CALEDONIAN SOCIETY
Dates: c. 1930
Location: Newcastle

CALLAN PARK
Dates: c. 1912
Location: Hospital Ground, Callan Park
Colours: Maroon and gold vertical striped shirts

CALLAN PARK CHURCH OF ENGLAND
Dates: c. 1940
Location: Hospital Grounds, Callan Park

CAMDEN
Dates: 1943
Location: Camden Showground; Onslow Park (1944)
Colours: Blue shirts

CAMDEN HAVEN
Dates: c. 1922
Location: Camden Haven

CAMDEN MAGPIES
Dates: c. 1943
Location: Camden Showground
Colours: Black and white shirts

CAMDEN WARATAHS
Dates: c. 1943
Location: Camden Showground

CAMPBELLTOWN
Dates: c. 1940
Location: Campbelltown

CAMPSIE ALBIONS
Dates: c. 1923
Location: Campsie

CAMPSIE THISTLE
Dates: c. 1920
Location: Hospital Ground, Campsie
Colours: Black shirts with white band

CANLEY HEIGHTS
Dates: 1948
Location: Sydney

CANLEY VALE
Dates: c. 1929
Location: Hartley's Oval, Canley Vale

CANN'S SPORTING BLUES
Dates: 1940
Location: District Park, Newcastle
Notes: Played in the Newcastle City Houses and Works Soccer Association competition.

CANOWINDRA
Dates: c. 1928
Location: Canowindra

CANTERBURY
Dates: 1885
Location: Campsie Recreation Ground
Colours: Navy blue shirts; blue and gold striped shirts
Nickname: The 'Burys; Cantabs; Belmore Boys

CANTERBURY-BANKSTOWN
Dates: 1943
Location: Blick Oval, Canterbury
Colours: Black and gold shirts with white shorts and black and gold socks.
Titles/Honours: Priest Cup 1946; State League Cup 1946; Miller Cup 1946

CANTERBURY DISTRICT
Dates: 1910
Location: Canterbury

CANTERBURY-MARRICKVILLE
Dates: 1886; 1943
Location: Arlington Oval, Dulwich Hill, Sydney
Colours: Blue and gold vertically striped shirts with white shorts and blue and gold socks

CANTERBURY PARK ALBIONS
Dates: c. 1920
Location: Leger Reserve, Canterbury Racecourse

CARDIFF
Dates: 1910
Location: Cardiff Park, Cardiff
Colours: Orange shirts with white shorts and orange socks; maroon shirts
Titles/Honours: North Second Division 1948

CARDIFF LOCO
Dates: 1934
Location: Cardiff Park
Notes: An amalgamation of the Cardiff and Loco clubs

CARDIFF LOCO WORKS
Dates: c.1941
Location: District Park, Newcastle
Notes: Played in the Newcastle City Houses and Works Soccer Association
Titles/Honours: *Telegraph* Shield 1928-33

CARDIFF UNITED
Dates: c. 1939
Notes: Club played in the Newcastle Protestant Churches competition.

CARLINGFORD HOSTEL

Dates: c. 1940
Location: St. Hillier's Ground, Auburn
CARLTON
Dates: c. 1919
Notes: Carlton played in the Rechabite competition.
CARLTON KANGAROOS
Dates: c. 1924
Location: Sydney
Notes: This team played in the St George Association competition.
CARLTON METHODIST
Dates: c. 1923
Location: Sydney
CARRINGTON BLACKWATCH
Dates: 1887
Location: Burwood, Newcastle
Colours: Black shirts with a gold sash; red and black shirt.
Notes: Formed by Scottish migrants who worked at the Mosquito Island colliery.
CARPET MANUFACTURERS
Dates: c. 1939
Location: Sydney
Notes: Competed in the City Houses competition in the early 1940's.
CASINO
Dates: c. 1932-1934; c. 1949
Location: Memorial Park, Casino
CASTLE HILLS
Dates: c. 1929
Location: Castle Hills
CASUALS
Dates: c. 1948
Location: Sydney
CATHERINE HILL BAY
Dates: c. 1939
Location: Catherine Hill
Colours: Black and white hooped shirts
Notes: Club played in the Newcastle Protestant Churches competition.
CATHOLIC YOUTH CLUB
Dates: 1945
Location: Fitzroy Flats, Goulburn
Colours: Scarlet and gold shirts
Titles/Honours: League winners 1945; Williams Cup 1945
Notes: Catholic Youth Club, Norths, Railways and Joy Club formed a League in Goulburn in 1945.
CENTENNIALS
Dates: c. 1902
Location: Moore Park
CENTRAL SPORT
Dates: c. 1925
Location: Sydney
CENTRAL TENNIS CLUB
Dates: c. 1940

Location: South Coast
CESSNOCK
Dates: 1906-1936
Location: Cessnock Sports Ground
Colours: Gold shirt with black 'V' with white shorts and black and gold hooped socks
Nickname: The 'Nocks
Titles/Honours: Hampdon Cup 1910; Northern Premiership 1926; State Premiership, 1928-29, State League Premiers 1929: State Cup 1929; Kerr Cup 1923, 1927, Ellis Cup 1927; Hampdon Cup 1910; Stevenson Cup 1927, 1929, 1939
Notes: First called Cessnock Starlights. From 1908 the club was briefly named Cessnock Mountaineers. Merged with Aberdare to form Cessnock Caledonian in 1937.
CESSNOCK CALEDONIAN
Dates: 1937
Location: Cessnock Sports Ground; Pit Paddock
Notes: This club was formed with the merger of the Cessnock and Aberdare clubs.
Titles/Honours: Alliance Cup 1948
CESSNOCK MOUNTAINEERS
Dates: 1908
Location: Cessnock Sports Ground
Notes: Re-named Cessnock in 1909.
CESSNOCK STARLIGHTS
Dates: 1907
Location: Cessnock Sports Ground
Colours: Black shirts with green hoops
Notes: Re-named Cessnock Mountaineers in 1908.
CESSNOCK WEST END
Dates: c. 1922
Location: Cessnock
CHALMERS CITY
Dates: c. 1922
Location: Hurlstone Park
Notes: This club played in the Protestant Churches 'A' Grade competition in 1922.
CHARLESTOWN
Dates: c. 1945
Location: Charlestown
CHARLESTOWN GAMBLERS
Dates: c. 1904
Location: Charlestown
Colours: Black and gold halved shirts with white shorts
CHATSBURY SLATE QUARRY
Dates: 1926-1927
Location: Goulburn
Notes: The team comprised of Welsh miners who originally called their team Dinorwic, after a Welsh mining town.
CHELSEA
Dates: c. 1948
Location: Sydney

CHESTER HILL
Dates: c. 1932
Location: Chester Hill
Titles/Honours: Southern Districts Soccer Football Association Premiers 1934

CHISWICK
Dates: 1915
Location: Chiswick
Notes: Chiswick played in the Club League.

CHRIST CHURCH
Dates: c. 1941
Location: Gladesville
Notes: Played in the Protestant Chrurches Football Association.

CHULLORA LOCO
Dates: c. 1947
Colours: Back and red shirts
Notes: Team from the Signals Branch of the Railways Department.

CHULLORA ELECTRIC CAR SHOP
Dates: 1931
Location: Ibrox Park
Notes: Club was formed within the railway workshop.
Titles/Honours: Telegraph Shield 1934; Toohey's Cup 1934

CHUNG HWA
Dates: 1944
Location: Sydney
Notes: Club consisted of Chinese players

CHURCH OF CHRIST
Dates: c. 1940
Location: Auburn

CITIZENS
Dates: c. 1939-1940
Location: Gladstone Ground, Broken Hill
Notes: Replaced Juventus in senior competition, 1940.

CITY COUNCIL
Dates: 1919
Location: Sydney
Notes: First played Second League soccer in Sydney in 1919.

CLEVELAND UNITED
Dates: c. 1944
Location: Sydney

CLIFFORD LOVE
Dates: c. 1939
Location: Sydney
Nickname: The Cornflour Boys
Notes: Clifford Loved manufactured cereals. The club played in the City Houses Competition.

CLUB ITALIA
Dates: 1937
Location: Easton Park, Sydney
Notes: Club represented the Italian community.

CLYDE ENGINEERING
Dates: 1936-1937
Location: Granville
Notes: Formerly named the Granville club. Renamed Granville in 1938

CLYDE RECREATION CLUB
Dates: c. 1903
Location: Granville
Titles/Honours: Granville Senior Association premiers 1903

COALCLIFF
Dates: c. 1937
Location: Coalcliff
Titles/Honours: Association Premiership 1937
Notes: Competed in the Southern Miners Association competition.

COALDALE SURF CLUB
Dates: c. 1944
Location: Coaldale

COCKATOO NAVAL DOCKYARD
Dates: 1910-1921
Location: Lorrimer's Paddock, Leichhardt; Five Dock; Ibrox Park, Leichhardt
Colours: White shirts with a black shield
Nickname: The Dock; The Dockyarders; The Islanders
Notes: Absorbed many players from the Balmain Kiaora club. The team was re-named Commonwealth Dockyard in 1922.

COCKBURN
Dates: 1913-1913
Location: Cockburn
Notes: Participated in the Broken Hill and District Football Association Championship for only one year.

COCKLE CREEK SULPHIDE WORKS
Dates: c. 1929
Location: Cockle Creek

COFFS HARBOUR
Dates: c. 192
Location: Coffs Harbour

COLEDALE BLUEBELLS
Dates: c. 1911
Location: Thirroul
Colours: Blue and gold shirts; red and blue shirts (1945)
Notes: The initial team largely consisted of Scottish migrants.

COLEDALE
Dates: c. 1940
Location: St James Park, Coledale

COLEDALE MAGPIES
Dates: c. 1913
Location: St James Park, Coledale

COLEDALE SCOTS
Dates: c. 1913
Location: Coledale
Colours: Black shirts with white shorts

COMBOYNE
Dates: 1922
Location: Comboyne

COMMONWEALTH AIRCRAFT FACTORY
Dates: c. 1944
Location: Sydney

COMMMONWEALTH DOCKYARD
Dates: 1922
Location: Ibrox Park
Colours: White shirts

COMMONWEALTH STEEL PRODUCTS
Dates: 1939
Location: District Park, Newcastle
Notes: Played in the Newcastle City Houses and Works Soccer Association competition.

COMRADES
Dates: c. 1913
Location: Newcastle
Notes: Played in the Newcastle Second League

CONCORD
Dates: 1914
Location: Concord

CONCORD CENTRAL
Dates: c. 1930
Location: Edward Park

CONCORD DISTRICT
Dates: 1931; 1936
Location: Concord; Edward Park
Colours: White shirts with a black 'V'

CONCORD PRESBYTERIAN
Dates: c. 1940
Location: Concord

CONCORD SCOTTISH
Dates: 1934
Location: Edward Park; Goddard Park

CONDONG
Dates: c. 1914
Location: Condong

COOLAMON
Dates: 1924-1925
Location: Kindra Park, Wagga
Titles/Honours: Cootamundra Cup 1924-5
Notes: Cootamundra Cup was played between Coolamon, Cootamundra, Temora and Wagga clubs.

COOLAMON CALEDONIAN
Dates: 1926
Location: Coolamon

COOMA
Dates: 1908
Location: Cooma

COOTAMUNDRA
Dates: 1913; 1925; 1949
Location: The Flat; Fisher Park, Cootamundra
Colours: Blue shirt with a white 'V' (1925); blue and white 'halved' shirts with white shorts and blue socks (1949)

CORAKI
Dates: 1911
Location: Coraki

COREEN COLLEGE
Dates: 1881-1882
Location: Woollahra
Notes: Team founded by John Walter Fletcher, founder of the Wanderers club. Fletcher was the headmaster of the school.

CORINTHIANS
Dates: c. 1924
Location: Hopetoun Park

CORRIMAL
Dates: 1891-1940; 1942
Location: Thorne's Paddock (1891); Musgrave's Paddock (1902); Memorial Park (1919); Woonona Oval, Woonona; McCabe Park
Nickname: The Coasters; 'Mals
Colours: Blue shirts (1891); red shirts (1903); Red and white shirts (1923); gold shirts (1929); red and white shirts (1942)
Titles/Honours: Bode's Cup 1892; South Coast Premiers 1906, 1908, 1910-1911; Charity Cup 1911; South Coast Challenge Cup 1911; Nurse Cup 1911; Tooth Cup 1931, 1935; Langridge Cup 1936; Sydney Cup 1942; Gibson Cup 1943; Sheehan Cup 1943; State Premiership 1943; 2nd Division winners 1945; State Cup 1947

CORRIMAL MINERS
Dates: c. 1937
Location: Memorial Park, Corrimal
Titles/Honours: Sneddon Cup 1939
Notes: Played in the Southern Miners Association competition.

CORRIMAL RANGERS
Dates: 1925-1947
Location: Memorial Park, Corrimal
Titles/Honours: State Association Premiers 1943; State League Cup 1947
Colours: Red and white quartered shirts with white shorts
Notes: In 1947 Corrimal Rangers amalgamated with Corrimal Rovers. The new club was called Rangers.

CORRIMAL ROVERS
Dates: c. 1945-1947
Location: Corrimal
Colours: Red and white shirts
Notes: In 1947 Corrimal Rovers amalgamated with Corrimal Rangers to become Rangers club.

CORRIMAL ST ANDREWS
Dates: 1945
Location: Corrimal
Colours: Grey and red shirts

CORRIMAL THISTLES
Dates: c. 1921

COUNCIL UNITED
Dates: 1934
Location: Goulburn
Notes: Players were Depression era council relief workers.

COWRA
Dates: 1926
Location: Cowra
Titles/Honours: Fitzgerald Cup 1927

CRITERION
Dates: 1939
Location: Wagga

C.R.M
Dates: c. 1939
Location: Illawarra

CROMPTON PARKINSON
Dates: c. 1940
Location: Sydney
Notes: Crompton Parkinson manufactured electrical goods. The club competed in the City Houses competition in the early 1940's.

CRONULLA
Dates: 1923
Location: Woolooware Oval, North Cronulla
Colours: White shirt with a blue collar

CRONULLA WARATAH
Dates: c. 1932
Location: Cronulla

CROOKWELL
Dates: c. 1924
Location: Crookwell Park Oval

CROYDON BAPTISTS
Dates: c. 1932
Location: Croydon

CRESCENT
Dates: c. 1903
Location: Auburn
Notes: Crescent played in the Granville competition.

CULLEN BULLEN
Dates: 1925
Location: Cullen Bullen
Colours: Maroon shirts

CULLEN RANGERS
Dates: 1915
Location: Cullen Bullen

CUMBERLAND
Dates: c. 1910
Location: Cumberland
Notes: Cumberland played in the Granville Association competition.

CUMBERLAND UNITED
Dates: c. 1949
Location: Sydney
Colours: Red and white shirts

D. COHEN LTD
Dates: 1939
Location: District Park, Newcastle
Titles/Honours: J.G. Arthur Cup 1939
Notes: Played in the Newcastle City Houses and Works Soccer Association.

DACEYVILLE ROVERS
Dates: c. 1925
Location: Daceyville

DAPTO
Dates: 1894; 1929
Location: Reed Park, Dapto
Colours: Royal blue shirts; blue and gold shirts (1923)
Titles/Honours: Division II Champions of Illawarra District 1929

DAVID JONES
Dates: c. 1947
Location: Lukes Park, Burwood
Notes: Club of the David Jones department store.

DEE WHY
Dates: c. 1926
Location: Duncum's Reserve, Dee Why
Colours: Blue and yellow shirts

DE BAVAY
Dates: c. 1914
Location: Newmarket Ground, Broken Hill

DE HAVILIAND
Dates: c. 1938.
Location: Sydney
Notes: De Havilland was the works team of the De Havilland aircraft firm.

DENVRIERE WELSH
Dates: 1926
Location: Chatsbury
Notes: Club of the NSW Slate Company, Chatsbury colliery.

DISTRICT UNEMPLOYED ASSOCIATION
Dates: c. 1933
Location: Lithgow

DOONSIDE
Dates: 1935
Location: Doonside
Titles/Honours: Granville District Competition winners 1935.

DRAKE, HMS
Dates: 1912
Location: Lyne Park, Rose Bay
Notes: HMS *Drake* replaced HMS *Powerful* as the British naval entry in the Sydney First League Rawson Cup Association competition.

DOWLING STREET DEPOT
Dates: c. 1924
Location: Domain Ground
Colours: Black shirts
Notes: Club was a member of the Tramway League.

DRUMMOYNE

Dates: 1913; 1943
Location: Blick Oval; Drummoyne Oval; Lambert Park (1949)
Colours: Black and white striped shirts; gold shirts with white shorts (1947); red and blue shirts (1949)
Nickname: *The Drums*
Titles/Honours: Metropolitan League Premiers 1945

DRUMMOYNE SCOTS
Dates: c. 1942
Location: Drummoyne

DUBBO
Dates: 1930
Location: White Bridge Ground, Dubbo
Colours: Royal blue shirts and white shorts
Nickname: *Old Contemptibles*
Titles/Honours: Hilda Ott Trophy 1930; Power Cup 1931.

DUBBO AND DISTRICT
Dates: 1930
Location: White Bridge Recreation Ground, Dubbo
Colours: Red shirts with white shorts
Notes: Changed name to Macquarie District in 1931
Titles/Honours: Hilda Ott Cup 1930

DUDLEY ATHLETIC
Dates: 1896
Location: Ocean View Park
Colours: Black shirt with a white collar (1947)

DUDLEY THISTLES
Dates: c. 1923
Location: Dudley
Colours: Black and white shirts
Titles/Honours: State Premiership 1944; Sheahan Cup 1944; Newcastle Cup winners 1948

DUDLEY-WHITEBRIDGE
Dates: 1941
Location: Ocean View Park, Dudley
Colours: Black shirts with white trim
Titles/Honours: Alan Burns competition winners 1942; Sheahan Cup 1944; State Alliance Cup 1946
Notes: A one year amalgamation of the Dudley and Whitebridge clubs

DULWICH HILL UNITED
Dates: 1919
Location: Crescent Oval, Dulwich Hill
Colours: Black shirts with white stripes; black and gold vertical striped shirts (1923)
Titles/ Honours: Charity Cup 1920

DULWICH HILL BAPTISTS
Dates: c. 1914
Location: Dulwich Hill
Colours: Maroon shirts

Nickname: *Dulie*
Notes: This club played in the Protestant Churches 'A' Grade competition.

DULWICH HILL SCOTTISH
Dates: c. 1936
Location: Dulwich

DUNDAS
Dates: c. 1929
Location: Dundas
Nickname: *The Rosebuds*

DUNLOP PERDRIAU
Dates: c. 1937
Location: Gladesville Sports Ground
Nickname: *Dunperd*
Colours: Green and blue shirts
Notes: The works team of the tyre company. Played 'A' grade in the City Houses Association in 1938.

DUNOON
Dates: 1914
Location: Dunoon, Northern Rivers

DUNGOG
Dates: c. 1920
Location: Dungog

DUTCH EAST INDIES
Dates: 1944
Location: Sydney
Notes: Most players were Indonesian. The club competed in the NSW Minor League.

DYRAABA
Dates: 1932
Location: Dyraaba

EARLS
Dates: c. 1928
Location: Rydalmere

EARLWOOD
Dates: c. 1939
Location: Earlwood

EARLWOOD WANDERERS
Dates: 1946
Location: Earlwood Oval, Earlwood
Colours: Black and yellow striped shirts with black shorts

EAST ARMIDALE
Dates: c. 1932
Location: Armidale

EAST GRETA
Dates: 1896-1903; 1913
Location: Greta
Colours: Black shirts with gold hoops
Notes: In 1903 East Greta joined with the new club of Heddon Greta.

EAST LAMBTON RANGERS
Dates: 1933
Location: East Lambton
Colours: Blue and gold shirts
Titles/Honours: Bargain Arcade Cup 1934

EASTERN SUBURBS
Dates: 1918
Location: Centennial Park; Sydney Cricket Ground
Colours: Red, white and blue shirts
Notes: Most players were from the Rose of Denmark Lodge.

EASTWOOD UNITED
Dates: 1949
Location: Richards Oval, Lismore
Colours: Red and white shirts

EAST SYDNEY
Dates: 1903-1908
Location: Epping Grounds; Sydney Cricket Ground No. 2
Colours: Blue shirts with red sleeves and white cuffs and collar
Notes: Club became Sydney District.

EGG BOARD
Dates: 1941
Location: District Park, Newcastle
Notes: Played in the Newcastle City Houses and Works Soccer Association.

ELECTRIC LAMP MANUFACTURERS
Dates: 1939
Location: District Park, Newcastle
Notes: Played in the Newcastle City Houses and Works Soccer Association.

ELECTRIC SUPPLY DEPARTMENT
Dates: 1939
Location: District Park, Newcastle
Notes: Played in the Newcastle City Houses and Works Soccer Association.

ELLANONG
Dates; 1926
Location: Ellanong

ELONG ELONG
Dates: c. 1930
Location: Elong

EMBROYOS
Dates: 1885
Location: Newcastle

E.R. & S.
Dates: c. 1945
Location: Wollongong
Colours: White shirts

ERMINGTON ROSEBUDS
Dates: c. 1929
Location: Dundas

ERSKINEVILLE HOLY TRINITY
Dates: c. 1947
Location: Erskinville

ERSKINEVILLE ROVERS
Dates: c. 1939
Location: Erskineville
Notes: Competed in the St George Association competition.

ERSKINEVILLE WARATAH
Dates: c. 1898
Location: Erskineville Oval

EUCHAREENA
Dates: c. 1932
Location: Recreation Ground, Euchareena

EXCELSIOR MINERS LODGE
Dates: c. 1939
Location: South Coast
Notes: Competed in the Southern Miners Association competition.

EXETER
Dates: c. 1929
Location: Exeter

EX-IMPERIAL
Dates: 1946
Location: Sydney Cricket Ground No. 2
Colours: Blue shirts
Notes: Club consisted of British players.

F. ASH LTD
Dates: 1941
Location: District Park, Newcastle
Notes: Played in the Newcastle City Houses and Works Soccer Association competition.

FAIRFIELD
Dates: 1910; 1922; 1930
Location: Fairfield
Colours: Blue and white shirts (1930)
Titles/Honours: SDSA Premiers 1931, 1933; Challenge Cup 1931

FAIRFIELD COMBINED
Dates: c. 1947
Location: Fairfield Park
Titles/Honours: Southern District Champions 1947

FAIRFIELD RSL
Dates: c. 1947
Location: Knight Park, Fairfield

FAIRFIELD UNITED
Dates: 1946
Location: Knight Park, Fairfield
Colours: Black and white halved shirts

FAIRY MEADOW
Dates: c. 1945
Location: Fairy Meadow
Titles/Honours: South Coast Premiership 1945

FAIRY MEADOW ROSEBUDS
Dates: c. 1913
Location: Fairy Meadow
Colours: Red and green shirts

FEDERAL
Dates: c. 1932
Location: Federal
Colours: Black and white shirts
Titles/Honours: Northern Rivers District Football Association Premiers 1932

FERNDALE

Dates: c. 1920
Location: John Street
Notes: Ferndale played in the Granville Association.
FERNHILL UNITED
Dates: 1925
Location: Fernhill, Illawarra
Nickname: The 'Hills
FIRE BRIGADE
Dates: 1939
Location: Duke of Kent Park, Wagga
Colours: Red shirts with dark blue shorts and red socks with blue tops.
FIRE BRIGADES
Dates: c. 1923
Location: Mascot
FITZROY
Dates c. 1935
Location: Sydney
FIVE DOCK METHODIST
Dates: c. 1923
Location: The Flat
FLINDERS
Dates: c. 1909
Location: Bode's Ground, Wollongong
Colours: Black and gold shirts
FORD
Dates: 1942
Location: Sydney
Notes: Works team of Ford Motor Company. Competed in Granville Association competition.
FOREST HILL
Dates: c. 1945
Location: Forest Hill
FORT MACQUARIE DEPOT
Dates: c. 1924
Location: Sydney
Colours: Maroon and gold shirts
Nickname: Fort Mac
Notes: Club was a member of the Tramway League.
4/3 BATTALION
Dates: 1935
Location: Sydney
FREDERICK ASH PTY LTD
Dates: c. 1939
Location: Newcastle
Colours: Cream and green shirts
Titles/Honours: Wakely Cup, Newcastle Houses 'B' grade Premiers 1940
Notes: This club represented a hardware manufacturer.
FROGHOLLOW
Dates: 1941-1942
Location: Wollongong
Nickname: 'Hollow
Notes: Club was renamed Woonona Rovers in 1943.

GARDEN ISLAND
Dates: 1908-1912; 1922
Location: Crescent Oval; Lyne Park, Sydney
Nickname: The Sailors: The Islanders
Colours: Royal blue shirts
GAS COMPANY
Dates: c. 1947
Location: Sydney
GENERAL ELECTRIC COMPANY
Dates: 1940
Location: Auburn
GERRINGONG
Dates: c. 1922
Location: Gerringong
GILGANDRA
Dates: 1929
Location: Recreation Ground, Gilgandra
Colours: White shirts
Nickname: The Gils
GLADESVILLE
Dates: c. 1912
Location: Brereton Park, Sydney
Colours: Maroon shirts; Black and gold striped shirts
Nickname: The 'Villes
Titles/Honours: Southern Premiership 1920
GLADESVILLE HOSPITAL
Dates: c. 1912
Location: Gladesville Hospital
Colours: Black and red vertical striped shirts (1922)
GLADESVILLE PRESBYTERIAN
Dates: c. 1932
Location: Gladesville
GLADESVILLE-RYDE
Dates: 1924
Location: Gladesville Sports Ground, Sydney
Colours: White shirts; yellow shirts with a black 'V' and black shorts; white shirts (1949)
Nickname: The Jockeys; 'Villes
Titles/Honours: Cronin Cup 1925-6; Metropolitan Knock-Out Cup 1925-6; Gardiner Cup 1927; Sunlight Cup 1927
GLEBE
Dates: 1900 - 1914
Location: Glebe, Sydney
Colours: Red shirts
Titles/Honours: Metropolitan Series winners 1908, 1910: Gardiner Cup 1906; Rawson Cup 1908, 1910
GLEBE ARCADIA
Dates: c. 1922
Location: Glebe
GLEBE BLACK WATCH
Dates: 1885
Location: Glebe
Notes: Changed name to Burwood United in 1887.

GLEBE UNITED
Dates: c. 1914
Location: Jubilee Park
Notes: Played Second League soccer in Sydney from 1919.

GLEBE WANDERERS
Dates: 1946
Location: Wentworth Park, Glebe
Colours: Blue shirts

GLEN DAVIS
Dates: 1939
Location: Glen Davis

GLEN INNES
Dates: 1920
Location: Showground, Glen Innes

GLENFIELD
Dates: 1936
Location: Glenfield Park

GLOBE WORSTED MILLS
Dates: c. 1937
Location: Sydney
Colours: Green shirts with a gold 'V' and gold cuffs.
Titles/Honours: First Division Premiership - Sydney District League 1941
Notes: Works team of a woolen mill located in Marrickville. Played in the Sydney and District League in 1938.

***GOLDEN HIND*, HMS**
Dates: 1939-1945
Location: Sydney Cricket Ground No 2 Oval (1945)
Colours: White shirt with blue collars and cuffs with a commodore flag on breast. Blue socks with white tops
Notes: Players were Royal Marines from the British ship. The team was admitted in the First Division in 1945. The ship left Australia at the end of the season.

GOODYEAR
Dates: 1934-1940
Location: Lidcombe Oval, Sydney
Colours: Blue and gold shirts
Nickname: The Tyre Boys
Titles/Honours: State Champion 1937-1939
Notes: Factory team of the Goodyear Tyre Company.

GOOLGOWI
Dates: 1927
Location: Goolgowi

GOONELLABAH STARS
Dates: 1949
Location: Goonellabah

GORDON MARR
Dates: c. 1939
Location: Gladesville Sports Ground
Notes: An engineering company. Works team took part in the City Houses Competition.

GOSFORD UNITED
Dates: 1924
Location: Gosford

GOULBURN
Dates: 1913; 1921; 1934
Location: North Goulburn Park
Colours: Black and gold shirts

GOULBURN AMATEUR SWIMMING CLUB
Dates: 1948
Location: Fitzroy Flats, Goulburn

GOULBURN CALEDONIAN
Dates: 1924-1925
Location: Victoria Park, Goulburn
Nickname: The Scotties

GOULBURN CITY
Dates: 1946
Location: North Goulburn Flat, Goulburn

GOULBURN RAILWAY
Dates: 1922
Location: North Goulburn Park
Colours: Black and gold shirts
Notes: Successor club to Goulburn Rovers.

GOULBURN ROVERS
Dates: 1913-1921
Location: Goulburn
Colours: Black and amber shirts with black shorts

GOULBURN SOUTH
Dates: c. 1934
Location: Goulburn

GOULBURN WEST
Dates: c. 1934
Location: Goulburn

GOULBURN WOOLEN MILLS
Dates: 1924
Location: Goulburn
Nickname: The Woolies

GRACE BROTHERS
Dates: c. 1944
Location: Gladesville Sports Ground
Colours: Green and gold shirts
Titles/Honours: St Peters Cup 1938
Notes: A prominent department store in Sydney. They absorbed some Auburn players in 1944.

GRAFTON CITY
Dates: 1933
Location: Grafton
Colours: Blue and white vertically striped shirts
Location: Fisher Park, Grafton

GRANVILLE
Dates: 1885-1936 ; 1938
Location: Clyde Oval ; Lidcombe Oval (1943) ; Colquhoun Park ; Garside Park, Granville ; MacArthur Park (1949)
Colours: White shirts with a blue star (1886); Black and white striped shirts with black shorts and black socks with white tops

Nickname: The Magpies; Clydesiders
Titles/Honours: Rainsford Trophy 1885-86; Metropolitan Premiership 1904, 1914-1915, 1923-1926; Gardiner Cup 1904, 1914, 1922; State Championship 1904, 1914, 1922; Lincoln Cup 1923; Sydney Cup 1933, 1941, 1948; Miller Cup 1948
Notes: Club was formed by iron workers from the Clyde Engineering Works. Most original players hailed from Ayrshire. Named Granville-Clyde in the late 1930's and then Clyde Engineering in 1936-1937. Granville did not compete in the years 1917-1918 due to the exigencies of WWI.

GRANVILLE BAPTIST
Dates: c. 1940
Location: Granville
Titles/Honours: Protestant churches competition 3rd Grade 'F' Division winners 1940'

GRANVILLE CALEDONIAN
Dates: c. 1923
Location: Granville

GRANVILLE CENTRALS
Dates: c. 1931
Location: Granville
Titles/Honours: Argus Cup 1931; Cottam Cup 1932

GRANVILLE - CLYDE
Dates: c. 1937 - c. 1939
Location: Granville
Nickname: The Magpies
Notes: Formerly the Granville club'

GRANVILLE DISTRICT
Dates: 1924
Location: Granville

GRANVILLE HOLROYD
Dates: 1919
Location: Granville
Notes: Sydney Second League soccer from 1919.

GRANVILLE PIRATES
Dates: c. 1913
Location: Granville

GRANVILLE RANGERS
Dates: c. 1920
Location: Granville
Colours: Black and white shirts

GRANVILLE SHAMROCK
Dates: c. 1903
Location: Harvey's Ground; Berry Street, Granville
Notes: Shamrock played in the Granville competition.
Titles/Honours: GDFA Shield 1940; Angus Cup 1940

GRANVILLE TWO BLUES
Dates: c. 1921

Location: Granville
Colours: Light and dark blue shirts

GREEN GROCERS
Dates: 1940
Location: District Park, Newcastle
Titles/Honours: Second division 'A' section winners 1941
Notes: Played in the Newcastle City Houses and Works Soccer Association.

GRETA BLACKWATCH
Dates: 1887-1888
Location: Greta
Notes: Players were from the Mosquito Colliery.

GRETA BLUEBELLS
Dates: 1886-1891
Location: Greta Park
Colours: White shirts with a blue sash

GRETA CAMEOS
Dates: 1900
Location: Greta

GRETA MAIN
Dates: c. 1947
Location: Greta

GREYSTANES
Dates: c. 1929
Location: Greystanes

GRIFFITH
Dates: 1924; 1931
Location: Rural School Ground, Griffith
Colours: Two blues (light and dark) quartered shirts; black shirts with white shorts and black socks (1926)
Titles/Honours: MIA Championship 1925; Bacon Cup (regional championship) 1925

GUILDFORD CONGREGATIONAL CHURCH
Dates: c. 1930
Location: Guildford

GUILDFORD UNITED
Dates: 1932-1934; 1948
Location: Yennora; Guildford Park
Colours: Blue shirts; blue and gold shirts (1949)
Titles/Honours: SDSA Premiers 1932; Knock-out Cup winners 1932-3; Granville Association Metropolitan Premiers 1948

GUILDFORD WANDERERS
Dates: c. 1932
Location: Guildford Park

GUNDAROO
Dates: 1933
Location: Gundaroo
Notes: Club played in the Australian Capital Territory competition.

GUNNNEDAH
Dates: c. 1921
Location: Gunnedah
Titles/Honours: New England Cup 1924; Challenge Cup 1926

GULLY LINE MAGPIES
Dates: c. 1932
Location: Adamstown
Colours: Black and white shirts
Titles/Honours: Farr's Market Cup 1933; Referee Cup 1933; Martin Hassett Cup 1933

GUNNEDAH
Dates: c. 1925
Location: Gunnedah

GWYNNEVILLE
Dates: c. 1926
Location: Bode's Ground; Wiseman Park

HAKOAH
Dates: 1939-
Location: Wentworth Park, Glebe
Colours: Sky blue shirts with white shorts and blue and white socks
Notes: One of the first 'ethnic' clubs to be formed in Sydney.

HAMILTON
Dates: 1931
Location: Tramway Ground, Hamilton

HAMILTON ATHLETIC
Dates: 1886-1891; 1901-1923
Location: Hamilton, Newcastle region.
Colours: White shirts with a blue sash; red and white shirts (1919)
Titles/Honours: Rainsford Trophy 1887
Notes: The club disbanded when the coal trade waned. Many players transferred to Carrington Blackwatch and Adamstown.

HAMILTON METHODIST
Dates: 1924
Location: Hamilton
Notes: Played in the Newcastle Protestant Churches competition.

HAMILTON NORTH
Dates: c. 1927
Location: Hamilton
Notes: Club changed name to Hamilton Rovers in 1943.

HAMILTON ROVERS
Dates: c. 1933
Location: Hamilton
Notes: Previously the Hamilton North club. In 1948 Hamilton Rovers combined with New Lambton to form New Lambton-Hamilton Rovers.

HAMPTON IRONSIDES
Dates: c. 1912
Location: Hampton

HANWOOD
Dates: 1924
Location: Hanwood Oval
Notes: Hanwood withdrew from the Murrumbidgee Irrigation Area competition after the 1924 season.

HARDEN IMPERIALS
Dates: c. 1913
Location: Harden

HARDEN RAILWAY
Dates: c. 1924
Location: Harden

HARDYS LTD
Dates: 1925
Location: Bolton Park, Wagga
Colours: Black and white shirts
Titles/Honours: Wagga District Soccer Association Champions 1925, 1927-8; Hardy Cup 1927-1928; Maples Cup 1927-1928
Notes: Hardy's Ltd was a building company.

HARDY'S HOTSPURS
Dates; 1926
Location: Bolton Park, Wagga
Notes: Sponsored by Hardy's Limited.

HARRIS PARK
Dates: c. 1918
Location: Harris Park

HARTLEY VALE
Dates: 1892
Location: Hartley Vale, Blue Mountains region

HAWKESBURY AGRICULTURAL COLLEGE
Dates: c. 1922
Location: Richmond

HEATON
Dates: c. 1928-1930
Location: Heaton

HEBBURN
Dates: 1918- 1921
Location: Hebburn
Colours: Light blue shirt with a yellow star on the left breast

HEDDON GRETA
Dates: 1904-1906
Location: Greta, Hunter region
Colours: White shirts with a black ribbon

HEDDON GRETA ROOKS
Dates: 1906-1909
Location: Greta
Colours: White shirts with a yellow sash

HELENSBURGH ROVERS
Dates: 1890-1909; 1913
Location: Helensburgh, Illawarra region
Colours: Black and gold shirts with black shorts
Nickname: The 'Burghs
Titles/Honours: South Coast Final Winners 1893, 1903

HELENSBURGH TOWN
Dates: c. 1914
Location: Helensburgh
Titles/Honours: Metropolitan Premiers 1928; Tooth Cup 1930

HELENSBURGH WANDERERS
Dates: c. 1914
Location: Helensburgh

HILL END
Dates: c. 1914
Location: Hill End
HILLS DISTRICT
Dates: c. 1939
Location: Hills District
HILLSIDE
Dates: c. 1929
Location: Hillside
Colours: Blue shirts with white shorts
HOLMESVILLE
Dates: c. 1918
Location: Newcastle Show Ground
Colours: Black and gold shirts
Titles/Honours: 3rd Grade Premiership 1925
HOLMESVILLE STARS
Dates: c. 1906
Location: Holmesville
Colours: Black and gold shirts
HOLROYD
Dates: c. 1910
Location: Granville Park No. 1
HOLROYD UNITED
Dates: c. 1920
Location: Granville Park
Colours: Red and white shirts
HONEYSUCKLE
Dates: c. 1925
Location: Newcastle
HORDERNIANS
Dates: c. 1924
Location: Lambert Park
Nickname: The Counter Jumpers
Notes: Club side of the Anthony Hordern department store.
HORNSBY ATHLETIC
Dates: 1921
Location: Wahroonga Grammar School; Waitara Oval (1923)
Colours: Blue shirts
Notes: Joined Sydney Metropolitan Second League in 1921.
HUGHES POTTERIES
Dates: 1939
Location: District Park, Newcastle
Notes: Played in the Newcastle City Houses and Works Soccer Association.
HUME PIPE
Dates: c. 1938
Location: Darcy Park
Notes: Works team of the Hume Pipe Company.
HURLSTONE PARK METHODISTS
Dates: c. 1922
Location: Hurlstone Park
HURLSTONE PARK WANDERERS
Dates: 1924

Location: Hurlstone Park Reserve (Ewen Park)
Colours: Blue and white striped shirts
HURSTVILLE FELLOWSHIP
Dates: c. 1913
Location: Hurstville
HURSTVILLE RECHABITES
Dates: c. 1917-1920
Location: Hurstville
HURSTVILLE UNITED
Dates: c. 1920
Location: Dumbleton Park
Colours: Maroon and gold shirts
ILLAWARRA ROVERS
Dates: 1888
Location: Scarborough Park Illawarra (1945)
Notes: Formerly name St George Soccer Club. Absorbed the Kogarah Rovers club in 1946.
ILLAWARRA TROJANS
Dates: c. 1939
Location: South Coast
INCH STREET
Dates: c. 1942
Location: Lithgow
Titles/Honours: WDSA 2nd Division premiers 1941
INVERELL
Dates: c. 1921
Location: Inverell
INVICTA
Dates: 1935
Location: Pottery Green, Lane Cove
ISLINGTON
Dates: 1924
Location: Wickham Park
ITALIAN CLUB
Dates: c. 1939
Location: Sydney
JENOLAN CAVES BLUE STARS
Dates: c. 1914
Location: Lithgow Region
JERRIGONG
Dates: 1922
Location: Jerrigong
JERVIS BAY
Dates: 1922
Location: Jervis Bay
JESMOND METHODIST
Dates: c. 1939
Location: Jesmond
Notes: Club played in the Newcastle Protestant Churches competition.
JESMOND RANGERS
Dates: c. 1922
Location: Jesmond
Colours: Gold and black quartered shirts
JEWISH CLUB

Dates: 1931
Location: Sydney
Colours: Blue shirts
Nickname: *The Blues*
Notes: Club played in the Judean League.

JOADJA CREEK SOUTHERN CROSS
Dates: 1887
Location: Joadja, South Coast, NSW
Titles/Honours: Atkinson Price Challenge Cup 1887; Finalist Gardiner Cup 1887
Notes: Club was formed by Scottish miners who mined shale oil for kerosene.

JESMOND move to p251 after Jervis Bay
Dates: c. 1925
Location: Jesmond
Colours: Yellow and black squared shirts (1927)

JOLLY BOYS
Dates: 1931
Location: Waratah
Notes: Players were from the Waratah-Mayfield Unemployed Association.

JOY CLUB
Dates: 1945
Location: Fitzroy Flats, Goulburn

JUDEAN ATHLETIC CLUB
Dates: c. 1927
Location: Moore Park

JUDEAN WARATAHS
Dates: 1928
Location: Moore Park
Colours: Royal blue shirts with a white 'V' neck

JUNEE
Dates: c. 1924
Location: Junee, Riverina region

JUNEE INSTITUTE
Dates: c. 1947
Location: Junee

JUVENTUS
Dates: 1940
Location: Broken Hill
Notes: Club exited competition mid-season.

KADIMAH
Dates: 1934
Location: Canterbury
Notes: Kadimah played in the Judean League. Kadima means 'forward' in Hebrew.

KAHIBAH
Dates: 1925- c. 1931
Location: Kahibah

KANDOS WANDERERS
Dates: 1923
Location: Kandos Cement Works Sports Ground.
Notes: Played in Lithgow competition. Club sponsored by the Kandos Cement Company.

KANGAROO VALLEY
Dates: 1922
Location: Kangaroo Valley, Illawarra Region

KAPOOKA
Dates: c. 1945
Location: Wagga
Notes: Players were soldiers from the army base. Team played in the Wagga Soccer Association competition.

KATOOMBA
Dates: 1923-1926
Location: Falls Reserve, Blue Mountains
Colours: Black and white shirts
Nickname: *The Kays*
Titles/Honours: Lloyd Cup 1924

KATOOMBA COLLEGE
Dates: 1885
Location: Katoomba, Blue Mountains Region
Notes: Club was founded by J.W. Fletcher, who was the headmaster of Katoomba College. Competed in the Southern British Football Association Cup in 1886.

KEARSLEY
Dates: 1924-1927; 1937-1948
Location: Kearsley Park
Titles/Honours: South Maitland champions 1941

KEIRA
Dates: c. 1937
Location: Keira
Notes: Played in the Southern Miners Association competition.

KEIRAVILLE
Dates: c. 1917
Location: Keiraville

KEMBLA
Dates: c. 1937
Location: Port Kembla
Notes: Played in the Southern Miners Association competition.

KEMBLAWARRA
Dates: 1939
Location: Kemblawarra

KEMPSEY
Dates: c. 1949
Location: Kempsey

KENMORE HOSPITAL
Dates: c. 1922
Location: Goulburn

KENTUCKY
Dates: c. 1920
Location: Kentucky, New England region

KEWPIES
Dates: c. 1920-1939; 1941
Location: Colquehoun Parkt
Colours: Black shirts
Honours/Titles: Granville District Association winners 1938-39

KIAMA
Dates: 1922
Location: Kiama, Illawarra Region

THE FOUNDATION YEARS 1859-1949

KILLINGSWORTH VIOLETS
Dates: c. 1907
Location: Killingsworth
Nickname: The Kills
Colours: Blue and gold shirts

KITCHENS
Dates: c. 1939
Location: Hordernians Sports Ground
Nickname: The Soapies
Notes: Kitchens were a soap manufacturer. The club played in the Sydney City Houses Association competition.

KLONDYKE COLLLIERY
Dates: c. 1942
Location: Blackstone, North Ipswich

KOGARAH ATHLETIC
Dates: c. 1922
Location: Dillon's Reserve, Ramsgate
Colours: Blue and white shirts

KOGARAH DISTRICT
Dates: c. 1912
Location: Moorefield

KOGARAH-HURSTVILLE
Dates: c. 1912
Location: Penshurst

KOGARAH RANGERS
Dates: c. 1938
Location: Kogarah

KOGARAH RECHABITES
Dates: c. 1919
Location: Kogorah

KOGARAH ROVERS
Dates: c. 1941-1945
Location: Kogarah
Notes: Was absorbed by the Illawarra Rovers club in 1946.

KOGARAH YOUNG MEN'S INSTITUTE
Dates: c. 1926
Location: Kogarah
Colours: Maroon and gold shirts

KRAGINE RANGERS
Dates: c. 1949
Location: Kragine

KURRI KURRI
Dates: 1904
Location: Central Park, Kurri Kurri; Gould Park (1931): Drill Hall (1936)
Colours: White shirts; green and white shirts; red, white and blue vertical striped shirts with white shorts and red socks with blue tops (1919); royal blue (c. 1929); red, white and blue shirts with white shorts (1932)
Nickname: The Cooks; Tricolours; Blue Brigade
Titles/Honours: Runner up State premiership 1929; Maitland Premiership 1943, Stevenson Cup 1923, 1928, 1935, 1943-1944.
Notes: First part time professional club from Northern New South Wales in 1929. Kurri Kurri and Weston were derby competitors.

KURRI KURRI COOPERATIVE SOCIETY
Dates: 1940
Location: District Park, Newcastle
Notes: Competed in the Newcastle City Houses and Works Soccer Association.

KURRI NORTH
Dates: 1923
Location: Kurri

KYOGLE
Dates: 1933
Location: Kyogle

LACHLAN RANGERS
Dates: 1920
Location: Waterloo Oval
Colours: Royal blue shirts with a gold sash
Notes: This club played in the Protestant Churches 'A' Grade competition in 1922.
Titles/Honours: PCSFA First Grade champions 1921, 1922. In 1923 the club entered the Senior Competition.

LADYSMITH
Dates: 1927
Location: Bolton Park, Wagga Wagga
Colours: White shirts and shorts with blue and red socks
Titles/Honours: Maples Charity Shield 1930

LAKE MACQUARIE
Dates: 1912; 1938
Location: Cardiff; Speers Point Oval
Colours: White shirts with white shorts and white socks; blue and gold quarters with white shorts (1947)
Nickname: The Lakesiders
Titles/Honours: Newcastle Cup 1946; Northern Premiership 1947; State Premiership 1947; O'Brien Shield 1947
Notes: Lake Macquarie was admitted to the NSW State Soccer League in 1941.

LAKE VIEW
Dates: c. 1925
Location: Griffith
Notes: Successor to the Boolaroo club (1912) and Speers Point club (1932).

LAKEMBA CONGREGATIONAL
Dates: 1921
Location: Lakemba
Colours: Red and white shirts
Notes: This club played in the Protestant Churches "A" Grade competition.

LAKEMBA METHODIST
Dates: c. 1922
Location: Sydney
Nickname: The Lakes
Notes: This club played in the Protestant Churches 'A' Grade competition in 1922.

LAMBTON THISTLES
Dates: 1885
Location: Lambton
LANCASHIRE BROTHERHOOD
Dates: 1923
Location: Sydney
LANCASHIRE SOCIETY
Dates: c. 1913 -1922
Location: Riverside Park, Marrickville; Sports Ground; North Sydney Oval
Colours: Maroon shirts
Nickname: The Immigrants
Titles/Honours: Dewar Cup 1914
LANE COVE
Dates: c. 1920
Location: Tantillion Park
LANES LTD
Dates: c. 1941
Location: Newcastle
Titles/Honours: Hotel Bennett Cup 1941
Notes: Played in the Newcastle City Houses and Works Soccer Association competition.
LANAWANNA
Dates: c. 1923
Location: Lanawanna
LANGLEA
Dates: c. 1919
Location: Langlea
Notes: Langlea played in the Rechabite competition.
LANSVALE
Dates: c. 1946
Location: J. Hartley's Oval, Lansvale (1947)
Colours: Royal blue and gold shirts
LEETON
Dates: 1924
Location: Nursery Paddock, Leeton; Leeton Associated Football Ground (1930)
Titles/Honours: Area Competition Winners 1924; Bacon Cup 1925; Maple Charity Shield 1926, 1931-2; Southern Districts Challenge Cup 1927
LEGION SERVICEMEN
Dates: 1946
Location: Gladstone Ground, Broken Hill
Notes: Clubs was also referred to as Ex-Servicemen.
LEICHHARDT
Dates: 1923
Location: Leichhardt, Sydney
Colours: White shirts; blue shirts (1949)
Titles/Honours: Sheahan Cup 1942; State League Cup 1943
LEICHHARDT-ANNANDALE
Dates: c. 1936
Location: Lambert Park, Sydney
Colours: Red shirts with white shorts and red and white hooped socks (1947)
Nickname: The 'Hardts; Dales
Honours/Titles: State League Premiers 1946, 1949; State Association Cup 1941; State League Cup 1943, 1948, 1949; Southern Premiership 1942; 1947; Sheahan Cup 1942; Priest Cup 1947; O'Brien Shield 1948
LEICHHARDT METHODIST
Dates: c. 1932
Location: Leichhardt
Titles/Honours: Protestant Churches Competition Premiers 1932
LEICHHARDT ROYALS
Dates: c. 1938
Location: Leichhardt
LEICHHARDT SWIMMERS
Dates: c. 1939
Location: Leichhardt
LEICHHARDT WARATAHS
Dates: c. 1936
Location: Easton Park
LEURA
Dates: c. 1923
Location: Leura
LGT ROVERS
Location: Wallsend
Dates: 1932
Colours: Red shirts
Notes: LGT was a club patron.
LIDCOMBE
Dates: 1923
Location: John St, Lidcombe
Colours: Light blue and dark blue shirts; scarlet shirts (1925)
Nickname: The Lids
LIDCOMBE-BERALA PRESBYTERIAN
Dates: c. 1944
Location: Lidcombe
LIDCOMBE CONGREGATIONAL
Dates: c. 1940
Location: Lidcolmbe
LIDCOMBE NORTH METHODIST
Dates: 1940
Location: Lidcombe
LIDCOMBE PRESBYTERIAN
Dates: c. 1940
Location: Lidcombe
LIFESAVING CLUB
Dates: c. 1913
Location: Wollongong
LILLESHALL RANGERS
Dates: c. 1913
Location: Lilleshall
LILYFIELD RANGERS
Dates: c. 1924
Location: Lilyfield

LILYFIELD UNITED
Dates: c. 1926
Location: Lilyfield
Colours: Blue and white shirts

LILYFIED LATTER DAY SAINTS
Dates: 1920
Location: Lilyfield
Notes: This club played in the Protestant Churches 'A' Grade competition.

LISMORE ATHLETIC
Dates: 1914
Location: Recreation Ground
Colours: Black and white vertical striped shirts with white shorts

LISMORE CITY
Dates: c. 1932; 1936; 1939
Location: Police Paddock, Dawson Street
Titles/Honours: Association Premiers Le Clare Cup 1933

LISMORE METHODISTS OK
Dates: 1949
Location: Lismore

LITHGOW
Dates: 1907; c. 1936-1937
Location: Hermitage Flat Paddock, Lithgow (1907)
Colours: White shirts; green shirts with white shorts (1936)
Notes: Lithgow entered the Sydney District League competition in 1936.

LITHGOW DISTRICT UNEMPLOYED ASOCIATION (LDUA)
Dates: 1933
Location: Lithgow

LITHGOW HOTSPURS
Dates: c. 1948
Location: Lithgow
Titles/Honours: Coal Board Trophy 1948

LITHGOW IRONWORKS ATHLETIC
Dates: 1919-1923
Location: Lithgow
Titles/Honours: Langlands Cup 1920-21

LITHGOW RAILWAY SHOP
Dates: c. 1930
Location: Lithgow
Titles/Honours: Railway and Tramway Institute's Shield 1930

LITHGOW SCOTS
Dates: c. 1919
Location: Lithgow

LITHGOW SCOTTISH
Dates: 1937
Location: Lithgow Recreation Reserve
Notes: The Lithgow club amalgamated with the Scottish Social Club to form the Lithgow Scottish club.

LITHGOW STEELWORKS
Dates: c. 1947
Location: Lithgow

LITHGOW THISTLE
Dates: 1912-
Location: Lithgow
Titles/Honours: Langlands Cup 1912, 1919, 1922, 1924, 1926

LITHGOW TOWN
Dates: c. 1915
Location: New Road Ground

LITHGOW UNITED
Dates: 1912
Location: Hooper's Gully

LITHGOW WANDERERS
Dates: c. 1947
Location: Lithgow

LITHGOW WARATAHS
Dates: c. 1932
Location: Lithgow
Titles/Honours: Loch Cup 1932; Tooth Cup 1932; Fitzpatrick Cup 1932

LITHGOW WORKMAN'S CLUB
Dates: 1947
Location: Old Showground, Lithgow

LIVERPOOL UNITED
Dates: c. 1920
Location: Liverpool
Colours: Black and gold shirts

LOCHINVAR
Dates: 1925
Location: Lochinvar

L.O.L. 46
Dates: c. 1922
Location: Five Dock
Notes: Club competed in the Protestant Churches 'A' Grade competition in 1922.

LOUTH PARK
Dates: c. 1930
Location: Newcastle

LUSTRE HOSIERY
Dates: c. 1940
Location: Sydney
Notes: Works team of the Paddington based hosiery factory. Competed in the City Houses competition in the early 1940's.

LYSAGHTS-ORB
Dates: 1930
Location: Mayfield Park, Mayfield
Colours: Green shirts whith white shorts and green socks with white tops (1947)
Titles/Honours: South Coast Premiers 1939-40; Langridge Shield 1939; Toot Cup 1939; Newcastle Senior League 1944; 2nd and 3rd Division Champions 1945
Notes: Previously named Lysaght United.

LYSAGHTS
Dates: c. 1941

Colours: Green and white shirts
Location: MacCabe Park, Wollongong (1945)

LYSAGHTS UNITED
Dates: 1921-1929
Location: Mayfield Park, Newcastle
Notes: Lysaghts United became Lysaghts-Orb in 1930. Lysaghts was a sheet metal company.

MACCABEAN GYM
Dates: 1932
Location: Canterbury Velodrome
Notes: Club played in the Judean League

MACCABEAN SOCCER CLUB
Dates: c. 1927
Location: Moore Park
Colours: Black and white shirts; sky blue shirts with a gold shield
Titles/Honours: Winners of Judean League, 1927-1929

MACCABI
Dates: 1949
Location: Queen's Park
Notes: Club played in the Judean League.

MACQUARIE DISTRICT
Dates: 1931
Location: White Bridge Soccer Ground, Dubbo
Colours: Red shirts
Titles/Honours: Draper Cup, 1932; Edward Evers Cup 1933
Notes: Formerly the Dubbo and District club.

MAITLAND
Dates: 1912
Location: Maitland Park

MAITLAND MAIN
Dates: c. 1937
Location: Maitland
Colours: White shirts and black shorts
Titles/Honours: Charity Cup 1939

MAITLAND UNITED
Dates: 1924
Location: Cessnock Sports Ground
Colours: Green shirts and white shorts, with black socks with green tops.

MALLEABLE CASTINGS
Dates: c. 1924
Location: Primrose Park
Nickname: The Bendy Irons

MALLEYS
Dates: c. 1947
Location: Sydney
Colours: Red and yellow shirts
Notes: Factory team of the Malleys washing machine company.

MALTINE ROVERS
Dates: c. 1914
Location: Sydney

MALVERN HILL METHODIST
Dates: c. 1940

Location: Malvern Hill

MANLY
Dates: 1922
Location: Manly Oval; Brookvale Park; Miller's Reserve
Colours: Red and blue shirts; yellow and black shirts (1949).

MANLY RETURNED SAILORS AND SOLDIERS
Dates: c. 1924
Location: Curl Curl

MARCUS CLARKS
Dates: 1939
Location: District Park, Newcastle
Notes: Played in the Newcastle City Houses and Works Soccer Association.

MARRICKVILLE AVOCA
Dates: c. 1922
Location : Marrickville
Colours: Red and navy blue shirts

MARRICKVILLE BAPTISTS
Dates: c. 1947
Location: Marrickville

MARRICKVILE CONGREGATIONAL
Dates: c. 1947
Location: Marrickville

MARRICKVILLE PIONEER
Dates: 1894
Location: Moore Park

MARRICKVILLE ROVERS
Dates: c. 1915
Location: Marrickville

MARULAN
Dates: c. 1924
Location: Marulan
Colours: Maroon and gold shirts
Titles/Honours: Munro Cup 1934; Byrne Cup 1934-5; Gordon-Graham Cup 1935.
Notes: Marulan played in the Berrima District, Southern Highlands and later Goulburn competitions.

MARULAN MAGPIES
Dates: 1947
Location: Marulan
Titles/Honours: Byrnes Cup 1948; Goulburn Premiers 1949

MARULAN ROVERS
Dates: 1946-1947
Location: Marulan

MARYLANDS
Dates: c. 1922
Location: Wallsend
Colours: Maroon and gold shirts

MASCOT
Dates: 1916-1917
Location: Mascot Park
Notes: Withdrew from League in 1917.

THE FOUNDATION YEARS 1859-1949

MASCOT ROVERS
Dates: 1914
Location: Mascot
MAY STREET METHODIST
Dates: c. 1937
Location: Sydney
MAYFIELD METHODIST
Dates: c. 1939
Location: Mayfield
Notes: Played in the Newcastle Protestant Churches competition.
MAYFIELD THISTLE
Dates: 1931
Location: Mayfield Park, Waratah
Colours: Green and purple shirts
MCDOWELLS
Dates: c. 1940
Location: Sydney
Notes: Played in the City Houses competition in the early 1940's.
MCKELLAR'S ATHLETIC
Dates: c. 1940
Location: Lithgow
Titles/Honours: WDSA Premiership 1941
MCLEANS RIDGES
Dates: c. 1932
Location: McLean's Ridge
MEADOWBANK
Dates: c. 1937
Location: Meadowbank
MEADOWS
Dates: c. 1929
Location: South West Sydney
MENDOORAN
Dates: c. 1929
Location: Mendooran
MAY STREET METHODISTS
Dates: c. 1939
Location: Sydney
MEREWETHER ADVANCE
Dates: 1894; 1909
Location: Speedway Ground; Adamstown Park
Colours: White shirts with a red sash
Titles/Honours: Northern District BFA Badge 1911, 1914-1915, Ellis Cup 1903, 1913-1915; Kerr Cup 1914; State Association Cup 1943, 1944
MERRAMIE
Dates: 1925
Location: Merramie
MERRY FARMERS
Dates: c. 1905
Location: Granville
MERRYLANDS
Dates: c. 1929
Location: Merrylands Park Oval
Colours: Green and gold shirts
Titles/Honours: All Age Knock Out winners 1935
MERRYLANDS SENIORS
Dates: c. 1912
Location: Merrylands
METAL MANUFACTURERS
Dates: c. 1941
Location: Wollongong
Titles/Honours: Langridge Shield 1941
METHODIST
Dates: 1912
Location: Sydney
Notes: Club of the South Sydney Methodist Mission.
METHODIST KIA-ORA
Dates: c. 1924
Location: Lithgow
Colours: Red and white shirts
METRO-VICK
Dates: c. 1920
Location: Sydney
METROPOLITAN RAILWAY INSTITUTE
Dates: c. 1939
Location: Frazer Park, Sydenham
METTERS
Dates: 1910- 1949
Location: Jubilee Oval; Dulwich Hill (1933); Arlington Oval; Henson Park (1947) Lambert Park
Colours: Blue and white halved shirts (1922); sky blue shirts with a white 'V' and white shorts and blue socks (1947);
Nickname: *The Stovies*
Titles/Honours: State Premiership 1940-41, 1944; State Cup 1935, 1938, 1940; Sheahan Cup 1939; Everson Cup 1940; Sydney Cup 1940; District Cup 1940; Jubilee Cup 1940
Notes: Metters manufactured *Kookaburra* stoves. Metters was the first part time professional team in Sydney in 1928.
The Metters club merged with Canterbury in 1949 to form Metters-Canterbury.
METTERS-CANTERBURY
Dates: 1949
Location: Arlington Park
Colours: Blue shirts
Notes: Merger of the Metters and Canterbury clubs.
MILITIA
Dates: 1939
Location: Duke of Kent Park, Wagga Wagga
MILLFIELD
Dates: 1948
Location: Millfield
MINMI
Dates: c. 1922
Location: Minmi
Colours: White shirts

MINMI CLIPPERS
Dates: c. 1910
Location: Minmi
MINMI RANGERS
Dates: 1883-1911
Location: Minmi Football Reserve, Minmi, Northern New South Wales
Colours: White shirts with white shorts and white socks; white shirts with a blue sash and red socks (1886); black and red shirts (1905)
Titles/Honours: Ellis Cup 1888-1889, 1893, 1895; 1898; Gardiner Cup 1892; Northern Premiership 1886-1888, 1890, 1892-1893, 1898
Notes: First club formed outside Sydney in New South Wales. For the first five seasons the team was comprised of Scottish miners. Lost senior status in 1911. Minmi is an aboriginal word for 'large water lilly'.
MINMI REMNANTS
Dates: c. 1920
Location: Minmi
MINMI SQUASHERS
Dates: c. 1906
Location: Minmi
Colours: White shirts with a blue band
MINMI STARLIGHTS
Dates: c. 1906
Location: Minmi
Colours: Green shirts with a red star
MINMI THISTLES
Dates: 1894
Location: Minmi
Colours: Blue shirts with a white sash.
Notes: Club was only in existence for one year.
MINMI WANDERERS
Dates: c. 1908
Location: Minmi
MILITIA
Dates: 1939
Location: Duke of Kent Ground, Wagga Wagga
MITTAGONG
Dates: 1896; 1919; 1938
Location: Sports Ground, Mittagong
Colours: Black and white striped shirts with white shorts and black socks with white tops.
MITTAGONG ROVERS
Dates: 1893
Location: Mittagong
MOLONG
Dates: 1931
Location: Molong
MONA VALE
Dates: c. 1949
Location: Mona Vale

MOORE'S CLIPPERS
Dates: c. 1909
Location: Newcastle
Colours: Red and white shirts
MORRISON AND BEARBYS
Dates: 1941
Location: District Park, Newcastle
Notes: Played in the Newcastle City Houses and Works Soccer Association competition.
MORISETT
Dates: c. 1913
Location: Morisett
Notes: Played in Newcastle First League.
MORISETT HOSPITAL
Dates: c. 1928
Location: Morrisett
Titles/Honours: Couper Cup 1928-9
MORTDALE BRICK-BATS
Dates: c. 1912
Location: Judd's Paddock, Mortdale
Nickname: The Brickies
MORTDALE THISTLE
Dates: 1928
Location: Mortdale
Notes: Formerly named Caledonian Celtics.
MORTLAKE WANDERERS
Dates: c. 1913
Location: Mortlake
MORT'S ESTATE
Dates: c. 1933
Location: Lithgow
Titles/Honours: Loch Cup 1933
MOSS VALE
Dates: 1896; c. 1914; 1934-5
MOSS VALE MILITIA
Dates: 1937
Location: New Park, Moss Vale
Colours: White shirt with a red 'V' (1938)
MOUNT KEMBLA
Dates: 1893-1902
Location: Mount Kembla
MOUNT VICTORIA
Dates: 1890
Location: Mount Victoria School
Notes: Mainly played matches against the Katoomba Club.
MULLUMBIMBY
Dates: 1933
Location: Mullumbimby
MURDOCHS
Dates: c. 1940
Location: Sydney
Notes: Played in the City Houses competition in the early 1940's.
MURRAMI
Dates: 1924
Location: Murrami

Titles/Honours: Maple Hospital Shield 1932; Tooth Cup 1932-3
MURWILLUMBAH UNITED
Dates: 1912
Location: Murwillumbah
MUSCLE CREEK
Dates: 1924
Location: Muscle Creek
MUSWELLBROOK
Dates: 1924-1928
Location: Recreation Park Ground; Bowman Park
Colours: Blue shirts
Nickname: The Brook
MYOCUM
Dates: 1933
Location: Myocum
Colours: Black and white shirts
Nickname: The Magpies
MYOCUM-MULLUMBIMBY
Dates: 1934
Location: Myocum
Colours: Black and white shirts
Nickname: The Magpies
Notes: Amalgamation of Myocum and Mullumbimby clubs.
NAIRN'S LINOLEUM WORKS
Dates: c. 1928
Location: Nairn's Ground, Auburn
Notes: Nairns was a Scottish owned linoleum firm which established a factory in Auburn in 1927.
NAPREDEK
Dates: 1936-1941; 1947
Location: Gladstone ground, Zinc Oval Broken Hill; Alma Oval
Titles/Honours: Premiers 1939-1940; Horrie Edwards Cup 1947; Knock-out Cup 1940; Middleton Cup 1940, 1948; Broken Hill Championship 1939-1940, 1949
Notes: Club was formed by Croatian/Yugoslav miners. The name means *Progress*. The club name changed to All Nations Stars for the 1944 season, but reverted to the original name thereafter.
NARANDERA
Dates: c. 1924
Location: Narandera
NARRABRI
Dates: c. 1921
Location: Narrabri
NARROMINE
Dates: c. 1930
Location: Narromine
NAVAL COLLEGE
Dates: 1925
Location: Jervis Bay
NAVY

Dates: 1900-1908; c. 1918
Location: Lyne Park, Rose Bay
Colours: Navy blue shirts
Nickname: The Blue Jackets; Fleet; Tars
Notes: Players were from various British and Australian navy vessels. Australian ships included HMAS *Australia*, HMAS *Brisbane* and HMAS *Sydney*.
NEATH
Dates: 1913-1926
Location: Neath
Colours: Blue and gold striped shirts
NEATH-ABERMAIN UNITED
Dates: 1927
Location: Neath
NESTANGLO
Dates: c. 1944
Location: Sydney
NEW CHUM
Dates: c. 1942
Location: Ebbw Vale
NEW CRUSADERS
Dates: c. 1922
Location: Cook's River, Sydney
NEW LAMBTON
Dates: 1914; 1940; 1946-1948
Location: Hobart Park; New Lambton Oval
Colours: Black and gold shirts; gold shirts with a black 'V' (1947)
Titles/Honours: Northern Alliance Premiership 1946; State Alliance Premiership 1946
Notes: New Lambton and Hamilton Rovers combined in 1948 to form New Lambton-Hamilton Rovers.
NEW LAMBTON CHATROCKS
Dates: c. 1921
Location: New Lambton
NEW LAMBTON-HAMILTON ROVERS
Dates: 1948
Location: New Lambton Oval
Notes: Teams of New Lambton and Hamilton Rovers were previously independent.
NEWBOLD
Dates: 1939
Location: District Park, Newcastle
Notes: Played in the Newcastle City Houses and Works Soccer Association.
Titles/Honours: First division premiers 1941
NEWCASTLE ABBOTOIRS
Dates: c. 1939
Location: Newcastle
Notes: Played in the Newcastle City Houses and Works Soccer Association competition.
NEWCASTLE CITY
Dates: c. 1921- 1923; 1939-1940
Location: District Park; Mitchell Park
Colours: Green and white shirts

Notes: Previously named Waratah-Mayfield. The early 1920s club merged with Hamilton to form the Newcastle-Hamilton club of 1923.

NEWCASTLE CIVIC
Dates: c. 1940
Location: Newcastle
Titles/Honours: *Telegraph* Shield 1940-41
Notes: Competed in the State Railways Soccer Championship.

NEWCASTLE AND SUBURBAN CO-OP
Dates: c. 1941
Location: Newcastle
Notes: Played in the Newcastle City Houses and Works Soccer Association competition.

NEWCASTLE DEPOT
Dates: c. 1924
Location: No 1 Ground, Newcastle
Colours: Blue and white shirts
Titles/Honours: Winners of Tramway League 1924; 1932
Notes: Club was a member of the Tramway League.

NEWCASTLE-HAMILTON
Dates: 1923
Location: Newcastle
Colours: Red and white shirts
Notes: Club represented a merger between the Newcastle City and Hamilton clubs.

NEWCASTLE TRANSPORT
Dates: c. 1925
Location: Newcastle
Titles/Honours: State Transport Premiership 1925

NEWCASTLE UNITED
Dates: c. 1914
Location: Newcastle
Colours: Black and white shirts

NEWNES BLUES
Dates: 1922
Location: Newnes
Colours: Blue shirts

NEWNES MAGPIES
Dates: 1922
Location: Newnes
Colours: Black and white shirts
Titles/Honours: Newnes Champions 1922

NEWNES REDS
Dates: 1922
Location: Newnes
Colours: Red shirts

NEWTOWN
Dates: 1909-1914
Location: Sydenham
Nickname: The Newts
Titles/Honours: Premiership 1913

NEWTOWN
Dates: c. 1924
Location: Newcastle

NEWTOWN
Dates: 1925-1928
Location: Shaw Street Recreation Ground, Wagga Wagga
Colours: Red and white striped shirts (1926)
Titles/Honours: Wagga District Soccer Association Champions 1926; Hardy Cup 1926

NEWTOWN DISTRICT
Dates: 1946
Location: Newtown
Colours: Sky blue shirts

NEWTOWN METHODISTS
Dates: c. 1941
Location: Newtown

NEWTOWN ROVERS
Dates: 1939
Location: Duke of Kent Ground, Wagga

NINETEEN MILE CAMP
Dates: c. 1927
Location: Nineteen Mile

NOLA
Dates: c. 1948
Location: Sydney
Notes: Yugoslav team of former players from Napredeks club in Broken Hill.

NOMADS
Dates: c. 1930
Location: Broken Hill

NORTH BEXLEY CHURCH OF CHRIST
Dates: c. 1947
Location: North Bexley

NORTH BROKEN HILL
Dates: 1913
Location: Western Oval; Alma Oval, Broken Hill

NORTH CROYDON METHODIST
Dates: c. 1940
Location: Croydon

NORTH GOULBURN
Dates: 1945
Location: Goulburn
Colours: Blue and gold shirts
Titles/Honours: Premiership 1948

NORTH ILLAWARRA ROVERS
Dates: 1888
Location: Thirroul

NORTH LISMORE MARAUDERS
Dates: c. 1949
Location: Lismore
Dates: 1888
Nickname: The Pines

NORTH SHORE
Dates: 1942
Location: Chatswood Oval; Sydney Cricket Ground No. 2 Oval (1945)
Colours: Red and black halved shirts with white shorts and blue and red socks (1947)

Nickname: The Shoremen
NORTH SHORE BRIDGE
Dates: c. 1929
Location: Sydney
NORTH SHORE GASWORKS
Dates: c. 1936
Location: Gore Hill Park, North Sydney
NORTH STRATHFIELD
Dates: c. 1943
Location: Strathfield
NORTH SYDNEY
Dates: 1908-1909; c. 1922
Location: Chatswood; Beauchamp Park; Sydney Cricket Ground No. 2
Colours: Green shirts; black and red striped shirts (1922)
Nickname: Norths
Notes: North Sydney was admitted to the NSW State Soccer League in 1941. Changed name to Willoughby St Stephens for one year in 1921.
NORTH SYDNEY DEPOT
Dates: c. 1924
Location: North Sydney
Colours: Red and blue shirts
Notes: Club was a member of the Tramway League.
NORTH SYDNEY RANGERS
Dates: 1897
Location: St Leonards Park Oval; North Shore Oval
NORTH WOLLONGONG
Dates: 1926
Location: Bodes Ground; Stuart Park Oval
Titles/Honours: Premiers 1936-37; Tooth Cup 1936, 1938; 1941; Division I Premiers 1946
NORTHERN SUBURBS
Dates: 1908-1909; 1928
Location: Naremburn Park; Lane Cove
Colours: Green shirts
NORTHS
Dates: c. 1913
Location: Western Oval, Broken Hill
Notes: Formerly named the Waverley club.
N.S.W. FIRE BRIGADES
Dates: 1920
Location: Lyne Park
Colours: Black shirts with a white 'V', front and back (1922)
N.S.W. POLICE
Dates: 1912-1913; c. 1949
Location: Police Barracks
Colours: Biscuit and blue shirts (1949)
Nickname: The Bobbies
Notes: Played in the Southern League Premiership in 1949
N.S.W. POLICE XI
Dates: c. 1934

Location: Arlington Oval; S.C.G.
Notes: Competed in the NSW Mid-Week Soccer Association competition
NURRAME
Dates: c. 1925
Location: Nurrame
OAKEY PARK CANARIES
Dates: c. 1940
Location: Oakey Park
OAKEY PARK RANGERS
Dates: c. 1920
Location: Oakey Park, Lithgow
Notes: Played in Lithgow competition
Titles/Honours: 2nd Division Lithgow Champions 1922; Pedersen Cup 1922
OAKLAND
Dates: 1911
Location: Oakland, near Lismore
OLD BULLI
Dates: c. 1937
Location: Bulli
Titles/Honours: Premiers Cup 1941
Notes: Played in the Southern Miners Association competition.
OLDTOWN
Dates: 1939
Location: Wagga
OLYMPIC
Dates: 1912
Location: Sydney
ORANGE
Dates: c. 1915
Location: Orange
Titles/Honours: Fitzpatrick Cup 1928, 1930; Edward Evers Cup 1930; Trundle and Parkes Cup 1930; Langlands Cup 1930; White Horse Whiskey Cup 1932; Western District Champions 1934
ORANGE GROVE
Dates: 1919-
Location: Easton Park
Notes: Orange Grove first played Second League soccer in Sydney in 1919.
ORANGE MILLS
Dates: c. 1934
Location: Orange
ORB CHAPEL
Dates: c. 1939
Location: Newcastle
Notes: Club played in the Newcastle Protestant Churches competition.
Titles/Honours: Dr Firth Pettinger trophy 1938
OUR BOYS
Dates: c. 1913
Location: Newcastle
Notes: Played in the Newcastle Second League.
PARA MEADOWS

Dates: 1888
Location: Para Meadow
PARKES
Dates: 1928
Location: Woodward Park, Parkes
PARKGROVE
Dates: 1887 – 1895
Location: Moore Park
Titles/Honours: Badge Series winners 1889-91; Gardiner Cup 1892
Notes: Parkgrove was formed by English players. It had a rivalry with the Caledonians club which was founded and by Scots.
PARRAMATTA
Dates: 1885
Location: Parramatta Park
Colours: Red and blue striped shirts
PARRAMATTA DISTRICT
Dates: 1916
Colours: Red and blue shirts
PARRAMATTA FEDERALS
Dates: c. 1903
Location: Sydney
Notes: Federal played in the Granville Association competition.
PARRAMATTA KIAORA
Dates: 1919
Location: Parramatta
PARRAMATTA METHODIST
Dates: c. 1946
Location: Parramatta
PARRAMATTA UNITED
Dates: c. 1920
Location: Parramatta Park No. 2
Colours: Maroon shirts
PAXTON ROVERS
Dates: c. 1930
Location: Paxton
Titles/Honours: Thompson Challenge Cup 1931-36; South Maitland Premiers 1938; Cup Champions 1938
PEAK HILL
Dates: 1929
Location: Peak Hill
PELAW MAIN
Dates: 1903-1909; 1918
Location: Pelaw Main
Nickname: Mains
Colours: White shirts with 3 inch sash (1903); white shirts with 3 inch yellow strip (1904); purple shirts (1906)
Titles/Honours: Newcastle Premiership 1907, 1918
PELAW MAIN CAMEOS
Dates: c. 1903
Location: Pelaw Main
PELAW MAIN VIOLETS

Dates: 1905
Location: Pelaw Main
PELICAN
Dates: c. 1933
Location: Pelican
Titles/Honours: Newcastle First Division Premiers 1934
PENGUIN, HMAS
Dates: c. 1926
Notes: Played in the NSW Mid-Week Soccer Association competition.
PENRITH DISTRICT
Dates: 1947
Location: Penrith Park
PENSHURST PRESBYTERIAN
Dates: c. 1927
Location: Penshurst
PENSHURST UNITED
Dates: c. 1914; c. 1920
Location: Penshurst Park; Hurstville Oval
Colours: White shirts with a green shield
Titles/Honours: St George Association Premiers 1925
PER WAY
Dates: c. 1938
Location: District Park, Newcastle
Titles/Honours: Premiers 1938; Referee Cup 1939
Notes: Played in the Newcastle City Houses and Works Soccer Association competition.
PERDRONIANS
Dates: c. 1929
Location: Sydney Cricket Ground
PETERSHAM
Dates: 1886; 1906-1907
Location: Leichhardt
Colours: White shirts
PHOEBE, HMS
Dates: 1904
Notes: Played in the Navy League in Sydney.
PINEVILLE
Dates: 1916
Location: Pineville
PINEVILLE RANGERS
Dates: 1923
Location: Easton Park
Colours: Green and gold shirts
PITT ROW
Dates: c. 1929
Location: Lidcombe Park; Jones Park (1944)
PLATTSBURG ROVERS
Dates: c. 1890
Location: Plattsburg
PLATYPUS, HMAS
Dates: c. 1921
Location: Sydney
Titles/Honours: Naval Soccer Challenge Cup 1921
POLICE

Dates: c. 1912
Location: Sydney
PORT KEMBLA
Dates: 1913
Location: Knopp's Ground Port Kembla
Colours: Red and green shirts
PORTLAND TOWN
Dates: 1912
Location: Portland
Notes: Played in Lithgow competition.
PORTLAND GRAND UNITED
Dates: 1926
Location: Portland
PORTLAND RIVERS
Dates: c. 1925
Location: Portland
POWERFUL, HMS
Dates: 1908-1911
Location: Naval Recreation Ground, Lyne Park, Rose Bay
Titles/Honours: Gardiner Cup 1910
Notes: HMS *Powerful* was a British naval vessel which took part in the Sydney First League Rawson Cup Premiership.
PREMIER
Dates: 1939
Location: St George area
PROGRESS
Dates: 1947
Location: Queens' Park
Notes: Club was previously called PJYS. (Progressive Jewish Youth Sports).
PROLETARIANS
Dates: 1933
Location: Warner's Bay
PROMETHEUS, HMS
Dates: c. 1905-1910
Location: Naval Recreation Ground, Lyne Park, Rose Bay.
Notes: HMS *Prometheus* was a British naval vessel at the Australian Station.
PROSPECT
Dates: c. 1929; 1934
Location: Prospect
PROTESTANT CHURCHES
Dates: c. 1943
Location: Mona Street Park, Auburn (1948)
PSYCHE, HMS
Dates: c. 1905-1912
Location: Sydney
Notes: British warship at the Australia station.
PUBLIC SERVICE
Dates: c. 1936
Location: Sydney
Notes: Team played in the mid-week Sydney Soccer Association competition.
PUNCH PARK

Dates: c. 1922
Location: Balmain
PUNCHBOWL
Dates: c. 1921
Location: Punchbowl Park
Colours: Black shirts with a gold sash
PYRMONT
Dates: c. 1910
Location: Wentworth Oval; Leichhardt Oval (1929); Wentworth Park (1949)
Colours: Blue shirts with white shorts and blue socks with white tops
Nickname: The Blues
Titles/Honours: Premiers 1921-1922; Sunlight Cup 1919-1920; Gardiner Cup 1904, 1908
PYRMONT-BALMAIN
Dates: 1946
Location: Pyrmont
Colours: Red and blue halved shirts
PYRMONT CALEDONIAN
Dates: c. 1896
Location: Pyrmont
PYRMONT CARLTON
Dates: 1894-1895
Location: Wentworth Park
PYRMONT CHURCH
Dates: c. 1912
Location: Pyrmont
Notes: Pyrmont Church played in the Club League, comprising non-district clubs.
PYRMONT LABOR
Dates: 1891
Location: Wentworth Park, Sydney
PYRMONT OLYMPIC
Dates: c. 1915
Location: Pyrmont
PYRMONT RANGERS
Dates: 1885-1909
Location: Forest Lodge Grounds; Wentworth Park, Glebe; University Oval
Colours: Maroon shirts with maroon socks; blue shirt with a gold sash crossed back and front; chocolate and white halved shirts (1922); blue shirts with a white 'V' and white cuffs (1924)
Nickname: The Monts
Titles/Honours: Sydney Metropolitan Premiers 1892, 1900-1901, 1903, 1905, 1907, 1909, 1918; Gardiner Cup 1889-1890, 1895, 1897; State Championship 1903; Rawson Cup 1907, 1909
Notes: Pyrmont Rangers became Pyrmont when the district system was introduced.
PYRMONT ROSEBUD
Dates: c. 1895
Location: Pyrmont
PYRMONT ROVERS
Dates: 1897
Location: Pyrmont

Titles/Honours: Gardiner Cup 1903
PYRMONT-SOUTH SYDNEY
Dates: 1925
Location: Redfern Oval
Notes: Succeeded Pyrmont club.
PYRMONT SWIMMERS
Dates: c. 1914
Location: Pyrmont
Titles/Honours: 2nd Division Premiers 1915; Sunlight Cup 1915.
PYRMONT-ULTIMO
Dates: 1944
Location: Wentworth Park
Colours: Red and blue halved shirts
PYRMONT VOLUNTEER
Dates: 1896-1903
Location: University Oval
Colours: Red and white striped shirts
Nickname: The Bulls
Titles/Honours: Ellis Cup 1897; Ellis Charity Challenge Cup 1897; Kerr Cup 1898, 1900; Gardiner Cup 1898.
PYRMONT WARATAHS
Dates: 1994
Location: Pyrmont
PYRMONT WEDNESDAY HALF-HOLIDAY
Dates: 1907
Location: Wentworth Park
Notes: Team played in a mid-week competition.
PYRMONT WHITE STARS
Dates: c. 1903
Location: Pyrmont
QUEANBEYAN
Dates: 1927-1932
Location: Queanbeyan Showground; Queanbeyan Park
Colours: White shirts
Titles/Honours: Canberra Cup 1929; White Horse Whiskey Cup 1930
Notes: Played in the Australian Capital Territory competition.
QUEANBEYAN CALEDONIANS
Dates: 1932
Location: Queanbeyan Showground
Notes: Played in the Australian Capital Territory Competition.
QUEANBEYAN WEST
Dates: 1932
Location: Queanbeyan Showground; Queanbeyan Park
Notes: Played in the Australian Capital Territory competition.
QUEENS PARK
Dates: 1894
Location: Leichhardt
QUIRINDI
Dates: c. 1924

Location: Quirindi
R.A.A.F
Dates: c. 1943
Location: Onslow Park
Titles/Honours: Camden District Soccer Association Shield 1943
R.A.A.F
Dates: 1949
Location: Duke of Kent Park, Wagga Wagga
Titles/Honours: Maples Charity Cup 1949
RAILWAY AND TRAMWAY INSTITUTE
Dates: 1922
Location: Railway Ground, Bathurst
RAILWAY
Dates: 1914-1915
Location: Sydney
Notes: Railway played in the Sydney Metropolitan Club League, for non-district teams.
RAILWAY INSTITUTE
Dates: 1939
Location: Frazer Park
RAILWAY COAL MINE
Dates: 1930
Location: Lithgow
Colours: Green shirts with gold letters RC over M on shield over left breast
Titles/Honours: Daily Telegraph Shield 1930; Premiers 1933; Langlands Cup 1933; Fitzpatrick Cup 1933
Notes: Team often referred to as State Mine.
RAILWAY PER WAY
Dates: 1939
Location: District Park, Newcastle
Titles/Honours: Referee Cup 1940
Notes: Played in the Newcastle City Houses and Works Soccer Association.
RAILWAY THISTLES
Dates: c. 1922
Location: Ibrox Park
RALEIGH PARK
Dates: 1927
Location: Raleigh Park, Kensington
RAMSGATE
Dates: c. 1926
Location: St George Sportsground
Colours: Maroon and gold shirts
RAMSGATE METHODIST
Dates: c. 1919
Location: Ramsgate
Notes: Ramsgate initially played in the Rechabite competition.
RANDWICK-COOGEE
Dates: c. 1927-1930
Location: Moore Park
Colours: Blue and white striped shirts; light and dark blue shirts (1929)

Notes: Randwick-Coogee competed in the Sydney Judean Soccer League competition from 1927.

RANGERS
Dates: c. 1930
Location: Broken Hill

RANGERS
Dates: 1947
Location: Corrimal

RATHMINES R.A.A.F
Dates: c. 1941
Location: Rathmines

RAYMOND TERRACE
Dates: c. 1915
Location: Raymond Terrace

RECHABITES
Dates: c. 1920
Location: Granville Park No. 1
Colours: Royal blue shirts

REDFERN UNITED
Dates: c. 1928
Location: Redfern

REDHEAD
Dates: 1921
Location: Mayfield
Titles/Honours: Bargain Arcade Cup 1933

REGENTS PARK
Dates: c. 1936
Location: Jensen Oval, Regents Park

REGENTS PARK BAPTIST
Dates: c. 1940
Location: Regent's Park

RETURNED SOLDIERS
Dates: c. 1918
Location: Toowoomba
Nickname: The Diggers

REVESBY ROVERS
Dates: c. 1924
Location: Revesby

RHONDDA
Dates: c. 1913; 1924
Location: Rhondda

RHYLSTONE
Dates: c. 1923
Location: Rhylstone

RICARDY
Dates: c. 1921
Location: Newcastle region

ROBINSVILLE
Dates: 1893
Location: Robinsville, Illawarra Region

ROCKDALE ARGYLE
Dates: c. 1926
Location: Rockdale
Colours: Blue and gold shirts

ROCKDALE SCOTTISH
Dates: c. 1932

Location: Moorefield Racecourse

ROCKDALE 2GB
Dates: c. 1939
Location: Rockdale

ROCKDALE UNITED
Dates: c. 1926
Location: Rockdale
Colours: Sky blue shirts

ROCKDALE WANDERERS
Dates: c. 1939
Location: Rockdale

ROSE BAY
Dates: c. 1925
Location: Rose Bay
Notes: Played in the Eastern Suburbs Association.

ROSE BAY-VAUCLUSE
Dates: c. 1939
Location: Rose Bay

ROSE OF DENMARK
Dates: 1918
Location: Sydney

ROSEBAY-VAUCLUSE
Dates: c. 1934
Location: Rose Bay

ROSEBUDS
Dates: c. 1911
Location: Bodes Ground, Wollongong
Nickname: The Buds

ROSEHILL
Dates: 1893-1895
Location: Rosehill
Colours: Navy blue shirt with a scarlet sash

ROTHBURY
Dates: 1919-1920
Location: Rothbury

ROVER
Dates: 1902
Location: Sydney
Titles/Honours: Kerr Cup 1902

ROVERS
Dates: c. 1920
Location: Granville Park

ROVERS
Dates: 1924
Location: The Entrance

ROYAL ARTHURS
Dates: c. 1907
Location: Show Ground, Broadmeadow
Colours: Black shirts with a green sash
Titles/Honours: Ellis Cup 1907

ROYAL AUSTRALIAN ENGINEERS
Dates: 1914
Location: Sydney

ROYAL NAVY
Dates: c. 1916- c. 1919
Location: Lyne Park, Rose Bay

Colours: Navy blue shirts
Titles/Honours: Gardiner Cup 1910
Nickname: Navals
Notes: The team comprised sailors from Royal Navy ships stationed in Sydney.

ROZELLE
Dates: 1900
Location: Easton Park
Colours: Black shirts
Nickname: The Roses; The Parrots; The West End
Titles/Honours: 2nd Grade winners 1909

ROZELLE DEPOT
Dates: c. 1924
Location: Rozelle
Colours: Red and white shirts
Notes: Club was a member of the Tramway League.

ROZELLE ROVERS
Dates: c. 1920
Location: Ibrox Park
Colours: Green and gold striped shirts

ROZELLE UNITED
Dates: c. 1920
Location: Five Dock Park

ROZELLE VALETA
Dates: c. 1913
Location: Rozelle

ROZELLE WYREEPI
Dates: c. 1915
Location: Rozelle

RUSHCUTTERS BAY DEPOT
Dates: c. 1922
Location: Rushcuttters Bay
Colours: Red, white and blue shirts; light blue shirts
Titles/Honours: Sydney Railway and Tramway League Premiers 1933

RUSSELL LEA
Dates: c. 1933
Location: Russell Lea

RUSSELL VALE
Dates: c. 1919
Location: Russell Vale
Colours: White shirts (1919); green shirts with a white 'V' (1945)

R. W. HANNAFORDS
Dates: c. 1947
Location: Cabra-Vale Park, Sydney (1948)

RYDALMERE
Dates: c. 1933
Location: Rydalmere

RYDALMERE
Dates: c. 1946
Location: Rydalmere Mental Hospital Grounds

RYDE
Dates: 1910; 1924

Location: Ryde
Colours: Maroon and gold shirts

RYDE METHODISTS
Dates: c. 1923
Location: Ryde

RYLANDS
Dates: 1939
Location: District Park, Newcastle
Notes: Club of the wire and nail manufacturer. Played in the Newcastle City Houses and Works Soccer Association.

ST AIDEN'S
Dates: c. 1922
Location: Wardell Road, Annandale
Colours: Blue and white shirts
Notes: This club played in the Protestant Churches 'A' Grade competition in 1922.

ST ALBANS
Dates: c. 1940
Location: Epping

ST ALBANS
Dates: c. 1923
Location: Ultimo

ST ANNE'S
Dates: c. 1922
Location: Clyde

ST ANDREW'S
Dates: 1933
Location: Police Paddock, Lismore
Colours: Blue shirts with white shorts

ST ANDREW'S PRESBYTERIAN
Dates: c. 1925
Location: Mayfield Park, Newcastle
Notes: Club played in the Newcastle Protestant Churches competition.

ST AUGUSTINE'S
Dates: c. 1939
Location: Stanmore

ST BEDE'S
Dates: c. 1923
Location: Drummoyne

ST CLEMENT'S
Dates: c. 1923
Location: Marrickville

ST GEORGE
Dates: 1910; 1921
Location: Moorefield Racecourse; St Edward Park; Rocky Point Road, Kogarah; Princes Highway, Carlton (1947)
Colours: White shirts with a red 'V'; red and white striped shirts (1922); red and white vertical striped shirt (1947)
Nickname: The Saints; Dragons
Titles/Honours: Southern and State title 1912; James Ross Charity Cup 1932; Sydney Cup 1932, 1945; State Cup 1933

ST GEORGE WARATAHS

Dates: 1920
Location: St George
Colours: Red and white striped shirts.
Notes: The Waratahs comprised players from three defunct team; St George District (Rockdale), San Souci and Hurstville Rechabites.

ST JOHN'S
Dates: c. 1941
Location: Glebe

ST. JOHN'S
Dates: c. 1927
Location: Penshurst

ST JOHN'S
Dates: c. 1912
Location: Rockdale

ST JOHN'S PARK
Dates: 1929
Location: St John's Park

ST MARK'S
Dates: 1939
Location: Granville
Notes: Competed in the Western Suburbs church competition.

ST MARY'S
Dates: c. 1947
Location: St Marys

ST MATTHEW'S CHURCH OF ENGLAND
Dates: c. 1941
Location: Botany
Notes: Played in the Protestant Churches Soccer Football competition.

ST OSWALD'S
Dates: c. 1941
Location: Haberfield
Notes: This club played in the Protestant Churches 'competition in 1922.

ST PATRICK'S
Dates: c. 1933
Location: Lithgow

ST PAUL'S
Dates: c. 1922
Location: Hurlstone Park; Bankstown Oval (1943)
Colours: Black and gold shirts
Titles/Honours: Final winners 1923
Notes: Played in the Protestant Churches 'A' Grade competition.

ST PAUL'S
Dates: c. 1940
Location: Scarborough Park

ST PETER'S
Dates: c. 1945
Location: Blair Park

ST PETER'S
Dates: c. 1940
Location: Burwood

ST PETERS KANGAROOS
Dates: c. 1926

Location: St Peters
Colours: Red and blue shirts

ST SILAS
Dates: c. 1923
Location: Sydney

ST STEPHEN'S
Dates: c. 1923
Location: Sydney

ST THOMAS
Dates: c. 1940
Location: Auburn

SANS SOUCI
Dates: c. 1919
Location: Sans Souci

SARGENTS
Dates: c. 1912
Location: Sydney
Nickname: The Cakes
Notes: Sargents played in the Club League, for non-district clubs. It was the club of the Sargent's pastry and cake firm.

SAWYER'S GULLY
Dates: 1926
Location: Sawyer's Junction

SEAHAMPTON SEAWEEDS
Dates: 1921
Location: Seahampton
Colours: Dark and light blue shirts

SCARBOROUGH
Dates: c. 1913
Location: Illawarra Park, Scarborough
Colours: Red and white shirts; Black shirts
Titles/Honours: H.J. Buckland Charity Cup 1913

SCHEYVILLE
Dates: c: 1931
Location: Scheyville

SCHOOL OF ARTS
Dates: c. 1926
Location: Lithgow

SCONE
Dates: 1924
Location: Scone

SCOTTISH
Dates: c. 1939
Location: Wolli
Notes: Club was a member of the St George Association.

SCOTTISH RIFLES
Dates: 1894
Location: Moore Park

SHIPPING
Dates: c. 1939
Notes: Played in the Newcastle City Houses and Works Soccer Association.

SINGLETON
Dates: c. 1931
Location: St John's Park Oval, Singleton

Colours: Sky blue shirts
SHAMROCK
Dates: c. 1910
Location: Sydney
SHIPPING COMPANIES
Dates: 1939
Location: District Park, Newcastle
Notes: Played in the Newcastle City Houses and Works Soccer Association.
SHOP ASSISTANTS
Dates: c. 1929
Location: Wagga Cricket Ground
SHORTLAND
Dates: c. 1934
Location: Shortland
S.T. LEIGH
Dates: c. 1917
Location: Sydney
Notes: S.T. Leigh and Company was involved in the construction industry with headquarters in Kensington.
SMALL ARMS FACTORY
Dates: c. 1913
Location: Recreation Oval, Lithgow
Titles/Honours: Langlands Premiership Cup 1925, 1927-8
SMITH SON AND REES
Dates: c. 1939
Location: Sydney
Notes: Company made automotive accessories. The club played in the Sydney City Houses competition.
SMITHFIELD
Dates: 1910; 1930
Location: Smithfield Park
Nickname: The Smithies
Notes: Smithfield first played in the Granville Association competition.
SMITHFIELD SPORTS
Dates: 1949
Location: Smithfield
SOUTH
Dates: c. 1945
Location: Zinc Oval, Broken Hill
Colours: White shirts
SOUTH BULLI
Dates: c. 1937
Location: Bulli
Notes: Played in the Southern Miners Association competition.
SOUTH CARDIFF
Dates: c. 1931
Location: Cardiff
Notes: Played in Newcastle 3rd Grade competition.
SOUTH CARLTON BAPTIST
Dates: c. 1947

Location: South Carlton
SOUTH HURSTVILLE METHODIST
Dates: 1927
Location: Hurstville
SOUTH ILLAWARRA
Dates: c. 1918
Location: Illawarra
SOUTH ROVERS
Dates: 1941; 1946
Location: Gladstone Ground, Broken Hill
SOUTH SYDNEY
Dates: c. 1903-1908; 1928
Location: St Peters Cricket Ground
SOUTH WOLLONGONG
Dates: c. 1922
Location: Wollongong
SOUTHERN PORTLAND
Dates: 1928
Location: Portland
Notes: All players were employed at the Portland Cement Works.
SPEERS POINT
Dates: 1929
Location: Goold Park, Speers Point
Nickname: The Fishermen; Lakesiders
Colours: Blue and gold shirts (1931)
Titles/Honours: Bargain Arcade Cup 1930
Notes: Speers Point amalgamated with the Boolaroo club in 1934. Club known as Boolaroo-Speers Point.
SPORTING BLUES
Dates: c. 1940
Location: Newcastle
Notes: Played in the Newcastle City Houses and Works Soccer Association.
SPRINGFIELD
Dates: 1936
Location: Springfield
Titles/Honours: Southern Districts Soccer Football Association Premiers 1936.
SPRINGWOOD
Dates: 1924
Location: Springwood
SPRINGWOOD WATTLES
Dates: 1924
Location: Springwood
S.T. LEIGH
Dates: c. 1928
Location: Waterloo
STANDARD TELEGRAPH AND WIRELESS (STC)
Dates: c. 1940
Location: Sydney
Notes: Competed in the City Houses competition in the early 1940s.
STANMORE PRESBYTERIAN
Dates: c. 1920-1922

Location: Stanmore
Notes: This club played in the Protestant Churches 'A' Grade competition.
STATE DOCKYARD
Dates: c. 1940
Location: Newcastle
STEELWORKS
Dates: c. 1939
Location: Wollongong
STEWART AND LLOYDS
Dates: 1940
Location: District Park, Newcastle
Titles/Honours: J.H. Wakeley Cup 1941
Notes: Team of the tube making company. Played in the Newcastle City Houses and Works Soccer Association competition.
STOCKTON METHODIST
Dates: 1924
Location: Stockton
STOCKTON ROVERS
Dates: 1887; 1925
Location: Ballast Ground; Lynn Oval, Stockton
Colours: Sky blue shirts (1887); Maroon and gold shirts (1925)
STONEWARE
Dates: c. 1947
Location: Swansea region.
Notes: Played in the Swansea Returned Soldiers League.
SULPHIDE WORKS
Dates: c. 1949
Location: Cockle Creek
SUMMERHILL
Dates: c. 1919
Location: Newcastle
SUNGLO WOOL
Dates: c. 1940
Location: Sydney
Notes: Competed in the City Houses competition in the early 1940's.
SUNLIGHT
Dates: c. 1910
Location: Birchgrove Oval; Sunlight Sports Ground
Colours: Blue and white striped shirts
Nickname: The Soaps
Titles/Honours: Berger Cup 1925
Notes: Works team of the Sunlight Soap Company.
SUPPLY
Dates: 1944
Location: Hay
SWANSEA
Dates: c. 1922
Location: Swansea
Colours: Amber and red shirts

SWANSEA-BELMONT
Dates: 1935; 1944
Location: Belmont Park
Colours: Green shirts with white shorts and green socks with white tops (1947)
Titles/Honours: Newcastle Premiership 1939; Daniels Cup 1944-45; Northern Division Premiers 1943, 1945
SWANSEA FOXES
Dates: c. 1947
Location: Swansea
Notes: Competed in the Swansea Returned Soldiers League
SWEETACRES
Dates: c. 1930
Location: Sydney
Notes: Sweetacres was a confectionary company.
SYDENHAM THISTLES
Dates; c. 1903
Location: Sydenham
SYDNEY
Dates: 1904
Location: Queen's Park; Sydney Cricket Ground No. 2
Colours: Black and white halved shirts; black and blue striped shirts (1922)
Titles/Honours: Rawson Cup 1912
Nickname: The Metropolitans
Notes: Formerly called YMCA.
SYDNEY
Dates: 1908
Location: Sydney
Colours: Royal blue shirts with white shorts
SYDNEY CALEDONIANS
Dates: c. 1915
Location: Sydney
Titles/Honours: Charity Cup 1916
SYDNEY DISTRICT
Dates: 1905
Location: Sydney
Colours: Red and green shirts
Notes: Succeeded the East Sydney club
Titles/Honours: Rawson Cup 1912
SYDNEY HARBOUR BRIDGE
Dates: c. 1926
Location: Waterloo Oval
SYDNEY MEAT PRESERVING CO.
Dates: 1939
Location: Granville region
SYDNEY RAILWAY INTERLOCKERS
Dates: c. 1910
Location: Sydney
Notes: Club played in the Sydney Second League.
SYDNEY TEACHERS COLLEGE
Dates: c. 1926

Location: Lyne Park, Rose Bay
Colours: Dark and light blue shirts
Notes: Played in the NSW Mid-Week Soccer Association competition.
SYDNEY THISTLES
Dates: 1893
Location: Sydney
Notes: Thistles played in the Metropolitan Premiership.
SYDNEY TRAMWAYS
Dates: c. 1929
Location: Sydney
SYDNEY UNITED SLATERS
Dates: 1915
Location: Sydney
Notes: Sydney United Slaters played in the Metropolitan League in 1915.
TAITS MASONIC ROVERS
Dates: c. 1944
Location: Gladstone Ground, Broken Hill
TALLANDOON
Dates: 1926
Location: Tallandoon
TALLIMBA
Dates: 1929
Location: Tallimba
Colours: Blue shirts with white shorts
TAMWORTH
Dates: 1922
Location: Tamworth Oval
TARRAWANNA SWEETHEARTS
Dates: 1913
Location: Tarrawanna, South Coast
Colours: white shirts with red heart; maroon shirts (1923); blue shirts (1945)
Notes: The team largely consisted of 'Geordie' players from North-East England.
TAREE
Dates: 1932
Location: Taree
Colours: Black and gold shirts and socks with white shorts
TAREE WANDERERS
Dates: c. 1949
Location: Taree
TAREN POINT RANGERS
Dates: c. 1924
Location: Taren Point
Colours: Sky blue shirts
Notes: Team played in the St George Association competition.
TATTERSALLS
Dates: 1947; 1949
Location: Fitzroy Flats, Goulburn
Notes: Team named after the local Tattersall's Hotel in Goulburn.
TAXATION

Dates: c. 1940
Location: Sydney
Notes: Played in the City Houses competition in the early 1940's.
TELARAH
Dates: c. 1920
Location: Talarah
TEMORA
Dates: c. 1913
Location: Recreation Ground, Temora
Titles/Honours: Corbett Cup 1913; Woods Cup 1926; McFadden Shield 1926
TEMORA RAILWAY AND TRAMWAY
Dates: 1925
Location: Temora
TEMPE DEPOT
Dates: 1924
Location: Tempe
Colours: Black and gold shirts
Notes: Club was a member of the Tramway League.
TEMPE RANGERS
Dates: c. 1924
Location: Tempe
Notes: This team played in the St George Association competition.
TEMPE PARK METHODIST
Dates: c. 1923
Location: Tempe
TEMPE ROVERS
Dates: c. 1936
Location: Easton Park
TENTERFIELD
Dates: 1922
Location: Queen's Park, Tenterfield
THE ENTRANCE
Dates: c. 1924
Location: Gosford
TERALBA RANGERS
Dates: c. 1906; 1924
Location: Teralba
Colours: White shirts with a blue hoop; black and gold shirts
Titles/Honours: Bryant Cup 1925; Newcastle championship 1939; First Division winners 1940; Air Force Cup 1941
TIGHES HILL
Dates: c. 1931
Location: Tighes Hill
THIRROUL BLUE BELL
Dates: 1887-1940; 1945
Colours: Royal blue shirts
Location: Figtree; Thirroul Park (1925)
Nickname: The Thistles
Titles/Honours: Kerr Cup 1905; Gardiner Cup 1928
THIRROUL ROVERS

Dates: 1892
Location: Thirroul
Colours: White shirts and shorts
THISTLE
Dates: 1893
Location: Moore Park, Sydney
TINGIRA, HMAS
Dates: c. 1913
Location: Sydney
Notes: Team played in the Eastern Suburbs Association.
TOONGABBIE
Dates: c. 1939-1949
Colours: Red and white vertical striped shirts
Location: Toongabbie
TORCH, HMS
Dates: 1904
Notes: Played in the Navy League in Sydney.
TORONTO
Dates: c. 1923
Location: Toronto
TOWN
Dates: c. 1945
Location: Zinc Oval, Broken Hill
TOWN HALL
Dates: 1918
Location: Sydney
TRAMWAY
Dates: 1906; 1914-1915
Location: Sydney
Notes: Tramway initially played in the Wednesday League. It later played in the Sydney Metropolitan Club League for non-district teams.
TRANSPORT
Dates: 1945
Location: Newcastle
Notes: Team of the Gordon Avenue depot of the Transport and Tramway Department. Played in the Newcastle City Houses and Works Soccer Association.
TRUNDLE
Dates: c. 1928
Location: Trundle
Titles/Honours: Power Cup 1929; Western Champions 1930
TRUNGLEY HALL
Dates: c. 1929
Location: Trungley Hall
TULLIBIGEAL
Dates: 1928
Location: Tullibigeal
TUMUT
Dates: 1914
Location: Tumut
Colours: White shirts with black shorts
TWO BLUES
Dates: c. 1920

Location: Clyde Oval, Granville
Colours: Light and dark blue striped shirts
ULLADULLA
Dates: 1895
Location: Ulladulla
ULTIMO
Dates: 1902
Location: University Oval
Nickname: *The Ults*
ULTIMO BULWARRA
Dates: c. 1914
Location: Ultimo
ULTIMO DEPOT
Dates: c. 1924
Location: Domain Ground
Colours: Black and white shirts
Notes: Club was a member of the Tramways League.
ULTIMO POWER HOUSE
Dates: 1907
Location: Ultimo
ULTIMO STARS
Dates: c. 1896
Location: Ultimo
UMBERUMBERKA
Dates: 1912-1913
Location: Broken Hill
Nickname: *The Umbers; Ums*
Notes: The club disbanded in 1913 as they could not find enough players to comprise a team in the Broken Hill competition.
UNDERCLIFFE SCOTTISH
Dates: c. 1932
Location: Prince Edward Park, Sydney; Scot's Park, Undercliffe
Titles/Honours: St. George Association Premiers 1932
UNITED FOUNDRIES
Dates: c. 1939
Location: District Park, Newcastle
Titles/Honours: Second Division premiers 1940
Notes: Funded by B.H.P. Played in the Newcastle City Houses and Works Soccer Association competition.
UNIVERSITY
Dates: c. 1917
Location: Sydney University
Colours: Blue and gold shirts
URALLA
Dates: c. 1920
Location: Uralla
URANQUINTY
Dates: c. 1945
Location: Uranquinty
VALE OF CLYDD
Dates: c. 1900
Location: Lithgow

Titles/Honours: Langlands Cup 1940; WDSA Premiership 1940
Notes: The team was based on the Colliery workers.

VAUCLUSE SALISBURY
Dates: c. 1925
Location: Vaucluse

VICARS WARATAH
Dates: 1927
Location: Alexandria Oval

VICTORIA PARK
Dates: 1915
Location: Victoria Park
Titles/Honours: Ellis Cup 1897; Kerr Cup 1898, 1900; Gardiner Cup 1898
Notes: Victoria Park played in the Metropolitan League in 1915.

VOLUNTEER
Dates: c. 1896-1903
Location: Sydney
Titles/Honours; Gardiner Cup 1898

VOLUNTEER
Dates: c. 1922
Location: Dundas

WADDINGTONS
Dates: 1942
Location: Clyde Oval
Titles/Honours: Granville District Cup winners 1942
Notes: Works team of Waddington's Paper Company, playing in the Granville District Association.

WAGGA
Dates: 1925
Location: Riverside Ground, Wagga Wagga
Colours: Royal blue and white striped shirts with white shorts

WAGGA CALEDONIAN
Dates: 1926-1939; 1949
Location: Bolton Park, Wagga Wagga
Colours: Royal blue shirts with a thistle and white shorts and blue socks
Nickname: The Thistles
Titles/Honours: Maples Charity Cup 1926, 1929; Bourne Shield Premiers 1929; Hardy Cup 1929

WAGGA EXPERIMENT FARM
Dates: 1925-1926
Location: Wagga Wagga
Colours: Black and white shirts
Nickname: The Magpies
Notes: Most of the team were young English migrants.

WAGGA HARRIERS
Dates: 1926
Location: Bolton Park, Wagga Wagga

WAGGA ROVERS
Dates: 1913
Location: Wagga

WAGGA TEACHERS COLLEGE
Dates: 1948
Location: Duke of Kent Park, Wagga Wagga
Colours: Red shirts with white shorts
Titles/Honours: Wagga Wagga and District Premiers 1948

WAGGA UNITED
Dates: 1939; 1948
Location: Duke of Kent Park, Wagga Wagga
Colours: Black shirts with black shorts and black socks with white tops. (1939); white shirts with black shorts and black socks with white tops.
Titles/Honours: Maples Charity Cup 1939

WAKEFIELD
Dates: c. 1923
Location: Wakefield

WALLAROO, HMS
Dates: c. 1905
Location: Sydney

WALLERAH SEABREEZERS
Dates: c. 1906
Location: Wallerah
Colours: White shirts with a black sash

WALLERRAWANG
Dates: c. 1923
Location: Wallerawang
Nickname: Wang

WALLSEND
Dates: 1889
Location: Federal Park; Wallsend Park No. 1; Crystal Palace, Wallsend
Colours: Red shirts with white shorts and red socks with white tops
Nickname: The Reds; Bolshies
Titles/Honours: Ellis Cup 1889; Denton Cup 1900; State League Premiership and Championship 1932-33, 1942, 1944; Kerr Cup 1921; Bargain Arcade Cup 1930; Robinson Cup 1937, 1939; Peters Cup 1937; Gardiner Cup 1944, 1947; State Cup 1937, 1942-1944; Sheahan Cup 1938, 1941; Daniels Cup 1932-1933, 1937-1939; Northern Premiers 1942; Miller Cup 1943; Priest Cup 1944; Victory Cup 1945; Stevenson Cup 1945;
Notes: Oldest club in Northern New South Wales. The club was called Wallsend Rovers from 1887 to 1888.
The derby between Wallsend and West Wallsend is one of the oldest, dating back to the 1890's.

WALLSEND GREAT BOULDERS
Dates: c. 1900
Location: Victoria Park

WALLSEND KIA ORA
Dates: 1922
Location: Wallsend
Colours: Dark and light blue shirts

WALLSEND MAZEPPAS
Dates: 1909
Location: Wallsend
Colours: Green and gold shirts

WALLSEND METHODIST
Dates: c. 1938
Location: Hamilton North
Titles/Honours: Presidents Trophy 1938
Notes: Club played in the Newcastle Protestant Churches competition.

WALLSEND MINERS' HOME
Dates: 1946
Location: Wallsend Park
Colours: Red, white and black shirts
Notes: The Miner's Home was a branch of the Grand United Order of Oddfellows.

WALLSEND ROVERS
Dates: 1887-1888
Location: Federal Park, Wallsend
Colours: Red shirt with a gold sash
Notes: Club named Wallsend after 1888.

WALLSEND MAZEPPAS
Dates: c. 1917
Location: Wallsend
Colours: Red and black shirts

WALLSEND ROVERS
Dates: c. 1931
Location: Wallsend
Notes: 3rd grade Newcastle club.

WALLSEND ROYALS
Dates: c. 1901
Location: Wallsend
Colours: White shirt with a red sash
Titles/Honours: Kerr Cup 1921

WALLSEND TINSLASHERS
Dates: c. 1932
Location: Wallsend

WANDERERS
Dates: 1880-1888
Location: Parramatta
Colours: White shirts with blue socks; red and blue halved shirts (1886)
Notes: The first official club formed in New South Wales.

WANDERERS
Dates: c. 1930
Location: Broken Hill

WARATAH
Dates: c. 1946
Location: Goulburn
Titles/Honours: Byrnes Cup 1946, 1949; Highland Society Cup 1946

WARATAH
Dates: c. 1932
Location: Lithgow Showground
Titles/Honours: Loch Cup 1932; Tooth's Cup 1932; Fitzpatrick Cup 1932

WARATAH-MAYFIELD
Dates: 1934
Location: Waratah Oval; YMCA Oval (1936)
Colours: White shirts with a waratah symbol and black shorts (1934); green and white shirts
Nickname: The 'Tahs
Notes: A successor to the Lysaght-Orb club.

WATER RATS
Dates: c. 1914
Location: Bodes Ground, Wollongong

WATTAMONDARA
Dates: 1927
Location: Wattamondara

WAVERLEY
Dates: 1921
Location: Alma Oval, Broken Hill
Colours: Red shirts with white shorts
Notes: Waverley changed name to Norths in mid- 1921.

WAVERLEY DEPOT
Dates: c. 1924
Location: Waverley
Colours: Maroon shirts
Notes: Club was a member of the Tramway League.

WELFARE FARM
Dates: 1938
Location: Yanco

WENTWORTH
Dates: 1916
Location: Wentworth
Notes: Wentworth played in the Metropolitan League in 1916.

WENTWORTHVILLE
Dates: c. 1930
Location: Wentworthville

WERRIS CREEK
Dates: c. 1920
Location: Werris Creek
Titles/Honours: Charity Cup 1921

WEST ARMIDALE
Dates: 1932
Location: Armidale

WEST BRITISH
Dates: 1921
Location: Broken Hill
Colours: White shirts with blue shorts; blue shirts with white shorts

WEST END PIRATES
Dates: c. 1909
Location: Newcastle

WEST END SLASHERS
Dates: c. 1940
Location: Newcastle

WEST MAITLAND
Dates: c. 1902
Location: West Maitland

Colours: White shirts
Titles/Honours: Gardiner Cup 1901
WEST MANLEY
Dates: c. 1928
Location: Manly
WEST RYDE
Dates: c. 1920
Location: Dundas Park
Colours: Blue and white shirts
WEST WYALONG
Dates: c. 1927
Location: West Wyalong
WEST SYDNEY
Dates: c. 1920
Location: Sydney
Colours: Blue and red halved shirts (1922)
Nickname: The Colonials
WEST QUEANBEYAN
Dates: 1932
Location: Queanbeyan Park, Queanbeyan
Notes: West Queanbeyan played in the Federal Capital Territory (ACT) competition.
WEST WALLSEND
Dates: 1940
Location: Johnson's Park, Wallsend
Colours: Blue shirts
WEST WALLSEND ATHLETIC
Dates: 1891-1896
Location: Federal Park, Wallsend
Colours: Light blue shirts and white shorts
Nickname: The Blues; Westy
Notes: Formed by Scottish miners who worked at the West Wallsend colliery. Club changed name to West Wallsend Bluebells in 1897.
WEST WALLSEND BLUEBELLLS
Dates: 1897-1938
Location: Johnston Park, Wallsend
Colours: Royal blue shirts with white trim and white shorts
Nickname: Westy
Titles/Honours: Northern District BFA Badge 1897-99, 1900-01, 1913, 1919-1921, 1925-1926; Gardiner Cup 1901, 1902, 1921, 1923, 1924, 1926; Ellis Cup 1898-1902, 1919-1921, 1925-1926; Denton Cup 1898-1899; Kerr Cup 1918, 1920; State League Cup 1931; Robinson Cup 1935-36
Notes: Succeeded West Wallsend Athletic.
WEST WALLSEND PRESBYTERIAN
Dates: c. 1939
Location: West Wallsend
Notes: Club played in the Newcastle Protestant Churches competition.
WEST WALLSEND WANDERERS
Dates: 1892
Location: Wallsend
Colours: Black and red shirts

Notes: Changed name to West Wallsend Athletic in 1893.
WEST WALLSEND WOODPECKERS
Dates: c. 1919
Location: Newcastle Showground
Colours: Red and black shirts
WEST WYALONG
Dates: c. 1928
Location: West Wyalong
WESTERN SUBURBS
Dates: c. 1908
Location: Sydney
WESTON ADVANCE
Dates: 1906-1945; 1947
Location: Weston Cricket Ground; The Homestead; Weston Worker's Park, Weston, Northern New South Wales
Colours: Black shirts with red hoops; black and white vertical striped shirts with black shorts and black socks with white tops (1909)
Nickname: The Geordies
Titles/Honours: Hemmings Cup 1917-1918; Gardiner Cup 1918; Ellis Cup 1923; Northern Premiership 1931; State League Premiership 1931, 1936; State Cup 1932, 1934, 1936; 1939; Stevenson Cup 1922, 1931-35-6, 1938, 1941-1942
Notes: Club was formed by immigrants from Newcastle-Upon-Tyne. In 1918 Hebburn amalgamated with Weston to create Weston United. Weston and Kurri Kurri were derby competitors.
WESTON ALBION
Dates: c. 1916
Location: Weston
Titles/Honours: Ellis Cup 1916
WESTON MAGPIES
Dates: c. 1917
Location: Weston
WESTON UNITED
Dates: 1918
Location: Weston
Titles/Honours: Gardiner Cup 1918
WETHERILL PARK ROVERS
Dates: 1924
Location: Wetherill Park
WHARF LABOURERS
Dates: c. 1947
Location: Newcastle
WHITBURN STARS
Dates: c. 1914
Location: Whitburn
WHITEBRIDGE
Dates: 1940
Location: Whitebridge Recreation Reserve
Colours: Black and white shirts
WHITEBRIDGE RANGERS

Dates: c. 1933
Location: Whitebridge
Colours: Black and white shirts
WILLOUGHBY
Dates: 1921
Location: Beauchamp Park
Notes: Was preceded and succeeded by the North Sydney club.
WINDING CREEK
Dates: c. 1908
Location: Winding Creek
WINGHAM RAMBLING LIONS
Dates: 1923
Location: Wingham
Colours: Royal blue and white vertical stripes with white shorts and royal blue socks with white tops
WOLGAN MAGPIES
Dates: 1922
Location: Old Showground, Wolgan
WOLGAN RANGERS
Dates: 1922
Location: Old Showground, Wolgan
WOLLI RANGERS
Dates: c. 1925
Location: Wolli
Colours: Red and white shirts
Titles/Honours: Tanner Cup 1926
Notes: This team played in the St George Association competition.
WOLLONGBAR EXPERIMENTAL FARM
Dates: 1914
Location: Wollongbar, Northern Rivers
WOLLONGONG
Dates: c. 1919; 1924
Location: Wollongong
Colours: White shirts with black hoops
WOLLONGONG
Dates: 1932
Location: McCabe's Park, Wollongong
Titles/Honours: Langridge Physical Culture Cup 1932
WOLLONGONG
Dates: 1939-1940
Location: Wollongong
Notes: Previously named the Lysaghts-Orb club.
WOLLONGONG CALEDONIANS
Dates: 1929-1930
Location: Bodes Ground, Wollongong
WOLLONGONG SENIOR
Dates: 1924
Location: Wollongong Showground
WOLLONGONG STEEL WORKS
Dates: 1936-1940
Location: McCabe Park, Wollongong
Colours: Blue and white quartered shirts
Nickname: The Steelies
Notes: Replaced Balgownie-Corrimal in the State inter-City Premiership in 1936.
WOLLONGONG SURF LIFE SAVING CLUB
Dates: c. 1913
Location: Wollongong
Colours: Blue and gold shirts
WOLLONGONG UNITED
Dates: 1923
Location: Bodes Ground, Wollongong
WOMBARRA
Dates: 1923
Location: Wombarra
Colours: Green shirts with white shorts
Notes: Wombarra is an Aboriginal term meaning 'Black Duck'
WONGAWILLI
Dates: c. 1943
Location: Dapto
WOOLLAHRA
Dates: c. 1949
Location: Woollahra
WONGARBON
Dates: 1930
Location: Wongarbon
WOOL BUYERS
Dates: c. 1936
Location: Sydney
Notes: Team played in the Mid-week Sydney Soccer Association competition.
WOOLWORTHS
Dates: c. 1939
Location: Hordernian's Sports Ground
Notes: Works team of the department store. Played in the City Houses competition in the early 1940s.
WOONONA
Dates: 1889; 1936
Location: Sharples Ground; Slacky Flat; Nicholson Park, Woonona
Colours: Red, white and blue shirts (1913) red and green shirts (1923); red shirts with blue sleeves (1944)
Nickname: The Coasters
Titles/Honours: South Coast Premiers 1904, Sydney Cup 1929, 1943, 1945; Sheahan Cup 1943; Langridge Physical Culture Shield 1936; Pallier Cup 1945
WOONONA-BULLI
Dates: c. 1914
Location: Balls Paddock, Woonona
Colours: Maroon and blue shirts; red shirts (1944); blue and red shirts (1949)
Titles/Honours: Nurse Cup 1914; Sydney Cup 1947
WOONONA PARK
Dates: 1923
Location: Woonona

Colours: Sky blue and white shirts
WOONONA ROVERS
Dates: 1943
Location: Woonona
Notes: This club was formerly named Frog Hollow.
WOONONA SWEETHEARTS
Dates: 1929
Location: Slacky Flat
WOONONA SURF CLUB
Dates: 1940
Location: Woonona Park
W.T. CARMICHAEL
Dates: c. 1948
Location: Mona Street Auburn, No. 2 Ground
Notes: W.T Carmichael was a stove manufacturer.
WUNDERLICH
Dates: c. 1928
Location: Granville Showground
Notes: Works team of Wunderlich Ltd, the building supplies company of Redfern.
YANCO
Dates: c. 1932
Location: Yanco
YELLOW CABS
Dates: 1924
Location: Sydney Cricket Ground
YENDA
Dates: 1924; 1931
Location: Yenda
Titles/Honours: Premiers Murrumbidgee Irrigation Area 1924; Bacon Cup 1933
YENNORA
Dates: c. 1946
Location: Yennora

YMCA
Dates: c. 1901-1919
Location: Moore Park; Cricket Ground No. 1.
Colours: Dark and light blue striped shirts
Nickname: The Christians; Triangles
Notes: Changed name in 1920 to become Sydney.
YMCA
Dates: c. 1912
Location: Western Oval, Broken Hill
YOUNG
Dates: 1912
Location: Young
YOUNG MEN'S CHRISTIAN SOCIETY
Dates: 1885
Location: Parramatta
YOUNG WALLSEND
Dates: 1892; 1924
Location: Young Wallsend Soccer Ground
Colours: Black shirts with a light coloured sash; black shirts and shorts (1922)
ZIG ZAG
Dates: 1909-1936
Location: Recreation Oval, Lithgow
Nickname: Zigies
Notes: Players consisted mainly of railway and colliery workers.
Titles/Honours: Langlands Cup 1923; Premiers 1924; Pedersen Cup 1927
ZINC CORPORATION
Dates: 1947
Location: Zinc Oval, Broken Hill; Gladstone Ground, Broken Hill
Notes: Company team of the local mining company.

Northern Territory

BLUES
Dates: c. 1945
Location: McMillan's Oval, Darwin
BOLSHIES
Dates: 1945
Location: Darwin
BUDERIM
Dates: c. 1924
Location: Buderim
CIVIL SERVICE
Dates: 1949
Location: Darwin
Colours: Black shirt with white patch and blue shorts

Notes: Club changed its name to Services in August, 1949.
COONAWARRA
Dates: 1949
Location: Town Oval, Darwin
Notes: This club did not complete the 1949 season.
CORINTHIANS
Dates: c. 1945
Location: Vestey's Oval, No. 2 Civil Ground, Darwin
Titles/Honours: Corinthians A won the Darwin Championship 1945
Notes: Corinthians fielded 'A' and 'B' teams in the First Division.

THE FOUNDATION YEARS 1859-1949

DARWIN CHINESE RECREATION CLUB
Dates: 1924
Location: Darwin Oval
Colours: Blue shirts; white shirts with yellow facings and socks with yellow tops; white shirt with black 'V' and black shorts (1949).

DARWIN INFANTRY BATTALION (D.I.B.)
Dates: c. 1940
Location: Parap

DARWIN ROVERS
Dates: 1934
Location: Darwin Oval

DARWIN UNITED
Dates: 1933-34
Location: Darwin Oval

EAST POINT
Dates: c. 1941
Location: Darwin
Titles/Honours: Knock out competition winners 1942

FIELD AMBULANCE
Dates: c. 1941
Location: Darwin

FIELD BATTERY
Dates: c. 1941
Location: Parap

FIELD BLUEBELLS
Dates: 1945
Location: Darwin

FLYING BOATS
Dates: c. 1945
Location: East Arm Oval, Darwin

FORTRESS
Dates: 1944
Location: Knuckey's Lagoon
Titles/Honours: NT Force Champion 1944

FRANCIS CAMP
Dates: 1949
Location: Francis Oval, Parap
Colours: White shirt with a red band and blue shorts
Notes: Francis Camp included recently arrived displaced persons from Europe. The club name was later abbreviated to Francis.

G DUCKETTO XI
Dates: 1919
Location: Parap, Darwin

GARRISON
Dates: c. 1934-1938
Location: The Oval, Darwin

HARDIES
Dates: c. 1945
Location: Winnellie, Darwin

HEAVIES
Dates: c. 1945
Location: Darwin

K9
Dates: 1949
Location: Darwin

KIWIS
Dates: 1944
Location: Fortress Ground

KOOKABURRAS
Dates: 1933
Location: The Oval, Darwin
Colours: Light and dark blue shirts with socks with blue tops
Nickname: 'Burras

KORDIES
Dates: c. 1945
Location: Melville Oval, Darwin

L and C
Dates: 1944
Location: Darwin

MAGPIES
Dates: 1933
Location: The Oval, Darwin
Colours: Black and white shirts with black socks with white tops

MEDIUMS
Dates: 1945
Location: Darwin

NAVY
Dates: 1945
Location: Melville Oval; Francis Grounds, Darwin
Colours: Red shirt with a black 'V' and white shorts (1949)
Titles/Honours: Cup winners 1944

NOMADS
Dates: c. 1945
Location: Civil Drome No. 1 Ground, Darwin

OIL TANKERS
Dates: c. 1924
Location: Darwin

OVALS
Dates: c. 1940
Location: Darwin

PIWITTS
Dates: c. 1945
Location: Civil Drome No. 2 Ground, Darwin

RAAF
Dates: 1944
Location: Darwin

RANGERS
Dates: c. 1945
Location: Civil Drome No. 1 Ground, Darwin

REFUGEES
Dates: c. 1945
Location: Civil Drome No. 3 Ground, Darwin

RYDER O BAILEY XI
Dates: 1919
Location: Darwin

SHAMROCKS
Dates: c. 1945

Location: Coonawarra, Darwin
SPITFIRES
Dates: c. 1945
Location: Civil Drome No. 3 Ground, Darwin
STUBBS
Dates: 1949
Location: Town Oval, Darwin
Colours: White shirt with a green sash and white shorts
Notes: This club did not complete the 1949 season.
STUART PARK
Dates: 1949
Location: Darwin
Titles/Honours: Winner of the McNab Shield 1949
TANKS UNITED
Dates: c. 1928 - c.1933
Location: The Oval, Darwin
Notes: Club was also referred to as Oil Tanks.
THISTLES
Dates: 1944
Location: Darwin
UNITED SERVICES
Dates: c. 1949
Location: Darwin
WANDERERS
Dates: c. 1924
Location: The Oval, Darwin
Colours: Blue shirts with white shorts
Titles/Honours: Darwin Association Premiers 1927
WARATAHS
Dates: c. 1927
Location: The Oval, Darwin
WINNELLIE BLUES
Dares: c. 1945
Location: Winnellie, Darwin
WORKSHOP
Dates: 1945
Location: Darwin
WRECKERS
Dates: c. 1945
Location: Darwin

Queensland

ABBEYWOOD
Dates: c. 1934
Location: Abbeywood
Titles/Honours: South Burnett Soccer Association Premiers 1934
ACKLAND RAMBLERS
Dates: c. 1926
Location: Ackland
Titles/Honours: Perkins & Co. Cup 1928
ALBION
Dates: 1912
Location: Albion Recreation Ground
ALBION ROVERS
Dates: c. 1912
Location: Maryborough
Notes: Most players were from the Albion Stove Works.
ALBION SWIFTS
Dates: 1889
Location: Old Goal Paddock, Rockhampton
ALDERLEY
Dates: c. 1929
Location: Alderley
ALLAN'S BACKYARD
Dates: c. 1941
Location: Ipswich
ALLIES
Dates: c. 1915
Location: Toowoomba

Titles/Honours: Friendly Societies Shield 1915-1917
ALLIGATOR CREEK
Dates: c. 1914
Location: Oolbun, Townsville
Notes: Formed by players from the Alligator Creek Meat Works.
ALLORA
Dates: c. 1925
Location: Allora Recreation Ground, Allora
ALLOWAYS
Dates: 1891
Location: The Dairy, Davies Park, West End, Brisbane.
Notes: The side included many rugby and Australian Rules players. Alloways failed to win a home match in two seasons.
ALOOMBA
Dates: c. 1935
Location: Aloomba
AMIENS
Dates: c. 1926
Location: Amiens State School Playground, Amiens
Colours: Red and white shirts
Titles/Honours: Ambulance Cup 1930, 1949; Tom Whelter Memorial Cup 1935; Perkins & Co Cup 1929; Pioneer Shield 1949
ANCHOR RANGERS

Dates: 1937; 1948
Location: Nobbs Street Ground, Rockhampton
ANNERLEY
Dates: 1946
Location: Ekibin Reserve
Colours: Royal blue shirts with a white 'V' and star on shirt
Nickname: The Boomerangs; The Stars
APPLETHORNE
Dates: c. 1945
Location: Applethorne
Notes: Played in the Stanthorpe District competition.
ARMY
Dates: 1941
Location: Maryborough
Colours: Khaki shirts and shorts
ARMY RECORDS
Dates: 1945
Location: Showgrounds Oval, Warwick
Notes: Team changed name to Warwick Diggers in August 1945.
ARMY SIGNAL CORPS
Dates: c. 1939-1940
Location: Brisbane
ASCOT TAXI
Dates: c. 1936
Location: Ascot
ASHTON
Dates: c. 1932
Location: Trebonne
ASTLEYS
Dates: c. 1917
Location: Hendra
ATHERTON
Dates: 1924
Location: Atherton
Colours: Blue and white shirts
Titles/Honours: Easter Cup 1934; Turner Cup 1934; Moses Cup 1934; Casey Premiership Cup 1934
ATHLETICS
Dates: 1889
Location: Brisbane
Notes: Athletics were formerly named St Andrews.
AUSTRALIAN NATIONAL AIRLINES (A.N.A.)
Dates: c. 1948
Location: Cairns
Titles/Honours: Anderson Cup 1948
AYR
Dates: c. 1948
Location: Ayr
BABINDA RANGERS
Dates: 1928
Location: Babinda
Titles/Honours: Kipps Shield 1929

BALGOWAN
Dates: c. 1929
Location: Balgowan
Titles/Honours: Perkins Cup 1928
BALLANDEAN
Dates: 1935
Location: Ballandean
Titles/Honours: Stanthorpe Soccer Association Premiers 1935; Bishop Cup 1935; Pioneer Shield 1936; Kearney Cup 1949
BALMORAL
Dates: c. 1919
Location: Moore Park, Hawthorne; Bulimba
BALLANDEAN
Dates: c. 1940
Location: Ballandean
BALNAGOWAN
Dates: c. 1925
Location: Balnagowan
BARALBA UNITED
Dates: 1923
Location: Baralba
Colours: Gold and black shirts with blue shorts and gold and black shorts
BARDON
Dates: 1926-1940
Location: Bowman Park, Brisbane
Colours: Maroon and white shirts
Titles/Honours: State Champions 1915
Notes: Bardon merged with Latrobe in 1941 for one season. Bardon fielded a senior team 1936-1939 and was notable for development of juniors.
BEAUDESERT
Dates: 1935
Location: Beaudesert
BEDFORD ROVERS
Dates: c. 1922
Location: Lang Park, Brisbane
BEERBURRUM
Dates: 1923
Location: Beerburrum
Notes: Team only played for one year in the North Coast Football Association competition.
BERSERKERS
Dates: c. 1882
Location: Eagan's Paddock, Rockhampton
Colours: Blue shirts with 'B.FC' on left breast
BINGERA
Dates: 1924
Location: South Kolan Oval
Nickname: Super stripes
BLACKBURN ROVERS
Dates: c. 1920
Location: Milton Reserve, Brisbane
BLACKHEATH COLLIERY

Dates: c. 1941
Location: Blackeath
BLACKSTONE ROVERS
Dates: 1886
Location: Thomas Reserve, Blackstone, Ipswich; Kalinga Park
Colours: Red and black striped shirts with white shorts and black socks with red tops.
Titles/Honours: WMBA FA Cup 1891; League Champions 1907, 1912, 1926, 1941; Charity Cup 1896, 1904; Challenge Cup 1896, 1904, 1912, 1926; Memmott Cup 1924; Ambulance Cup 1925; Tristram Shield 1926; G.H. Price Cup 1937; Tedman Cup 1937; Nissen Cup 1937; Brough Cup 1949
BLAIR ATHOL
Dates: c. 1912
Location: Blair Athol
BLUE AND WHITE CABS
Dates: c. 1936
Location: Heath Park, Brisbane
BOOGAN STARS
Dates: c. 1933
Location: Innisfail
Titles/Honours: Castor Cup 1933; Premiership Shield 1937-38; South Johnstone Ambulance Cup 1938
Notes: Team was largely comprised of players of Italian heritage.
BOONAH STATS
Dates: c. 1930
Location: Boonah
BOOVAL ENTERPRISES
Dates: c. 1894-1901
Location: Ipswich
Notes: Succeeded by Booval Rangers.
BOOVAL STARS
Dates: 1902-1946
Location: Cole Street Ground, Ipswich
Colours: Red and white shirts; black shirts with a white star (1938)
Titles/Honours: Premiership 1935; Challenge Cup 1936; Tristram Shield 1938
Notes: Booval Stars succeeded Booval Enterprises which was formed in 1894.
BOWEN CITY
Dates: 1924
Location: Bowen Recreation Ground
Colours: Maroon shirts
BOWEN RANGERS
Dates: c. 1924
Location: Bowen
Colours: Blue shirts
BOWEN HILLS
Dates: c. 1921
Location: Bowen Hills
BOWEN WATERSIDE WORKERS UNION

Dates: 1924
Location: Bowen
Colours: Red and white striped shirts
BOYNEWOOD
Dates: c. 1918
Location: Boynewood
BRILLIANT EXTENDED
Dates: c. 1908
Location: Charters Towers
BRISBANE CITY
Dates: 1915-1925; 1927
Location: Brisbane
Notes: Club absorbed Returned Soldiers in 1921.
Titles/Honours: 1st Grade Premiership 1925
BRISBANE GYMNASIUM
Dates: c. 1922
Location: Brisbane
BRISBANE NORTH
Dates: c. 1899
Location: Queen's Park
BRISBANE TRAMWAY ROVERS
Dates: c. 1927
Location: Brisbane
BROTHERS
Dates: c. 1938
Location: Brisbane
BROTHERS
Dates: c. 1948
Location: Cairns
BUDERIM
Dates: 1920
Location: Central Park, Buderim
Colours: Royal blue and white shirts
BULIMBA
Dates: c. 1910
Location: Bulimba
Titles/Honours: Charity Cup 1911-12
BULIMBA RANGERS
Dates: 1947
Location: Memorial Park, Balmoral
Colours: Black shirts with white band hoops
Titles/Honours: Charity Cup winners 1919; Senior Challenge Cup 1922
BUNDAMBA
Dates: 1940
Location: Bundamba
Notes: Temporarily replaced Bundamba Rangers.
BUNDAMBA RANGERS
Dates: 1886-1940; 1941
Location: Bundamba
Colours: Light blue shirts
Titles/Honours: Challenge Cup 1902; Premiership 1936-9; Tristram Shield 1946
BUNDABERG NATIVES
Dates: c. 1899

THE FOUNDATION YEARS 1859-1949

Location: Bundaberg
Titles/Honours: Premiership 1900
BUNDAMBA ROVERS
Dates: 1886
Location: Bundamba soccer ground, Ipswich
Colours: Sky blue shirts with white shorts; alternative colours maroon.
Titles/Honours: Queensland League title 1922, 1938
Notes: Merged with Latrobe in 1941 for one season.
BUNDABERG CITY UNITED
Dates: 1923
Location: Bundaberg
Colours: Maroon shirts with white shorts
BURRAM
Dates: 1894
Location: Burrum
BUSH RATS
Dates: c. 1933
Location: Rockhampton
Titles/Honours: Edgar Charity Cup 1933
Notes: Players were from the former 42nd Battalion. Club changed name to Corinthians in 1935.
CADETS
Dates: c. 1919
Location: Toowoomba
CAIRNS BREWERY
Dates: 1947
Location: Cairns
CAIRNS CALEDONIANS
Dates: 1936
Location: Cairns
CAIRNS NORTH
Dates: c. 1947
Location: North Cairns Reserve
CAIRNS RAILWAY ROVERS
Dates: c. 1915
Location: Cairns
CAIRNS RANGERS
Dates: c. 1907; 1923
Location: Norman Park, Cairns
Titles/Honours: Kipps Shield 1915
CAIRNS ROVERS
Dates: 1895
Location: Norman Park, Cairns
Colours: Black and white shirts
Titles/Honours: Cairns Premiership 1924
CAIRNS ROVERS
Dates: 1949
Location: Cairns
CAIRNS UNITED
Dates: 1913
Location: Norman Park
Colours: Black and gold shirts
Titles/Honours: Lifeguard Cup 1925

CAIRNS WANDERERS
Dates: c. 1928
Location: Cairns
Titles/Honours: Cairns District Soccer Association Premiers 1948
CALEDONIAN
Dates: 1892
Location: Athletic Reserve, Charters Towers
CALEDONIAN
Dates: 1946
Location: Langlands Park, Coorparoo
Colours: Red shirts with white sleeves and red and white socks
CALEDONIAN
Dates: c. 1934
Location: John Bell's property, Ipswich
Colours: Black and gold shirts
CALEDONIANS
Dates: c. 1913
Location: Kingsthorpe
Titles/Honours: Friendly Societies Shield 1913; Challenge Cup 1913; Ambulance Cup 1913; Hospital Cup 1913
CALL BACKS
Dates: c. 1892
Location: Bundamba
CAMERONS
Dates: c. 1937
Location: Mackay
Notes: This was an iron foundry team.
CAWARRAL
Dates: 1909
Location: Cawarrral
Titles/Honours: Wesley Hall Challenge Cup 1910-1911-1912.
CANNON PARK
Dates: c. 1935
Location: Norman Park, Cairns
CARSTAIRS
Dates: c. 1924
Location: Carstairs
CASUALS
Dates: c. 1921
Location: Toowoomba
CAWARRAL
Dates: c. 1910
Location: Cawarral
Titles/Honours: Wesley Hall Challenge Cup 1910-12; Charity Cup 1912
CAWDOR
Dates: c. 1919
Location: Toowoomba
Titles/Honours: Toowoomba Champions 1921; Charity Shield 1921; Friendly Societies Cup 1921
CELTIC
Dates: c. 1910
Location: Brisbane

CELTIC
Dates: c. 1925
Location: Gymnasium Ground, Rockhampton
Titles/Honours: Heiser Cup 1924

CENTRAL
Dates: c. 1949
Location: Drill Hall ground, Port Pirie

CHARTERS TOWERS
Dates: 1908
Location: Charters Towers
Notes: Most of the original Charters Towers players were Scottish miners.

CHRISTIAN BROTHERS
Dates: 1937
Location: Brisbane

CITIES
Dates: c. 1924
Location: Recreation Reserve, Bowen

CLAYFIELD ROVERS
Dates: c. 1919
Location: Hendra

CLEVELAND RANGERS
Dates: c. 1893
Location: Victoria Park, Townsville

CLIFTON
Dates: 1912
Location: Clifton

CLONCURRY
Dates: c. 1940
Location: The Reserve, Cloncurry

COLLINSVILLE HEARTS
Dates: c. 1925
Location: Collinsville
Colours: Black and white shirts

COLLINSVILLE ROVERS
Dates: c. 1926
Location: Collinsville

COLLINSVILLE THISTLE
Dates: c. 1926
Location: Collinsville
Titles/Honours: Windsor Cup 1927

COMMONWEALTH
Dates: c. 1940
Location: Victoria Park, Townsville

COOROY
Dates: 1926
Location: Cooroy Showground
Titles/Honours: Charity Cup winners 1926

CORINTHIANS
Dates: 1913
Location: Langlands Park, Coorparoo; Heath Park
Colours: White shirts with black shorts and black and white socks
Titles/Honours: Nissen Cup 1939; McDonald Cup 1939; Premiership 1940

CORINTHIANS
Dates: 1940
Location: Maryborough
Notes: Many players were from the White Star club.

COWLEY BROTHERS
Dates: c. 1933
Location: Boogan

DERRA
Dates: c. 1918
Location: Derra Recreation Ground

DIGGERS
Dates: 1919
Location: Brisbane

DIGGERS
Dates: c. 1948
Location: Cairns

DINMORE BUSH RATS
Dates: 1889
Location: New Chum, Ipswich
Colours: Navy blue shirts; black and gold vertical striped shirts with navy shorts and gold hooped socks
Titles/Honours: Champions 1892, 1895, 1898-1901, 1903, 1907, 1910, 1921; WMBA FA Cup 1892; Tristram Shield 1922, 1924, 1928; Challenge Cup 1895, 1898-1901, 1910, 1915; Hodgson Cup 1895; Charity Cup 1898-1899, 1909, 1910

DINMORE POTTERY
Dates: c. 1941
Location: Dinmore

DINMORE WANDERERS
Dates: c. 1924
Location: Dinmore
Colours: Black and gold shirts; maroon and white shirts (1925)
Titles/Honours: Callow Cup 1929; Tristram Shield 1933-1934; Telegraph Cup 1934

DUNDEE COLLIERY
Dates: c. 1942
Location: Ipswich

EDMONTON
Dates: c. 1948
Location: Edmonton

EAST BARRON
Dates: 1934
Location: East Barron
Colours: White shirts with blue shorts

EASTERN SUBURBS
Dates: 1938
Ground: Heath Park, Hilton Street, East Brisbane
Colours: Green and gold shirts
Titles/Honours: Tristram Shield 1945
Notes: Eastern Suburbs was formed after a merger of Pineapple Rovers, United Rangers and Shafston United.

EDMONTON
Dates: c. 1932; c. 1948
Location: Cairns
Titles/Honours: Diggers Cup 1949

ELLENA
Dates: c. 1919
Location: Milton
Notes: Played in 1st Grade, Brisbane.

ELLIOTT RANGERS
Dates: 1932
Colours: Red and white shirts
Notes: Played within the Bundaberg Soccer Association.

EMERALD
Dates: c. 1912
Location: Emerald

ESKGROVE
Dates: c. 1910
Location: Eskgrove
Nickname: 'Groves

ESTATES
Dates: c. 1940
Location: Victoria Park, Townsville

EVANS DEAKIN
Dates: c. 1938
Location: Brisbane

EVELYN
Dates: c. 1936
Location: Millaa Millaa
Titles/Honours: Ambulance Shield 1936; Wadsworth Cup 1936

EXCELSIORS
Dates: c. 1917
Location: New Farm Park

FAIRFIELD ROVERS
Dates: c. 1919; 1925
Location: Brisbane

FERNVALE
Dates: c. 1893
Location: Ipswich
Colours: White shirt with a blue sash

FISHERY FALLS
Dates: 1934-1938
Location: Deeral
Colours: Red and blue horizontal striped shirts.
Notes: Many players were of Italian origin.

FITZROY HORNETS
Dates: 1935
Location: Rockhampton
Colours: Red and black shirts with white shorts and black socks with red tops.
Titles/Honours: Edgar Charity Cup 1935
Notes: Previously named Fitzroy Rovers prior to 1935.

FITZROY RAMBLERS
Dates: 1886
Location: Archer Park, Rockhampton
Colours: White shirts with a scarlet sash and white shorts
Titles/Honours: Wesley Hall Challenge Cup 1900-1, 1922

FITZROY RANGERS
Dates: c. 1882
Location: Gymnasium Ground; Campbell Street Ground, Rockhampton
Colours: Red shirts with white shorts
Titles/Honours: Charity Cup 1929; Heiser Cup 1932, 1934; Wesley Hall Premiership Cup 1899, 1930-1931, 1934

FITZROY ROVERS
Dates: 1889
Location: Gymnasium Ground; Campbell Street, Rockhampton
Notes: Team changed name to Fitzroy Hornets in 1935. It absorbed the Valleys club in 1934.

FOUREX
Dates: 1939
Location: Hockey Ground, Maryborough

42nd BATTALION
Dates: c. 1931
Location: Rockhampton

FRENCHVILLE
Dates: 1948
Location: North Rockhampton High School

FRESHWATER
Dates: 1936
Location: Freshwater
Colours: Red shirts; blue and white striped shirts (1939)

GARGETT
Dates: c. 1926
Location: Gargett
Titles/Honours: Country British Football Association Premiers 1926

GENERAL MOTORS
Dates: c. 1927
Location: Brisbane

GLASSHOUSE MOUNTAINS
Dates: 1930
Location: Glasshouse Mountains

GLEN APLIN
Dates: c. 1930
Location: Glen Aplin
Titles/Honours: Bishop Cup 1949

GLEN ALLYN
Dates: c. 1921
Location: Glen Allyn
Colours: Green shirts

GLEN ALLYN
Dates: c. 1926
Location: Mr Clarke's Paddock, Glen Allyn
Colours: White shirts with blue shorts
Notes: Team played in the Atherton Tableland Football Association.

GOLDEN GROVE
Dates: c. 1925
Location: Atherton
Colours: Blue shirts with white shorts
Notes: Team played in the Atherton Tableland Football Association

GOODNA
Dates: c. 1875; 1913
Location: Goodna Asylum Ground
Notes: Most players worked at the Mental Asylum. Goodna (formerly Woogaroo) was the site of some of the earliest matches in Queensland.

GOOMBOORIAN
Dates: c. 1930
Location: Goomboorian

GOOMBUNGEE
Dates: 1913
Location: Goombungee

GOONDI ATHLETIC
Dates: c. 1927
Location: Goondi

GORDONVALE
Dates: c. 1926; 1933
Location: Gordonvale
Titles/Honours: Cairns League Premiership 1929; Brophy Trophy 1930; Lifeguard Cup 1932

GOSFORD MAGPIES
Dates: 1924
Location: Waterside Park, Gosford

GOWRIE
Dates: c. 1912
Location: Gowrie colliery

GRACEVILLE
Dates: c. 1928
Location: Graceville Recreation Reserve

GRAMMARS
Dates: c. 1908
Location: Townsville

GRAND ELEVEN
Dates: c. 1948
Location: Cairns

GRANGE THISTLE
Dates: 1919
Location: Lanham Park, Grange
Colours: Orange shirts with white shorts and orange socks with white tops; light blue shirts (1946)
Titles/Honours: League Champions 1923
Notes: Merthyr Thistle was the forerunner to the Grange Thistle club.

GREGORY ROVERS
Dates: c. 1913
Location: Brisbane

HABANA
Dates: c. 1926
Location: Habana

Notes: Club was formed by Maltese immigrants.

HALIFAX-MACKNADE
Dates: c. 1932
Location: Halifax
Notes: Players worked at the Macknade sugar mill.

HALY CREEK
Dates: c. 1930
Location: Haly Creek

HAMILTON
Dates: c. 1921
Location: Chapman's Paddock, Hamilton

HARBOR
Dates: c. 1936
Location: Queen's Park Mackay

HARLAXTON
Dates: c. 1917
Location: Toowoomba

HARTLEY
Dates: c. 1926
Location: Rockhampton

HAWTHORNE UNITED RANGERS
Dates: c. 1935
Location: Hawthorne

HELLENIC
Dates: 1949
Location: Milton Park, Milton
Colours: Blue and white striped shirts with blue and white socks

HIGHFIELDS
Dates: 1919
Location: Queen's Park, Toowoomba

HIVESVILLE
Dates: c. 1932
Location: Hivesville

HOLMESVILLE
Dates: c. 1924
Location: Holmesville

HOLY TRINITY
Dates: c. 1921
Location: Mackay

HOME HILL
Dates: 1923
Location: Home Hill

HOME HILL WANDERERS
Dates: 1925
Location: Home Hill

HOSPITAL
Dates: 1945
Location: Showgrounds Oval, Warwick

HOTSPURS
Dates: 1939
Location: Kangaroo Oval, Maryborough
Colours: Light blue and white shirts
Nickname: Spurs
Titles/Honours: Association Premiers 1939; Challenge Shield 1947; Premiership Shield 1949

THE FOUNDATION YEARS 1859-1949

HOWARD ROVERS
Dates: c. 1895; 1904
Location: Howard
Titles/Honours: Maryborough Association Premiership 1925, 1941; Steindl Cup 1926; Williams Cup 1940; Challenge Shield 1940

IDALIA ROVERS
Dates: c. 1910
Location: Victoria Park, Townsville
Titles/Honours: Dryborough Charity Shield 1911; Perry Trophy 1914

INGHAM
Dates: c. 1931
Location: Ingham
Titles/Honours: Noora Cup 1940

INGHAM TOWN ATHLETIC CLUB
Dates: c. 1936
Location: Ingham

INNISFAIL ASIATICS
Dates: 1947
Location: Wright's Park, Innisfail
Notes: This team was formed by native islanders.

INNISFAIL TOWN ATHLETIC
Dates: c. 1933
Location: East Innisfail

INNISFAIL UNITED
Dates: 1931
Location: East Innisfail Recreation Reserve, Innisfail
Colours: White jersey with a blue badge on heart and blue shorts
Titles/Honours: Noorla Cup No. 2 1938

INNISFAIL-GOONDI UNITED
Dates: c. 1932
Location: Goondi

INNISPLAIN
Dates: c. 1935
Location: Innisplain

IPSWICH CITY
Dates: 1891; 1925
Location: Ipswich
Colours: Light blue shirts (1925)

IPSWICH RAMBLERS
Dates: c. 1926
Location: Ipswich

IPSWICH RAILWAY
Dates: c. 1910
Location: Sandy Gallop

IPSWICH ROVERS
Dates: c. 1892
Location: Ipswich

IPSWICH WORKSHOPS
Dates: 1911
Location: Ipswich

ITHICA UNITED
Dates: c. 1929
Location: Lang Park, Brisbane

IRVINEBANK
Dates: c. 1897
Location: Irvinebank

JACKARANDA SPORTS
Dates: 1939
Location: Ipswich
Colours: Royal blue shirts with a gold 'V'

JOHNSTONE
Dates: c. 1947
Location: Wright's Park, Innisfail

JUBILEE STARS
Dates: c. 1936
Location: Brisbane

JUNCTION RANGERS
Dates: c. 1940
Location: Brisbane

KAIRI THISTLE
Dates: c. 1926
Location: Kairi
Colours: White shirt with a red sash and blue shorts; black shirt with white shorts

KANDANGA
Dates: 1949
Location: Kandanga

KANGAROO ATHLETIC
Dates: 1921
Location: Brisbane

KANGAROO POINT STARS
Dates: c. 1928
Location: Kangaroo Point

KANGAROOS
Dates: c. 1927
Location: Eskdale Park, Maryborough

KANOWNA
Dates: c. 1929
Location: Edmonton Sports Ground

KEDRON UNITED
Dates: 1921
Location: Kedron
Colours: Black shirts with a white horizontal band and white shorts

KENILWORTH
Dates: 1923
Location: Kenilworth
Titles/Honours: Power Silver Cup 1927

KIDAMAN CREEK
Dates: 1923
Notes: Team only played for one year in the North Coast Football Association competition.

KILCOY
Dates: 1915
Location: Kilcoy

KIN KIN
Dates: c. 1928
Location: Kin Kin

KINGAROY
Dates: c. 1928

Location: Kingaroy
KINGSTHORPE
Dates: c. 1936
Location: Kingsthorpe
KINGSTHORPE CALEDONIANS
Dates: c. 1913
Location: Kingsthorpe
Titles/Honours: Ambulance Cup 1913; Challenge Cup 1913; Hospital Cup 1913; Friendly Societies Shield 1913
KLIENTON ROVERS
Dates: 1907
Location: Polo Ground, Toowoomba
KURILPA RANGERS
Dates: c. 1929
Location: Kurilpa
KURILPA ROVERS
Dates: c. 1916
Location: Kurilpa
Notes: Played in Third Grade Competition.
LAKE'S CREEK
Dates: 1887
Location: North Rockhampton
Colours: Red shirts with white shorts
Nickname: The Gallant Highlanders
Titles/Honours: Wesley Hall Premiership Cup 1895-6, 1921, 1924; 1934
LATROBE
Dates: 1916-c.1970
Location: Gregory Park, Milton; Brisbane Cricket Ground; Lang Park
Colours: Red; green and gold halved shirts with white shorts and green and gold hooped socks; royal blue shirts (1935)
Titles/Honours: Tristram Shield 1925, 1927, 1929-1932; Charity Cup 1925; Moore Cup 1928; Brisbane Cup 1929; Challenge Cup 1929; Cup 1932; Premiers 1929, 1933; Hilton Shield 1935; Courier-Mail Challenge Cup 1935; Hilton Shield 1939
LATROBE
Dates: c. 1948
Location: Cairns
Titles/Honours: Charity Cup 1949
LEICHHARDT
Dates: c. 1938
Location: Mackay
MACKAY
Dates: 1914
Location: Victoria Park, Mackay
MACKAY ATHLETIC
Dates: 1923
Location: Mackay
MACKAY BUSHRATS
Dates: 1927
Location: Mackay

Notes: Bushrats absorbed the Country club in 1927.
MACKAY CORINTHIANS
Dates: c. 1925
Location: Queens Park, Mackay
Colours: White shirts with black shorts
Titles/Honours: City Premiers 1926
MACKAY COUNTRY
Dates: c. 1920 - c. 1925
Location: Mackay
MACKAY THISTLE
Dates: c. 1936
Location: Mackay
MACKAY WORKER-THISTLE
Dates: c. 1947
Location: Mackay
MACKAY NORTH ROVERS
Dates: 1947
Location: Mackay
Titles/Honours: Quinn Challenge Trophy 1947
MACKAY UNITED
Dates: c. 1924
Location: Queen's Park
Location: Mackay
MACKAY WANDERERS
Dates: c. 1938
Location: Mackay
Colours: White shirts
Titles/Honours: Coleman Trophy 1938; Premiership 1947
MACKAY WATERSIDE WORKERS UNION
Dates: 1924
Location: Mackay
Colours: Red shirts
Nickname: Watersiders
Titles/Honours: Ghodes Cup 1928; Ambulance Shield 1929
MCQUEENS COLLIERY
Dates: c. 1941
Location: Ipswich
MAIN ROADS COMMISSION
Dates: c. 1927
Location: Pomona
MALANDA GARDEN CITY
Dates: 1924
Location: Malanda
Colours: Maroon shirts with white shorts
Notes: Competed in the Atherton Tableland Football Association.
MALENY
Dates: c. 1926
Location: Maleny
MANLY UNITED
Dates: c. 1923
Location: Manly
Colours: Maroon and yellow shirts; blue and white striped shirts

MANLY-WYNNUM
Dates: c. 1928
Location: Memorial Park
MAPLETON
Dates: 1921
Location: School of Arts Ground, Mapleton
Titles/Honours: Robertson Cup 1928
MARBURG
Dates: 1934
Location: Marburg
Colours: Maroon shirts
MAREE
Dates: c. 1919
Location: Brisbane
Notes: Competed in Metropolitan Third Grade.
MAREEBA
Dates: c. 1895; 1947
Location: Mareeba
MARIAN
Dates: 1922
Location: Marian
Colours: Green shirts and white shorts
Titles/Honours: Gohdes Cup 1922, 1924; Soccer Union Cup 1924
MARY VALLEY
Dates: 1924
Location: Mary Valley
MARSH AND WEBSTERS
Dates: c. 1937
Location: Mackay
Notes: Marsh and Websters was a Mackay department store.
MARYBOROUGH CITY
Dates: 1945
Colours: White shirts with khaki shorts
MARYBOROUGH COLTS
Dates: 1947
Location: Location: Kangaroo Oval, Maryborough
MARYBOROUGH COMETS
Dates: c. 1949
Location: Maryborough
MARYBOROUGH GRANVILLE
Dates: 1947
Location: Maryborough
Titles/Honours: Premiership Shield 1947; Cup Winners 1948; White Challenge Shield 1949
MARYBOROUGH RANGERS
Dates: 1913
Location: Maryborough
Notes: Team was extant for one year.
MARYBOROUGH ROVERS
Dates: c. 1924
Location: Maryborough
MARYBOROUGH UNION
Dates: 1894

Location: The Reserve, Maryborough
MARYBOROUGH UNITED COMMERCIALS
Dates: 1939
Location: Kangaroo Oval, Maryborough
Nickname: Comms
Titles/Honours: F.Williams Memorial Cup winners 1947
MARYBOROUGH WANDERERS
Dates: 1926
Location: Maryborough
Notes: Club was formerly named Shipyards.
MARYBOROUGH WARATAHS
Dates: c. 1925
Location: Maryborough
MARYBOROUGH WHITE STARS
Dates: 1939-1941
Location: Hockey Ground, Maryborough
MEMERAMBI
Dates: c. 1928
Location: Memerambi
MERINDA HOTSPUR
Dates: 1925
Location: Merinda
Titles/Honours: Bowen Independent Cup 1925
MERTHYR
Dates: c. 1925
Location: New Farm Park
Titles/Honours: 2nd Grade Premiers 1925
MERTHYR THISTLE
Dates: 1911-1919
Location: New Farm Park
Notes: This club was a forerunner to the Grange Thistle club.
MERTON ROVERS
Dates: 1926
Location: Dutton Park Oval; Yeronga Park
Colours: Black and white quartered shirts with white shorts and black socks with white hoops
Titles/Honours: Tedman Cup 1934
METROPOLITAN FIRE BRIGADE (M.F.B)
Dates: 1923
Location: Brisbane
Notes: Players were from the Ann St station.
MICHELMORES
Dates: c. 1937
Location: Mackay
Notes: Club of a wholesale merchant.
MIDDLE RIDGE
Dates: c. 1913
Location: Athletic Ground, Toowoomba
Nickname: The Ridgers
Titles/Honours: Gibson Cup 1913; Knock-Out Cup 1913
MILL HILL
Dates: 1936
Location: Mill Hill
MILLS UNITED

Dates: c. 1908
Location: Mill Hill
MILTON
Dates: c. 1910
Location: Gregory Park; Lang Park, Brisbane
MINBIN ROVERS
Dates: c. 1924
Location: Minbin
MIRANI
Dates: 1925-1926
Location: Mirani
Notes: Team played for one season, then disbanded.
MIRRIWINNI
Dates: c. 1929
Location: Mirriwinni
MITCHELL
Dates: c. 1912
Location: Mitchell
MITCHELTON
Dates: 1920
Location: Mitchelton Sports Reserve
Colours: Green shirts with white collar
MONTE
Dates: c. 1894
Location: Silkstone, Ipswich
Titles/Honours: Cup Winners 1920
Colours: White shirts; red, white and blue shirts
MONTIES
Dates: c. 1904
Location: Charters Towers
MONTVILLE
Dates: c. 1922
Location: Montville
MOOLOOLAH
Dates: c. 1924
Location: Mooloolah Recreation Ground
MOOROOKA
Dates: c. 1910
Location: Moorooka
MOSSMAN
Dates: c. 1928
Location: Mossman
MOUNT CHALMERS
Dates: c. 1890
Location: Mount Chalmers
MOUNT COLLIERY
Dates: 1926-1927
Location: Warwick District
Nickname: The Colliers
Titles/Honours: Warwick and District Soccer Association Premiers 1926
Notes: The Warwick and District Soccer Association comprised the teams of Mount Colliery, Warwick, Allora and Tannymorel.
MOUNT ISA CORINTHIANS
Dates: c. 1940
Location: Mt Isa
Nickname: Corries
Titles/Honours: League Champions 1920, 1940, 1949; Challenge Cup 1915; Gray Cup 1939, Jeff Willan Cup 1939; Earl Castle Stewart Cup 1939
MOUNT ISA MAGPIES
Dates: c. 1934
Location: Mount Isa
MOUNT ISA RANGERS
Dates: c. 1939
Location: Mt Isa
Titles/Honours: Littlejohn Cup 1939
MOUNT ISA ROVERS
Dates: c. 1934
Location: Mount Isa
MOUNT ISA THISTLES
Dates: c. 1934
Location: Mount Isa
MOUNT MORGAN RANGERS
Dates: 1887-1911
Location: Mount Morgan
Colours: Red and white striped shirts
Titles/Honours: Stewart Cup 1888-1889; Wesley Hall Challenge Cup 1902
MOUNT MORGAN SWIFTS
Dates: c. 1890
Location: Mount Morgan
Colours: Blue shirts with white shorts
MOUNT MULLIGAN ROVERS
Dates: c. 1920
Location: Mount Mulligan
MOURILYAN
Dates: c. 1926
Location: Mourilyan
Colours: Red shirts
Titles/Honours: Lifeguard Cup 1929-30, McDonald Cup 1930; Premiers 1931, 1933, 1935; Hugh McIlrath Cup 1938; Clayton Cup 1938
Notes: Team was founded by members of the Italian community.
MOURILYAN ATHLETIC
Dates: c. 1933
Location: Mourilyan
MOURILYAN BROTHERS
Dates: c. 1933
Location: Mourilyan
Titles/Honours: Castor Cup 1935
MUNDUBBERAH
Dates: c. 1919
Location: Mundubberah
MUNGAR JUNCTION
Dates: 1894
Location: Mungar Junction
MURGON

Dates: c. 1928
Location: Murgon Recreation Ground
Titles/Honours: South Burnett Premiership 1929-1931; Miller Cup 1929
MUSGRAVE RANGERS
Dates: c. 1919
Location: Musgrave Park, Brisbane
NAMBOUR
Dates: 1921; 1923
Location: Nambour
Titles/Honours: McKiana Cup 1921, Hospital Cup 1921
NANANGO
Dates: 1913
Location: Nanango
NATIONALS
Dates: 1929
Location: Victoria Park, Townsville
NATIVES
Dates: c. 1919
Location: Brisbane
Notes: Competed in the Metropolitan Second Division.
NAVY
Dates: 1945
Location: Brisbane Exhibition Ground.
Notes: The navy fielded two teams, Nos 1 and 2 in the top metropolitan competition in Brisbane in 1945.
NAVY
Dates: 1941
Location: Maryborough
Colours: Blue and red striped shirts with white shorts
NERANG
Dates: c. 1923
Location: Nerang
NERIMBERA
Dates: c. 1926
Location: Nerimbera
Colours: Amber and black shirts
Nickname: *The Tigers*
Titles/Honours: Wesley Hall Challenge Cup 1920, 1926-1928, 1947-1949; Charity Cup 1925; Heiser Cup 1932
NEW CHUM
Dates: c. 1891
Location: New Chum
NEWTOWN
Dates: 1926
Location: Maryborough
NEWTOWN CADETS
Dates: 1906
Location: Toowoomba
Notes: By 1908 Toowoomba teams were competing for a trophy named the Citizens' Cup.
NEWTOWN UNITED

Dates: c. 1930
Location: Yaronga Park, Brisbane
NOBBY
Dates: c. 1928
Location: Nobby
NORMAN
Dates: 1889
Location: Drill Ground, East Brisbane
Titles/Honours: Challenge Cup 1894; Charity Cup 1895
NORMAN PARK
Dates: 1927
Location: Brisbane Cricket Ground
Nickname: *Parks*
Notes: Norman Park took the place of Pineapple Rovers in the QFA First Division in 1927.
Titles/Honours: Queensland Cup 1930
NORTH ARM
Dates: 1921
Location: W. Worthington's Paddock, North Arm
Colours: Blue shirts
Titles/Honours: Premiers, North Coast Association 1921; Power Cup 1923; Plint Cup 1923; Robinson Cup 1923
Notes: In 1921 the North Coast Association consisted of the North Arm, Buderim, Mapleton and Palmwoods clubs.
NORTH IPSWICH
Dates: 1906
Location: North Ipswich Reserve
Nickname: *The Royals*
NORTH JOHNSTONE
Dates: c. 1926
Colours: Black and white striped shirts
NORTH ROCKHAMPTON
Dates: 1948
Location: Rockhampton
NORTH ROVERS
Dates: 1947
Location: Mackay
NORTHERN DOWNS
Dates: c. 1932
Location: Toowoomba
Titles/Honours: Perkins Cup 1937
NORTHTOWN UNITED
Dates: 1926
Location: Ipswich
OAKEY
Dates: 1907
Location: Oakey Recreation Reserve
Titles/Honours: Downs Championship Cup 1908
OBI OBI
Dates: 1922
Location: Obi Obi
Titles/Honours: Premiers 1924; Power Cup 1924-1926

OSBORNE
Dates: c. 1924
Location: Osborne

OUR BOYS
Dates: 1927
Location: Bowen

OVERLANDERS
Dates: c. 1947
Location: Wright's Park Innisfail

OXLEY UNITED
Dates: 1912
Location: Dunlop's Paddock; Luckock's Paddock (1927); Cawonea Park (1934); Graceville Oval (1953); Dunlop Park, Corinda (1955)
Colours: Maroon shirts with white collars and white shorts
Nickname: The Boomerangs; Ramblers

PADDINGTON TRAMWAY
Dates: c. 1925
Location: Paddington

PALMWOODS
Dates: 1920
Location: Palmwoods
Notes: Palmwoods only played for one season in the North Coast Football Association competition and was replaced by Buderim.

PARK CHURCH
Dates: c. 1910
Location: Ipswich

PARK RANGERS
Dates: c. 1928
Location: Dutton Park, Brisbane

PAST GRAMMARS
Dates: c. 1927
Location: Maryborough

PAST NORTHS
Dates: 1919
Location: Queens Park, Toowoomba

PINE CREEK
Dates: 1924
Location: Pine Creek

PINEAPPLE ROVERS
Dates: 1912-1938
Location: Pineapple Ground, Kangaroo Park; Raymond Park; Heath Park
Colours: Black and gold shirts
Titles/Honours: Premiership 1919, 1924; Nissen Cup 1919; Charity Cup 1920, 1922, 1925; State League Champions 1924-5
Notes: In 1939 Pineapple Rovers and Shafston United dissolved to form the nucleus of the Eastern Suburbs club.

PINNACLE
Dates: c. 1926
Location: Pinnacle

POMPADOURS
Dates: c. 1928
Location: Ipswich

POSTAL INSTITUTE
Date: 1949
Location: McCook Park, Newmarket
Colours: Maroon and gold quartered shirts

POZIERES
Dates: c. 1926
Location: Pozieres

PRESBYTERIAN
Dates: c. 1924
Location: Maryborough

PROSERPINE
Dates: 1928
Location: Proserpine

PROSTON
Dates: c. 1930-1936; 1938
Location: Proston Recreation Reserve
Colours: Maroon shirts with white shorts and maroon and white socks

QUEENS PARK
Dates: 1884-1886
Location: Pineapple Ground, Brisbane
Colours: Blue and white shirts
Notes: One of the first three clubs formed in Queensland.

QUEENS PARK RANGERS
Dates: c. 1922
Location: Mackay
Colours: Maroon shirts
Titles/Honours: Gohdes Cup 1927

QUEENS PARK THISTLE
Dates: 1920
Location: New Farm Park
Notes: Club was formerly Merthyr Thistle

QUEENSLANDERS
Dates: 1886
Location: Brisbane

QUEENTON RANGERS
Dates: c. 1891
Location: Athletic Reserve, Townsville
Colours: Blue shirts with white shorts
Titles/Honours: Caledonian House Trophy 1892

RAAF ARCHERFIELD
Dates: 1941
Location: Archerfield

RACEVIEW ROYALS
Dates: c. 1907
Location: Raceview
Colours: Blue and white shirts

RAILWAY ROVERS
Dates: 1912
Location: Norman Park, Cairns

RANGERS
Dates: 1883-1888
Location: Brisbane
Colours: Red and white shirts; light blue shirts;
Titles/Honours: Queensland Champions 1884

Notes: Queensland's first club, founded by Andrew Rankine, and winner of the first Queensland championship.
REDBANK SEEKERS
Dates: 1935; 1945
Location: Morris Woollen Mills Ground, Redbank
Colours: Green and gold shirts
REDCLIFFE
Dates: 1928
Location: Wood Point Reserve
Colours: Royal blue and white quartered shirts with blue and white socks
REDFERN
Dates: c. 1936
Location: Redfern
REDLANDS UNITED
Dates: 1918
Location: Redlands Bay Sports Ground
Colours: Red and white shirts; black and gold quartered shirts with white shorts; red and white shirts (1924)
REEL CABS
Dates: c. 1926
Location: Brisbane
Notes: Club of a taxi company formed by returned soldiers from World War I.
RELIANCE
Dates: 1903
Location: Dinmore
RETURNED SOLDIERS
Dates: 1919-1920
Location: Queen's Park, Toowoomba
Nickname: The Diggers; Bully Beefs
Notes: Club merged with Brisbane City in 1921.
ROCKHAMPTON CORINTHIANS
Dates: 1935
Location: Campbell Street Ground, Rockhampton
Titles/Honours: Wesley Hall Premiership Cup 1935; Heiser Cup 1935
Notes: Club was formerly named Bush Rats.
ROCKHAMPTON ROVERS
Dates: c. 1931
Location: Rockhampton
ROCKHAMPTON THISTLE
Dates: c. 1925
Location: Campbell Street Ground, Rockhampton
Titles/Honours: Wesley Hall Cup 1925
ROCKHAMPTON UNITED
Dates: 1920
Location: Bullock Flat, Rockhampton
ROCKHAMPTON WARATAHS
Dates: c. 1936
Location: Rockhampton
Colours: Blue and gold shirts
Titles/Honours: Wesley Hall Cup 1938

ROMA
Dates: c. 1912
Location: Queen's Park, Roma
ROSALIE
Dates: c. 1921
Location: Rosalie
ROSEBANK
Dates: 1893
Location: Rosebank
Titles/Honours: Premiers 1893; Challenge Cup 1893, 1897; Charity Cup 1894, 1897
Notes: Rosebank was formed by a breakaway group from the Alloways club.
ROSEBELLS
Dates: c. 1912
Location: Ipswich
Colours: Green shirts
Titles/Honours: Callow Cup 1927; Ipswich Premiers 1932, 1933; Challenge Cup 1934
ROSEWOOD LIGHT HORSE
Dates: c. 1924
Location: Rosewood
ROSEWOOD RAMBLERS
Dates: c. 1924-1940
Location: Anzac Park, Rosewood
Colours: Black and white shirts with white shorts
Titles/Honours: Hetherington Cup 1924
ROYALS
Dates: c. 1901
Location: North Ipswich Reserve; Junction Park
Colours: Maroon shirts with white shorts
ROXY
Dates: c. 1940
Location: Victoria Park, Townsville
ST ANDREW'S
Dates: 1884-1888
Location: Pineapple Ground, Raymond Terrace
Colours: Dark blue shirts
Titles/Honours: Badge 1886
Notes: The name of the club was changed to Athletics in 1889.
ST BARNABAS
Dates: c. 1919
Location: Bulimba
ST HELEN'S
Dates: c. 1912-1940; c. 1945
Location: Ebbw Vale Park, Ebbw Vale
Colours: Green shirts with white shorts and white socks with green tops
Titles/Honours: Austral Cup 1926; Tedman Cup 1928; Challenge Cup 1929, 1931; Ipswich Premiers 1932; Java Cup 1932; G.H. Price Cup 1939; Tedman Cup 1939; League champions 1947-48; Tristram Shield 1948; Charity Cup 1948; Hilton Shield 1948-9

ST JOHN'S
Dates: 1912
Location: Townsville

ST MARY'S
Dates: c. 1935
Location: Brisbane

ST OSWALD'S
Dates: c. 1934
Location: Brisbane

ST PHILIP'S
Dates: c. 1917
Location: Brisbane

ST STEPHEN'S
Dates: 1913
Location: Newtown

SANDGATE
Dates: 1938
Titles/Honours: Ernie Brough Memorial Cup 1939

SANDGATE RAAF
Dates: 1939
Location: Sandgate

SANDHILLS SWIFTS
Dates: 1932
Colours: Green and gold shirts

SARINA
Dates: c. 1927-1937; 1947
Location: Sarina Recreation Ground

SAWMILLS
Dates: 1912
Location: Cairns

SCOTTISH RIFLES
Dates: 1887
Location: Cricket Ground, North Rockhampton
Colours: Blue and white shirts with white shorts
Titles/Honours: Charity Cup 1892

SCOTTVILLE RANGERS
Dates: c 1926
Location: Scottville

SEEKERS
Dates: c. 1935-1939; 1946
Location: Redbank
Colours: Green and gold shirts

SEVERNLEA
Dates: c. 1930
Location: Severnlea

SHAFSTON ROVERS
Dates: c. 1935-1938
Location: Thompson Estate, Stones Corner; Raymond Park, Kangaroo Point
Colours: Black shirts with white shorts
Titles/Honours: 2nd Grade Premiers 1922
Notes: In 1939 Shafston United and Pineapple Rovers dissolved to form the nucleus of the Eastern Suburbs club.

SHIPYARDS
Dates: 1926
Location: Maryborough
Notes: This team changed its name to Wanderers in 1926.

SILKSTONE PRESBYTERIANS
Dates: c. 1891
Location: Silkstone
Titles/Honours: Green Cup 1924

SOLDIERS
Dates: c. 1919
Location: Darling Downs
Nickname:: Diggers

SOMERSET DAM
Dates: 1938
Location: Somerset Dam
Colours: Saxe blue shirts with white shorts

STANTHORPE
Dates: c. 1936
Location: Stanthorpe

STANWELL
Dates: c. 1933
Location: Stanwell

SOUTH BRISBANE
Dates: 1894
Location: Davies Park, Brisbane
Notes: South Brisbane was formerly named the Alloways club.

SOUTH BRISBANE SCOTTISH
Dates: c. 1922
Location: Heath Park, Brisbane

SOUTH BURNETT
Dates: c. 1930
Location: South Burnett

SOUTH JOHNSTON
Dates: c. 1936
Location: South Johnstone
Colours: Black shirts with white 'V'
Titles/Honours: Premiership 1936

SOUTH TOWNSVILLE
Dates: 1929
Location: Victoria Park, Townsville

SOUTH WARD ROVERS
Dates: c. 1930
Location: Mackay
Titles/Honours: Biddle Cup 1931

SOUTH WARD WANDERERS
Dates: 1924
Location: Mackay
Colours: Red and black shirts with white shorts
Titles/Honours: Biddle Cup 1932

SOUTHPORT
Dates: c. 1923
Location: Southport

SOUTHS
Dates: c. 1908
Location: Townsville
Colours: Maroon shirts

THE FOUNDATION YEARS 1859-1949

SOUTHS UNITED
Dates: c. 1921
Location: Victoria Park, Townsville
Titles/Honours: Townsville Challenge Cup 1921-1922; Premiers 1924
STANTHORPE ROVERS
Dates: 1926
Location: McGregor Park, Stanthorpe
Colours: Blue and white shirts
STANWELL
Dates: c. 1933
Location: Stanwell
Colours: Blue shirts with white shorts
STARLIGHTS
Dates: c. 1924
Location: Gymnasium Ground, Rockhampton
STONE RIVER
Dates: c. 1931
Location: Stone River
SUMMIT HOTSPUR
Dates: c. 1936
Location: Warwick
Titles/Honours: Ambulance Cup 1936
SWIFTS
Dates: 1886
Location: Brisbane
Notes: Swifts only played for one season.
TANNYMOREL
Dates: 1912
Location: Tannymorel
Nickname: Tanny
TARINGA
Dates: c. 1934
Location: Taringa
TARINGA ROVERS
Dates: 1949
Location: Moore Park, Indooroopilly
Colours: Blue shirts
THE SUMMIT HOTSPURS
Dates: c. 1926
Location: The Summit Recreation Oval
Titles/Honours: Pioneer Shield 1935; Ambulance Cup 1935
THERESA
Dates: c. 1936
Location: Millaa Millaa
Titles/Honours: Blue Jay Cup 1936
THISTLE
Dates: 1887
Location: Lanham Park, Grange
Colours: Light blue shirts with white shorts
Nickname: The Scotsmen
Titles/Honours: Metropolitan Premiers 1926; Inter City Cup winners 1926
Notes: Thistle was an offshoot of St. Andrews.
TINANA ROVERS
Dates: c. 1924 -1925

Location: Tinana
Notes: In 1925 the Maryborough and District Soccer Association included the clubs Tinana, Walkers, Presbyterians, Wallaroos and Howard.
TOOMBUL UNITED
Dates: c. 1928
Location: Nundah Oval
Colours: Black and white striped shirts; orange shirts and black shorts (1934)
TOOWONG
Dates: c. 1913
Location: Toowong Sports Ground
Colours: Black and gold shirts
TOOWONG RECREATION
Dates: 1948
Location: Milton Park, Milton
Colours: Bottle green shirts with a gold V.
TOOWOOMBA
Dates: c. 1908
Location: Toowoomba
Titles/Honours: Perkins & Co Cup 1927
TOOWOOMBA CITY
Dates: c. 1907
Location: Athletic Grounds, Toowoomba
Colours: Maroon and white halved shirts
Nickname: The Townies
Titles/Honours: League Premiers 1921-1922
TOOWOOMBA CITY UNITED
Dates: 1923
Location: Athletic Grounds, Toowoomba
Colours: Maroon shirts with white shorts
Nickname: The Townies
TOOWOOMBA CORINTHIANS
Dates: c. 1912
Location: Toowoomba
TOOWOOMBA DIGGERS
Dates: 1919
Location: Toowoomba
Titles/Honours: Gilson's Cup 1920; Citizen's Cup 1920; Premiers Toowoomba League 1922-1925; Charity Cup 1925
TOOWOOMBA ELECTRICS
Dates: c. 1930
Location: Toowoomba
Notes: Team of the Toowoomba Electric Light and Power Company.
TOOWOOMBA HEATHER
Dates: c. 1911
Location: Toowoomba
TOOWOOMBA PARK RANGERS
Dates: c. 1913
Location: Toowoomba
TOOWOOMBA RANGERS
Dates: c. 1921
Location: Toowoomba
Colours: Red shirts with white shorts

TOOWOOMBA WARATAHS
Dates: 1910
Location: Polo Ground, Toowoomba

TORBANLEA
Dates: 1926
Location: Torbanlea
Colours: Yellow and black shirts
Titles/Honours: Steindl Cup 1926

TIGERS
Dates: c. 1947
Location: Townsville

TOOMBUL
Dates: c. 1934
Location: Toombul
Nickname: The Buls

TOOWONG
Dates: c. 1912
Location: Toowong Sports Ground
Nickname: The Cemetery Boys

TORBANLEA
Dates: 1893; c. 1925
Location: One Mile Ground, Torbanlea
Colours: Black and yellow shirts
Titles/Honours: Steindl Cup 1926

TOWNSVILLE
Dates: c. 1922
Location: Victoria Park, Ross Island

TOWNSVILLE CALEDONIANS
Dates: c. 1929
Location: Townsville

TOWNSVILLE ROVERS
Dates: c. 1940
Location: Victoria Park, Townsville

TOWNSVILLE THISTLE
Dates: c. 1908
Location: Townsville
Colours: White shirts

TOWNSVILLE TIGERS
Dates: c. 1947
Location: Townsville

TOWNSVILLE TROJANS
Dates: c. 1947
Location: Townsville

TRAMWAY ATHLETIC
Dates: c. 1928
Location: Lang Park, Brisbane

TULLY
Dates: 1931
Location: Tully
Colours: Red shirts with red socks and white tops.

TULLY CALEDONIANS
Dates: 1929
Location: Tully

TULLY ODDFELLOWS
Dates: 1929
Location: Tully

TULLY RANGERS
Dates: 1935
Location: Tully

UNDERGROUND
Dates: c. 1940
Location: Mt Isa
Titles/Honours: Mt. Isa Premiership 1939

UNEMPLOYED
Dates: c. 1933
Location: Innisfail

UNITED COMMERCIALS
Dates: 1939
Location: Hockey Ground, Maryborough

UNITED RANGERS
Dates: c. 1932
Location: Brisbane
Colours: Red shirts
Titles/Honours: Stewart Shield 1933

VALLEY
Dates: c. 1909-1933
Location: Campbell Street Ground, Rockhampton
Notes: Club was absorbed by Fitzroy Rovers in 1934.

VICE-REGALS
Dates: 1932
Location: Mackay
Titles/Honours: Mackay Premiers 1932; Watson Cup 1932; McGuire Cup 1934

VIOLET
Dates: 1921
Location: Brisbane
Colours: Navy blue with a spray of violet

WALKERS ATHLETIC
Dates: 1947
Location: Kangaroo Oval, Maryborough
Titles/Honours: Werder Kangaroo Oval Cup 1949

WALKERS COLLIERY
Dates: c. 1942
Location: Ipswich

WALKERS LTD
Dates: 1924
Location: Eskdale Park, Maryborough
Notes: An engineering company which had a foundry in Maryborough.

WALLANGARA
Dates: c. 1924
Location: Wallangara

WALLABY
Dates: c. 1916
Location: Raymond Park

WALLAROOS
Dates: c. 1920
Location: Yaronga Park, Brisbane

WALLAROOS
Dates: c. 1924

Location: Eskdale Park, Maryborough
Titles/Honours: Maryborough Association Shield 1926
WALLAROOS
Dates: c. 1890
Location: Rockhampton
WALLOON
Dates: c. 1909
Location: Walloon
Colours: Dark blue shirts with white shorts
WALTER REID AND CO
Dates: c. 1889
Location: Archer Park, Rockhampton
Colours: Maroon and white bars on shirt
Notes: Team of a prominent local merchant with many commercial interests in Rockhampton.
WARWICK
Dates: 1912- c. 1931; 1935
Location: Slade Park (1912) McLaughlin's Paddock; Queen's Park; Cunningham Park, Warwick
Colours: Red and white shirts
WARWICK DIGGERS
Dates: 1945
Location: Showground Oval, Warwick
Notes: Club was called 'Army Records' in early 1945.
WARWICK ROVERS
Dates: c. 1926
Location: Warwick
Colours: Blue and white shirts
WATERSIDE
Dates: 1922
Location: Brisbane
WATERSIDE WORKERS UNION
Dates: c. 1922
Location: Brisbane
WATSONVILLE
Dates: c. 1897
Location: Watsonville
WELLINGTON
Dates: c. 1895
Location: Pineapple Ground
Nickname: The 'Tons
Titles/Honours: Challenge Cup 1905, 1906, 1909
WEST BRISBANE AMATEUR ATHLETIC CLUB
Dates: 1923
Location: Brisbane
WESTERN SUBURBS
Dates: c. 1910-1913
Location: Polo Ground, Toowoomba
Colours: Red shirts with white shorts
Titles/Honours: Toowoomba Premiers 1910
WHITWOOD
Dates: c. 1892
Location: Whitwood Ground, Bundamba

Notes: Players were employees of the Stafford Brothers, Whitwood Colliery
WILSTON
Dates: 1922
Location: Wilston
WILSTON UNITED
Dates: 1948
Location: Finsbury Park, Newmarket
Colours: Navy shirts with black shorts and navy and white socks
WOLVI
Dates: c. 1928
Location: Wolvi
WOODVILLE COLLIERS
Dates: c. 1910
Location: Woodville
WOOGAROO ASYLUM
Dates: 1873
Location: Goodna
WOOLLOONGABBA LOCO
Dates: c. 1926
Location: Woolloongabba
Titles/Honours: Mid-Week Soccer Association Premiership 1927; Reel Cabs Cup 1927
WOOMBYE
Dates: c. 1921
Location: Woombye
WYANDRA SS
Dates: c. 1924
Location: Cairns
WYNNUM
Dates: 1921
Location: Wynnum
Colours: Black and white vertical striped shirts with black shorts and black socks with white tops
Nickname: The Bay
Titles/Honours: 2nd Division Champions 1938; G.H. Price Cup 1938; Tedman Cup 1938
Notes: Wynnum club absorbed most players from the Queen's Park club.
WYREEMA, SS
Dates: c. 1912
Notes: SS *Wyremma* (built 1908) was a steam ship active on the east coast, particularly in Queensland. The crew would stop at Cairns and other ports and play local teams.
YARGIN
Dates: 1934
Location: Yargin
Colours: White shirts with white shorts
YELLOW CABS
Dates: c. 1927
Location: Brisbane
YEPPOON
Dates: 1895; c. 1925
Location: Rockhampton

Notes: The Yeppoon based team was required to play all matches in Rockhampton.
YMCA
Dates: 1911; 1930; c. 1940
Location: Wembley Oval; Langlands Park, Brisbane
Colours: White shirts with maroon 'V', with white shorts and maroon and white hooped socks

Nickname: *The Triangles*
Titles/Honours: State League Champions 1934, 1936, 1946; Tristram Shield 1940
YMCA
Dates: c. 1908
Location: Townsville
Colours: Red shirts with white shorts

South Australia

ADELAIDE
Dates: 1902; 1904-1915
Location: South Parklands, Adelaide
Colours: White shirts with blue shorts
Titles/Honours: Cambridge Cup 1912-1914
Notes: Adelaide devolved from the South Adelaide club.
ADELAIDE TRAMWAYS COMPANY
Dates: c. 1914
Location: Adelaide
ADELAIDE UNITED
Dates: 1924
Location: Adelaide
Colours: Red and White
Nickname: *The Citizens*
Notes: Was absorbed by the North Adelaide club in 1925.
ADELAIDE UNIVERSITY
Dates: 1935
Location: Birkalla Oval; South Parklands
Notes: Players were students of Parkin College.
ALAWOONA
Dates: 1929
Location: Alawoona Oval
ASCOT PARK
Dates: 1922-1950
Location: Le Fevre Terrace; Harcourt Gardens
Colours: Green and black striped shirts
Nickname: *The Park*
Titles/Honours: Second Division Champions 1931
Notes: Ascot Park was formerly a rugby club.
ASCOT UNITED
Dates: c. 1926
Location: Ascot
Notes: Team played in the Suburban Soccer Association competition.
BARMERA
Dates: 1924
Location: Barmera Recreation Ground
Colours: Light and dark blue shirts (1928)

BERRI
Dates: c. 1924
Location: Berri Soccer Ground
Colours: White shirts
Titles/Honours: Rowe Cup winners 1927
BIRKALLA ROVERS
Dates: 1933
Location: Sportsville Bay Road, Plympton; Novar and Camden Recreation Ground (1946)
Colours: Gold shirts with black shorts and gold socks
Titles/Honours: Woodrow Shield 1935; Cambridge Cup 1935; 1st division Champions 1944-45, 1947; Presidents Cup 1944-1945, 1947; Pelaco Cup 1938, 1944; Pozza Cup 1946-1947
Notes: Birkalla is said to be an aboriginal word meaning 'level ground'.
BLACK FOREST
Dates: c. 1924
Location: Camden Recreation Ground
Notes: Black Forest played in the Seventh Division in 1947.
BLACK ROCK
Dates: c. 1924
Location: Black Rock
BLYTH
Dates: 1924
Location: Blyth Oval
BORDERTOWN
Dates: 1930
Location: Bordertown Show Ground
Colours: Red shirts with a white 'V', navy blue shorts, black socks with white tops.
BRITISH TUBE MILLS (BTM)
Dates: 1943-1944; 1947-1951
Location: Kilburn
Notes: BTM was a heavy engineering works making auto bodies.
BUTE
Dates: c. 1925
Location: Bute
CAMBRIDGE
Dates: 1906-1911

Location: Alberton Oval; Cheltenham, Adelaide
Colours: Light blue shirts and dark blue shorts
Nickname: *The Blues*
Titles/Honours: Premiers 1910; Webb-Harris Cup 1907, 1910-1911
Notes: Club changed name to Tandanya in 1912.

CAMDEN MAGPIES
Dates: 1943
Location: Camden Showground; Onslow Park (1944)
Notes: Camden played in the Seventh Division in 1947.

CENTRAL
Dates: 1949-1950
Location: South Parklands, Port Pirie

CENTRALS
Dates: c. 1932
Location: Port Lincoln

CHANDADAH
Dates: c. 1931
Location: Chandadah

CHELTENHAM
Dates: 1912-1924; 1929-1940
Location: Cheltenham; Woodville
Colours: Blue and white shirts
Nickname: Chelts
Titles/Honours: League title 1915, 1920-1921, 1923; Cambridge Cup 1915, 1920, 1922; Webb-Harris Cup 1920
Notes: In 1925 Cheltenham, Hindmarsh and Holden's United amalgamated to form the West Torrens Club. Cheltenham fielded only Australian born players in the 1920's.

CLARE GYMNASIUM
Dates: c. 1924
Location: Clare Oval

COHUNA
Dates: c. 1925
Location: Cohuna

COLONEL LIGHT GARDENS
Dates: c. 1946
Location: Adelaide
Notes: Competed in the Adelaide sixth division in 1946.

CRETE PARK THISTLES
Dates: 1949
Location: Soccer Ground, Whyalla
Titles/Honours: Whyalla Championship 1949

CRETE PARK WANDERERS
Dates: 1949
Location: Soccer Ground, Whyalla
Notes: Club comprised British migrants.

CUMBERLAND UNITED
Dates: 1943
Location: Hollywood Estate (Cumberland Park); Mortlock Park; Pearson's Estate, Edwardstown
Colours: White shirts with black shorts and black and white socks; chocolate and gold shirts (1947)
Nickname: *The Foxes*
Notes: Cumberland first fielded junior teams in 1941.

CUMMINS
Dates: 1933
Location: Recreation Oval, Cummins

CUNGENA
Dates: c. 1931
Location: Cungena

DAVENPORT UNITED
Dates: c. 1929
Location: Davenport Oval, Port Augusta
Titles/Honours: Port Pirie Leonard League Shield 1930

EAST TORRENS
Dates: 1925-1931
Location: Murray Park, Magill; Kent Town Oval
Colours: Maroon shirts
Notes: First President was Mr Penfold-Hyland of the wine making family.

EASTERN OTIOSE
Dates: c. 1935
Location: Adelaide

EASTERN UNITED
Dates: 1931
Location: Dequetteville Terrace, East Parklands
Notes: Third division club.

EDILLILIE
Dates: c. 1932
Location: Edillilie

EDWARDSTOWN
Dates: c. 1946
Location: Wayville West

ELMORE
Dates: c. 1925
Location: Elmore

EUREKA YOUTH LEAGUE
Dates: 1943
Location: Soccer Ground, Whyalla

GAWLER UNITED
Dates: 1911
Location: The Oval, Gawler

GLENELG
Dates: 1920-1931; 1939
Location: Camden Oval; Novar Gardens, Glenelg
Colours: Yellow and black shirts
Nickname: *The Seasiders*

GOODWOOD
Dates: c. 1923
Location: Camden

HALBURY
Dates: c. 1925
Location: Halbury

HARRIS SCARFE
Dates: 1936
Location: Adelaide
Notes: Club of the Harris Scarfe department store.

HELLENIC
Dates: 1939-1940
Location: South Terrace, Adelaide

HINDMARSH
Dates: 1905-1919; 1922-1925
Location: Hindmarsh Oval; East Parklands; Lindsay Circus Oval; Findon
Colours: Red and white shirts
Nickname: The Reds; Marshites
Titles/Honours: Premiers 1905, 1907, 1908-1909, 1913, 1924; Webb-Harris Cup 1908-09, 1915, 1919
Notes: Hindmarsh absorbed the members of the Woodville club. In 1925 Cheltenham, Hindmarsh and Holden's United amalgamated to form the West Torrens Club.

HOLDEN'S UNITED
Dates: 1924
Location: Adelaide
Titles/Honours: Cambridge Cup 1924
Nickname: The Body Builders
Notes: Factory team of the Holden Motor Body Builders.
Notes: In 1925 Cheltenham, Hindmarsh and Holden's United amalgamated to form the West Torrens Club.

HOLDFAST BAY
Dates: 1924; 1933
Location: Da Costa Park, Holdfast Bay
Colours: Black and yellow shirts
Nickname: *The Bays, The Tigers*

HOTSPUR
Dates: 1939
Location: West Parklands, Adelaide
Notes: Hotspur absorbed Westbourne Park Rovers in 1940.

HOYLES PLAINS
Dates: 1924
Location: Halbury

IMPERIAL SERVICES
Dates: 1923
Location: Mile End
Colours: Black shirts with white shorts
Notes: Changed name to West Adelaide in late 1924.

INDUSTRIALS
Dates: c. 1947
Location: Adelaide
Notes: Industrials played in the Seventh Division in 1947.

INVICTA
Dates: c. 1931
Location: Port Lincoln

JAVANESE
Dates: 1943
Location: Hart Street, Port Adelaide
Notes: Team disbanded during the 1943 metropolitan season.

JUVENTUS
Dates: 1946
Location: Cumberland Park, Adelaide
Colours: (1946) Navy blue shirts with a white 'J'; (1949) black and white striped shirts with white shorts.
Titles/Honours: Second Division Champions 1945
Notes: Founded initially by players from the Savoia club which existed in 1940. From 1946 the club was named Juventus.

KADINA
Dates: 1926
Location: Newton Oval, Kadina
Colours: Red shirts with white shorts

KANIVA TIGERS
Dates: c. 1930
Location: Kaniva

KINGSWOOD
Dates: 1927-1944; 1946
Location: Mortlock Park; Kingswood Oval (1929)
Colours: Royal blue shirts with white shorts
Titles/Honours: League Premiers 1933, 1946; Pelaco Cup 1935; Pozza Cup 1935
Notes: Club included many Italian players in the 1930's.

KINGSWOOD ALBION
Dates: 1938-1940
Location: Kingswood

KINGSWOOD-MORTLOCK PARK
Dates: 1928
Location: Mortlock Park

KIRTON POINT
Dates: 1932
Location: Port Lincoln

LANCASHIRE
Dates: 1927-c. 1934
Location: Swan Terrace, Adelaide; Barton Terrace, North Adelaide (1931)
Colours: Red and white shirts
Titles/Honours: Second Division Premiers 1930; Pelaco Cup 1931

LARGS ATHLETIC
Dates: 1932-1938
Location: Almond Tree Flat, Swansea
Colours: Black and amber shirts
Titles/Honours: Basse Cup 1932
Notes: Club initially named Osborne Athletic.

LEFEVRE
Dates: c. 1946
Location: Adelaide

LIPSON
Dates: c. 1935
Location: Lipson
LOCO
Dates: 1913-1914
Location: Adelaide
Notes: Railway workshop team.
LOCK 5
Dates: 1925-1926
Location: Renmark
Colours: Royal blue shirts
Titles/Honours: Minor premiers 1925
MAFFRA
Dates: c. 1925
Location: Maffra
MAGILL UNITED
Dates: 1912-1913
Location: Murray Park Oval
MAITLAND
Dates: c. 1926
Location: Maitland
MANNUM
Dates: 1925
Location: Mannum
MELITA
Dates: 1949
Location: Adelaide
Notes: Melita was formed by Maltese migrants.
MERIBAH
Dates: 1929
Location: Meribah
MINNIPA
Dates: c. 1931
Location: Minnipa
MISSION TO SEAMEN
Dates: c. 1926-1929
Location: Port Adelaide
Notes: Club formed for sailors working ashore. When club disbanded Rosewater Colts club was formed.
MOONTA
Dates: 1927
Location: Moonta
Notes: Moonta fielded Australian born players only.
MOOROOK
Dates: 1924
Location: Moorook
MORTLOCK PARK
Dates: 1928
Location: Mortlock Park soccer ground
Notes: Mortlock Park was a subsidiary club of Kingswood.
MURRAY BRIDGE
Dates: 1923-1924; 1928
Location: Murray Bridge Recreation Ground, Adelaide Road

NAILSWORTH
Dates: c. 1946
Location: Nailsworth
NAMBROK
Dates: c. 1925
Location: Nambrok
NEW ROVERS
Location: Adelaide
Notes: A Third Division team
NORTH ADELAIDE
Dates: 1898-
Location: South Parklands, Adelaide; Fitzroy Terrace, McKinnon Parade; Jubilee Oval
Colours: White shirts; Blue shirts with white shorts
Titles/Honours: Premiers 1903-6-8-14 -19-22; Sturt Cup 1928
Nickname: The Lillywhites
Notes: One of the first three clubs formed in Adelaide and winner of the first championship in 1903. Absorbed the Prospect and Adelaide United clubs in 1925.
NORTH ADELAIDE UNITED
Dates: c. 1929
Location: Adelaide
Colours: Red and white striped shirts
Titles/Honours: Third Division champions 1929; Sturt Shield 1930
NORTH ATHLETIC
Dates: 1929
Location: Adelaide
Colours: Red shirts
NORTH CAMDEN
Dates: c. 1927
Location: North Camden
NORTH UNITED
Dates: c. 1929
Location: LeFevre Terrace
NORTHUMBERLAND AND DURHAM
Dates: 1928-1944; 1946-1948
Location: Baulderstone's Estate, Clarence Park; West Park (1930) Allenby Gardens, Adelaide
Colours: Heliotrope (Light purple) shirt with a black 'V', white shorts and heliotrope and black socks.
Titles/Honours: League Champions 1938, 1943; Sturt Shield 1929; Pozza Cup 1938; Pelaco Cup 1943; League Champion 1943
NORWOOD
Dates: 1923-24; 1938-41; 1947-1953
Location: Norwood
Colours: Red and blue shirts
NORWOOD IMPERIALS
Dates: c. 1922
Location: Dequetteville Terrace, Kent Town

OLYMPIC
Dates: 1949
Location: Adelaide

OLYMPICS
Dates: 1947
Location: Crete Park, Whyalla

ORROROO
Dates: c. 1924
Location: Orroroo
Notes: Orroroo played in a sub association in matches against the Broken Hill clubs in western New South Wales.

OSBORNE ATHLETIC
Dates: 1928-1931
Location: Largs Reserve, Swansea
Colours: Black and amber shirts
Notes: Founded by employees of the South Australian Gas Company.
Club became Largs Athletic in 1932.

OTIOSE
Dates: 1931-1939
Location: Clarence Park
Titles/Honours: Second Division Champions 1937
Notes: Otiose comprised unemployed Australian youths.

PARK ALBION
Dates: 1936-1941; 1946
Location: Taylor's Road Ground; Allenby Gardens; West Thebarton
Titles/Honours: Second Division Champions 1938

PEAK UNITED
Dates: 1949
Location: Fitzroy Terrace, Adelaide
Notes: Company team of Peak Construction Company.

PENNINGTON ROVERS
Dates: 1938-1940
Location: Torrens Road, Woodville
Colours: Red and blue shirts with white sleeves

PERRY ENGINEERING
Dates: 1943-1948
Location: Hutt Street; Allenby Gradens, Adelaide
Nickname: The Engineers
Notes: Company was a foundry which built trains.

PETERBOROUGH
Dates: 1919; 1923
Location: Hillview Estate Recreation Ground
Colours: Yellow shirts with black shorts
Notes: The club was previously named Petersburg.

PETERSBURG
Dates: 1912-1914
Location: Petersburg Showground
Nickname: The Burgs
Notes: The town of Petersburg was re-named Peterborough after WWI. Petersburg played in a sub association in matches against the Broken Hill clubs in western New South Wales.

PIONEERS
Dates: 1893
Location: Adelaide

PLYMPTON
Dates: c. 1925
Location: Weigall Oval, Adelaide

POLICE
Dates: 1930
Location: Wayville West

PORT ADELAIDE
Dates: 1905-1914; 1920-1941; 1944
Location: Woodville Park; Cheltenham; Alberton; Swan Terrace; Fletcher Road Reserve, Semaphore (1925); Peterhead Reserve; ICI Oval, Ethelon
Colours: Black shirts with black shorts (1908); Black and white striped shirts with black shorts and black socks
Nickname: The Magpies; The Seasiders; The Dickers; The Portonians
Titles/Honours: First Division Title 1911-1913, 1926-1927, 1931, 1945; Sturt Shield 1925; State Cup 1926, 1933, 1945; Pelaco Cup 1926, 1945; Basse Cup 1926
Notes: Team originally named Woodville. Port Adelaide absorbed Cheltenham club in 1914 and the Semaphore club in 1925. Joined First Division in 1929.

PORT ADELAIDE COLTS
Dates: 1927
Location: Adelaide
Titles/Honours: Adelaide Suburban Soccer League Premiers 1927

PORT ALBION
Dates: 1936
Location: Port Albion

PORT LINCOLN
Dates: c. 1931
Location: Northern Grounds, Port Lincoln

PORT LINCOLN RANGERS
Dates: 1931
Location: Northern Grounds, Port Lincoln

PORT LINCOLN STAR
Dates: c. 1931
Location: Northern Grounds, Port Lincoln
Titles/Honours: West Coast League Champions 1931

PORT PIRIE
Dates: c. 1910
Location: Balmoral Road; Recreation Ground, Port Pirie

PORT PIRIE CALEDONIANS
Dates: 1932
Location: Drill Hall Ground, Port Pirie

THE FOUNDATION YEARS 1859-1949

PORT PIRIE MAGPIES
Dates: 1924 - c. 1947
Location: Balmoral Road Oval, Port Pirie
Colours: Black and white shirts

PORT PIRIE RAMBLERS
Dates: 1924
Location: Military Oval ; Maytown Oval, Port Pirie
Colours: Blue shirts with white shorts
Titles/Honours: Leonard Cup 1927

PORT PIRIE ROVERS
Dates: 1924
Location: Balmoral Road Oval; Maytown Oval, Port Pirie

PORT PIRIE SOCCER CRICKET
Dates: 1927
Location: Port Pirie

PORT PIRIE STARS
Dates: 1931
Location: Drill Hall Ground, Port Pirie
Notes: Port Pirie Stars disbanded after one season.

PORT PIRIE THISTLES
Dates: 1926
Location: Balmoral Road Oval; Maytown Oval, Port Pirie
Titles/Honours: Leonard Cup 1928, 1931; Leonard League Shield 1931

PORT PIRIE UNITED
Dates: 1930
Location: Port Pirie
Titles/Honours: Port Pirie Cup 1930

PORT PIRIE WARRIORS
Dates: 1928
Location: Balmoral Road Oval, Port Pirie

PORT PRESBYTERIAN THISTLE
Dates: 1930-1941; 1948
Location: John Hart Reserve; Largs Bay; Hindmarsh Oval
Colours: Blue shirts with a yellow 'V'
Titles/Honours: League Champions 1934-35-37; Pelaco Cup 1934
Notes: Club founded by Presbyterian Church members.

PORT PIRIE UNITED
Dates: 1930
Location: Drill Hall Oval, Port Pirie
Titles/Honours: Port Pirie Soccer Association Cup 1930

PORT THISTLE
Dates: c. 1932
Location: Hindmarsh Oval
Colours: Dark blue shirts
Titles/Honours: First Division Premiers 1934; Pelaco Cup 1934; Moulden League Premiership Cup 1935

POSTAL INSTITUTE
Dates: 1943; 1948-52
Location: West Terrace, Adelaide

PROSPECT UNITED
Dates: c. 1920- 1924
Location: Prospect
Titles/Honours: Basse Cup 1921; Moulden Challenge Cup 1921; Webb-Harris Cup 1921; State Cup 1923
Notes: Club was absorbed by the North Adelaide club in 1925.

PSYCHE, HMS
Dates: c. 1908-1910
Notes: Played matches against local clubs when in port.

PULTENEY OLD SCHOLARS
Dates: 1927-1928; 1930-33
Location: Wayville West, Adelaide
Notes: Club based on ex-students from Pultney Grammar School.

QUORN
Dates: c. 1922; 1943
Location: Quorn

RAILWAYS
Dates: c. 1932
Location: Port Pirie

RAL RAL
Dates: 1925
Location: Renmark
Colours: White shirts, shorts and socks
Notes: Players in the club were from the Block E and Chaffey areas.

RAMBLERS
Dates: 1925
Location: Mount Barker
Colours: Blue shirts with white shorts

RANGERS
Dates: 1893; 1924
Location: Adelaide

RENMARK TOWN
Dates: 1896- c. 1912; 1924
Location: Renmark
Colours: Blue and white shirts; black and white striped shirts with white shorts and black socks with white tops (1927)
Titles/Honours: Upper Murray Association Premiers 1925
Notes: By 1925 Renmark were part of the Upper Murray Soccer Association with the teams of Berri, Ral Ral and Lock 5.

RICHMOND
Dates: c. 1946
Location: Camden Recreation Ground

RIVERTON
Dates: 1924
Location: Riverton Recreation Ground

RUBERY OWN KEMSLEY (R.O.K)
Dates: 1949
Location: Adelaide

Notes: R.O.K was a subsidiary of a British owned engineering company.

ROSEWATER COLTS
Dates: 1928-1933
Location: Hardwick Estate, Rosewater Plains, Adelaide
Notes: Succeeded the Mission to Seamen Institute club. Initially a Third Division side.

ROYAL AUSTRALIAN AIR FORCE (RAAF)
Dates: c. 1942
Location: Port Pirie

ST LEONARD'S
Dates: c. 1946
Location: Wayville West. Adelaide

ST PETER'S
Dates: 1912-1915; 1924
Location: St Peters
Colours: Blue shirts with white shirts
Titles/Honours: Second Division Champions 1914

SAVOIA
Dates: 1940
Location: South Terrace, Adelaide
Notes: First Italian based club in Adelaide.

SAVOY
Dates: 1946
Location: South Parklands, Port Pirie
Titles/Honours: Inaugural PPSA competition 1949
Notes: Savoia, Central and Wanderers were a part of the inaugural Port Pirie Soccer Association. Savoy was formed by Italian migrants.

SCOUTS
Dates: c. 1948
Location: Whyalla

SEAMANS MISSION
Dates: c 1922
Location: Adelaide

SEMAPHORE
Dates: 1923-1924
Location: Fletcher Road Reserve, Semaphore; Hart Street, Semaphore
Colours: Navy blue shirts
Notes: Semaphore broke away from Port Adelaide in 1923 and then re- amalgamated with the Port Adelaide Club.

SNOWTOWN
Dates: c. 1925
Location: Snowtown Oval

SOCCER CRICKET CLUB
Location: Port Pirie
Dates: 1927-1928

SOUTH ADELAIDE
Dates: 1902
Location: Hutt Street Ground; South Parklands
Colours: Blue and white shirts with white shorts:
Titles/Honours: Cambridge Cup 1921; Second Division Champions 1936, 1947; Woodrow Shield 1936; Hugh Pozza Cup 1936
Notes: One of the first three clubs formed in Adelaide. South Adelaide played the first match of the British Football Association League against Woodville on April 25, 1903.

SOUTH AUSTRALIAN RAILWAYS INSTITUTE
Dates: 1928-1935; 1937
Location: Railway Recreation Grounds, West Terrace, Adelaide
Colours: Green and yellow shirts
Titles/Honours: Premiership and Woodrow Shield 1928; Second Division Champions 1934; Pelaco Cup 1930, 1933; Pozza Cup 1946
Notes: A successor club to Locos.

SOUTH CELTIC
Dates: 1920
Location: Hutt Street Ground, Adelaide
Notes: Club formed by the South Adelaide Club to replace YMCA in League in 1920.

SOUTHERN UNITED
Dates: 1930
Location: Cohen Avenue, Plympton.

STURT
Dates: 1904; 1911-1914; 1919; 1946
Location: Wayville; Hawthorn Oval (1925); Mortlock Park Oval, Colonel Light Gardens (1927)
Colours: Dark blue and light blue halved shirts; green shirts with white shorts (c.1920)
Titles/Honours: Albert Shield 1926; State League Champions 1940, 1948-1949; Cambridge Cup 1919; Pelaco Cup 1936-1937, 1941

TANDANYA
Dates: 1912-1913
Location: Adelaide
Colours: Brown shirts with a blue band
Nickname: The Tans
Notes: Tandanya in Aboriginal means 'place of the red kangaroo'. The club was previously named Cambridge.

TEROWIE
Dates: 1913
Location: Terowie
Notes: Terowie played in a sub association in matches against the Broken Hill clubs in western New South Wales.

THE WEIR
Dates: c. 1925
Location: The Weir

THEBARTON RAMBLERS
Dates: 1947-1954
Location: Taylors Road, Thebarton

THE FOUNDATION YEARS 1859-1949

Colours: Green and white shirts
THEVENARD
Dates: c. 1931
Location: Thevenard
TRAMWAYS
Dates: 1914-20, 1933-1940
Location: Adelaide
TROJAN THISTLE
Dates: 1943
Location: Adelaide
TUMBY BAY
Dates: c. 1931
Location: Tumby Bay
UNDERDALE ROVERS
Dates: c. 1939
Location: Allenby Gardens, Underdale
UNIVERSITY
Dates: 1935
Location: South Parklands (University Ground)
Colours: Black shirts with a white 'V'
UNLEY UNITED
Dates: 1928-1935
Location: West Wayville, Adelaide
Colours: Red shirts
Notes: Players were ex-students of Unley high and Goodwood central schools.
WAIKERIE
Dates: 1924
Location: Waikerie
WALLABY
Dates: 1909
Location: Cheltenham, Adelaide
Colours: Violet and gold shirts
WALLAROO RANGERS
Dates: 1926
Location: Wallaroo
Colours: Black and gold shirts
WANDERERS
Dates: 1949-1951
Location: South Parklands, Port Pirie
WARILDA
Dates: 1912
Location: Adelaide
WELLAND UNITED
Dates: 1924
Location: Welland
WEST ADELAIDE
Dates: 1925-1939; 1946
Location: Jubilee Oval; Mile-End; Hindmarsh Oval
Colours: Red and black striped shirts with black shorts and red and black socks
Titles/Honours: Second Division Champions 1929; League Champions 1930.
Notes: The club was formed by members of the Imperial and Welland clubs.

WEST TORRENS
Dates: 1925-1942; 1945-1979
Location: East Parklands; Hindmarsh Oval, Adelaide (1926)
Colours: Blue and gold shirts
Titles/Honours: League Champions 1925, 1928-1929, 1932, 1939, 1941; Cambridge Cup 1925; Pelaco Cup 1927, 1928; Pozza Cup 1934
Notes: The West Torrens Club was an amalgamation of the Cheltenham, Hindmarsh, and the Holden United clubs.
WEST UNITED
Dates: 1927-1932
Location: West Parklands, Adelaide; Weigall Oval, Plympton
Notes: West United was formerly the West Adelaide United club.
WESTBOURNE PARK ROVERS
Dates: 1939-1940
Location: Wayville West; Kingswood Oval
Notes: Team was absorbed by Hotspurs in 1940.
WHYALLA
Dates: 1923; 1940
Location: Whyalla
Colours: Black shirts with a white 'V' and white shorts.
WHYALLA CALEDONIANS
Dates: c. 1944
Location: Soccer Ground, Whyalla
Titles/Honours: Association Shield 1945
WHYALLA BLAST FURNACE
Dates: 1940
Location: Whyalla
Notes: Blast Furnace fielded two teams in the local 1940 Whyalla competition.
WHYALLA DODGERS
Dates; 1944
Location: Soccer Ground, Whyalla
WHYALLA ROVERS
Dates: 1940
Location: Soccer Ground, Whyalla
Colours: Black shirt with a white 'V' and white shorts
Titles/Honours: League winners 1943
WHYALLA SHIPYARDS
Dates: 1941
Location: Whyalla
Titles/Honours: Ken Reed Cup 1943; Sneath Cup 1943
Notes: Shipyards usually fielded two teams in the local competition.
WHYALLA WAVERLEY
Dates: 1949
Location: Crete Park
WOODSIDE UNITED
Dates: c. 1949
Location: Woodside

Notes: Woodside was formed by European migrants from the Woodside Camp.
WOODVILLE
Dates: 1903-1905
Location: Woodville
Colours: Black shirts
Titles/Honours: League Champions: 1904
Notes: One of the first three clubs formed in South Australia. Played on ground where Queen Elizabeth Hospital now stands. Changed name to Port Adelaide in 1905.
WOODVILLE NORTH
Dates: 1949
Location: Woodville
YARCOWIE
Dates: 1925
Location: Yarcowie
YATINA
Dates: 1923
Location: Yatina
YORKETOWN
Dates: 1925
Location: Yorketown
Colours: White shirts and blue shorts
YMCA
Dates: 1893; 1911-1913; 1919; 1929-1930
Location: North Park Lands, Frome Road, Adelaide
YMCA
Dates: 1927
Location: Balmoral Road Oval, Port Pirie

Tasmania

ALL BLACKS
Dates: c. 1926
Location: Launceston
Titles/Honours: Leeson Cup 1926
ANGLESEA
Dates: 1898-1909
Location: Hobart
Notes: Anglesea teams were from the army barracks.
ARMY
Dates: c. 1941
Location: Hobart
ASTON
Dates: c. 1941
Location: Hobart
ATHLETIC
Dates: c. 1914
Location: Rose Bay, Hobart
AUSTRALIAN NEWSPRINT MILLS (A.N.M.)
Dates: 1949
Location: New Norfolk
BEACONSFIELD
Dates: 1948
Location: Beaconsfield
BEACONSFIELD ROVERS
Dates: 1946
Location: Beaconsfield
BEREA YOUTH CLUB
Dates: 1944
Location: Domain No. 2, Hobart
Titles/Honours: 'C' grade premiers 1945
BLACK DIAMONDS
Dates: c. 1932
Location: St Marys
BLUE CRUSADERS
Dates: 1931-1933
Location: Hobart
Notes: Blue Crusader became the Excelsior club in 1933.
BLUE RANGERS
Dates: 1948
Location: Beaconsfield
BRIGHTON OLYMPIANS
Dates: 1948
Location: Brighton
BURNIE UNITED
Dates: 1913; 1922-1929; 1930
Location: South Burnie Recreation Ground
CADBURYS
Dates: 1921-1926; 1948
Location: Claremont
Titles/Honours: Falkinder Cup 1922
Notes: Team comprised of workers from the Cadbury chocolate factory at Claremont. Also called Cadbury Fry Pascall Athletic (C.F.P. Athletic) in 1922.
CAMBURN
Dates: 1940
Location: Hobart
Titles/Honours: Division 'C' Premiers 1944; Honeysett Cup 1944; Knock-out Cup 1944
CASCADE BREWERY
Dates: 1931-1938
Location: South Hobart Ground
Colours: Red and green shirts
Nickname: The Brewery
Titles/Honours: State Premiers 1931; Division I Premiership 1934; State Premiership 1931, 1932, 1934-1935
Notes: Factory team of Cascade Brewery. Club was a breakaway from the South Hobart club.

THE FOUNDATION YEARS 1859-1949

CITY UNITED
Dates: 1914; 1940
Location: Hobart
Nickname: The Citizens; Tigers

CITY UNITED
Dates: 1930
Location: Launceston

CORINTHIAN ROVERS
Dates: 1940
Location: Hobart
Notes: Corinthian Rovers represented the disbanded West End Club.

CORINTHIANS
Dates: 1910-1925
Location: Cornelian Bay; Rose Bay, Hobart
Colours: Green shirts
Nickname: The Amateurs
Titles/Honours: Southern Champion 1913-1914; State Champion 1913-1914; Falkinder Cup 1920
Notes: Corinthians took over the Hobart YMCA club in 1912.

CORNWALL
Dates: 1929-1932
Location: Association Ground, Cornwall
Notes: Many players worked at the Cornwall colliery.
Colours: Blue shirts

DERWENT UNITED
Dates: 1923-1929
Location: South Hobart, Hobart

DEVONPORT GYMNASIUM
Dates: 1930-1932
Location: Devonport Oval

ELLIOTT
Dates: c. 1914
Location: Elliott

ELPHIN
Dates: 1914-1925; 1927-1930; 1931
Location: Fry's Paddock, Elphin, Launceston
Colours: Royal blue shirts with white shorts
Nickname: The Swifts
Titles/Honours: Northern Premiership 1914, 1920, 1923-1924, 1927-1928; Linney Barber Cup 1927

EXCELSIOR
Dates: 1933
Location: Hobart
Notes: Formerly Blue Crusaders. The team of the Haywards Excelsior Biscuit Factory.

EX-NAVY
Dates: 1946
Location: Hobart

FINGAL
Dates: 1930-1932
Location: Fingal

GLEBE
Dates: 1934-1938

Location: No. 1 Domain Ground; Moonah Sports Ground, Hobart

GLENORCHY
Dates: c.: 1947
Location: Glenorchy

GORMANSTON
Dates: 1923
Location: Gormanston

GUNNERS
Dates: 1900-1903
Location: Hobart, Tasmania
Titles/Honours: Hobart competition 1902
Notes: One of three clubs which formed the first competition in Tasmania. The Gunners comprised a regiment from Anglesea Barracks.

HOBART
Dates: 1908
Location: Clare Street, Hobart
Colours: Light blue shirts (1912); blue and gold shirts (1914)
Nickname: Light blues; Townies
Titles/Honours: Southern League 1910; Falkinder Charity Cup 1945

HOBART ATHLETIC
Dates: 1924-33
Colours: Blue shirts with white shorts
Titles/Honours: Southern Premiers 1928, 1930; State champions 1928; Charity Cup 1930

HOBART WATERSIDE WORKERS
Dates: c. 1915
Location: Hobart

HUTCHINS OLD BOYS
Dates: 1932-1935, 1937-8
Location: South Hobart Ground

INTERNATIONAL
Dates: 1945
Location: Butler's Gorge

INVERMAY
Dates: 1922-1938, 1946-1954
Location: Launceston
Colours: Dark blue and white halved shirts
Titles/Honours: Northern Champions 1924-9; McClymont Cup 1925-1928; Linney Barber Cup 1929; Booth Cup 1929, 1946; Morris Joseph Cup 1929; Northern Premiership 1946, 1949; State Premiership 1947
Notes: The team withdrew from the 1931 competition. Briefly named Invermay United in the late 1930's.

KOONYA
Dates: 1913
Location: Koonya

LAUNCESTON UNITED
Dates: 1912-1918
Location: Windsor Park, Launceston

LINDISFARNE

Dates: c. 1914
Location: Lindisfarne
LAUNCESTON TECH OLD BOYS
Dates: 1946
Location: Launceston
LAUNCESTON WATERSIDE WORKERS
Dates: 1947
Location: Goderich St, Launceston
Titles/Honours: 'B' grade Premiership 1947; Knockout Cup 1947
LINDISFARNE
Dates: c. 1916
LOVETT UNITED
Dates: 1914
Location: Lovett
METRO-CLAREMONT
Dates: 1941
Location: Pascal Recreation Ground, Claremont
Colours: Blue and gold shirts with white shorts and blue socks
Titles/Honours: Faulkner Cup 1948; South Tasmania Premiers 1949
METROPOLITAN
Dates: 1938-1947
Location: Hobart
MOONAH
Dates: 1948
Location: Moonah
MOUNT NELSON
Dates: 1947
Location: Bell Street, New Town
NAVAL AND MILITARY
Dates: c. 1924
Location: Cornwall Ground, Cornwall
NAVY ATHLETIC
Dates: 1934-1939
Location: Hobart
NEW NORFOLK
Dates: 1908- c. 1910; 1934
Location: New Norfolk; Kensington Park Race Course
NEW TOWN
Dates: 1934
Location: New Town
NORFOLK UNITED
Dates: 1948
Location: New Norfolk
NORTH ESK
Dates: c. 1914-1938
Location: Cornwall Ground; York Park, Launceston; Fry's Paddock
Colours: Green shirts
Titles/Honours: Northern Champions 1913, 1922
NORTH HOBART
Dates: 1935-1939
Location: Hobart

NORTH LAUNCESTON
Dates: 1938-1939
Location: Inveresk
OLD VIRGILIANS
Dates: 1934-1939
Location: South Hobart
OONGANA
Dates: c. 1912
Location: Cypress St Ground, Launceston
OTC
Dates: c. 1944
Location: South Hobart Ground
PALOONA, SS
Dates: 1910
Location: Clare Street, Hobart
Notes: SS *Paloona* was a New Zealand registered passenger ship which fielded a team in the Hobart competition in 1910.
PATONS AND BALDWIN
Dates: 1922
Location: Coronation Park, Launceston
Titles/Honours: Northern Champions 1925-1926, 1930, 1939; State Champions 1926, 1930; McClymont Cup 1947
Notes: Works team of the Paton and Baldwin knitting mills.
PREMAYDENA
Dates: 1913
Location: Premaydena
PUBLIC SCHOOL OLD BOYS
Dates: 1934
Location: No. 1 Domain Ground, Hobart
QUEENSTOWN PIONEERS
Dates: 1923
Location: Recreation Ground, Queenstown
Colours: Navy blue and gold shirts
RAPSON
Dates: 1929-1930
Location: Grammar School, Launceston
Notes: Works team of the Rapson tyre factory.
ROSEVEARS
Dates: 1913
Location: Recreation Ground, Rosevears
ROYAL AUSTRALIAN NAVAL RESERVE (R.A.N.R.)
Dates: 1925-1934; 1940
Location: Lindisfarne
Titles/Honours: Falkinder Charity Cup 1940
Notes: Was absorbed by Hobart Athletic in 1934.
ST GEORGE
Dates: 1911-1923
Location: Risdon; Clare Street, Hobart
Colours: Red shirts with white shorts
Nickname: The Saints; Georgians; Reds
Titles/Honours: Southern and State Champions 1912

Notes: Team was formed by Rev. Brain, rector of St George's Church in Battery Point.

ST MARYS
Dates: 1930-1932
Location: St Marys Recreation Ground
Colours: Black and white shirts
Nickname: *The Magpies; Tigers*

SANDY BAY
Dates: 1900; 1922
Location: Queensborough Ground, Hobart
Colours: Blue and white striped shirts; black and white striped shirts
Titles/Honours: Southern Champions, 1924-1925, 1927, 1933, 1936, 1938-1939; State Champions 1924-1925, 1927, 1933, 1936, 1938-1939; Falkinder Charity Cup 1925, 1935, 1941, 1946, 1948; Knock-out Cup 1942-1943, 1945
Nickname: *Bay; Magpies*
Notes: One of three teams to comprise the first competition in Tasmania. The team was comprised of army volunteers, 'C' Company Sandy Bay Rifles. Rivals of South Hobart Club.

SNAX ROVERS
Dates: 1933-1936
Location: No. 1 Domain Ground, Hobart.
Titles/Honours: Division III Cup winners 1934
Notes: Snax was the works team of Haywood's, a biscuit manufacturer.

SOUTH HOBART
Dates: 1910 to date
Location: Cornelian Bay; South Hobart Ground, Washington Street
Colours: Dark red shirt with white 'V' (1913); dark and light blue shirts; red and blue shirts
Titles/Honours: Honeysett Cup 1914; Southern Champions 1919-1923, 1926, 1929, 1945-1947; State Champions 1920-1923, 1929, 1946-1948; Falkinder Charity Cup 1942-1943, 1948
Notes: Founded by J.J.B. Honeysett and the oldest continuous club in Tasmania.

SOUTH HOBART WANDERERS
Dates: 1925-1928
Location: Lindisfarne

SOUTH LAUNCESTON
Dates: 1918-1925, 1945-1962
Location: St. Leonards Reserve
Colours: Red and white striped shirts with white shorts and red socks

SOUTH LAUNCESTON
Dates: c. 1926
Location: Launceston

SOUTHERN TASMANIAN ARTILLERY
Dates: 1897
Location: Hobart

SPARTANS
Dates: 1916
Location: Hobart

TABERNACLE
Dates: 1927-1931
Location: Cornwall Ground, Launceston
Colours: Black and yellow shirts
Nickname: *Tabs*
Titles/Honours: Harry Cobern Cup 1930; Stewart Cup 1930

TAMAR
Dates: 1907-1935
Location: Cornwall Ground; Cypress Street, Launceston
Colours: Blue and white shirts; maroon shirts (1931)
Titles/Honours: Northern Championship 1912-1913, 1922, 1931-1934

TAMAR ATHLETIC
Dates: 1948
Location: Coronation Park

TAMAR VALLEY
Dates: 1915
Location: Rosevears
Notes: Club was previously named West Tamar.

TECHNICAL COLLEGE
Dates: c. 1941
Location: Hobart

THISTLE
Dates: 1934
Location: Launceston
Titles/Honours: Hopwood Cup 1932; Stewart Cup 1932; Booth Cup 1935; Butler Cup 1939

TITAN
Dates: 1947-1951
Location: Northall Park, Moonah.
Notes: The Titan team was the works team of the Titan nail factory.

TRINITY BRITISH ASSOCIATION FOOTBALL CLUB
Dates: 1900-1903
Location: Hobart, Tasmania
Titles/Honours: Winner of the Hobart competition 1900-01.
Notes: The first soccer club in Tasmania, founded by the Reverend Richard Taylor with a number of clergymen as players.

UNIVERSITY
Dates: 1898-1901
Location: Hobart

WANDERERS
Dates: 1913-1915
Location: Rose Bay; Domain Ground, Hobart
Nickname: *The Zebras*
Titles/Honours: Nurse Cup 1913

WANDERERS ATHLETIC
Dates: 1949
Location: Hobart
Notes: Wanderers Athletic was comprised of British migrants.

Titles/Honours: Falkinder Trophy 1949
WARATAH
Dates: c. 1930
Location: Hobart
WELLINGTON
Dates: c. 1924
Location: Launceston
WEST END UNITED
Dates: 1930-1939
Location: West End, Hobart
Notes: West End disbanded and was re-named Corinthian Rovers in 1940.
WEST TAMAR
Dates: 1913-1914
Location: Rosevears
Nickname: *The River Eleven*
Notes: Club changed name to become Tamar Valley in 1915.
WESTRALIA, SS
Dates: 1908-1915

Titles/Honours: Southern Champions 1911
Notes: Team represented the steam ferry S.S. *Westralia*. It could only play on alternate weeks due to voyages.
WOMBATS
Dates: c. 1912
Location: Launceston
WYNYARD ROVERS
Dates: c. 1914
Location: Wynyard
YMCA
Dates: 1908-1912; 1919
Location: Hobart
Nickname: *The Young Men*
Notes: Club was absorbed by Corinthians.
YMCA
Dates: c. 1908 -1912; 1919
Location: Launceston

Victoria

A.I.F. ST KILDA
Dates: 1943
Location: St Kilda
Notes: Team consisted of army enlistments. Withdrew after one season.
AIR FORCE
Dates: 1926
Location: Melbourne
ALBERT PARK
Dates: c. 1912-1915; c. 1922
Location: Middle Park, Melbourne
Nickname: *The Park*
Colours: Blue and white striped shirts with white shorts
Titles/Honours: Dockerty Cup 1922; 2nd Division Premiers 1926
Notes: Albert Park changed name to Glenroy in 1931.
ALEXANDRA TOWN
Dates: 1922
Location: Showgrounds, Alexandra
ALPHINGTON
Dates: c. 1928
Location: Alphington
ALTONA
Dates: 1947
Location: Altona
ANGLO-AUSTRALIAN ASSOCIATION
Dates: 1883
Location: Richmond Ground
Notes: Team was formed prior to the first competition year in Victoria.

APOLLO ATHLETIC
Dates: 1935
Location: Fawkner Park
Notes: Club was formed by the Greek community. Briefly named Greek Club.
AUSTRAL
Dates: c. 1924
Location: Middle Park, Melbourne
Notes: Austral only fielded Australian born players.
AUSTRALIAN PAPER MILLS (A.P.M.)
Dates: 1947
Location: Morwell
BABINDA RANGERS
Dates: c. 1928
Location: Cairns
BALLARAT STURT ROVERS
Dates: 1927
Location: Ballarat
Titles/Honours: Madden Cup 1928
BAMAWM
Dates: c. 1913
Location: Rochester Recreation Reserve
Titles/Honours: Northern League champions 1925
BEACONSFIELD, HMAS
Dates: 1945
Location: Melbourne
BENALLA
Dates: c. 1930
Location: Benalla
BENDIGO
Dates: 1902
Location: Upper Reserve, Bendigo

Notes: There were two teams formed in June, 1902 within the Bendigo club. Teams 'A' and 'B' played matches against each other. Club only played during the year of 1902.

BENDIGO CITY
Dates: 1923
Location: Golden Square Recreation Reserve; Showgrounds, Bendigo
Titles/Honours: Northern District Association Cup winners 1925

BENTLEIGH
Dates: c. 1926-1932
Location: Bentleigh

BIRMINGHAM-VICTORIA
Dates: 1912
Location: Middle Park, Melbourne
Nickname: The Brums
Notes: Most players were English migrants from Birmingham.

BIRREGURRA
Dates: 1926
Location: Birregurra
Notes: Played in the Colac District League.

BOORT
Dates: c. 1926
Location: Boort

BOROUGH UNITED
Dates: c. 1925
Location: Borough

BOX HILL
Dates: 1922
Location: Springfield Park; Wembley Park, Box Hill South, Surrey Park
Colours: Blue shirts with white shorts and blue socks
Nickname: The Hillmen
Titles/Honours: Champions 1918; 3rd Division Premiership 1926; State League Champions 1948
Notes: Formed by British migrants and the second oldest club in Victoria.

BRADFORD COTTON MILLS
Dates: 1946
Location: Henry Turner Reserve, Footscray
Nickname: The Spinners

BRIGHTON CITY
Dates: 1924
Location: Hurlingham Park
Colours: Maroon jersey with blue collar and white shorts; black and white hooped shirts and black shorts (1949)
Nickname: The Seasiders
Titles/Honours: Dockerty Cup 1933, 1937, 1943-1944; League Premiers 1949
Notes: Initially entered the Fourth Division of the Metropolitan League. Attained First Division status in 1931.

BRISBANE, HMAS
Dates: c. 1926
Location: Geelong

BROADFORD
Dates: 1925
Location: Broadford

BROWN COAL MINE
Dates: c. 1933
Location: Morwell district
Titles/Honours: Central Gippsland Soccer League Premiers 1933

BRUNSWICK UNITED
Dates: 1915
Location: Brunswick Cricket Ground
Nickname: The Wicks
Titles/Honours: First Division Champions 1931

BURNS
Dates: 1911
Location: Melbourne

CAMBERWELL
Dares: 1936-1937
Location: Camberwell

CAMBRIAN UNITED
Dates: c. 1914
Location: Albert Park, Melbourne
Nickname: The Welshmen
Notes: The team was comprised of Welsh players.

CAMPERDOWN
Dates: 1926
Location: Cressy Road Ground, Camperdown
Colours: Light blue shirts with white shorts
Notes: Played in the Colac District League.

CARDROSS
Dates: c. 1928
Location: Mildura

CARLTON
Dates: 1884
Location: Carlton Cricket Ground
Colours: Red and black shirts

CARLTON UNITED
Dates: 1908
Location: Middle Park
Titles/Honours: Dockerty Cup 1910

CARWARP
Dates: c. 1929
Location: Carwarp

CAULFIELD
Dates: c. 1921
Location: East Caulfield Reserve, Melbourne

CELTIC
Dates: c. 1927
Location: Wonthaggi

CERBERUS, HMAS
Dates: 1915
Location: Melbourne

COBDEN

Dates: c. 1926
Location: Cobden
COBURG
Dates: 1914
Location: West Coburg Reserve
COBURG UNITED
Dates: 1946
Location: Coburg
COLAC THISTLE
Dates: 1925
Location: Colac
Titles/Honours: Madden Cup 1926
COLLINGWOOD
Dates: 1925-1940
Location: Collingwood, Melbourne
Notes: Formerly named Yarra Falls Spinning Mills.
COROROOKE
Dates: 1926
Location: Cororooke
Notes: Played in the Colac District League.
CROYDON
Dates: c. 1926
Location: Croydon
DEER PARK
Dates: c. 1929
Location: Deer Park
DOOKIE COLLEGE
Dates: c. 1927
Location: Dookie
EAST GEELONG
Dates: 1928
Location: Geelong
ECHUCA
Dates: c. 1924
Location: Echuca
EILDON WEIR
Dates: 1922
Location: Eildon Weir
EIGHTH AUSTRALIAN EMPLOYMENT CORP (8th A.E.C)
Dates: 1945
Location: Melbourne
Notes: Military team comprising ex Austrian and German youths from the ship SS *Dunera*.
ELMORE
Dates: 1910
Location: Elmore
ELSTERNWICK GREEK CLUB
Dates: 1932
Location: Elsternwick
Notes: Club amalgamated with Prahran in 1936.
ESSENDON CITY
Dates: 1923-1927
Location: Essendon, Melbourne
FEDERAL WOOLEN MILLS
Dates: 1929-1930

Location: Federal Mills Ground, Geelong
Titles: Winner Geelong and Western Districts League 1929, 1930; Caledonian Shield 1929; Madden Cup 1929
FIFERS
Dates: 1949
Location: Melbourne
Notes: Fifers, a Scottish based club, was formed by the Fifeshire Association of Victoria.
FITZROY
Dates: 1909
Location: Albert Park
FLINDERS NAVAL DEPOT
Dates: c. 1924
Location: Crib Point, Orrong Park (1928)
Titles/Honours: First Division Champions 1928; Dockerty Cup 1924, 1926, 1928
Notes: Players were from British ships stationed at Flinders Naval Depot.
FOOTSCRAY
Dates: 1912-1913
Location: Ammunition Flat, Footscray
Notes: Footscray became the Northumberland and Durham club in 1914.
FOOTSCRAY THISTLE
Dates: 1914
Location: Yarraville
Titles/Honours: First Division Champions 1924-1926, 1929-1930, 1932; Dockerty Cup 1932
FOOTSCRAY UNITED
Dates: c. 1919-1934
Location: Barkly Street, Footscray.
Titles/Honours: Dockerty Cup 1919, 1927, 1929
FORD RECREATION CLUB
Dates: 1926-1928
Location: Geelong
Notes: Club comprised employees of the Ford Motor Company, Geelong.
FOROUGH UNITED
Dates: c. 1925
Location: Forough
GEELONG CALEDONIAN
Dates: 1927
Location: Manifold Heights, Geelong
GEELONG CITY
Dates: 1914
Location: Baker's Oval; Geelong West reserve
Titles/Honours: Premiers Geelong League 1926; Caledonian Shield 1926; Madden Cup 1927
GEELONG UNITED
Dates: 1923-1925; 1934
Location: Hope Street, Geelong West
Colours: Royal blue shirts with a white band from shoulder to hip
GEORGE CROSS
Dates: 1947

Location: Royal Park, Melbourne
Colours: Red and white striped shirts
Notes: George Cross was established by the Maltese community in Melbourne.

GINO LISA
Dates: 1935- c. 1939
Location: Royal Park, Carlton
Colours: Black shirts with white shorts
Notes: This club played matches against the Savoia club. It represented an Italian Fascist group.

GLENMAGGIE WEIR
Dates: c. 1925
Location: Glenmaggie Weir

GLENROWAN
Dates: c. 1925
Location: Glenrowan

GLENROY
Dates: 1931-1934
Location: Glenroy
Notes: Formerly the Albert Park club.

GORDONVALE
Dates: c. 1928
Location: Cairns

GOULBURN VALLEY
Dates: c. 1936
Location: Goulburn Valley

GREENSBOROUGH
Dates: 1910
Location: Greensborough

HAKOAH
Dates: 1927
Location: Exhibition Oval; Princes Park (1929); Olympic Park; Middle Park, Melbourne
Colours: Sky blue shirts with white shorts and blue and white socks
Titles/Honours: 1st Division Premiers 1931-1932, 1934-1935, 1938; Australia Cup 1934; Dockerty Cup 1935.
Notes: The earliest Jewish based club formed in Australia. From 1943 to 1945 Hakoah merged with Moreland to form Moreland-Hakoah.

HAWTHORN
Dates: 1915
Location: Auburn

HEIDELBERG
Dates: 1925
Location: James Park, Rosanna
Titles/Honours: 4th Division Premiers 1926

HORSHAM
Dates: 1924; 1927
Location: Horsham Show Grounds, Horsham

IMPERIAL CHEMICAL INDUSTRIES (I.C.I.)
Dates 1938-1940
Location: Deer Park
Nickname *The Imperials*
Colours: Blue shirts with white shorts

Notes: This club was formerly known as Nobels and reverted to the Nobels name after 1940.

IRYMPLE
Dates: 1912
Location: Mildura
Colours: Blue and white shirts
Titles/Honours: Mildura Premier League 1912-1913

JUVENTUS
Dates: 1948
Location: Melbourne
Colours: Black and white striped shirts with white shorts
Titles/Honours: Victorian Third Division champions 1949

KARAWINNA SOUTH
Dates: c. 1929
Location: Karawinna

KATANDRA WEST
Dates: c. 1932-1933
Location: Katandra
Titles/Honours: League Cup 1932; Tongala Hospital Cup 1932-1933

KERANG
Dates: c. 1912; 1925
Location: Kerang

KEW
Dates: 1914
Location: Kew

KILCUNDA
Dates: 1927
Location: Kilcunda
Notes: Kilcunda played in the Wonthaggi Soccer Association competition.

KINGSVILLE
Dates: c. 1929
Location: Kingsville

KORUMBURRA
Dates: c. 1895; 1929
Location: Korumburra

KOYUGA
Dates: 1926
Location: Koyuga
Colours: Blue and white shirts

KYABRAM
Dates: 1914; 1926
Location: Kyabram Reserve
Notes: Kyabram played in the Goulburn Valley League with Koyuga, Lancaster and Tongala.

KYVALLEY
Dates: c. 1914
Location: Kyvalley

LAKE KANGAROO
Dates: c. 1930
Location: Lake Kangaroo
Notes: Swan Hill District Soccer Association member.

LANCASTER
Dates: 1926
Location: Lancaster
Colours: Maroon shirts
Titles/Honours: Goulburn Valley League Premiers 1927

LANCASHIRE AND YORKSHIRE
Dates: 1925-1926
Location: Melbourne

LETTERKENNY
Dates: 1910
Location: Letterkenny
Nickname: The Kennies

LINCOLN MILLS
Dates: 1923-1925
Location: Coburg

LISMORE
Dates: 1926
Location: Lismore
Notes: Played in the Colac District League.

MACEDONIANS
Dates: c. 1948
Location: Yarra Park, Melbourne

MAFFRA
Dates: 1925
Location: Maffra

MALVERN UNITED
Dates: c. 1929-1932
Location: Malvern

MANCHESTER
Dates: 1912
Location: Melbourne

MELBOURNE, HMAS
Dates: c. 1927
Location: Geelong
Notes: Team played in the Geelong competition

MELBOURNE MANX
Dates: 1935
Location: Melbourne

MELBOURNE ROVERS
Dates: c. 1887
Location: Scotch College Ground
Colours: Blue shirts

MELBOURNE THISTLE
Dates: 1912
Location: Mowling Flat
Colours: Blue shirts
Titles/Honours: First Division Champions 1914-15, 1924-6, 1929-1930, 1932; Dockerty Cup 1914-1915, 1919, 1925, 1927, 1929-1930 Fist Division Champions 1936-1937-1941; Dockerty Cup 1941, 1945

MELBOURNE UNIVERSITY
Dates: c. 1948
Location: Melbourne

MELBOURNE WELSH
Dates: c. 1925

Location: Melbourne
Colours: Red shirts

MERBEIN
Dates: c. 1913
Location: Merbein
Nickname: The Magpies

MERRIGUM
Dates: c. 1928
Location: Merrigum

MERRINEE
Dates: c. 1929
Location: Merrinee

METTERS
Dates: c. 1948
Location: West Footscray, Melbourne

METROPOLIS
Dates: c. 1930
Location: Geelong

MIDDLE PARK
Dates: 1910
Location: Melbourne
Notes: Factory team of Dunlop Rubber Works.

MILDURA
Dates: 1896; 1911
Location: Recreation Ground; 9th Street, Mildura
Colours: White shirts

MINYIP
Dates: c. 1927
Location: Minyip

MIRBOO NORTH
Dates: c. 1914
Location: Mirboo

MIRBOO SOUTH
Dates: c. 1914
Location: Mirboo

MOONEE PONDS
Dates: 1923
Location: Moonee Valley Racecourse

MOOROOPNA
Dates: c. 1928
Location: Recreation Ground, Mooroopna
Colours: White shirts with a red band and blue shorts (1932)
Titles/Honours: F.C. Johns Cup 1934; Tongala Hospital Cup 1929, 1934

MOORABBIN
Dates: 1912
Location: Morabbin
Notes: Formerly known as Sandringham United.

MOORABBIN CITY
Dates: 1949
Location: Moorabbin
Colours: Black and white quartered shirts with black shorts.

MORELAND
Dates: 1934
Location: Campbell Reserve, East Coburg

Notes: Moreland was a break away club from Brunswick. Moreland merged with Hakoah from 1945 to 1946, to become Moreland-Hakoah. The clubs subsequently split and were reconstituted.
Titles/Honours: First Division Champions 1937, 1946

MORWELL BRIDGE
Dates: c. 1938
Location: Morwell

MORWELL METHODISTS
Dates: c. 1944
Location: Morwell

MORWELL PRESBYTERIANS
Dates: c. 1944
Location: Morwell

MORWELL RANGERS
Dates: c. 1944
Location: Morwell

MORWELL UNITED
Dates: 1933
Location: Morwell
Colours: Light blue shirts with white shorts

MOYHU
Dates: c. 1929
Location: Moyhu
Titles/Honours: Ledger Cup 1925

NAMBROK
Dates: c. 1925
Location: Nambrok

NAVAL COLLEGE
Dates: c. 1914
Location: Naval College Ground, Geelong
Titles/Honours: Dockerty Cup 1928

NETHERLANDS
Dates: 1943
Location: Melbourne
Notes: This club consisted of Dutch servicemen from the Netherlands East Indies playing in the metropolitan first division. Withdrew after one season.

NETTLEFOLDS
Dates: c 1930-1931; 1934
Location: McIntrye Road, Sunshine
Nickname: The Screws
Notes: Nettlefolds is a manufacturer of hardware.
Titles/Honours: 3rd Division Premiership 1935

NEWPORT
Dates: 1923
Location: Newport Recreation Reserve

NOBELS
Dates: 1929
Location: Deer Park, Sunshine
Titles/Honours: State championship 1938; Dockery Cup 1938-40
Notes: Nobels was founded by the British ICI chemical company and entered the metropolitan Division 4. It entered Division 1 in 1938. Club was known as ICI in 1939-40.

NORTH GEELONG
Dates: c. 1926
Location: Geelong

NORTH MELBOURNE METHODISTS
Dates: 1935
Location: Melbourne

NORTH MELBOURNE PRESBYTERIANS
Dates: 1935-1938
Location: North Melbourne

NORTH WONTHAGGI THISTLE
Dates: c. 1927
Location: Wonthaggi
Titles/Honours: League Cup 1927

NORTHCOTE CITY
Dates: c. 1922
Location: Merri Park, Northcote

NORTHCOTE HIGH SCHOOL OLD BOYS (N.H.S.O.B.)
Dates: c. 1937-1938
Location: Northcote, Melbourne

NORTHUMBERLAND AND DURHAM UNITED
Dates: 1914
Location: Riverbank Ground, Footscray; Footscray Park
Colours: Yellow and black shirts
Titles/Honours: First Division Champions 1919-20, 1922
Notes: The club was formerly known as Footscray.

OAKLEIGH TOWN
Dates: 1926
Location: Oakleigh
Notes: Withdrew from Fourth Division of Metropolitan League within the season.

OLYMPIC
Dates: 1946
Location: Melbourne

OSBORNE HOUSE
Dates: 1920
Location: Geelong
Nickname: The Submarines
Notes: Players came from a naval submarine school in Geelong and were from the submarine J4.

OVERSEAS
Dates: 1926
Location: Geelong

PARK RANGERS
Dates: 1946
Location: Olympic Park; Middle Park, Melbourne
Colours: Maroon shirt with white collar and cuffs.
Notes: Park Rangers was name chosen by South Melbourne United Juniors when the entered the senior grades.
Titles/Honours: Dockerty Cup 1948

PASCOE VALE

Dates: c. 1927
Location: Pascoe Vale
POWLETT RIVER
Dates: 1910
Location: Powlett River
Notes: Location of the State coal mine
PRAHRAN
Dates: 1884
Location: Fawkner Park; Middle Park; Como Park, South Yarra
Colours: Maroon; Alternative: white
Titles/Honours: Beaney Cup 1885; George and George Challenge Cup 1887; Champions 1927; First Division Champions 1939, 1942, 1944-1945 Dockerty Cup 1942
Notes: Prahran absorbed the Elsternwick club in 1936.
PRAHRAN CITY
Dates: 1925
Location: Fawkner Park, Prahran; Toorak Park (1928)
Notes: Former name of club was Windsor.
PRESTON
Dates: c. 1913-1915; 1926
Location: Bell Park, Preston
PRESTON TECHNICAL SCHOOL OLD BOYS
Dates: 1942
Location: Preston
QUEENSCLIFF
Dates: 1926
Location: Geelong
RAAF
Dates: 1939
Location: Melbourne
RAAF ASCOT VALE
Dates: c. 1944
Location: Ascot Vale
RAAF LAVERTON
Dates: c. 1942
Location: Laverton
RAAF POINT COOK
Dates: 1925
Location: Point Cook
REDCLIFFE
Dates: c. 1925
Location: Redcliffe
REDHILL
Dates: c. 1925
Location: Redhill
RESERVOIR
Dates: c. 1935
Location: Reservoir
RICHMOND
Dates: 1884
Location: Warehouseman's Cricket Ground; Richmond Cricket Club Oval; Richmond Park
Titles/Honours: George and George Challenge Cup 1884-85
RINGWOOD
Dates: 1946
Location: Bedford Park
Nickname: The Warehousemen
ROCHESTER
Dates: c. 1933
Location: Rochester
ROVERS
Dates: 1913
Location: Mildura region
ROYAL CALEDONIANS
Dates: 1927
Location: Melbourne
Titles/Honours: First Division Champions 1933; Dockerty Cup 1934
RUPANYUP
Dates: c. 1927
Location: Rupanyup Recreation Ground
ST DAVID'S
Dates: c. 1920-1925; 1935-1938
Location: Melbourne
Notes: St David's was based on players from a Welsh church.
ST JOHN'S
Dates: c. 1944
Location: Morwell
ST KILDA
Dates: c. 1909
Location: Albert Park; Middle Park, Melbourne
Titles/Honours: First Division Champions 1923; Dockerty Cup 1911, 1923
SALE UNITED
Dates: c. 1925
Location: Sale Football Ground
SANDRINGHAM
Dates: c. 1936
Location: Sandringham
SANDRINGHAM CITY
Dates: 1948
Location: Ludstone Street Ground
SANDRINGHAM UNITED
Dates: 1911
Location: Hampton
Notes: Changed name to Moorabbin in 1912
SAVOIA
Dates: 1933 - c. 1936
Location: Melbourne
Colours: Light blue shirts with white shorts
Notes: Savoia (Savoy) were one of the first major clubs established by Italians.
SHEPPARTON
Dates: 1926
Location: Shepparton
Colours: Royal blue shirts with white shorts and black socks

THE FOUNDATION YEARS 1859-1949

SHEPPARTON EAST
Dates: 1926
Location: Law's Paddock; Shepparton Show Ground
Titles/Honours: Goulburn Valley League Champions 1930-1932; Joseph Karsten Cup 1933-1934; S.H. Ghent League Cup 1934.
Notes: Shepparton East initially fielded 'A' and 'B' teams in local competition.

SHEPPARTON TOWN
Dates: 1932
Location: Show Ground, Shepparton

SIXTH AUSTRALIAN EMPLOYMENT CORP (6th A.E.C.)
Dates: 1945
Location: Melbourne

SHEPPARTON UNITED
Dates: 1934
Location: Billy Goat Flat; Drill Hall Reserve; Victory Park, Shepparton

SOUTH MELBOURNE
Dates: 1884; 1936-1939
Location: Carlton Cricket Ground; Fawkner Park; Middle Park, Melbourne
Colours: Blue shirts

SOUTH MELBOURNE
Dates: 1948
Location: Middle Park
Colours: White shirts with white shorts and white socks with blue tops.

SOUTH MELBOURNE UNITED
Dates: 1936-1942; 1944
Location: Langridge Street, Middle Park
Colours: Red shirts with white shorts
Titles/Honours: Charity Cup 1948

SOUTH UNITED
Dates: c. 1946
Location: Campbell Reserve, Melbourne

SOUTH YARRA
Dates: 1928
Location: Fawkner Park, South Yarra
Titles/Honours: Dockerty Cup 1947
Notes: South Yarra were formed when Prahran Juniors, too old to play junior soccer, formed the South Yarra club.

SPOTSWOOD
Dates: c. 1914
Location: Spotswood

SPRINGVALE
Dates: 1928
Location: Springvale
Nickname: The Vale

STANHOPE
Dates: 1924; 1929
Location: Stanhope
Notes: Joined Goulburn Valley Soccer League in 1929.

STRATFORD
Dates: c. 1925
Location: Stratford

SUNSHINE UNITED
Dates: 1912; 1924-1935; 1944
Location: Garden Reserve; Railway Reserve; Sunshine Park
Nickname: The Harvesters
Titles/Honours: First Division Champions 1947

TALLANDOON
Dates: 1926
Location: Tallandoon

TARANGO
Dates: c. 1929
Location: Tarango

TONGALA
Dates: 1914; 1926
Location: Tongala
Colours: Black and white shirts
Titles/Honours: Goulburn Valley Soccer League Premiers 1931

TRESCO
Dates: c. 1928
Location: Tresco
Notes: Tresco played in the Swan Hill District Association.

UNDERA
Dates: 1927
Location: Undera

UNION JACK
Dates: c. 1925
Location: Albert Park, Melbourne
Colours: Blue shirts with white shorts
Notes: Club was formed by British players.

UNION JACK
Dates: 1927
Location: Hope Street Ground, Geelong
Notes: Club was formed by British players.

UNIVERSITY HIGH SCHOOL OLD BOYS
Dates: c. 1941
Location: Fawkner Park, Melbourne

VALLEY MILLS
Dates: c. 1926
Location: Geelong

VICTORIA POLICE
Dates: 1949
Location: Melbourne
Colours: Red shirts with white shorts

WALLABIES
Location: Brunswick
Dates: c. 1911

WANGARATTA
Dates: c. 1926
Location: Wangaratta

WARRACKNABEAL
Dates: 1926
Location: Warracknabeal

WARRNAMBOOL
Dates: 1912
Location: Friendly Societies Park, Warrnambool
WELSH UNITED
Dates: 1921
Location: Middle Park
WERRIBEE UNITED
Dates: 1924
Location: Werribee
Notes: Joined the Melbourne Districts League in 1927.
WEST MELBOURNE
Dates: c. 1929
Location: Melbourne
WEST SALE
Dates: c. 1943
Location: Sale
WESTERN SUBURBS
Dates: 1946
Location: Sunshine Park, Sunshine
WHITFIELD RANGERS
Dates: c. 1925
Location: Whitfield
WHOROULY
Dates: c. 1929
Location: Whorouly
WINDSOR
Dates: 1915; 1932-1934
Location: Melbourne
Colours: Purple shirt with old gold sash
WILLAH
Dates: c. 1929
Location: Willah
WILLIAMSTOWN
Dates: 1884-1911
Location: Garden Reserve
Colours: Blue shirts
Nickname: The Blues
Titles/Honours: First Division Champions 1911
Notes: The team had a connection with the Nugget Polish Company. The team merged with Yarraville to become Williamstown-Yarraville in 1912.
WILLIAMSTOWN DISTRICT
Dates: 1948
Location: Maddox St Ground, Newport
Nickname: 'Towns
WILLIAMSTOWN-YARRAVILLE
Dates: 1912
Location: Yarraville
Notes: Previously named the Williamstown club.
Titles/Honours: Dockerty Cup 1912
WINDSOR
Dates: 1915-1924
Location: Middle Park
Colours: Purple shirts with a gold sash
Notes: Windsor changed its name to Prahran City in 1925.

WINDSOR
Dates: 1932
Location: Windsor
WINTON
Dates: c. 1925
Location: Winton
WONTHAGGI
Dates: 1914
Location: Wonthaggi
WONTHAGGI CALEDONIANS
Dates: c. 1927
Location: Wonthaggi
WONTHAGGI CELTIC
Dates: c. 1927
Location: Wonthaggi
WONTHAGGI MAGPIES
Dates: c. 1926
Location: Wonthaggi
Titles/Honours: Webb Cup 1926; Dockerty Cup 1931
WONTHAGGI MANCHESTER UNITY
Dates: c. 1930
Location: Wonthaggi
WONTHAGGI RANGERS
Dates: 1910
Location: Wonthaggi
WONTHAGGI ROVERS
Dates: c.1935
Location: Wonthaggi
WOODLANDS
Dates: c. 1948
Location: Chelmsworth Park, Ivanhoe
YALLOURN
Dates: 1923
Location: Yallourn No. 3 Oval
YALLOURN REDS
Dates: c. 1933
Location: No. 3, Briquette Oval, Yallourn
YALLOURN ROVERS
Dates: c. 1934
Location: No. 3, Briquette Oval, Yallourn
YALLOURN WANDERERS
Dates: c. 1934
Location: No. 3, Briquette Oval, Yallourn
YALLOURN WHITES
Dates: 1933
Location: No. 3, Briquette Oval, Yallourn
YARAMBA
Dates: c. 1929
Location: Yaramba
YARK UNITED
Dates: 1922
Location: Yark
YARLOOP
Dates: 1901-1913
Location: Yarloop
Nickname: The Timber Jerkers

YARRA FALLS SPINNING MILLS
Dates: 1923-1924
Location: Yarra Falls
Notes: Changed name to Collingwood in 1925.
YARRAVILLE
Dates: c. 1909-1911.
Titles/Honours: First Division Champions 1913; Dockerty Cup 1913
Notes: The team merged with Williamstown to form Williamstown-Yarraville in 1912.
YARRAVILLE WANDERERS
Dates: 1895

Location: Melbourne
YEO
Dates: 1926
Location: Yeo
YCWM
Dates: c. 1948
Location: Broadmeadows
YMCA
Dates: 1923
Location: Bendigo

Western Australia

ACTON PARK RANGERS
Dates: c. 1930
Location: Acton Park, Acton
Colours: Black and white shirts
Nickname: The Magpies
Titles/Honours: Premiership 1931; Hart Trophy 1933
AGNEW
Dates: c. 1938
Location: Agnew
ALBANY
Dates: c. 1930
Location: Parade Street Ground, Albany
ALBANY EAST
Dates: c. 1932
Location: Albany
ALBANY NORTH
Dates: c. 1932
Location: Albany
ALBANY RANGERS
Dates: c. 1920
Location: Parade Ground, Albany
Titles/Honours: Challenge Cup 1921
ALBANY SOCCER
Dates: c. 1924
Location: Albany
ALBION
Dates: c. 1913
Location: Perth Road Ground, Albany
Colours: White shirts with blue shorts
ALEXANDRA
Dates: c. 1931
Location: Alexandra Bridge
ALPINE TAXIS
Dates: c. 1929
Location: Perth
ARDATH
Dates: 1926
Location: Ardath

Colours: Blue shirts
Titles/Honours: Jacoby Ardath Challenge Premiership Cup 1929
Notes: Ardath played in the Bruce Rock Soccer Association.
ARGYLES
Dates: c. 1925
Location: Albany
ARMADALE
Dates: 1925-1930
Location: Armadale
Titles/Honours: Second League Premiers 1927
ASCENSIONS
Dates: 1912
Location: Perth
AUGUSTA
Dates: c. 1928
Location: Augusta Recreation Ground
Titles/Honours: Association Cup 1930
AUGUSTA-MARGARET
Dates: c. 1936
Location: Augusta
Titles/Honours: W.A. Association Trophy 1936
AUSTRALS
Dates: c. 1911; 1932
Location: Margaret River
Notes: Team comprised of Australian players.
AUSTRALS
Dates: 1908
Location: Perth
AZZURRI
Dates: 1949
Notes: Azzurri was supported by the Italian community. Played in the Third Division.
BABAKIN
dates: c. 1926
Location: Babakin
BADGEBUP
Dates: 1922

Location: Badgebup
Nickname: The Pups
BALLANDONG RANGERS
Dates: 1924
Location: Forrest Park, York
BALLIDU
Dates: c. 1923
Location: Ballidu Show Ground
Titles/Honours: Sizmur Cup 1927; Country Cup 1927
Notes: Ballidu, Pithara and Moora played in a local competition.
BALMORAL RANGERS
Dates: c. 1946
Location: Fraser Park
Titles/Honours: Cronshaw Cup 1946
BARBERTON UNITED
Dates: 1914
Location: Ranfurly Park, Barberton
BASSENDEAN WANDERERS
Dates: c. 1926-1931
Location: Pickering Park; Recreation Reserve, Bassendean
BASSENDEAN UNITED
Dates: 1932-1935
Location: Hays Swamp
BASSENDEAN ZORA
Dates: 1931
Location: Recreation Reserve, Bassendean
BAYSWATER
Dates: c. 1926
Location: Bayswater Oval
Titles/Honours: Cronshaw Cup 1927
BEACONSFIELD GYMNASIUM
Dates: c. 1912
Location: Beaconsfield
BELMONT
Dates: c. 1939
Location: Perth
BENCUBBIN
Dates: c. 1926
Location: Bencubbin
BERKSHIRE VALLEY
Dates: 1914
Location: Berkshire Valley
BELMONT
Dates: c. 1946
Location: Perth
BENCUBBIN
Dates: c. 1928
Location: Bencubbin
BEVERLEY UNITED
Dates: c. 1930
Location: Beverley
BLACKBOY SPURS
Dates: c. 1931
Location: Blackboy

BLACKWOOD ROVERS
Dates: c. 1927
Location: Blackwood
BLYTH'S PARK RANGERS
Dates: c. 1923
Location: Blyth's Park
BODDINGTON
Dates: c. 1933
Location: Boddington
BONNY ROCK
Dates: c. 1931
Location: Bonny Rock
BORDEN
Dates: c. 1924
Location: Borden
Colours: Blue shirts
Nickname: The Dens
Titles/Honours: Hospital Cup 1925, 1929; Charity Cup 1927
BORNHOLM
Dates: c. 1933
Location: Bornholm
BOSCABEL
Dates: c. 1926
Location: Boscabel
BOULDER CITY
Dates: 1897; 1900 -1914; 1929
Location: Boulder Recreation Reserve; Golden Gate Football Ground; Commonwealth Park; Hamilton Street; Launceston Ground, Boulder
Colours: Black shirts; Blue and white shirts
Nickname: The Tigers
Titles/Honours: Hahn League Cup 1905; County Week Winners 1934, 1936-1937; League Premiers 1936-1937; Bland Cup 1936; Casey Cup 1940; Nicholson Cup 1940
BOULDER MINES
Dates: 1898
Location: Boulder Lake View and Boulder Junction Ground; Hamilton Street Reserve; Forrest Street Reserve
Colours: Maroon shirts
BOULDER MINES WARRIORS
Dates: 1932
Location: Commonwealth Ground, Boulder
BOWGADA
Dates: 1930
Location: Bowgada
BOYANUP
Dates: 1923
Location: Boyanup Cricket Ground
BOYUP BROOK ROVERS
Dates: c. 1933
Location: Boyup Brook Ground
BRAMLEY RANGERS
Dates: c. 1929
Location: Bramley

Nickname: The Tigers
Titles/Honours: Shield winners 1933
BRAMLEY UNITED
Dates: c. 1933
Location: Margaret River Recreation Ground
Colours: Black and white shirts
Titles/Honours: Dr Taylor Thomas Cup 1933, 1934; League Shield 1934; Challenge Shield 1934
BRIDGETOWN
Dates: 1914; 1925
Location: Recreation Ground, Bridgetown
Colours: White shirts with blue shorts (1925)
Nickname: The Bridgetonians
BRIDGETOWN WARRIORS
Dates: 1913
Location: Bridgetown Recreation Ground
BRITISH
Dates: 1912
Location: Narrogin
Notes: Changed name to Narrogin in late 1912.
BROOKTON
Dates: 1926
Location: Brookton
Nickname: The Tigers
BRUCE ROCK
Dates: c. 1921
Location: Bruce Rock
Titles/Honours: Jacoby Ardath Challenge Premiership Cup 1927-1928, 1930
BUINGUP
Dates: c. 1929
Location: Buingup
Titles/Honours: Carter Shield 1929
BULLFINCH
Dates: c. 1921
Location: Collie
BUNBURY
Dates: 1904; 1911-1931
Location: Recreation Ground, Bunbury
Colours: Red and blue shirts
Nickname: The Mariners
Notes: Bunbury Soccer Association ceased in 1931. The club played friendly matches.
BUNBURY THISTLES
Dates: c. 1928
Location: Bunbury
BUNTINE
Dates: 1926
Location: Buntine
Titles/Honours: Premiership 1929
BUREKUP
Dates: c. 1926
Notes: Played in Yarloops District League.
BURNBANK ATHLETIC
Dates: c. 1919
Location: Burnbank

BURNGUP
Dates: 1927
Location: Burngup
BURNLEY
Dates: c. 1911-1914
Location: Perth Road Ground, Albany
Colours: Black and white shirts
BUSSELTON CALEDONIANS
Dates: 1929
Location: Show Grounds, Busselton
Nickname: Callies
BUSSELTOWN COLTS
Dates: 1937
Location: Busselton
BUSSELTOWN ROVERS
Dates: c. 1932
Location: Recreation Ground, Busseltown
Titles/Honours: League Cup 1932
BUSSELTON TOWN
Dates: 1922; 1925
Location: Bovell's Paddock; Brockman's Paddock, Recreation Ground, Busseltown
Colours: Green shirt with white shorts
Titles/Honours: Association champions 1929, 1930; Busseltown Centenary Soccer Cup 1937
Notes: In 1929 the Busselton Soccer Association consisted of the following clubs; Busseltown Town, Busseltown Caledonians, Willyabrup, Yalyalup and Yoongarilup.
CALEDONIAN
Dates: 1913-1916; 1921-1941; 1946
Location: Fremantle Park; Polo Ground, East Fremantle (1920); Mann Oval, Mosman Park, (1925)
Colours: Primrose and pink striped shirts with white shorts (1913); royal blue shirts with white shorts and red socks (1929); dark blue shirts with white shorts (c. 1947)
Nickname: Callies
Titles/Honours: League Cup 1926, 1933; First Division Champions 1926, 1927, 1933, 1941, 1946-1947, 1949; Challenge Cup 1927, 1935-1936, 1938-1940, 1949; Charity Cup 1927, 1929, 1936, 1937-1939, 1940-1941, 1949; League Cup 1933
Notes: Team was formed by the Fremantle Caledonian Society.
CALEDONIANS
Dates: c. 1910
Location: Collie
CALINGIRI
Dates: 1924; 1934
Location: Calingiri
CAMBRIAN UNITED
Dates: 1913
Location: Kalgoorlie
Nickname: The Welshmen

CANARIES
Dates: c. 1925
Location: Pemberton district
CANNA
Dates: c. 1926
Location: Canna
CANNING
Dates: c. 1946
Location: Canning
CANNNING VALE
Dates: c. 1935
Location: Canning Vale
CARDIFF ROVERS
Dates: 1910
Location: Collie
CARMARTHAN
Dates: c. 1929
Location: Carmanthan
Titles/Honours: League Premiers 1937; Richmond Cup 1937; Nockholds Cup 1937; Clarke Cup 1938
CARNAHMAH
Dates: 1927
Location: Carnamah
CARSCOTS
Dates: c. 1940
Location: Carscots
CASUALS UNITED
Dates: 1899-1925
Location: The Esplanade, Perth
Colours: Black shirts; red and white striped shirts
Nickname: The Geordies
Titles/Honours: Charity Cup 1914; Challenge Cup 1921, 1928
Notes: Most of the team were from North East England.
CATTERICK
Dates: c. 1933
Location: Catterick
CENTRALS
Dates: c. 1935-1936
Location: Walpole district
Notes: Walpole, Tingledale, Hazlewood and Centrals comprised the Walpole and District Soccer Association.
CHAPMAN'S HILL
Dates: c. 1927
Location: Chapman's Hill
CIRCLE VALLEY
Dates: 1928
Location: Circle Valley
CITY UNITED
Dates: 1905-1918
Location: Wellington Square, Perth; Victoria Park; The Esplanade
Colours: Blue and gold shirts

Titles/Honours: First Division Champions 1906, 1908, 1913; Charity Cup 1908, 1911; Challenge Cup 1909
Notes: Club merged with Perth City to form Perth City United in 1918.
CIVIL SERVICE
Dates: 1896
Location: Lord Street Ground, Perth
Colours: Black and red halved shirts with navy blue shorts
Titles/Honours: First Division Champions 1898; Challenge Cup 1898-1900, 1902-03; Charity Cup 1905
Notes: Civil Service played the first match under British Association Rules in Perth against the Perth club on 30 May, 1896.
CIVIL SERVICE
Dates: 1913
Location: Geraldton
Titles/Honours: Premiers 1913
Notes: Joint 1913 Premiers with Geraldton Town
CLAREMONT
Dates: c. 1908
Location: Claremont
Colours: Red shirts
Nickname: The 'Monts
Titles/Honours: Division One 1910, 1912, 1919, 1923; Charity Cup 1909, 1921, 1925; Challenge Cup and Shield 1908, 1910, 1912-1913, 1915, 1920
CLAREMONT GLEBE
Dates: c. 1912
Location: The Esplanade
Titles/Honours: Second Division Champion 1914
CLAREMONT MENTAL HOSPITAL (C.M.H.)
Dates: c. 1938
Location: Claremont Hospital Grounds
Notes: Successor club to Hospital for the Insane
CLAREMONT-NORTH COTTESLOE
Dates: c. 1931
Location: Claremont
CLAREMONT TRAINING COLLEGE
Dates: 1908
Location: Claremont
CODGATOTINE
Dates: c. 1925
Location: Codgatotine
COKERNUP
Dates: c. 1914
Location: Cokernup
COLLIE BOOMERANGS
Dates: c. 1904
COLLIE BULLFINCH
Dates: c. 1923
Location: Collie Recreation Ground

THE FOUNDATION YEARS 1859-1949 321

COLLIE BURN
Dates: 1912
Location: Collie Recreation Ground
Colours: Black and white striped shirts
Nickname: The Caledonians; Burnites
COLLIE CO-OPERATIVES
Dates: c. 1923
Location: Collie Recreation Ground
COLLIE RANGERS
Dates: 1906
Location: Collie
Titles/Honours: West Australian League Champions 1911
COLLIE SHOTTS
Dates: c. 1923
Location: Collie Recreation Ground
COLLIE THIISTLE
Dates: 1910
Location: Collie
COLLIE TOWN
Dates: c. 1903
Location: Collie
Colours: Blue shirts
Nickname: The Colliers; Royals
Titles/Honours: Country Week Champions 1924; 1928; Collie Cup 1948
COOKERNUP UNITED
Dates: 1914
Location: Cookernup
COOLGARDIE PIONEERS
Dates: c. 1894
Location: Coolgardie Recreation Reserve
COOMBERDALE
Dates: c. 1914
Location: Coomberdale
COOPERATIVE
Date: 1921-1927
Location: Collie
CORINTHIA
Dates: c. 1931
Location: Corinthia
CORINTHIANS
Dates: 1921
Location: Parade Ground, Albany
Titles/Honours: Albany British Football Premiers 1921
CORINTHIANS
Dates: 1931
Location: Corinthia Recreation Reserve
Notes: Players were from the Corinthia Gold mine. The team played in the Yilgarn League.
CORINTHIANS
Dates: 1901
Location: Fremantle
CORINTHIANS
Dates: 1926
Location: Northcliffe and Pemberton region

CORRIGIN
Dates: 1925
Location: Corrigin Recreation Ground
Titles/Honours: Kulin Carnival Cup 1930
COTTESLOE
Dates: 1896
Location: Cottesloe
COTTESLOE
Dates: 1949
Location: Cottesloe
COWARAMUP
Dates: c. 1933; 1939
Location: Cowaramup
Colours: Blue shirts
COWARAMUP UNITED
Dates: 1933
Location: Cowaramup
CRANBROOK
Dates: c. 1928
Location: Cranbrook
CRUSADERS
Dates: 1896
Location: Weld Square; Russell Square; Cottesloe, Perth
CUBALLING
Dates: c. 1913
Location: Wardering Football Ground
CUE
Dates: 1902
Location: Cue
DALWALINNU
Dates: c. 1926
Location: Dalwalinnu
DARLING RANGE
Dates: c. 1930-1932
Location: Darling Range
DATATINE
Dates: c. 1923
Location: Datatine
DAY DAWN
Dates: c. 1902
Location: Cremorne Ground, Day Dawn
Nickname: The Dawnites
DENMARK
Dates: 1928
Location: Show Ground, Denmark
Colours: Blue shirts
Titles/Honours: Clark Cup 1931
DIXVALE
Dates: c. 1931
Location: Dixvale
Titles/Honours: Smith-Tuckey Cup 1938
DOWERIN
Dates: c. 1929
Location: Dowerin
DRUMIN
Dates: c. 1926

Location: Drumin
DUMBLEYUNG
Dates: c. 1929
Location: Dumbleyung
DWELLINGUP WANDERERS
Dates: c. 1912
Location: Dwellingup
EAST ALBANY
Dates: 1932
Location: Parade Ground, Albany
Colours: Red shirts and white shorts
EAST CLAREMONT
Dates: c. 1929-1930; 1936-1940; 1945
Location: College Park
Titles/Honours: First Division Champions 1940; Second League Premiers 1936; Caris Challenge Cup 1936
EAST TINGLEDALE
Dates: c. 1931
Location: Tingledale
EAST WEST ALBANY
Dates: c. 1924
Location: Ulster Road Reserve, Albany
ELECTRIC AND GAS DEPARTMENT
Dates: c. 1932
Location: Perth
Titles/Honours: Caris Challenge Cup 1932
ELLEKER
Dates: c. 1924
Location: Elleker
EMU HILL
Dates: c. 1922
Location: Mr Coyne's Paddock, Emu Hill
EWINGTON
Dates: c. 1923
Location: Collie Recreation Ground
Titles/Honours: Collie Premiership League Champions 1927; Bland Cup 1935
EX-STUDENTS
Dates: 1905
Location: Wellington Square, Perth
Colours: Purple and green shirts
Titles/Honours: League Cup 1906
FAIRBRIDGE
Dates: c. 1931
Location: Fairbridge
FOREST GROVE
Dates: c. 1933
Location: Margaret River
FORREST
Dates: 1924
Location: Holyoake
FRANKLAND RIVER
Dates: c. 1932
Location: Frankland River
FREMANTLE
Dates: c. 1903-1913

Location: Stephen's Ground; Polo Ground Fremantle
Nickname: The Portsiders
Titles/Honours: Charity Cup 1912
FREMANTLE ALBION
Dates: 1905
Location: Fremantle Park
Notes: Successor club to Fremantle Richmond.
FREMANTLE CITY
Dates: 1935
Location: Stephen Street Reserve
Titles/Honours: Caris Challenge Cup 1946, 1949
FREMANTLE HOTSPUR
Dates: 1908
Location: Fremantle
FREMANTLE RANGERS
Dates: c. 1927-1934
Location: Fremantle
Titles/Honours: Caris Challenge Cup 1927, 1930
FREMANTLE RICHMOND
Dates: 1914
Location: Fremantle
Notes: Successor club to Fremantle
FREMANTLE ROVERS
Dates: 1906
Location: Fremantle Park
Titles/Honours: Charity Cup 1906; Challenge Cup 1907
FREMANTLE TRAINING COLLEGE
Dates: c. 1908
Location: Fremantle
FREMANTLE WANDERERS
Dates: 1896-1914
Location: Cottesloe
Titles/Honours: Division One Champions 1896-1897, 1897, 1899, 1901; Challenge Cup 1901
GABBIN
Dates: c. 1926
Location: Gabbin
GALENA
Dates: c. 1925
Location: Galena
GERALDTON RANGERS
Dates: c. 1920
Location: Geraldton
Titles/Honours: Hansen Cup 1923; Robinson Cup 1933
GERALDTON THISTLE
Dates: 1913
Location: Queen's Park, Geraldton
Titles/Honours: Geraldton Association Premiership 1915, 1920, 1922-1923, 1928, 1936, 1939; Hansen Cup 1932-1933, 1936; League Bowl 1936; McNamara Cup 1936

GERALDTON TOWN
Dates: 1913
Location: Queen's Park, Geraldton
Colours: Red shirts with white shorts
Titles/Honours: Premiers 1913; Hansen Cup 1915, 1928
Notes: Joint 1913 Premiers with Civil Service.

GLENARTY
Dates: c. 1930
Location: Karridale
Nickname: The Glens
Notes: Glenarty played in the Augusta-Margaret River Association which comprised Glenarty, Kudarup, Margaret, Rosabrook, Cowaramup and Warner Glen.

GNOWANGERUP
Dates: c. 1914; 1927
Location: Show Ground, Gnowangerup
Colours: Red and white shirts
Nickname: The Gnows
Titles/Honours: Premiership 1925; Charity Cup 1928

GOOMALLING UNITED
Dates: c. 1927
Location: Goomalling

GORDON RIVER
Dates: c. 1928
Location: Gordon River

GOSNELLS AND DISTRICT
Dates: c. 1932
Location: Gosnells

GREENBUSHES
Dates: 1914
Location: Mill Ground, Greenbushes
Nickname: The 'Bushes

GREENFIELDS WANDERERS
Dates: c. 1933
Location: Greenfields, Mandurah

GUILDFORD
Dates: 1901-1914; 1926-1934; 1937
Location: Guildford
Colours: White shirt with a red 'V' and black shorts (1930)
Titles/Honours: Caris Challenge Cup 1937

GUILDFORD UNITED
Dates: 1934
Location: Guildford

GUTHA
Dates: c. 1926
Location: Gutha

GWALIA
Dates: 1925
Location: Tower Hill Ground, Gwalia
Colours: Red shirts; amber and black shirts (1929)

GWALIA-LEONORA WANDERERS
Dates: c. 1927
Location: Tower Hill Ground, Gwalia
Colours: Blue shirts; royal blue shirts with white facings (1929)

GWALIA VALLEY
Dates: c. 1914
Location: Gwalia
Nickname: The Welshmen

GYMNASIUM CLUB
Dates: 1932-1933; 1938
Location: Denmark
Colours: Red and black shirts and socks
Nickname: Gyms
Titles/Honours: H. Piesse Cup 1933

HADFIELD
Dates: c. 1926
Location: Hadfield

HAMILTON HILL
Dates: 1933
Location: Hamilton Hill

HANNAN'S CORINTHIANS
Dates: 1897
Location: Recreation Ground, Kalgoorlie

HARRINGTON ROVERS
Dates: 1931
Location: Harrington

HARVEY
Dates: 1914; 1923; 1926-1927; c. 1929
Location: Harvey Recreation Ground
Colours: Olive green shirts with white shorts (1927)
Titles/Honours: League Cup 1926; Challenge Shield 1926

HATFIELD STEEL WORKS
Dates: c. 1926
Location: Hatfield

HAZELVALE
Dates: c. 1946
Location: Hazelvale

HAZELWOOD
Dates: c. 1931
Location: Hazelwood
Colours: Black and white shirts
Nickname: The Magpies
Notes: In 1931 the Hazelwood Association League competition comprised Hazelwood, and East and West Tingledale clubs.

HIGH SCHOOL
Dates: c. 1908
Location: Perth

HOFFMAN'S MILL
Dates c. 1926
Location: Hoffman
Notes: Played in the Yarloops District League

HOLYOAKE
Dates: c. 1914; 1924
Location: Holyoake Recreation Ground (1925)

HOSPITAL FOR THE INSANE (H.F.I)

Dates: c. 1919 - c. 1937
Location: Claremont Hospital Grounds
Titles/Honours: Caris Challenge Cup 1924, 1928
Notes: Club succeeded by Claremont Mental Hospital in 1947.

IMPERIAL EX-SERVICEMEN
Dates: 1949
Location: Perth

JALBURRAGUP ROVERS
Dates: c.1927
Location: Jalbarragup

JANDAKOT
Dates: c. 1914
Location: Jandakot

JARNADUP
Dates: 1914
Location: Jarnadup

JINDONG
Dates: 1931
Location: Jindong

JOLLY ROGER
Dates: c. 1945
Location: Perth
Titles/Honours: Division One Champions 1945
Notes: Team of the British warship HMS *Adamant*.

KALAMUNDA
Dates: c. 1928
Location: Kalamunda Reserve

KALGOORLIE
Dates: 1900; 1910
Location: Kalgoorlie Oval; Gala Ground
Colours: Chocolate and light blue shirts
Notes: The Kalgoorlie Association included Boulder City, Boulder Mines, Kanowna and Coolgardie Pioneer.

KALGOORLIE CALEDONIANS
Dates: 1929
Location: Commonwealth Reserve, Kalgoorlie
Colours: Royal blue shirts

KALGOORLIE RANGERS
Dates: c. 1936
Location: Hamilton Street Reserve, Kalgoorlie
Titles/Honours: Casey Cup 1937

KALGOORLIE ROVERS
Dates: 1903
Location: Half-way Ground, Kalgoorlie

KALGOORLIE CITY
Dates: 1933
Location: Kalgoorlie

KALGOORLIE UNITED
Dates: 1933
Location: Kalgoorlie

KALGOORLIE WARRIORS
Dates: c. 1932
Location: Kalgoorlie

KANOWNA
Dates: c. 1898
Location: Kanowna Reserve

KARDARLUP
Dates: c. 1929
Location: Kardarlup

KARLGARIN
Dates: c. 1927
Location: Karlgarin

KARRIDALE
Dates: c. 1929
Location: Karridale

KATANNING
Dates: 1914
Location: Show Ground, Katanning
Colours: White shirts with a red 'V' and blue shorts
Titles/Honours: Joy Shield 1927

KATANNING NORTH
Dates: 1912
Location: Katanning

KATANNING SOUTH
Dates: 1912
Location: Katanning
Colours: Red shirts

KELLERBERRIN
Dates: 1932-1934
Location: Kelleberrin

KENTDALE
Dates: 1933
Location: Kentdale

KING RIVER
Dates: c. 1930
Location: Strathmore

KIRRUP
Dates: c. 1927
Location: Kirrup

KOJONUP
Dates: 1914
Location: Kojonup Recreation Ground
Colours: Blue shirts

KONDININ
Dates: 1928
Location: Kondinin

KOOLANOOKA
Dates: c. 1929
Location: Koolanooka
Titles/Honours: Perenjori District Soccer Association Premiers 1929
Notes: Team played in the Wolgan Line League.

KOORDA
Dates: c. 1926
Location: Koorda
Notes: Koorda was part of the Mt Marshall Soccer Association. Other clubs included Bencubbin, Drumin, Gabbin, Mandiga and Newcarlbeon.

THE FOUNDATION YEARS 1859-1949

KORRELOCKING
Dates: 1926
Location: Korrelocking
Colours: Amber and black shirts
Titles/Honours: Lindsay Cup 1928; Williams Shield 1928

KUDARUP
Dates: c. 1928-1930; 1933
Location: Kudarup

KULIN ATHLETIC
Dates: 1927
Location: Kulin Recreation Ground
Titles/Honours: Dunstan Cup 1929

KULJA
Dates: c. 1930
Location: Kulja

KUNUNOPPIN
Dates: 1932
Location: Kununoppin

LAKE BIDDY
Dates: c. 1927
Location: Lake Biddy

LAKE GRACE
Dates: c. 1927
Location: Lake Grace Soccer Ground
Titles/Honours: Cup winners 1927

LAKESIDE
Dates: c. 1935
Location: Lakeside

LATHAM
Dates: c. 1926
Location: Latham

LEEDERVILLE
Dates: 1913-1915
Location: Leederville

LEONORA ROVERS
Dates: 1925
Location: Soccer Ground, Leonora

LEONORA WANDERERS
Dates: 1925
Location: Soccer Ground, Leonora

LORA
Dates: c. 1931
Location: Lora

MACCABEAN
Dates: 1931-1971
Location: The Esplanade
Nickname: The Maccies
Titles/Honours: Third League Champion 1935; Challenge Shield 1946
Notes: Example of an early 'ethnic' club backed by the Jewish community.

MACEDONIA
Dates: 1949
Location: College Park, Perth
Notes: Played in the Third Division.

MADDINGTON
Dates: c. 1934-1935
Location: Maddington
Notes: Maddington disbanded in 1935 and their place in the metropolitan league was taken by South Perth. Maddington was re-named South Perth.

MANDIGA
Dates: c. 1926
Location: Mandiga

MANIMUP
Dates: 1914
Location: Manimup

MARGARET RIVER
Dates: c. 1929; 1940
Location: Margaret River
Colours: Black and white shirts
Nickname: The Magpies
Titles/Honours: Augusta-Margaret River Soccer Football Association Premiership Shield 1929; Northern Division League champions 1931; Challenge Cup winners 1931; Cup winner 1948

MARGARET RIVER BOYS (M.R.B.)
Dates: c. 1929
Location: Margaret River

MAYLANDS ATHLETIC
Dates: 1924-1930
Location: Wellington Square; Maylands Oval
Titles/Honours: League Champions 1928; Challenge Cup 1928; Flick Cup and Shield 1928; Second Division champions 1930

METRICUP
Dates: c. 1931
Location: Metricup
Nickname: The Robins
Titles/Honours: Margaret River Champions 1936-37; League Premiership Shield 1946; Challenge cup winners 1946

MIDLAND
Dates: c. 1940
Location: Muirfield Park, Midland

MIDLAND JUNCTION OLYMPIC
Dates: c. 1901
Location: Midland Reserve
Titles/Honours: Charity Cup 1903

MIDLAND (LOCO) WANDERERS
Dates: 1910; 1925
Location: Muirfield Park, Midland
Colours: Red shirts with white shorts
Titles/Honours: Buttsworth Cup 1931; Caris Challenge Cup 1931; Eastern Division Champions 1934
Notes: Often referred to as Loco Wanderers.

MOONYOONOOKA
Dates: c. 1913
Location: Moonyoonooka

MOORA

Dates: 1914
Location: Moora Recreation Reserve
MOORA THISTLE
Dates: 1925
Location: Moora
Colours: Royal blue shirts and white shorts
MOORINE ROCK
Dates: c. 1930
Location: Moorine Rock
MORAWA
Dates: 1927
Location: Morawa
MORNINGTON
Dates: c. 1914; 1926
Location: Mornington
MORNINGTON MILLS
Dates: c. 1914
Location: Wokalup
MOUNT BARKER
Dates: c. 1913
Location: Mount Barker
Nickname: The Barkerites
MOUNT HAWTHORN
Dates: c. 1945
Location: Mt Hawthorn
MOUNT HELENA
Dates: c. 1931
Location: Mount Helena Oval
Colours: Red shirts
MOUNT LAWLEY
Dates: c. 1945
Location: Perth
MOUNT LYELL
Dates: 1929
Location: Mount Lyell
MOUNT MAGNET
Dates: c. 1906
Location: Mount Magnet
Titles/Honours: Pettigrew Cup 1906
MOUNT MARSHALL
Dates: c. 1929
Location: Mount Marshall
Titles/Honours: Country Week champions 1929
MUNDIJONG
Dates: c. 1925
Location: Mundijong
Nickname: The Timber Workers
Titles/Honours: Second League Champions 1926
MUNTADJIN
Dates: 1929
Location: Muntadjin
Titles/Honours: Jacoby Cup 1931
MURADUP
Dates: 1914
Location: Muradup Sports Ground
Colours: Green shirts with white shorts

Titles/Honours: Joy Shield 1926
Notes: Muradup was part of the Katanning District Soccer Association. Other teams in the Association were Badgebup, Katanning and Kojunup.
MYALUP
Dates: c. 1931
Location: Myalup
Titles/Honours: Edwards Cup 1932
NANNUP
Dates: c. 1927
Location: Nannup
NARALING
dates: c. 1935
Location: Naraling
NAREMBEEN
Dates: c. 1922-c. 1929
Location: Narembeen
Colours: Royal blue shirts and white shorts
NARLINGUP
Dates: c. 1927
Location: Narlingup
NARROGIN
Dates: 1912
Location: Narrogin Sports Ground
Colours: Black and white striped shirts with white shorts (1913)
Notes: Originally named British in early 1912.
NEEDILUP
Dates: c. 1923
Location: Needilup
NEWCARLBEON
Dates: c. 1926
Location: Newcarlbeon
NEWTON BEACH
Dates: c. 1926
Location: Newton Beach
NEWTOWN UNITED
Dates: 1927
Location: Vasse
NINGHAN
Dates: c. 1929
Location: Ninghan
NOOMBLING
Dates: 1926
Location: Noombling
NORNALUP
Dates: c. 1930
Location: Nornalup
NORSEMAN BUTTERFLIES
Dates: c. 1934
Location: Norseman
NORTH ALBANY
Dates: 1932
Location: Parade Ground, Albany
NORTH COTTESLOE
Dates: c. 1925; 1949

Location: Cottesloe
NORTH COTTESLOE ATHLETIC
Dates: c. 1922
Location: Cottesloe Oval
Nickname: The Surfers
Titles/Honours: Caris Challenge Cup 1925
NORTH DALWALLINU
Dates: c. 1923
Location: North Dalwallinu
NORTH PERTH
Dates: 1924
Location: Woodville Reserve; Leederville Oval
Colours: Blue and white halved shirts
Nickname: The Northerners
Titles/Honours: Second League Champion 1929; Division One 1948; Charity Cup 1947-1948; Challenge Cup 1947.
NORTH PERTH RANGERS
Dates: 1908
Location: Perth
Titles/Honours: 2nd Division Metropolitan Champions 1908
NORTH WAILKI
Dates: c. 1933
Location: North Wailki
NORTHERN CASUALS
Dates: 1912-1914; 1920-1940; 1949
Location: Perth
Nickname: The Geordies
Titles/Honours: Charity Cup 1913, 1924, 1930; First Division League Championship 1930, 1932; Challenge Cup 1924-1926, 1928, 1932; Ambulance Cup 1932
Notes: Club of the Northumberland and Durham Association.
NORTHAM
Dates: 1900; 1912
Location: Northam
NORTHAMPTON
Dates: 1932
Location: Northhampton
Titles/Honours: Premiers Geraldton Association 1933; Hampton Cup 1936
NORTHCLIFFE
Dates: c. 1926
Location: Northcliffe
Titles/Honours: Country Week champions 1926
NYABING RANGERS
Dates: 1929
Location: Nyabing
OLYMPIC
Dates: 1901
Location: Midland Junction, Perth; Loton's Paddock
Nickname: Ollies; Pics
Titles/Honours: Charity Cup 1903
ONGERUP

Dates: c. 1921
Location: Ongerup
Titles/Honours: Champions 1921, 1928, 1932; O'Meehan Shield 1925; Hospital Cup 1934
OSBORNE PARK
Dates: 1926; c. 1945
Location: Osborne Park Agricultural Show Ground
PALMER'S FIND
Dates: c. 1935
Location: Palmer's Find
PALMYRA
Dates: c. 1918
Location: Palmyra
PEMBERTON RAILWAYS
Dates: c. 1925
Location: Pemberton
PERENJORI
Dates: 1927
Location: Perenjori
Colours: Yellow and black shirts
Notes: Perenjori, Bowgada and Morawa formed a league in 1930.
PERTH
Dates: 1896-1918
Location: Weld Square, Perth
Colours: White shirts with blue shorts
Titles/Honours: Champions Division One 1899, 1902, 1905; Charity Cup 1904; Challenge Cup and Shield 1904; Presentation Cup 1912
Notes: Perth were the oldest club in the capital. Perth amalgamated with the City United club in 1919.
PERTH CITY ROVERS
Dates: c. 1922
Location: South Perth
PERTH CITY UNITED
Dates: 1919; 1948
Location: Perth
Colours: Blue and gold shirts
Titles/Honours: Division One Champions 1920, 1922, Charity Cup 1919; Division Two champions 1949
Notes: Club a merger of junior club Perth City and City United.
PERTH CORINTHIANS
Dates: 1947
Location: Perth
PERTH ELECTRICITY AND GAS DEPARTMENT.
Dates: c. 1932
Location: Perth
PERTH GAS WORKS
Dates: c. 1925
Location: Forrest Park
PERTH GLEBE RANGERS
Dates: 1906-1928

Location: Perth
Colours: Dark blue shirts with white shorts
Titles/Honours: First Division Champions 1911; Charity Cup 1907; Challenge Cup 1906, 1908
PERTH RANGERS UNITED
Dates: c. 1910
Location: Perth
Colours: Green and white shirts
PERTH ROVERS
Dates: 1948
Location: Perth
PERTH SWAN
Dates: 1908
Location: Perth
Titles/Honours: Division Three Premiers 1908
PERTH VOLUNTEERS
Dates: 1897
Location: Perth
PICCADILLY
Dates: 1932
Location: Kalgoorlie
Notes: The Piccadilly Club was named after the Piccadilly Hotel, Kalgoorlie.
PICKERING BROOK
Dates: c. 1933
Location: Pickering Brook, Perth
PINGELLY-MOURAMBINE
Dates: 1926
Location: Mourambine
Colours: White shirts with blue shorts
Titles/Honours: Brookton-Pingelly League Champions 1926
PINJARRA
Dates: 1929
Location: Pinjarra
Colours: White shirts with white shorts and black socks with white tops (1930); black shirts with white shorts and black and white socks (1932)
PITHARA
Dates: 1923
Location: Pithara
PORT RANGERS
Dates: 1896
Location: Fremantle
QUEEN'S PARK
Dates: 1936
Location: Queen's Park
Titles/Honours: Caris Challenge Cup 1940-1941
Notes: Formerly the Welshpool club until 1935.
QUEENS PARK RANGERS
Dates: 1909
Location: Queen's Park, Geraldton
Titles/Honours: Premiers Geraldton Association, 1915; Hansen Cup 1939, 1947
RAILWAYS
Dates: c. 1928

Location: Bunbury
Titles/Honours: Bunbury Soccer Association Premiers 1930
RECREATION
Dates: c. 1934
Location: Boulder
Notes: Club named after the Recreation Hotel, Boulder.
RETURNED SOLDIERS
Dates: c. 1926
Location: Pemberton District
Notes: Club was a member of the Northcliffe and Pemberton District Association Football League. Other members were Corinthians, Pemberton Roads and Bridges, Spartans and Wasps.
ROADS AND BRIDGES
Dates: c. 1926
Location: Pemberton District
ROCKY GULLY
Dates: c. 1932
Location: Rocky Gully
ROSABROOK
Dates: c. 1929
Location: Rosabrook
ROSELLA
Dates: c. 1931
Location: Rosa Brook
Nickname: The Parrots
ROTHSAY
Dates: c. 1935
Location: Rothsay
ROYAL ARTILLERY
Dates: c. 1941
Location: Perth
ROYAL AUSTRALIAN AIR FORCE (RAAF)
Dates: 1941-1946
Location: The Esplanade, Perth
ROYAL AUSTRALIAN GARRISON ARTILLERY (R.A.G.A)
Dates: c. 1911
Location: Albany
Nickname: The Forts
ST JOSEPH'S ATHLETIC
Dates: c. 1934
Location: Show Grounds, Bussleton
SABINA VALE
Dates: c. 1933
Location: Sabina Vale
SALMON GUMS
Dates: 1934
Location: Salmon Gums
SCADDEN
Dates: 1928
Location: Scadden
SCOTSDALE
Dates: c. 1929

Location: Scotsdale
Nickname: Scots
Titles/Honours: Clarke Cup 1933
Notes: In 1929 Scotsdale played in a Denmark District Soccer Association competition against the Denmark, Carmarthen and Nornalup clubs.

SHACKLETON-ARGYLE
Dates: c. 1926
Location: Shackleton
Titles/Honours: Pennant 1926

SHAMROCK ROVERS
Dates: c. 1932
Location: Kalgoorlie

SHENTON PARK RANGERS
Dates: c. 1946
Location: Subiaco

SHOTTS
Dates: 1921
Location: Collie
Titles/Honours: League Cup 1925; Challenge Cup 1925; Charity Cup 1925

SOMERSET HILL
Dates: c. 1931-1933
Location: Somerset Hill
Nickname: The Hills

SOUTH BELMONT
Dates: c. 1932
Location: Peet Park, South Belmont

SOUTH BUNBURY
Dates: c. 1925
Location: Bunbury

SOUTH PERTH
Dates: 1936
Location: South Perth Oval
Titles/Honours: Challenge Cup 1948.
Notes: South Perth subsumed the Maddington club in 1935.

SOUTHERN CROSS
Dates: 1896
Location: Southern Cross
Colours: White shirts with dark shorts
Nickname: The 'Cross

SPARTA
Dates: 1933
Location: Commonwealth Reserve, Kalgoorlie; Launceston Ground
Colours: White 'S' on black shirts
Titles/Honours: League Premiers 1935
Notes: Team mostly comprised of Yugoslav players.

SPARTANS
Dates: c. 1926
Location: Pemberton District

SPEARWOOD
Dates: 1914
Location: Spearwood

SPEARWOOD ROVERS
Dates: 1931-1934; 1938
Location: Spearwood
Colours: White shirt with a black 'V' and white shorts with black socks with white tops.
Titles/Honours: Caris Challenge Cup 1938; Challenge Cup 1941

SPEARWOOD UNITED
Dates: 1929
Location: Fruitgrowers Reserve
Titles/Honours: Charity Cup 1941

STOCKTON
Dates: c. 1926; c. 1938
Location: Collie
Titles/Honours: League Cup 1947; Collie Cup 1947; Charity Cup 1947

STONEHOUSE CAMP
Dates: c. 1932
Location: Harvey

SUBIACO
Dates: 1910
Location: Onslow Road, Subiaco (1926)
Colours: Black and white shirts
Nickname: Suby
Titles/Honours: Divisional Champions 1934

SUBIACO-JOLIMONT
Dates: c. 1923
Location: Subiaco

SWANS
Dates: 1907
Location: Perth

SWAN ATHLETIC
Dates: 1945
Location: McDonald Park, Perth
Notes: Players were from the Yugoslav community. Many players were from the Swan Valley club.

SWAN VALLEY
Dates: 1931
Location: Herne Hill; Gingin Road, Perth
Titles/Honours: Charity Shield 1946
Notes: Players were of Yugoslav origin.

SWANBOURNE
Dates: c. 1925
Location: Perth

TAMBELLUP
Dates: c. 1928
Location: Tambellup

TAXI
Dates: c. 1928
Location: Perth

TAYLOR'S WELL
Dates: c. 1935
Location: Taylor's Well

THISTLE UNITED
Dates: 1921
Location: Perth Road Ground, Albany

THISTLE UNITED

Dates: 1912-1940
Location: Forrest Park, Perth
Nickname: The Jags
Titles/Honours: First Division Champions 1914-15, 1921, 1925;
Charity Cup 1913, 1915, 1921, 1929;
Presentation Cup 1913;
Challenge Cup and Shield 1914;
Wanderers Cup 1914-1915
Notes: Club with support from the Scottish community.

TINGLEDALE
Dates: c. 1946
Location: Tingledale
Titles/Honours: Frankland Shield 1948; W. Vigus Cup 1948

TOODYAY
Dates: 1925
Location: Toodyay

TOOLBRUNUP
Dates: 1915
Location: Toolbrunup

TOOLIBIN
Dates: 1913
Location: Toolibin Lake
Colours: Green shirts

TOWNS
Dates: 1921
Location: Collie

TRAINING COLLEGE
Dates: 1907-1925
Location: Claremont
Colours: Green and gold shirts
Titles/Honours: First Division Champions 1909

TRAYNING
Dates: c. 1932
Location: Trayning

UNIONS
Dates: c. 1934
Location: Agusta

UNITED
Dates: 1911
Location: Albany
Colours: Red shirts
Titles/Honours: Albany Association Premiership 1913

UNITED
Dates: c. 1922
Location: Collie

UNITED KINGDOM NATIVES ASSOCIATION (U.K.N.A.)
Dates: 1926
Location: Bassendean
Nickname: The Natives

UNITED PRESS
Dates: c. 1929
Location: The Esplanade

UNITED TRANSPORT
Dates: c. 1929
Location: Perth

UNIVERSITY
Dates: 1949
Location: Broadway, Perth
Titles/Honours: Third Division Champions 1949

UPPER SWAN
Dates: c. 1922
Location: Perth
Nickname: The Grape Merchants; Swans

VICTORIA PARK
Dates: 1926-1940
Colours: Black and amber striped shirts
Titles/Honours: First Division Champions 1928-1929, 1931, 1934-1939;
Charity Cup 1926, 1928-1931-1932, 1934, 1937;
Busselton Centenary Cup 1933, 1936;
Association Cup 1936-1937

WAGIN
Dates: c. 1912; 1929
Location: Wagin

WALLSEND
Dates: 1910
Location: Collie

WALPOLE
Dates: c. 1935-1937; 1946
Location: Walpole Oval

WANDERERS
Dates: c. 1920
Location: Parade Ground, Albany

WANDERERS UNITED
Dates: c. 1925
Location: Perth

WARNER GLEN
Dates: c. 1930
Location: Karridale

WAROONA
Dates: 1926
Location: Waroona Show Ground

WASPS
Dates: c. 1926
Location: Pemberton district

WELBUNGIN
Dates: c. 1929
Location: Welbungin

WELLINGTON MILL
Dates: c. 1912
Location: Wellington Mill

WELSH SETTLEMENT
Dates: c. 1914
Location: Moora district

WELSHPOOL
Dates: c. 1931
Location: Welshpool
Notes: Welshpool changed name to Queen's Park in 1936.

WEST ALBANY
Dates: 1932
Location: Parade Ground, Albany
Colours: Black shirts and white shorts

WEST BUSSELTON COLTS
Dates: 1938
Location: West Busselton

WEST COLLIE
Dates: 1910
Location: Collie
Colours: Black and white shirts
Titles/Honours: Premiers 1912

WEST COLLIE RANGERS
Dates: 1910
Location: Collie

WALLSEND
Dates: 1910
Location: Collie

WEST DENMARK
Dates: c. 1932-1937
Location: Denmark

WEST PERTH
Dates: 1931
Location: Wellington Square

WEST TINGLEDALE
Dates: c. 1931
Location: Tingledale
Titles/Honours: Association Cup 1932; Association Shield 1932

WEST-TON
Dates: 1928
Location: Collie
Notes: Amalgamation of the Stockton and Westralia clubs.

WESTRALIA
Dates: 1921-1927
Location: Collie

WESTRALIAN
Dates: 1912
Location: Collie

WICKEPIN
Dates: 1927

WILGOYNE
Dates: c. 1930
Location: Wilgoyne
Location: Spackman's Paddock, Wickepin

WILLIAMS BAY
Dates: c. 1931
Location: Williams Bay

WILLYABRUP
Dates: c. 1928
Location: Willyabrup
Colours: Red shirts with white shorts
Titles/Honours: Premiers 1928

WILUNA CASUALS
Dates: c. 1932
Location: Wiluna

WILUNA RANGERS
Dates: c. 1932
Location: Wiluna

WILUNA THISTLE
Dates: c. 1932
Location: Wiluna

WILUNA TOWNS
Dates: c. 1932
Location: Wiluna

WOKALUP
Dates: 1926
Colours: Black and white shirts
Titles/Honours: Yarloops District Challenge Shield 1927

WONGAN HILLS
Dates: 1929
Location: Wongan Hills

WOODLANDS
Dates: 1924
Location: Woodlands

WOOLEN MILLS
Dates: 1925
Location: Albany

WORSLEY
Dates: 1913
Location: Worsley

WUBIN
Dates: c. 1926
Location: Wubin

WYALCATCHEM
Dates: 1920; 1927
Location: Wyalcatchem
Colours: Blue shirts with white shorts
Titles/Honours: Lindsay Cup 1927

YALYALUP
Dates: c. 1929-1930
Location: Yalyalup
Colours: Royal blue shirts with white shorts

YARLOOP
Dates: c. 1911
Location: Yarloop
Titles/Honours: Harvey-Yarloop Association Premiers 1927;
Cup winners 1927

YEALERING
Dates: 1927
Location: Yealering
Nickname: The Lakesiders
Titles/Honours: Association Cup 1930

YELBENI
Dates: c. 1929
Location: Yelbeni
Titles/Honours: Dampier Association Premiers 1932
Notes: Yelbeni was part of the Dampier Soccer Association comprising Yelbeni, Trayning, Kununoppin and Nungarin clubs.

YMCA
Dates: c. 1913
Location: Katanning
YMCA
Dates: c. 1911
Location: Perth
YOONGARILLUP
Dates: 1928
Location: Yoongarillup Oval
Colours: Blue and yellow shirts with white shorts
Nickname: The Blues
YORK
Dates: c. 1912
Location: York

YORK THISTLE
Dates: 1924
Location: Forrest Park, York
YUNA
Dates: c. 1930
Location: Yuna
Titles/Honours: Globe Brewery Cup 1936
ZORA
Dates: 1931
Location: Osborne Park
Notes: Zora was formed by Yugoslav players.

About Peter Kunz

Peter Kunz is a retired Canberra-based librarian and researcher who has worked for cultural institutions such as the National Library of Australia and the National Film and Sound Archive. From the late 1960s he played amateur soccer in Canberra and was also a soccer referee and a correspondent for the *Soccer World* newspaper in the 1970s. His principal interest has been historical research, which has led to investigation of the early development of soccer in Australia as well as the curation of Australian soccer memorabilia. Son of an Australian mother and a Hungarian immigrant, Peter's formative years were spent in Sydney in the early 1960s watching and supporting the St George-Budapest soccer club.

fairplaypublishing.com.au

www.ingramcontent.com/pod-product-compliance
Lightning Source LLC
Chambersburg PA
CBHW051934290426
44110CB00015B/1969